A Handbook of Critical Approaches to Literature

FOURTH EDITION

WILFRED L. GUERIN
EARLE LABOR
LEE MORGAN
JEANNE C. REESMAN
JOHN R. WILLINGHAM

New York • *Oxford*
OXFORD UNIVERSITY PRESS
1999

Oxford University Press

Oxford   New York
Athens   Auckland   Bangkok   Bogotá   Buenos Aires   Calcutta
Cape Town   Chennai   Dar es Salaam   Delhi   Florence   Hong Kong   Istanbul
Karachi   Kuala Lumpur   Madrid   Melbourne   Mexico City   Mumbai
Nairobi   Paris   São Paulo   Singapore   Taipei   Tokyo   Toronto   Warsaw

and associated companies in
Berlin   Ibadan

Copyright © 1992, 1999 by Oxford University Press, Inc.

Copyright © 1966, 1979 by Wilfred L. Guerin, Earle Labor, Lee Morgan,
and John R. Willingham

Published by Oxford University Press, Inc.,
198 Madison Avenue, New York, New York 10016
http://www.oup-usa.org

Library of Congress Cataloging-in-Publication Data
A handbook of critical approaches to literature / Wilfred L. Guerin
. . . [et al.] — 4th ed.
p. cm.
Includes bibliographical references and index.
ISBN 0–19–509955–9 (paper)
1. Criticism.   I. Guerin, Wilfred L.
PN81.G8   1998
801'.95—dc21   97–30003
                                      CIP

Printing (last digit): 9 8 7 6 5 4

Printed in the United States of America
on acid-free paper

TO OUR FIRST CRITICS

Jeannine Thing Campbell
Carmel Cali Guerin
Rachel Higgs Morgan
Sylvia Kirkpatrick Steger
Grace Hurst Willingham

Contents

Preface   *xi*

1. **Getting Started: The Precritical Response**   *1*
   I. Setting   6
   II. Plot   7
   III. Character   7
   IV. Structure   8
   V. Style   9
   VI. Atmosphere   10
   VII. Theme   11

2. **Traditional Approaches**   16
   I. **Nature and Scope of the Traditional Approaches**   *16*
      A. Textual Scholarship: A Prerequisite to Criticism   *18*
      B. Types of Traditional Approaches   *21*
         1. Historical-Biographical   *22*
         2. Moral-Philosophical   *25*

   II. **The Traditional Approaches in Practice**   *27*
      A. Traditional Approaches to Marvell's
         "To His Coy Mistress"   *27*
         1. The Text of the Poem   *27*
         2. The Genre of the Poem   *28*
         3. Historical-Biographical Considerations   *30*
         4. Moral-Philosophical Considerations   *32*

B. Traditional Approaches to *Hamlet*   33
   1. The Text of the Play   33
   2. A Summary of the Play   36
   3. Historical-Biographical Considerations   37
   4. Moral-Philosophical Considerations   41
C. Traditional Approaches to *Adventures of Huckleberry Finn*   42
   1. Dialect and Textual Matters   43
   2. The Genre and the Plot of the Novel   43
   3. Historical-Biographical Considerations   45
   4. Moral-Philosophical Considerations   50
D. Traditional Approaches to "Young Goodman Brown"   51
   1. The Text of the Story   52
   2. The Genre and the Plot of the Story   52
   3. Historical-Biographical Considerations   54
   4. Moral-Philosophical Considerations   57
E. Traditional Approaches to "Everyday Use: for your grandmama"   60
   1. The Plot of the Story   60
   2. Historical-Biographical Considerations   61
   3. Moral-Philosophical Considerations   65

3. The Formalistic Approach   70

I. Reading a Poem: An Introduction to the Formalistic Approach   70

II. The Process of Formalistic Analysis: Making the Close Reader   73

III. A Brief History of Formalistic Criticism   76
   A. The Course of a Half Century   76
   B. Backgrounds of Formalistic Theory   77
   C. The New Criticism   80

IV. Constants of the Formalistic Approach: Some Key Concepts, Terms, and Devices   82
   A. Form and Organic Form   83
   B. Texture, Image, Symbol   85
   C. Fallacies   87
   D. Point of View   87
   E. The Speaker's Voice   89
   F. Tension, Irony, Paradox   90

V. The Formalistic Approach in Practice   91
   A. Word, Image, and Theme: Space-Time Metaphors in "To His Coy Mistress"   91
   B. The Dark, the Light, and the Pink: Ambiguity as Form in "Young Goodman Brown"   96

1.Virtues and Vices   *98*
2. Symbol or Allegory?   *100*
3. Loss upon Loss   *101*
C. Romance and Reality, Land and River: The Journey as
Repetitive Form in *Huckleberry Finn*   *104*
D. Dialectic as Form: The Trap Metaphor in *Hamlet*   *110*
1. The Trap Imagery   *110*
2. The Cosmological Trap   *111*
3. "Seeming" and "Being"   *113*
4. "Seeing" and "Knowing"   *116*
E. Irony and Narrative Voice: A Formalistic Approach to
"Everyday Use: for your grandmama"   *118*

VI. **Limitations of the Formalistic Approach**   *121*

4. The Psychological Approach: Freud   ***125***

I. **Aims and Principles**   ***125***
A. Abuses and Misunderstandings of the Psychological
Approach   *126*
B. Freud's Theories   *127*

II. **The Psychological Approach in Practice**   ***134***
A. *Hamlet:* The Oedipus Complex   *134*
B. Rebellion against the Father in *Huckleberry Finn*   *137*
C. "Young Goodman Brown": Id versus Superego   *141*
D. *The Turn of the Screw:* The Consequences of Sexual
Repression   *144*
E. Death Wish in Poe's Fiction   *148*
F. Love and Death in Blake's "Sick Rose"   *149*
G. Sexual Imagery in "To His Coy Mistress"   *150*
H. Morality over the Pleasure Principle in "Everyday
Use"   *153*

III. **Other Possibilities and Limitations of the Psychological
Approach**   ***155***

5. Mythological and Archetypal Approaches   ***158***

I. **Definitions and Misconceptions**   ***158***

II. **Some Examples of Archetypes**   ***160***
A. Images   *161*
B. Archetypal Motifs or Patterns   *165*
C Archetypes as Genres   *166*

III. **Myth Criticism in Practice**   ***167***
A. Anthropology and Its Uses   *168*
1. The Sacrificial Hero: Hamlet   *171*

2. Archetypes of Time and Immortality: "To His Coy
Mistress"   *175*
B. Jungian Psychology and Its Archetypal Insights   *177*
1. Some Special Archetypes: Shadow, Persona,
and Anima   *180*
2. "Young Goodman Brown": A Failure of
Individuation   *182*
3. Syntheses of Jung and Anthropology   *184*
C. Myth Criticism and the American Dream: Huckleberry
Finn as the American Adam   *186*
D. "Everyday Use": The Great [Grand]Mother   *191*

IV. Limitations of Myth Criticism   *193*

6. Feminist Approaches   *196*

I. Feminism and Feminist Literary Criticism:
Definitions   *196*

II. Historical Overview and Major Themes in Feminist
Criticism   *198*

III. Four Significant Current Practices   *200*
A. Gender Studies   *200*
B. Marxist Feminism   *202*
C. Psychoanalytic Feminism   *203*
D. Minority Feminist Criticism   *208*

IV. The Future of Feminist Literary Studies: Some Problems
and Limitations   *212*

V. Five Feminist Approaches   *215*
A. The Marble Vault: The Mistress in "To His Coy
Mistress"   *215*
B. Frailty, Thy Name Is Hamlet: Hamlet and Women   *217*
C. Men, Women, and the Loss of Faith in "Young Goodman
Brown"   *223*
D. Women and "Sivilization" in *Huckleberry Finn*   *225*
E. "In Real Life": Recovering the Feminine Past in
"Everyday Use"   *230*

7. Cultural Studies   *239*

I. What Is "Cultural Studies"?   *239*

II. Three Ways to Study Culture   *245*
A. British Cultural Materialism   *245*
B. The New Historicism   *247*
C. American Multiculturalism   *253*
1. African American Writers   *256*

2. Latina/o Writers   *260*
3. American Indian Literature   *263*
4. Asian American Writers   *267*

III. Cultural Studies in Practice   **270**
  A. Two Characters in *Hamlet:* Marginalization with a Vengeance   *270*
  B. "To His Coy Mistress": Implied Culture versus Historical Fact   *276*
  C. "The Lore of Fiends": Hawthorne and His Market   *278*
  D. Telling the Truth, "Mainly": Tricksterism in *Huckleberry Finn*   *283*
  E. Cultures in Conflict: A Story Looks at Cultural Change   *292*

8. Additional Approaches   *302*

  I. Aristotelian Criticism (Including the Chicago School)   *304*

  II. Genre Criticism   *307*

  III. Source Study and Related Approaches (Genetic Criticism)   *311*

  IV. The History of Ideas   *315*

  V. Rhetoric, Linguistics, and Stylistics   *319*

  VI. The Marxist Approach   *327*

  VII. Structuralism and Poststructuralism, Including Deconstruction   *331*
    A. Structuralism: Context and Defintion   *331*
    B. The Linguistic Model   *332*
    C. Russian Formalism: Extending Saussure   *334*
    D. Structuralism, Lévi-Strauss, and Semiotics   *335*
    E. French Structuralism: Codes and Decoding   *337*
    F. British and American Interpreters   *339*
    G. Poststructuralism: Deconstruction   *340*

  VIII. Phenomenological Criticism (The Criticism of Consciousness)   *343*

  IX. Dialogics   *349*

  X. Reader-Response Criticism   *355*

Epilogue   *369*

Appendixes   *373*

Andrew Marvell, "To His Coy Mistress"   *373*
Nathaniel Hawthorne, "Young Goodman Brown"   *375*
Alice Walker, "Everyday Use: for your grandmama"   *388*

Index   *397*

Preface

This book, now in its fourth edition, has been from the first the product of our shared conviction that the richness of great literature merits correspondingly rich responses—responses that may be reasoned as well as felt. Corollary to this conviction is our belief that such responses come best when the reader appreciates a great work from as many perspectives as it legitimately opens itself to. Nothing, of course, replaces the reader's initial *felt* responses: the sound of poetry on both the outer and the inner ear; the visions of fiction in the mind's eye; the kinesthetic assault of "total theater." But human responses seldom remain dead-level: they reverberate through multiple planes of sensibility, impelled toward articulation—in short, toward criticism. To answer the inevitable classroom questions, "Why can't we simply *enjoy* this poem [story, novel, play]? Why must we spoil the fun by criticizing?" we would rejoin, "The greatest enjoyment of literary art is never simple!" Furthermore, we should recall, in T. S. Eliot's words, "that criticism is as inevitable as breathing, and that we should be none the worse for articulating what passes in our minds when we read a book and feel an emotion about it."

Eliot's reminder was instrumental in the genesis of the first edition of *A Handbook of Critical Approaches* in the early 1960s, when the four original coauthors were colleagues in the English Department at Centenary College of Louisiana. At that time we had become sensitive to the problems of teaching literary analysis to young college students in the absence of a comprehensive yet elementary guide to some of the major critical approaches to works of literature. No work of that sort existed at the time, yet students clearly could have profited from a more formalized and contemporary introduction to the serious study of literature than they generally had received in lower levels of education. We found that most lower– and many upper–division students were entering and emerging from courses in literature still unenlightened about the most rewarding critical techniques that a keen reader could apply to good imaginative writing. Even students whose exposure to literature had been extensive often possessed only a narrow and fragmented concept of such interpretive approaches. Consequently, one of our first aims—then and now—has been to help establish a healthy balance in the student's critical outlook. We—a group that now includes another collaborator—still fervently believe that any college or university student—or, for that matter, any advanced high school student—should have at hand the main lines of the most useful approaches to literary criticism.

With these assumptions in mind, we marked off our areas of concern and laid claim to fill the need we sensed. We have been gratified with the success of that claim, indicated by the acceptance of the book by our professional colleagues and by thousands of students throughout the land and abroad. (The book has now been published in Spanish, Portuguese, Japanese, Chinese, and Korean [besides an English version in Korea].) However, there has also been an acceptance we did not anticipate. Our original concern was to offer critical approaches to students in the early years of college work, but we have found that in instance after instance the book is being used at upper–division levels and in graduate classes. Even so, this extended use has not precluded the book's acceptance by numerous high school teachers as well.

We hope that in this fourth edition we have preserved that versatility, and we have worked strenuously to improve upon it. Since the publication of our first edition in the mid-1960s, we have witnessed a veritable explosion of critical theories, along with a radical expansion and revision of the literary canon. These extraordinary developments have prompted corresponding revisions in each succeeding edition of our handbook. For example, our prologue in the third edition has now been expanded to a full chapter which includes not only precritical comments on "To His Coy Mistress," *Hamlet*, "Young Goodman Brown," and *Huckleberry Finn*, but also a reader-response approach to Alice Walker's "Everyday Use: for your grandmama." This opening discussion of Walker's widely celebrated classic signals one of the most substantial additions to this fourth edition: because of its accessibility (it is eminently readable) and its richness of interpretive susceptibility, "Everyday Use" nicely complements the other four major works we have treated in detail in each of our preceding editions; and because of its succinctness, the complete story is conveniently reprinted in our Appendixes, along with "To His Coy Mistress" and "Young Goodman Brown." Moreover, Walker's story responds to our increasingly felt need to recognize the canonical significance of women writers, especially those who represent the cultural diversity of our literature. Our recognition of this diversity is further manifested by the addition of our full chapter on cultural studies, composed of sections on British cultural materialism, new historicism, and multiculturalism, and including detailed treatments of all five major works as well as specific mention of other works that represent this burgeoning literary phenomenon. This fully packed seventh chapter replaces our previous chapter on structuralism and poststructuralism, which are now discussed in our eighth chapter along with several other important approaches, coming full circle to our opening discussion of reader-response criticism. In this concluding chapter we have, as before, surveyed various additional approaches in such a way that students may find both orientation and bibliographical guides to expanding their critical horizons. These Quick Reference guides are provided handily at the end of each section in chapter 8, just as they are included at the end of each preceding chapter (rather than being relegated to the back of the book as in our previous editions).

Note also that we have often included additional helpful entries for works not discussed in the text, especially in those sections that treat more contemporary critical emphases.

Despite these changes, our aim in this new edition is still

much the same as it was in the first three editions: to provide a basic introduction to the major critical-interpretive perspectives that a reader beginning a serious study may bring to bear on literature. This book describes and demonstrates the critical tools that have come to be regarded as indispensable for the sensitive reader; these tools are what we call "approaches." Furthermore, because this is a *handbook* of critical approaches, we have tried to make it suggestive rather than exhaustive. We make no claim to being definitive; on the contrary, the book's value lies, in part, in opening the student's eyes to the *possibilities* in literature and criticism. Today we read much about heuristics, the process of discovery. This sense of discovery was important in the previous editions, and it continues to be important here.

But heuristics can be guided, and for that reason we have selected seven main approaches to literary criticism, all of which we consider viable not only for the critical expert but also for the critical neophyte. These approaches constitute the first seven chapters of our handbook. Each of these chapters begins with an introduction to and definition of a particular interpretive approach, usually followed by a detailed application of that approach to the same five major works—two British and three American, one of which is African American—representing the following genres: poetry, drama, novel, and short story. Each chapter also includes comments on other literary works cited as occasional illustrations, thereby effectively extending the handbook's application beyond the five works treated more extensively, while at the same time permitting the student to apply the various critical approaches to the works thus briefly mentioned. There is no rigid sequence from chapter to chapter, and the five major works are not all treated with the same degree of detail in each chapter, since not all works lend themselves equally well to a given approach. Consequently, one important aspect of our treatment of critical reading should be the student's recognition of the need to select the most suitable approach for a given literary work.

Chapter 1, "Getting Started: The Precritical Response," discusses the reader's initial involvement with a work of literary art, emphasizing the importance of this unique personal aesthetic experience. Chapter 2 considers the cluster of perspectives generally accepted as traditional—the biographical, the historical, the moralistic, and the philosophical—with some attention to textual matters and to the time-honored technique of interpretive summary. Chapter 3 deals with the formalistic approach, which has come to be especially associated with the New Criticism. Chapter 4 presents a treatment of psychology in literature, focusing on traditional Freudian concepts. Chapter 5 moves into the realm of cultural myths and archetypal patterns as they are manifested in literature, with particular attention to the archetypal theories of C. G. Jung. Chapter 6 serves as an extensive introduction to the feminist approach, with its rich sociological and political as well as aesthetic implications. The feminist approach includes such varying attitudes as those of neo-Freudians, Marxists, and deconstructionists, since these are sometimes amalgamated with the reformation of sexist attitudes in literary criticism. Chapter 7 addresses one of the liveliest and widest-ranging recent developments in the teaching of literature, cultural studies, with special attention to examples of American multiculturalism in the works of African American, Latina/o, American Indian, and Asian American writers. In chapter 8 we discuss ten additional approaches; to conserve space, we do not attempt in this succinct survey to treat the five major works chosen for detailed analyses in the seven preceding chapters.

These five works were chosen because they lend themselves exceptionally well to multiple interpretations and because they will make the beginning student aware of the joys of reading at increasingly higher levels of ability. Two of them—*Adventures of Huckleberry Finn* and *Hamlet*—are easily available in paperback, if not in the student's literature anthology. The other three—"To His Coy Mistress," "Young Goodman Brown," and "Everyday Use"—are included in this book. Regardless of the availability of these five works, we hope that this book will serve as a model or guide for the interpretation of many literary works. In short, while our handbook possesses an integrity of its own, it may be used most instructively as a complementary text in conjunction with an anthology or a set of paperbacks.

This handbook may be read from cover to cover as a continuous unit, of course, but it has been organized for both flexibility and adaptability. For example, although it is primarily organized by "approaches" rather than genres, at the beginning of a course the instructor may assign the introductory section of each chapter, later assigning the section of each of the seven main chapters that deals with a certain genre. Thus, the instructor who decides to begin with the short story may assign "Young Goodman Brown" and "Everyday Use" along with the introductory sections of selected chapters and the accompanying discussions of these two stories. Another possible strategy is to have students read several literary works early in the term and discuss them in class without immediate recourse to this handbook. Then they might read this text, or pertinent sections of it, and bring their resulting new insights to bear on the literature read earlier, as well as on subsequent readings. This double exposure has the advantage of creating a sense of discovery for the perceptive reader.

For the continuing success of this handbook over the past four decades, we owe many thanks. Our debt to the canon of literary scholarship—the breadth and depth of which is reflected in the Quick Reference sections of this text—is obvious, and we acknowledge it with gratitude. Equally considerable is our debt to the many friends and colleagues whose assistance and suggestions have helped to insure this success. To these we give special thanks: Laurence Perrine, William B. Allmon, James A. Gowen, Donald F. Warders, Arthur Schwartz, Richard Coanda, James Wilcox, Kathleen Owens, Czarena Stuart, Irene Winterrowd, Yvonne B. Willingham, Mildred B. Smith, Melinda M. Carpenter, Alyce Palpant, Jeanette DeLine, Betty Labor, Ruby George, Mary McBride, Robert C. Leitz III, Stephen J. Mayer, Karl-Heinz Westarp, Donald Hannah, Ellen Brown, Bernard Duyfhuizen, Michael L. Hall, David H. Jackson, Jefferson Hendricks, Kyle Labor, Phillip Leininger, Bettye Leslie, Teresa Mangum, Barry Nass, Steven Shelburne, Frederick C. Stern, Keith G. Thomas, David Havird, John Hardt, Harry James Cook, Donald Kummings, Gayle Labor, Earl Wilcox, Kevin Harty, James Lake, Sue Brown, Helen Taylor, Sura Rath, Ed Odom, John Reesman, Garry Partridge, Debbie López, Elia DeLeon, Douglas Bruster, Gena Dagel Caponi, John Kucich, Louis Mendoza, Denise Walker, Kim Chapman, Bridget Drinka,

Linda Woodson, Susan Streeter, Alan E. Craven, and Raymond T. Garza.

Once again we wish to express our appreciation for the constant and thoughtful support from the staff of Oxford University Press, particularly our editor, D. Anthony English, and our production editor, Terri O'Prey.

Finally, we are most deeply indebted to Patty Roberts, without whose untiring efforts in helping to prepare our manuscript this edition might never have come forth.

W. L. G.
E. L.
L. M.
J. C. R.
J. R. W.

· 1 ·

Getting Started:
The Precritical Response

It may come as a surprise to contemporary students to learn that well into the nineteenth century, courses in British and American literature were not offered in universities. For centuries in western Europe, only the literature of classical antiquity was thought to have sufficient merit for systematic study. Yet it was inevitable that literature should one day become a part of the academic curriculum. Anything that could so move and interest large numbers of people, including the most cultivated and enlightened, and that had such obvious and pronounced didactic uses was in the judgment of academicians bound to be worthy of intellectual analysis. Such a view may well have motivated educators to make literature an academic subject: it "taught" something; it was a source of "knowledge." In any event, once literature was established in the curriculum, it was subjected to the formal discipline of criticism, which ultimately consisted of taking it apart (and putting it back together again) to see how and why as well as what it was and meant.

A popular opinion has it that because literary "technicians" have so rigorously pursued their studies, many "common readers" (a term that Dr. Samuel Johnson contributed to the lexicon) shy away from the rich and pleasurable insights that balanced, intelligent literary criticism can lead to. Whatever the reason, many students not innately hostile to literature may well have come almost to despise it, certainly to dread it in school, and to think of it in the same category as quantum physics, Erse philology, macroeconomic theory, or—worse yet—English grammar.

Some professional critics have apparently sympathized with this negative view of the effects of criticism and have espoused subjective and appreciative critical criteria that bear scrutiny in such a discussion as this. A generation ago, for example, Susan Sontag in "Against Interpretation" mounted a frontal attack on most kinds of contemporary criticism, which, she maintained, actually usurp the place of a work of art (13–23). In her free-swinging assault Sontag was at once defending a precritical response somewhat similar to the one elaborated in this chapter and asserting that critical analysis was the desecration of an art form. She saw art as the uninhibited creative spirit in action, energetic and sensual. She saw criticism—at least, most of it—as a dry-as-dust intellectual operation, the intent of which is to control and manage art and the method of which was to reduce the work of art to *content* and then to interpret that. Her approach is highly provocative and stimulating. Yet despite some last-minute disclaimers that she is not condemning all critical commentary and some advice to critics to pay more attention to *form,* it is difficult to escape the conclusion that in her opinion interpretation impoverishes art and that its practice for a number of decades by most academic and professional critics had been unquestionably harmful. She concluded with the pronouncement that "in place of a hermeneutics we need an erotics of art."

Such a view would seem to place her in general agreement with Leslie Fiedler, who, addressing a national convention of the College English Association in the early seventies, advocated "ecstatics" as a response to literature. Professor Fiedler would make the gut reaction the be-all and end-all of art. The traditionally accepted standards and classics were in his view elitist, academic opinions and productions that had been forced on the reading public, who demonstrably prefer sentimental literature, horror stories, and pornography—all of the Pop variety. Such popular writings produce almost exclusively emotional effects—particularly feelings of pathos, terror, and sexual titillation. They cause readers, said Fiedler, "to go out of control, out of [their] heads." He continues by pointing out that we do have a traditional name for the effect sought, and at its most successful achieved, by Pop; the temporary release from the limits of rationality, the boundaries of the ego, the burden of consciousness; the moment of privileged insanity[;] that traditional name is, of course, "Ekstasis," which Longinus spoke of in the last centuries of the Classic Era, not in terms of Popular Art or High Art, which in fact cannot be distinguished in terms of this concept; but of *all* art at its irrational best—or, to use his other favorite word, most "sublime."

That political principles underlie Fiedler's position is clear in his closing remarks:

Once we have made *ekstasis* rather than instruction or delight the center of critical evaluation, we will be freed from the necessity of ranking mass-produced and mass-distributed books in a hierarchal order viable only in a class-structured society, delivered from the indignity of having to condescend publicly to works we privately relish and relieved of the task of trying to define categories like "high" and "low," "majority" and "minority" which were from the beginning delusive and unreal. (3–8)

Both Sontag's and Fiedler's points of view are instructive for readers interested in familiarizing themselves with the variety of critical responses to a literary work. Whether one subscribes to them in their entirety or in part or disagrees with them categorically, they are invigorating polemics that can spark further intellectual exchange on the issue in the classroom, in the learned journals, and in magazines and newspapers.

Subjective, less rational responses to literature in the classroom have not gone unchallenged. Among the earliest spirited rebuttals were J. Mitchell Morse's "Are English Teachers Obsolete?" (9–18); Ann Berthoff's "Recalling Another Freudian Model—A Consumer Caveat" (12–14); and Eva Touster's "Tradition and the Academic Talent" (14–17). And John Ciardi in the second edition of *How Does a Poem Mean?* emphatically condemns appreciation and free association in discussing poetry in the classroom, calling the one "not useful," the other "permissive and pointless," and both together "dull" (xix–xxi).

Perhaps as a result of this controversy, a dilemma has arisen in the classroom for some teachers of literature, namely, whether to discuss material in an essentially subjective manner—the extreme of which could be relativistic and nonrational—or whether to employ the tools of logical and intellectual analysis. We believe that these options do not necessarily constitute a dilemma.

There is unquestionably a kind of literary analysis that is like using an elephant gun to shoot a gnat. It is practiced by riders of all kinds of scholarly hobbyhorses and may manifest itself in such ways as ascertaining the number of feminine rhymes in *The Rape of the Lock* or instances of trochees in book 4 of *Paradise Lost* or the truth about Hamlet's weight problem. The early pages of Charles Dickens's *Hard Times* illustrate the imagination-stifling effect of one such technique. Thomas Gradgrind, patron of a grammar school in an English industrial town, is listening to a class recite. He calls on one of the pupils, "girl number twenty," for the definition of a horse. "Girl number twenty" (in Gradgrind's world there is no personal identity—nor are there any militant feminists) cannot produce the expected rote answer. A better-conditioned classmate can: "'Quadruped. Graminivorous. Forty teeth, namely twenty-four grinders, four eye-teeth and twelve incisive. Sheds coat in the spring; in marshy countries sheds hoofs, too. Hoofs hard, but requiring to be shod with iron. Age known by marks in mouth.' 'Now girl number twenty,' said Mr. Gradgrind, 'You know what a horse is.'" It hardly needs pointing out that such a definition would not do justice to the likes of Bucephalus, Pegasus, Black Beauty, Traveller, or Flicka. But absorption with extraneous, irrelevant, or even too practical considerations that detract from aesthetic perception seems to be an occupational disease of many literary critics. This appears to be a problem, however, rather than a dilemma, and its solution is among the several aims of this book.

Our purpose in this chapter is to show that the precritical response is not only desirable but indeed essential in the fullest appreciation of literature. In doing so, we do not mean to suggest that analysis or expertise detracts from aesthetic sensitivity any more than we mean to suggest that a *pre*critical response is an unworthy one. It is a truism to say that our senses can sometimes mislead us, hence the need to analyze literature that is being studied as well as read for pure pleasure.

We maintain that knowledge, even of a specialized kind, is not in and of itself a deterrent to the enjoyment of literature. On the contrary, this book is predicated on the assumption that such knowledge and the intelligent application of several interpretive techniques can enhance the pleasure that the common reader can derive from a piece of literature.

Let us illustrate with an analogy. A college student in an American university decides to take in a film on a Friday evening as a reward for a week of grinding study. She rounds up a group of friends similarly disposed, and they head for a nearby mall, the site of a huge theater where eight films are being shown simultaneously in different auditoriums. The sheer joy of weekend freedom and the anticipation of an attractive choice of films afford an ecstasy denied to many. Even that pleasure is heightened by the sight of hordes of other students laughing and clowning about their release from labs and libraries into the wonderful world of cinema. America's future business and professional leaders are stocking up on mouthwatering tubs of hot buttered popcorn and mammoth cups of soft drinks before disappearing into dark caverns full of luxuriously upholstered reclining theater seats, there to thrill vicariously to torrid love scenes, gory detective brutality, wild and crazy comedy, complex psychological drama, and amazing tales of the future. Everything combines to immerse them in a pool of sensation.

Not far away from these avid fans, a smaller, somewhat less flamboyant group of students are making their way into one of the auditoriums, but they lack none of the other group's excitement and anticipation. They are members of one of the university's film classes, and they are accompanied by their professor. They are thoroughly informed on the history of moviemaking; they know both classic and contemporary films; they understand the technical operations of the camera and its myriad effects; they are familiar with acting styles, past and present. On the level of sense experience, they are receiving the same impressions as the other group of students. But because of their special knowledge, they *comprehend* what they are witnessing. Their knowledge does not dim their pleasure; it does not nullify any precritical, amateur response. It may even intensify it; it certainly complements it. For there is no real opposition of responses here. These more knowledgeable movie-goers do not say to themselves at one point, "Now we're *feeling*," and at another, "Now we're *knowing*." By this stage the knowing is almost as instinctive as the feeling.

What the academic critic needs to keep always in mind is that the precritical response is not an inferior response to literature. (After all, we may be sure that Shakespeare did not write *Hamlet* so that scholarly critical approaches to it could be formulated.) Rather, the precritical response employing primarily the senses and the emotions is an indispensable one if pleasure or delight is the aim of art. Without it the critic might as well be merely proofreading for factual accuracy or correct mechanical form. It may be said to underlie or even to drive the critical response.

▪ I. SETTING

The students' precritical response to a film parallels the common reader's precritical response to literature. The generic 1990s Americana locale of *Scream* corresponds to the *setting* of the work of literature (the antebellum South of *Huckleberry Finn*; Puritan Massachusetts in "Young Goodman Brown"; Cavalier England in "To His Coy Mistress"; eleventh-century Denmark in *Hamlet*; the Deep South of the 1970s in "Everyday Use").

Precritical responses to setting in the works to be dealt with in this handbook are likely to be numerous and freewheeling. One reader of *Huckleberry Finn* will respond to the nostalgia of an earlier, rural America, to the lazy tempo and idyllic mood of Huck and Jim's raft trip down the Mississippi. Still another will delight in the description of the aristocratic Grangerfords' bourgeois parlor furnishings or the frontier primitivism of Arkansas river villages and the one-horse plantation of the Phelpses. The Gothic texture of the New England forest in "Young Goodman Brown" will sober some readers, as will the dark and brooding castle of Hamlet. The actual setting of "To His Coy Mistress" must be inferred (a formal garden? the spacious grounds of a nobleman's estate? some Petit Trianon type of apartment?), but romantically connotative settings such as the "Indian Ganges" and the "tide of Humber" are alluded to, as are macabre or mind-boggling places like "marble vaults" and "deserts of vast eternity." The primitive living conditions of the Johnsons in "Everyday Use" will be altogether unfamiliar to most modern young readers, even to those in the South.

▣ II. PLOT

The students' uncomplicated view of an individual film equals the reader's precritical response to the *conflict* (*plot*) involving *protagonist* and *antagonist* (Hamlet versus his uncle; Clint Eastwood versus hoods and drug dealers). Readers who delight in action will thrill to the steps in Hamlet's revenge, even when it lights on the innocent, and will feel the keen irony that prevents him from knowing his Ophelia to be true and guiltless and from enjoying the fruit of his righteous judgment. Such time-honored plot ingredients as the escape, the chase, the capture, the release—sensationally spiced with lynching, tar-and-feathering, swindling, feuding, murder, and treachery—may form the staple of interest for precritical readers of *Huckleberry Finn*. Such readers will also be rooting for the white boy and his black slave friend to elude their pursuers and attain their respective freedoms. Enigma and bewilderment may well be the principal precritical response elicited by the plot of "Young Goodman Brown": is Brown's conflict an imaginary one, or is he really battling the Devil in this theological *Heart of Darkness*? Or in "To His Coy Mistress," will the young Cavalier prevail with his Coy Mistress to make love before they are crushed in the maw of Time?

▣ III. CHARACTER

The young moviegoers assess, after a fashion, the roles of the actors. Although these are frequently cultural stereotypes, they bear some analogy to the common reader's commonsense character analysis of literary figures (the self-effacing, sacrificial nature of Sidney Carton in *A Tale of Two Cities*, the matter-of-fact courage and resourcefulness of Robinson Crusoe, the noble but frustrated humanity of John Savage in *Brave New World*). Precritical reactions to the characters in "To His Coy Mistress" will no doubt vary with the degree to which the reader subscribes to situation ethics or adheres to a clearly articulated moral code. Strict constructionists will judge the male aggressor a wolf and the woman a tease at best. Libertines will envy the speaker his line. Feminists will deplore the male-chauvinist exploitation that is being attempted. Although characters more complex than the tornado-chasing team in *Twister* appear in *Huckleberry Finn*, a precritical perusal of the book will probably divide them into good (those basically sympathetic to Huck and Jim) and bad (those not). Similarly, the dramatis personae of *Hamlet* will be judged according to whether they line up on the side of the tormented Hamlet or on that of his diabolically determined uncle. In more complex character analysis, the simplistic grouping into good and bad will not be adequate; it may in fact necessitate an appreciation of ambiguity. From this viewpoint, Gertrude and Polonius and Rosencrantz and Guildenstern appear more weak and venal than absolutely vicious. Complexity also informs the character treatment of Dee and her mother in "Everyday Use." The former is not merely the stock figure of the young black civil rights leader of the 1970s any more than her mother is a latter-day female Uncle Tom. Just as ambiguity was prominent in the plot of "Young Goodman Brown," so does it figure largely in a reader's precritical evaluation of character. Brown may appear to be a victim of trauma, an essentially shallow man suddenly made to seem profoundly disturbed.

▪ IV. STRUCTURE

The students' awareness of the major complications and developments of a film plot such as that of *The English Patient* and the importance of each to the outcome is akin to the reader's or viewer's unconscious sense of *plot structure*, the relatedness of actions, the gradual buildup in suspense from a situation full of potential to a climax and a resolution (as in Macbeth's rise to be king of Scotland through foul and bloody means and the poetic justice of his defeat and death by one he had wronged). A precritical response to the structure of "To His Coy Mistress" could certainly involve the recognition of the heightening intensity, stanza by stanza, of the lover's suit—from the proper and conventional complimentary forms of verbal courting to more serious arguments about the brevity of life and, finally, to the bold and undisguised affirmation that sexual joy is the central goal of the lover's life. The common reader can discern the plot development in *Hamlet* step by step, from mystery, indecision, and torment to knowledge, resolute action, and catharsis. He or she may be fascinated by the stratagems that Hamlet and Claudius employ against each other and amused by the CIA-like techniques of Polonius to ferret out Hamlet's secret. Spellbinding horror and, later, cathartic pathos are possible emotions engendered by the climax and dénouement of this revenge tragedy. The episodic plot of *Huckleberry Finn* is somehow coherent even though precritical readers must confront in rapid order thrill, suspense, danger, brutality, outrage, absurdity, laughter, tears, anger, and poetic justice as they respond to Huck and Jim's attempts to elude capture; the side-splitting charlatanism as well as the sinister and criminal behavior of the King and the Duke; wrecked steamboats; tent revivals; feuding, shooting in the street, and thwarted lynching; and finally the mixed triumph of the heroes. The structural stages in "Young Goodman Brown" may result in ambivalent reactions by the reader: on the one hand, plain recognition of the destructive effects of the events of the plot on Brown; on the other, bewilderment as to whether the events really took place or were all fantasy.

■ V. STYLE

The acting technique in a film may be realistic, as is Morgan Freeman's in *Seven*, or it may be stylized, as in the case of Jim Carey's Ace Ventura. It has its counterpart in the verbal *style* of a literary work (the spare, understated prose of Hemingway; the sophisticated wit of *The Importance of Being Earnest;* the compressed, highly allusive idiom of poets like Eliot and Yeats; the crude, earthy plain talk of Norman Mailer's *The Naked and the Dead*, John Updike's *Couples,* and Kurt Vonnegut's *Slaughterhouse-Five*). The precritical reader feels it in the Pike County dialect of *Huckleberry Finn*, its vocabulary and rhythms seemingly ringing true in every line; in the urbane diction, learned allusion, and polished couplets of "To His Coy Mistress"; in the magnificent blank verse of *Hamlet,* alternately formal and plain, yet somehow organic and right for both dramatic action and philosophical soliloquy; in the solemn, cadenced phraseology of "Young Goodman Brown," echoing what one imagines Puritan discourse to have been like, both in and out of the pulpit, its lightest touches still somehow ponderous; and in the wry, folksy dialogue and internal commentary of "Everyday Use."

▪ VI. ATMOSPHERE

Defined as the mood or feeling that permeates an environment, *atmosphere* is a further common ingredient in the two parts of our analogy. Several factors combine to create it: in Steven Spielberg's movie *The Lost World*, the physical setting, the terror, the acting itself; in a literary work, such similar factors as the eerie locales and stormy weather in Mary Shelley's *Frankenstein* and Emily Brontë's *Wuthering Heights*, the panic of the green troops in Stephen Crane's *Red Badge of Courage*, the suspense and terror in Edgar Allan Poe's "Tell-Tale Heart," the indifference and listlessness of the characters in William Faulkner's "That Evening Sun."

The five works that we are emphasizing for precritical responses afford interesting possibilities. "To His Coy Mistress," which on the surface seems to have fewer overt atmosphere-producing elements, in fact has a fairly pronounced atmosphere (or atmospheres, since there are shifts). The atmosphere results from the diction and the tone the speaker employs. The formal honorific "Lady" and its implied politeness create, if not a drawing-room atmosphere, a stylized one where there is romantic badinage, where gallants wax hyperbolic in a formulary way, and where fair maidens drop their eyes demurely or, if hyperbole becomes too warm, tap male wrists with a delicate fan. It is a mannered, controlled, ritualistic atmosphere. But in the second stanza, compliments give way to a professorial lecture as the aggressive male grows impatient with coyness carried too far, hence a dispiriting philosophical discussion about the brevity of life and the nothingness of afterlife. Finally, in the third stanza, the atmosphere becomes electric and potentially physical as the diction becomes explicitly erotic.

In *Huckleberry Finn*, on a very obvious plane, setting contributes to atmosphere. The Mississippi River, sleepy villages, small towns, one-horse plantations, Victorian parlors: all combine to present an essentially "normal" nineteenth-century-Americana kind of security along with zest for life. Diction, character, and costume, however, also function to add subtle features to the atmosphere: the casual use of expressions like "nigger" and "harelip" (most of our nineteenth-century ancestors did not share our aversion to using racial epithets or to making fun of physical deformity); the toleration and acceptance of violence, cruelty, and inhumanity observable in conversation and exposition; the radical inconsistency of basically decent, religious people breaking up slave families while evincing genuine affection for them and concern for their welfare. The amalgam of their shocking and sometimes contradictory attitudes and actions results in an utterly convincing atmosphere.

Both setting and plot make for a gloomy, foreboding atmosphere in *Hamlet* and "Young Goodman Brown." The Shakespearean drama opens with sentries walking guard duty at midnight on the battlements of a medieval castle where a ghost has recently appeared. It is bitter cold and almost unnaturally quiet. Though later the scene changes many times, this atmosphere persists, augmented by the machinations of the principals, by dramatic confrontations, by reveries on death, by insane ravings, and finally by wholesale slaughter. In only slightly less melodramatic form, Hawthorne's story takes the reader to a witches' sabbath deep in the forests of seventeenth-century Massachusetts, where a cacophony of horrid sounds makes up the auditory background for a scene of devilish human countenances and eerie, distorted images of trees, stones, clouds. The protagonist's ambiguous role in the evil ceremony, which ruins his life, adds to the dark atmosphere pervading the story. In "Everyday Use," setting (the humble cabin of country blacks in modern rural Georgia) and tension (between conservative rural blacks and their "emancipated" kinswoman) combine to form an atmosphere of latent and ultimately overt conflict.

▪ VII. THEME

The often rich and varied underlying idea of the action is the *theme*. In a film, theme may be no more than "Bust those drug dealers!" "Zap those aliens!" "Go for it!" In a literary work, theme may be as obvious as the message in *Uncle Tom's Cabin* that "Slavery is cruel and morally degrading and must go" or the implicit point of *Robin Hood* that "Some rich folks deserve to be taken from, and some poor folks need to be given to." These scarcely compare with such profound thematic implications as those in *Macbeth, The Scarlet Letter,* or "The Love Song of J. Alfred Prufrock." As theme is a complex aspect of literature, one that requires very intentional thinking to discern, it is not likely to elicit the precritical response that the more palpable features do. This is not to say that it will not be felt. Twain's criticisms of slavery, hypocrisy, chicanery, violence, philistine aesthetic taste, and other assorted evils will move both the casual reader and the scholar. So will Marvell's speaker's cavalier defiance of all-conquering Time. The poignancy of young Hamlet's having to deal with so many of life's insolubles at once and alone is certainly one of the play's major themes, and is one available at the precritical level of response. There are others. Despite complexity and ambiguity, the precritical reader will sense the meaning of faith and the effects of evil in "Young Goodman Brown" as two of the more urgent themes in the story. So will he or she perceive the ambivalence in accepting and rejecting one's heritage in "Everyday Use."

None of these feelings, whether at a movie or in private reading, is contingent upon a technical knowledge of motion pictures or a graduate degree in the humanities. Without either, people may appreciate and respond precritically to both Oscar-award-winning films and the cold setting of Jack London's "To Build a Fire," to the sequence of events that causes Oedipus to blind himself, or to the phantasmagoric atmosphere of horror pervading Poe's "Masque of the Red Death."

In short, regardless of the extent to which close scrutiny and technical knowledge aid in literary analysis, there is no substitute for an initial personal, appreciative response to the basic ingredients of literature: setting, plot, character, structure, style, atmosphere, and theme. The reader who manages to proceed without that response sacrifices the spontaneous joy of seeing any art object whole, the wondrous sum of myriad parts.

The precritical approach, then, is the one taken by the aforementioned "common reader"—literate, sensitive, interested in literature but lacking the technical skills of academic criticism. It is an approach which, as we have just claimed, produces satisfaction—even joy—and appreciation.

Another personal approach, similar in a number of respects, is reader-response. This approach, which has been around in various forms for some five decades, has, during that period, been valorized by sophisticated critics whose position we shall elaborate in chapter 8. Here let us examine the "personal" dimensions of reader-response theory as a variant of precritical analysis. As its name implies, readers "respond" on the basis of their identity and their experience. For example, the Ivy League-educated scion of a meat-packing fortune is going to react differently to Upton Sinclair's *The Jungle* from the young union laborer whose family has suffered from strikes and layoffs.

We shall illustrate by positing two hypothetical readers of Alice Walker's "Everyday Use." The first is, let us say, Tricia, a twenty-year-old African American, female, junior pre-med student in a large Southern university noted for academic excellence. This young woman comes from an upper middle-class family; both parents are working professionals with advanced degrees. Proud of the achievements of her parents and of her own self in a society where it is sometimes difficult for members of minority groups to attain success, Tricia is understandably sympathetic with those who have remained in the underclass into which her grandparents were born. To her, the female narrator of the story is a heroic figure who has faced the ugliness of racial bigotry and been wounded but not defeated or overly embittered by it. Tricia appreciates how the narrator has taken the simplest, humblest, least dramatic tokens of her family's heritage—churns, benches, quilts—and had her spirits lifted and kept aloft by their practical and symbolic value. Tricia perceives that the narrator's wisdom and understanding are on a par with her heroism in that she does not condemn her talented young daughter for seeing racial matters in an angry light, for changing her original name to an African one, for traveling with a Muslim man who sports a wild-looking hairdo and beard, for dressing and adorning herself unconventionally, and for seeing the few artifacts of the family household as quaint and potentially pricey folk art. Indeed, Tricia's sympathies, pretty much those of any middle-class person, all lie with the narrator, whose common sense, reasonableness, wisdom, and goodness impress her much more favorably than Dee/Wangero's more flamboyant and rebellious rejection of everything in her heritage.

Our second hypothetical reader, Ibrahim, is an eighteen-year-old African American male freshman in a large metropolitan university in the Northeast. Ibrahim was born and grew up in the ghetto, exchanging his birth name for an Arabic one during high school, when he became a convert to the Nation of Islam. Inspired by the confrontational and fiery rhetoric of such figures as Malcolm X and Louis Farrakhan, Ibrahim is now unsympathetic with more traditional civil rights groups like the NAACP. He sees Dee/Wangero as a strong kindred spirit, a true revolutionary determined not to be held back by any sentimental attachment to family. To Ibrahim, the narrator in "Everyday Use" and Maggie are ignorant country blacks, content to live in a slave setting and too fearful of whites even to resent the deprivation caused by whites. He regards their "triumph" at the end and the debunking of Wangero and Hakim-a-barber, their behavior, and everything they represent as capitulation to irredeemable white racism.

For the other works that this handbook treats in detail—"Coy Mistress," *Hamlet*, *Huckleberry Finn*, and "Young Goodman Brown"—let us posit only one reader, a white female graduate of an average high school in a small Midwestern town now in her freshman year in a liberal arts college. The curriculum in her high school reflected an anticlassical, pro-contemporary bias on the part of state department textbook committees with a concomitant reduction of traditional requirements in older literature. She has, for example, read no Shakespeare. Nor has she read any seventeenth-century poets like Milton or Donne. Finally, she has read no literature that contained rural black dialect of the nineteenth century. She is, therefore, reacting in puzzlement, shock, and incomprehension as she studies the works listed above. Because she is a member of a nondenominational Protestant church, the theological issues in the Hawthorne story strike her as antiquarian and irrelevant, as do the attitudes toward sex in "Coy Mistress" and *Hamlet*. In short, her responses to these classics of English and American literature are affected by her education, her home life, and the attitudes of an increasingly secular and sexually permissive society.

These three hypothetical examples emphasize an important tenet of reader-response: the belief that readers interpret literature in the light of their experiences and convictions and thus that their varying interpretations are valid. It may be difficult for many students to escape the conclusion that from this point of view a piece of literature may have as many "meanings" as it has readers or that it may mean "anything." However, as we hope to make clear in the following chapters, a great work of literature is not a mere ink blot. Though it may be in one sense inexhaustible of meaning, truly valid interpretation must be supportable by contextual evidence. In other words, while we respect—indeed, encourage—creative, imaginative reader-responses, our ultimate aim is never to read anything *into* the work, but to find everything we profitably can *in* the work.

Quick Reference

Berthoff, Ann. "Recalling Another Freudian Model—A Consumer Caveat." *The CEA Critic* 35 (May 1973): 12–14.

Ciardi, John. *How Does a Poem Mean?* 2nd ed. Boston: Houghton Mifflin, 1975.

Fiedler, Leslie. "Is There a Majority Literature?" *The CEA Critic* 36 (May 1974): 3–8.

Morse, J. Mitchell. "Are English Teachers Obsolete?" *The CEA Critic* 36 (May 1974): 9–18.

Sontag, Susan. "Against Interpretation." *The Evergreen Review,* 1964. Reprinted in *Against Interpretation and Other Essays.* New York: Dell, 1969.

Touster, Eva. "Tradition and the Academic Talent." *The CEA Critic* 33 (May 1971): 14–17.

▪ 2 ▪

Traditional Approaches

I. NATURE AND SCOPE OF THE TRADITIONAL APPROACHES

Some years ago, a story was making the rounds in academic circles and was received in good humor by all the enlightened teachers of literature. A professor of English in a prestigious American university, so the story goes, entered the classroom one day and announced that the poem under consideration for that hour was to be Andrew Marvell's "To His Coy Mistress." He then proceeded for the next fifty minutes to discuss Marvell's politics, religion, and career. He described Marvell's character, mentioned that he was respected by friend and foe alike, and speculated on whether he was married. At this point the bell rang, signaling the end of the class. The professor closed his sheaf of notes, looked up, smiling, and concluded, "Damn' fine poem, men. Damn' fine."

The story was told to ridicule the type of criticism that once dominated the study of literature and that is still employed in some classrooms even today. In this approach the work of art frequently appeared to be of secondary importance, something that merely illustrated background. Such an approach often (many would say inevitably) led to the study of literature as essentially biography, history, or some other branch of learning, rather than as art.

Well into the twentieth century, however, a new type of liter-

16

ary analysis emerged in which the literary work per se (that is, as a separate entity divorced from extrinsic considerations) became the dominant concern of scholars. The New Critics, as the proponents of this position were called, insisted that scholars concentrate on the work itself, on the text, examining it as art. This method revolutionized the study of literature. It frequently divided critics and teachers into opposing factions: those of the older school, for whom literature provided primarily an opportunity for exercising what they perceived to be the really relevant scholarly and cultural disciplines (for example, history, linguistics, and biography) and the New Critics, who maintained that literature had an intrinsic worth, that it was not just one of the means of transmitting biography and history. Now that the controversy has lessened, the rationale of the New Criticism seems to have put into clearer focus what a poem or play or piece of fiction is trying to do; it has unquestionably corrected many wrongheaded interpretations resulting from an unwise use of the older method. To this extent it has expanded our perception and appreciation of literary art.

Nevertheless, in their zeal to avoid the danger of interpreting a literary work solely as biography and history—the end result of the traditional method, they thought—many twentieth-century followers of New Criticism have been guilty of what may well be a more serious mistake, that of ignoring any information not in the work itself, however helpful or necessary it might be. Fortunately, the most astute critics have espoused a more eclectic approach and have fused a variety of techniques. They have certainly insisted on treating literature as literature, but they have not ruled out the possibility of further aesthetic illumination from traditional quarters. Oscar Cargill, in the introduction to his *Toward a Pluralistic Criticism*, endorsed the eclectic approach unequivocally:

> I have always held that any method which could produce the meaning of a work of literature was a legitimate method. . . . I came to the conclusion that . . . the critic's task was . . . to procure a viable meaning appropriate to the critic's time and place. Practically, this meant employing not any one method in interpreting a work of art but every method which might prove efficient. (xii–xiv)

In any event, while we may grant the basic position that literature is primarily art, it must be affirmed also that art does not exist in a vacuum. It is a creation by someone at some time in history, and it is intended to speak to other human beings about some idea or issue that has human relevance. Any work of art for that matter will always be more meaningful to knowledgeable people than to uninformed ones. Its greatness comes from the fact that when the wisest, most cultivated, most sensitive minds bring all their information, experience, and feeling to contemplate it, they are moved and impressed by its beauty, by its unique kind of knowledge, and even by its nonaesthetic values. It is surely dangerous to assume that a work of art must always be judged or looked at or taught as if it were disembodied from all experience except the strictly aesthetic. Many literary classics are admittedly autobiographical, propagandistic, or topical (that is, related to contemporary events). These concerns are, in fact, central to one of the most recent theoretical approaches—the new historicism (see chapter 7).

Thus, although we have not yet elaborated these critical methods, let us be aware from the outset that in succeeding chapters we will be dealing with some widely divergent interpretive approaches to literature and that, regardless of what newer modes of analysis may be in the ascendant, the traditional methods retain their validity.

A. Textual Scholarship: A Prerequisite to Criticism

Before we embark upon any interpretive ventures, we should look to that branch of literary studies known as textual criticism. In the words of James Thorpe, author of one of the best modern books on the subject, *Principles of Textual Criticism*, textual criticism has as its ideal the establishment of an *authentic* text, or the "text which the author intended" (50). This aim is not so easy to achieve as one might think, however, and it is a problem not only with older works, where it might be more expected, but also in contemporary literature. There are countless ways in which a literary text may be corrupted from what the author intended. The author's own manuscript may contain omissions and errors in spelling and mechanics; these mistakes may be preserved by the text copyists, be they scribes or printers, who may add a few of their own. Or, as has often happened, copyists or editors may take it upon themselves to improve, censor, or correct what the author wrote. If the author or someone who knows what the author intended does not catch these errors during proofreading, they can be published, disseminated, and perpetuated. (Nor does it help matters when authors themselves cannot decide what the final form of their work is to be but actually release for publication several different versions or, as is frequently the case, delegate broad editorial powers to others along the line.) So many additional mishaps can befall a manuscript in the course of producing multiple copies for the public that, to quote Thorpe again, the "ordinary history of the transmission of a text, without the intervention of author or editor, is one of progressive degeneration" (51). Shocking as such an assertion may sound, it is nevertheless true and can be documented.

We frequently assume that the text before us has come down unchanged from its original form. More often than not, the reverse is the case; what we see is the result of painstaking collation of textual variants, interpretation, and emendation or conjecture. Because it is pointless to study inaccurate versions of anything, from economic theories to works of literature, except with a view to ascertaining the true (that is, the authorial) version, our debt to textual criticism is well-nigh incalculable. For example, the student who uses the eight-volume Chicago edition of *The Canterbury Tales,* a collation of scores of medieval manuscripts, should certainly appreciate the efforts of precomputer scholars. Similarly, the studies of W. W. Greg, A. W. Pollard, Fredson Bowers, Charlton Hinman, Stanley Wells, Garry Taylor, and a host of others have gone far toward the establishment of a satisfactory Shakespearean text. This type of scholarship should create in the student a healthy respect for textual criticism and expert editing, and well it might, for as Thorpe has aptly phrased it, "where there is no editing the texts perish" (54).

Textual criticism plays an especially important role in studying the genesis and development of a piece of literature. Thus it has enabled us to see how Ezra Pound's editorial surgery transformed T. S. Eliot's *The Waste Land* from a clumsy and diffuse poem to a modern classic. (The poem still presents textual problems, however, because Eliot himself authorized versions containing substantive differences.) Other famous textual cases include Dickens's two endings for *Great Expectations:* after seeing the first "unhappy" ending in proof, Dickens wrote another and authorized only it. Later editors have published the first version as having more aesthetic integrity, but Dickens never authorized it. Thomas Hardy made so many substantive character and plot alterations in the four versions of *The Return of the Native,* all of which he authorized for publication between 1878 and 1912, that James Thorpe understandably asks, "Which is the real *Return of the Native?*" (34). Moreover, textual criticism is, contrary to what ill-informed people may think, anything but an essentially mechanical operation. Although its practitioners are very much concerned with such matters as spelling, punctuation, capitalization, italicization, and paragraphing (accidentals, as they are called in textual criticism) in the establishment of an authentic text, they deal with much more than close proofreading. They must be highly skilled in linguistics, literary history, literary criticism, and bibliography, to mention only the most obvious areas.

However, though textual critics must and do make aesthetic judgments, not only in accidentals but also in substantives (actual verbal readings), they do so in order to establish by means as scientific as possible an authentic text for the literary critic, who may then proceed to interpret and evaluate. Textual criticism is therefore treated in this book not as a traditional interpretive approach to literature but as an indispensable tool for further meaningful analysis. This relationship between textual and strictly interpretive criticism may be expressed in a surgical metaphor: textual critics are the first in a team of critics who prepare the literary corpus for further study. Nevertheless, we should not push any analogy between textual criticism and science too far. Textual critics are not and should not be considered scientists. They have no predetermined or inviolable laws that they can use to come out with an authentic text. Perhaps it would be more accurate to concede that textual critics are scientists of sorts; they simply are not exact scientists (that is, ones dealing in an exact science). They are, more precisely, a combination of scientist and artist. As A. E. Housman says, textual criticism is the "science of discovering error in texts and the art of removing it" (2).

Thorpe, however, is highly critical of any scientific claims for textual criticism. Indeed, one of the main points of his book is the failure of textual studies to measure up to their alleged scientific status. Somewhat resignedly he concludes:

> It would be cheerful to be able to report that a mastery of sound principles, an application of effective methods, and an exercise of conscientious care will enable the textual critic to reach the ideal which is incorporated in the first principle of his craft. But it would not be true. In textual criticism, the best that one can do is to cut the losses, to reduce the amount of error, to improve or clarify the state of textual affairs, to approach the ideal. After all has been done that can be done, however, the results of textual criticism still are necessarily imperfect. (55)

Whether one agrees with Thorpe or with those who view textual criticism as less tentative and more scientific, all critics can agree on one thing: it is far more preferable to have a version of a literary work that textual criticism can make available to us than to have one that has not been subjected to the rigorous methodology of that discipline.

Another especially thorough and incisive discussion of this subject is D. C. Greetham's *Textual Scholarship: An Introduction.* In addition to a narrative account of the history of the field, there are explanations and illustrations covering the the spectrum of textual scholarship. And, though it deals with such technical material as enumerative and research bibliography, descriptive and analytical bibliography, paleography and typography, historical and textual bibliography, textual criticism and textual theory, and scholarly editing, Greetham's book is as accessible to the nonspecialist undergraduate as it is to the literary scholar and editor.

B. Types of Traditional Approaches

We present two types of traditional critical approaches to literature, the historical-biographical and the moral-philosophical; each will be defined, discussed, and subsequently applied to each of the five works selected for emphasis. Early in the discussions of each work we will also treat textual matters, summarizing the narrative line of the literary work and making some nontechnical observations about genre. (The generic approach will receive additional attention in chapter 8.) These steps may be thought of as preliminaries to traditional literary analysis and can certainly be useful in other interpretive approaches as well.

1. Historical-Biographical

Although the historical-biographical approach has been evolving over many years, its basic tenets are perhaps most clearly articulated in the writings of the nineteenth-century French critic H. A. Taine, whose phrase *race, milieu, et moment,* elaborated in his *History of English Literature,* bespeaks a hereditary and environmental determinism. Put simply, this approach sees a literary work chiefly, if not exclusively, as a reflection of its author's life and times or the life and times of the characters in the work.

At the risk of laboring the obvious, we will mention the historical implications of William Langland's *Piers Plowman,* which is, in addition to being a magnificent allegory, a scorching attack on the corruption in every aspect of fourteenth-century English life—social, political, and religious. So timely, in fact, were the poet's phrases that they became rallying cries in the Peasants' Revolt. John Milton's sonnet "On the Late Massacre in Piedmont" illustrates the topical quality that great literature may and often does possess. This poem commemorates the slaughter in 1655 of the Waldenses, members of a Protestant sect living in the valleys of northern Italy. A knowledge of this background clarifies at least one rather factual reference and two allusions in the poem. Several of Milton's other sonnets also reflect events in his life or times. Two such are "On His Blindness," best understood when one realizes that the poet became totally blind when he was forty-four, and "On His Deceased Wife," a tribute to his second wife, Katherine Woodcock. Milton was already blind when he married her, a fact that explains the line, "Her face was veiled." In fact, Milton affords us an excellent example of an author whose works reflect particular episodes in his life. *Samson Agonistes* and *The*

Doctrine and Discipline of Divorce may be cited as two of the more obvious instances.

A historical novel is likely to be more meaningful when either its milieu or that of its author is understood. James Fenimore Cooper's *Last of the Mohicans,* Sir Walter Scott's *Ivanhoe,* Charles Dickens's *Tale of Two Cities,* and John Steinbeck's *Grapes of Wrath* are certainly better understood by readers familiar with, respectively, the French and Indian War (and the American frontier experience generally), Anglo-Norman Britain, the French Revolution, and the American Depression. And, of course, there is a very real sense in which these books are *about* these great historical matters, so that the author is interested in the characters only to the extent that they are molded by these events.

What has just been said applies even more to ideological or propagandist novels. Harriet Beecher Stowe's *Uncle Tom's Cabin,* Frank Norris's *The Octopus,* and Upton Sinclair's *The Jungle* ring truer (or falser as the case may be) to those who know about the antebellum South, railroad expansion in the late nineteenth century, and scandals in the American meat-packing industry in the early twentieth century. Sinclair Lewis's satires take on added bite and fun for those who have lived in or observed the cultural aridity of *Main Street,* who have been treated by shallow and materialistic physicians like some of those in *Arrowsmith,* who have sat through the sermons and watched the shenanigans of religious charlatans like Elmer Gantry, or who have dealt with and been in service clubs with all-too-typical American businessmen like Babbitt. Novels may lend themselves somewhat more readily than lyric poems to this particular interpretive approach; they usually treat a broader range of experience than poems do and thus are affected more by extrinsic factors.

It is a mistake, however, to think that poets do not concern themselves with social themes or that good poetry cannot be written about such themes. Actually, poets have from earliest times been the historians, the interpreters of contemporary culture, and the prophets of their people. Take, for example, a poet as mystical and esoteric as William Blake. Many of his best poems can be read meaningfully only in terms of Blake's England. His "London" is an outcry against the oppression of man by society: he lashes out against child labor in his day and the church's indifference to it, against the government's indifference to the indigent soldier who has served his country faithfully, and against the horrible and unnatural consequences of a social code that represses sexuality. His "Preface" to *Milton* is at once a denunciation of the "dark Satanic Mills" of the Industrial Revolution and a joyous battle cry of determination to build "Jerusalem/In England's green and pleasant Land." It has been arranged as an anthem for church choirs, is widely used in a hymn setting, and was sung in London in the 1945 election by the victorious Labour party. The impact of the Sacco and Vanzetti case upon young poets of the 1920s or of the opposition to the war in Vietnam upon almost every important American poet in the 1960s resulted in numerous literary works on these subjects. Obviously, then, even some lyric poems are susceptible to historical-biographical analysis.

Political and religious verse satires like John Dryden's in the seventeenth century and personal satires like Alexander Pope's in the eighteenth century have as one of their primary purposes the ridiculing of contemporary situations and persons. Dryden propounds his own Anglican faith and debunks the faith of both Dissenters and Papists in *Religio Laici*. Later, when he had renounced Anglicanism and embraced Roman Catholicism, he again defended his position, and in *The Hind and the Panther* he attacked those who differed. His *Absalom and Achitophel* is a verse allegory using the biblical story of Absalom's rebellion against his father, King David, to satirize the Whig attempt to replace Charles II with his illegitimate son, the Duke of Monmouth. Pope's *Dunciad* is certainly a satire against all sorts of literary stupidity and inferiority, but it is also directed against particular literary people who had the bad fortune to offend Pope. All these works may be understood and appreciated without extensive historical or biographical background. Most readers, however, would probably agree with T. S. Eliot that "No poet, no artist of any art, has his complete meaning alone" (from "Tradition and the Individual Talent") and with Richard D. Altick that "almost every literary work is attended by a host of outside circumstances which, once we expose and explore them, suffuse it with additional meaning" (5).

The triumph of such verse satires as those of Dryden and Pope is that they possess considerable merit as poems, merit that is only enhanced by their topicality. That it should ever have been necessary to defend them because they were topical or "unpoetic" is attributable to what Ronald S. Crane calls, in *A Collection of English Poems, 1660–1800,* the tyranny of certain Romantic and Victorian "presuppositions about the nature of poetry" and the "inhibitions of taste which they have tended to encourage." He mentions among such presuppositions the notions that

> true poetry is always a direct outpouring of personal feeling; that its values are determined by the nature of the emotion which it expresses, the standards being naturally set by the preferences of the most admired poets in the nineteenth-century tradition; that its distinctive effort is "to bring unthinkable thoughts and unsayable sayings within the range of human minds and ears"; that the essence of its art is not statement but suggestion. (v)

In short, even topical poetry can be worthwhile when not limited by presuppositions that make poetry a precious, exclusively personal, even esoteric thing.

2. Moral-Philosophical

The moral-philosophical approach is as old as classical Greek and Roman critics. Plato, for example, emphasized moralism and utilitarianism; Horace stressed that literature should be delightful and instructive. Among its most famous exemplars are the commentators of the age of neoclassicism in English literature (1660–1800), particularly Samuel Johnson. The basic position of such critics is that the larger function of literature is to teach morality and to probe philosophical issues. They would interpret literature within a context of the philosophical thought of a period or group. From their point of view Jean-Paul Sartre and Albert Camus can be read profitably only if one understands existentialism. Similarly, Pope's *Essay on Man* may be grasped only if one understands the meaning and the role of reason in eighteenth-century thought. Such teaching may also be religiously oriented. Henry Fielding's *Tom Jones,* for example, illustrates the moral superiority of a hot-blooded young man like Tom, whose sexual indulgences are decidedly atoned for by his humanitarianism, tenderheartedness, and instinctive honor (innate as opposed to acquired through training). Serving as foils to Tom are the real sinners in the novel— the vicious and the hypocritical. Hawthorne's *Scarlet Letter* is likewise seen essentially as a study of the effects of secret sin on a human soul—that is, sin unconfessed before both God and man, as the sin of Arthur Dimmesdale with Hester Prynne, or, even more, the sin of Roger Chillingworth. Robert Frost's "Stopping by Woods on a Snowy Evening" suggests that duty and responsibility take precedence over beauty and pleasure.

A related attitude is that of Matthew Arnold, the Victorian critic, who insisted that a great literary work must possess "high seriousness." (Because he felt that Chaucer lacked it, Arnold refused to rank him among the very greatest English poets.) In each instance critics working from a moral bent are not unaware of form, figurative language, and other purely aesthetic considerations, but they consider them to be secondary. The important thing is the moral or philosophical teaching. On its highest plane this is not superficially didactic, though it may at first seem so. In the larger sense, all great literature teaches. The critic who employs the moral-philosophical approach insists on ascertaining and stating *what* is taught. If the work is in any degree significant or intelligible, this meaning will be there.

It seems reasonable, then, to employ historical-biographical or moral-philosophical analyses among other methods (such as textual study and recognition of genre) in getting at the total meaning of a literary work when the work seems to call for them. Such approaches are less likely to err on the side of over-interpretation than are more esoteric methods. And overinterpretation is a particularly grievous critical error. A reader who stays more or less on the surface of a piece of literature has at least understood part of what it is about, whereas a reader who extracts interpretations that are neither supportable nor reasonable may miss a very basic or even key meaning. Obviously, a dull, pedestrian, uniformly literal approach to literary analysis is the antithesis of the informed, imaginative, and creative approach that this book advocates. But it must be remembered that, brilliant and ingenious criticism notwith-standing, words in context, though they may mean many things, cannot mean just anything at all. Daring, inventive readings of metaphorical language must have defensible ratio-nales if they are to be truly insightful and convincing.

The enemies of the traditional approach to literary analysis have argued that it has tended to be somewhat deficient in imagination, has neglected the newer sciences, such as psy-chology and anthropology, and has been too content with a commonsense interpretation of material. But it has neverthe-less performed one valuable service: in avoiding cultism and faddism, it has preserved scholarly discipline and balance in literary criticism. We do not mean that we favor traditional criticism over predominantly aesthetic interpretive aproaches. We do suggest, however, that any knowledge or insight (with special reference to scholarly disciplines like history, philoso-phy, theology, sociology, art, and music) that can help to ex-plain or clarify a literary work ought to be given the fullest possible chance to do so. Indeed, in some sense these ap-proaches represent a necessary first step that precedes most other approaches.

Readers who intend to employ the traditional approaches to a literary work will almost certainly employ them simultane-ously. That is, they will bring to bear on a poem, for instance, all the information and insights these respective disciplines can give in seeing just what the poem means and does.

▪ II. THE TRADITIONAL APPROACHES IN PRACTICE

A. Traditional Approaches to Marvell's "To His Coy Mistress"

1. The Text of the Poem
Some words on textual problems in Andrew Marvell's "To His Coy Mistress" will set the stage for our consideration of the poem. One of these problems is the last word in this couplet:

> Now therefore, while the youthful hue
> Sits on thy skin like morning dew.

Instead of "dew," the first edition of the poem had "glew,"
which we now know is a dialectal variant of "glow," although
it was earlier thought to be another spelling of "glue," a senseless reading in the context. "Lew" (dialectal "warmth") was
also suggested as a possibility. But when someone conjectured
"dew," probably in the eighteenth century, it was apparently
so happy an emendation that virtually all textbooks have long
printed it without any explanation. The first edition of this
handbook followed those textbooks. But two modern texts restore the earliest reading. Both Louis Martz's *Anchor Anthology
of Seventeenth-Century Verse* and George de F. Lord's *Andrew
Marvell, Complete Poetry* print "glew" (meaning "glow") as
making more sense in the context and being quite sound linguistically. Two other words in the poem that must be explained are "transpires" and "instant" in this couplet:

> And while thy willing soul transpires
> At every pore with instant fires.

In each case, the word is much nearer to its Latin original than
to its twentieth-century meaning. "Transpires" thus means literally "breathes forth," and "instant" means "now present"
and "urgent." Admittedly, this sort of linguistic information
borders on the technical, but an appreciation of the meaning
of the words is imperative for a full understanding of the
poem.

2. The Genre of the Poem

Most critics are careful to ascertain what literary type or genre
they are dealing with, whether a poem (and if so, what particular kind), a drama, a novel, or a short story. This first
step—the question "What are we dealing with?"—is highly
necessary, because different literary genres are judged according to different standards. We do not expect, for example, the
sweep and grandeur of an epic in a love lyric, nor do we expect the extent of detail in a short story that we find in a novel.
From a technical and formal standpoint, we do expect certain
features in particular genres, features so integral as to define
and characterize the type (for example, rhythm, rhyme, narrative devices such as a point-of-view character, and dramatic

devices such as the soliloquy). The lyric, the genre to which "Coy Mistress" belongs, is a fairly brief poem characterized primarily by emotion, imagination, and subjectivity.

Having ascertained the genre and established the text, the employer of traditional methods of interpretation next determines what the poem says on the level of statement or, as John Crowe Ransom has expressed it, its "paraphrasable content." The reader discovers that this poem is a proposition, that is, an offer of sexual intercourse. At first it contains, however, little of the coarseness or crudity usually implied in the word *proposition*. On the contrary, though impassioned, it is graceful, sophisticated, even philosophical. The speaker, a courtier, has evidently urged an unsuccessful suit on a lady. Finding her reluctant, he is, as the poem opens, making use of his most eloquent line. But it is a line that reveals him to be no common lover. It is couched in the form of an argument in three distinct parts, going something like this: (1) If we had all the time in the world, I could have no objection to even an indefinite postponement of your acceptance of my suit. (2) But the fact is we do not have much time at all; and once this phase of existence (that is, life) is gone, all our chances for love are gone. (3) Therefore the only conclusion that can logically follow is that we should love one another now, while we are young and passionate, and thus seize what pleasures we can in a world where time is all too short. After all, we know nothing about any future life and have only the grimmest observations of the effects of death.

This is, as a matter of fact, a specious argument, viewed from the rigorous standpoint of formal logic. The fallacy is called denying the antecedent, in this case the first part of the conditional statement beginning with "if." The argument goes like this: If we have all the time and space in the world, your coyness is innocent (not criminal). We do not have all the time and space in the world. Therefore, your coyness is not innocent. Both premises are true, and the conclusion is still false. The lady's coyness may not be innocent for other reasons besides the lovers' not having all the time and space in the world. The male arguer undoubtedly does not care whether his argument is valid or not as long as it achieves his purpose. As Pope so well expressed it in *The Rape of the Lock*:

For when success a Lover's toil attends,
Few ask, if fraud or force attained his ends. (2.33–34)

3. Historical-Biographical Considerations

We know several facts about Marvell and his times that may help to explain this framework of logical argument as well as the tone and learned allusions that pervade the poem. First, Marvell was an educated man (Cambridge B.A., 1639), the son of an Anglican priest with Puritan leanings. Because both he and his father had received a classical education, the poet was undoubtedly steeped in classical modes of thought and literature. Moreover, the emphasis on classical logic and polemics in his education was probably kept strong in his mind by his political actions. (He was a Puritan, a Parliamentarian, an admirer of Oliver Cromwell, a writer of political satires, and an assistant to John Milton, who was Latin secretary to the government.) That it should occur, therefore, to Marvell to have the speaker plead his suit logically should surprise no one.

There is, however, nothing pedantic or heavy-handed in this disputatious technique. Rather, it is playful and urbane, as are the allusions to Greek mythology, courtly love, and the Bible. When the speaker begins his argument, he establishes himself in a particular tradition of love poetry, that of courtly love. No one would mistake this poem for love in the manner of "O my love's like a red, red rose" or "Sonnet from the Portuguese." It is based on the elevation of the beloved to the status of a virtually unattainable object, one to be idolized, almost like a goddess. This status notwithstanding, she is capable of cruelty, and in the first couplet the speaker accuses her of a crime, the crime of withholding her love from him. Moreover, because she is like a goddess, she is also capricious and whimsical, and the worshiper must humor her by following the conventions of courtly love. He will complain (of her cruelty and his subsequent pain and misery) by the River Humber. He will serve her through praise, adoration, and faithful devotion from the fourth millennium B.C. (the alleged time of Noah's flood) to the conversion of the Jews to Christianity, an event prophesied to take place just before the end of the world. Doubtless, this bit of humor is calculated to make the lady smile and to put her off her guard against the ulterior motive of the speaker.

However pronounced courtly love may be in the opening portion of the poem (the first part of the argument), by the time the speaker has reached the conclusion, he has stripped the woman of all pretense of modesty or divinity by his accusation that her "willing soul" literally exudes or breathes forth ("transpires") urgent ("instant") passion and by his direct allusion to kinesthetic ecstasy: "sport us," "roll all our strength," "tear our pleasures with rough strife/Thorough the iron gates of life" (the virginal body). All of this is consistent with a speaker who might have been schooled as Marvell himself was.

Many allusions in the poem that have to do with the passage of time show Marvell's religious and classical background. Two have been mentioned: the Flood and the conversion of the Jews. But there are others that continue to impress the reader with the urgency of the speaker's plea. "Time's winged chariot" is the traditional metaphor for the vehicle in which the sun, moon, night, and time are represented as pursuing their course. At this point, the speaker is still in the humorous vein, and the image is, despite its serious import, a pleasing one. The humor grows increasingly sardonic, however, and the images become in the second stanza downright repulsive. The allusions in the last stanza (the conclusion to the argument or case) do not suggest playfulness or a Cavalier attitude at all. Time's "slow-chapped [slow-jawed] power" alludes to the cannibalism of Kronos, chief of the gods, who, to prevent ever being overthrown by his own children, devoured all of them as they were born except Zeus. Zeus was hidden, later grew up, and ultimately became chief of the gods himself. The last couplet,

> Thus, though we cannot make our sun
> Stand still, yet we will make him run,

suggests several possible sources, both biblical and classical. Joshua commanded the sun to stand still so that he could win a battle against the Amorites (Josh. 10:13). Phaeton took the place of his father, the sun, in a winged chariot and had a wild ride across the sky, culminating in his death (Ovid, *Metamorphoses*). Zeus bade the sun to stand still in order to lengthen his night of love with Alcmene, the last mortal woman he embraced. In this example it is, of course, easy to see the appropriateness of the figures to the theme of the poem. Marvell's speaker is saying to his mistress that they are human, hence mortal. They do not have the ear of God as Joshua had, so God will not intervene miraculously and stop time. Nor do they possess the power of the pagan deities of old. They must instead cause time to pass quickly by doing what is pleasurable.

In addition to Marvell's classical and biblical background, further influences on the poem are erotic literature and Metaphysical poetry. Erotic poetry is, broadly speaking, simply love poetry, but it must emphasize the sensual. In "Coy Mistress" this emphasis is evident in the speaker's suit through the references to his mistress's breasts and "the rest" of her charms and in the image of the lovers rolled up into "one ball." The poem is Metaphysical in its similarities to other seventeenth-century poems that deal with the psychology of love and religion and—to enforce their meaning—employ bizarre, grotesque, shocking, and often obscure figures (the Metaphysical conceit). Such lines as "My vegetable love should grow," the warning that worms may violate the mistress's virginity and that corpses do not make love, the likening of the lovers to "amorous birds of prey," and the allusion to Time's devouring his offspring ("slow-chapped") all help identify the poem as a product of the seventeenth-century revolt against the saccharine conventions of Elizabethan love poetry. As for its relation to vers de société, "To His Coy Mistress" partakes more of the tone than the subject matter of such poetry, manifesting for the most part wit, gaiety, charm, polish, sophistication, and ease of expression—all of these despite some rough Metaphysical imagery.

4. Moral-Philosophical Considerations

An examination of what "Coy Mistress" propounds morally and philosophically reveals the common theme of *carpe diem*, "seize the day," an attitude of "eat and drink, for tomorrow we shall die." Many of Marvell's contemporaries treated this idea (for example, Robert Herrick in "To the Virgins, To Make Much of Time" and Edmund Waller in "Go, Lovely Rose"). This type of poetry naturally exhibits certain fundamental moral attitudes toward the main issue this poem treats—sex. These attitudes reflect an essentially pagan view. They depict sexual intercourse as strictly dalliance ("Now let us sport us while we may"), as solely a means of deriving physical sensations. Although not a Cavalier poet, Marvell is here letting his speaker express a more Cavalier (as opposed to Puritan) idea.

One more aspect of the historical background of the composition of the poem may be helpful in understanding its paradoxically hedonistic and pessimistic stance. The seventeenth century, it should be remembered, was not only a period of intense religious and political struggle, but a period of revolutionary scientific and philosophical thought. It was the century when Francis Bacon's inductive method was establishing itself as the most reliable way of arriving at scientific truth; it was the century when the Copernican theory tended to minimize the uniqueness and importance of the earth, hence of man, in the universe; it was the century when Thomas Hobbes's materialism and degrading view of human nature tended to outrage the orthodox or reflective Christian. Given this kind of intellectual milieu, readers may easily see how the poem might be interpreted as the impassioned utterance of a man who has lost anything resembling a religious or philosophical view of life (excluding, of course, pessimism). The paradox of the poem consists in the question of whether the speaker is honestly reflecting his view of life—pessimism—and advocating sensuality as the only way to make the best of a bad situation or whether he is simply something of a cad—stereotypically male, conceited, and superior, employing eloquence, argument, and soaringly passionate poetry merely as a line, a devious means to a sensual end. If the former is the case, there is something poignant in the way the man must choose the most exquisite pleasure he knows, sensuality, as a way of spitting in the face of his grand tormentor and victorious foe, Time. If the latter, then his disturbing images of the female body directed at his lady only turn upon him to reveal his fears and expose his lust. A feminist reading, as in chapter 6, sees the rhetoric of the poem very differently than does a traditional reading.

B. Traditional Approaches to *Hamlet*

1. The Text of the Play
Few literary works have received the amount and degree of textual study that Shakespeare's *Hamlet* has. There are some

obvious reasons for this. To begin with, even the earliest crude printings, shot through with the grossest errors, revealed a story and a mind that excited and challenged viewers, producers, readers, critics, and scholars—so much so that the scholars decided to do everything possible to ascertain what Shakespeare actually wrote. The other reasons are all related to this one. Shakespearean editors ever since have realized the importance of establishing an accurate text if students and audiences are to discover the meaning of *Hamlet*.

It is difficult at this remove in time for college students embarking on a serious reading of *Hamlet* to realize that the beautiful anthology or the handy paperback before them, each edited by an eminent authority, contains the product of nearly four hundred years of scholarly study of four different versions of *Hamlet* and that it still includes some moot and debatable readings. Besides questionable readings, there are a number of words whose meanings have changed over the years but that must be understood in their Elizabethan senses if the play is to be properly interpreted. To be sure, modern editors explain the most difficult words, but occasionally they let some slip by or fail to note that reputable scholars differ. Obviously, it is not possible here to point out all the variants of a given passsage or to give the seventeenth-century meaning of every puzzling construction, but the student can catch at least a glimpse of the multiplicity and the richness of interpretations by examining some of the more famous ones.

One of the best-known examples of such textual problems occurs in act I, scene ii: "O that this too too solid flesh would melt." This is perhaps the most common rendering of this line. The word "solid" appears in the first folio edition (1623) of Shakespeare's complete works. Yet the second quarto edition (1604–5), probably printed from Shakespeare's own manuscript, has "sallied," a legitimate sixteenth-century form of "sully" (to dirty, or make foul). These words pose two rather different interpretations of the line: if one reads "solid," the line seems to mean that Hamlet regrets the corporeality of the flesh and longs for bodily dissolution in order to escape the pain and confusion of fleshly existence. If, on the other hand, one reads "sullied," the line apparently reveals Hamlet's horror and revulsion upon contemplating the impurity of life and, by extension, his own involvement in it through the incest of his mother. J. Dover Wilson, in *What Happens in "Hamlet,"* sees "sullied flesh" as the clue to many significant passages in the play (for example, to Hamlet's imaginations "foul as Vulcan's stithy"); to his preoccupation with sexuality, particularly with the sexual nature of his mother's crime; and to his strange conduct toward Ophelia and Polonius. This view becomes even more credible when one considers Hamlet's seemingly incomprehensible remark to Polonius in act II, scene ii, where he calls the old man a "fishmonger" (Elizabethan slang for "pimp"); implies that Ophelia is a prostitute by referring in the same speech to "carrion" (Elizabethan "flesh" in the carnal sense); and warns Polonius not to let her "walk i' the sun" (that is, get too close to the "son" of Denmark, the heir apparent, him of the "sullied flesh" and "foul" imaginations). Wilson explains Hamlet's ambiguous remark as obscene because Hamlet is angry that Polonius would stoop to "loose" his daughter to him (as stockmen "loose" cows and mares to bulls and stallions to be bred) in order to wheedle from him the secret of his behavior, and he is angry and disgusted that his beloved would consent to be used in this way. Hence his later obscenities to her, as in act III, scene i, when he tells her repeatedly to go to a "nunnery" (Elizabethan slang for "brothel").

One final example must suffice to illustrate the importance of textual accuracy in interpreting this piece of literature. In the second quarto the speeches of the officiant at Ophelia's funeral are headed "Doct." This is probably "Doctor of Divinity," the term that one editor of *Hamlet*, Cyrus Hoy, inserts in the stage directions (86). The "Doctor of Divinity" reading was one reason for J. Dover Wilson's asserting positively that Ophelia's funeral was a Protestant service, contrary to the way directors often stage it. Indeed, the point seems to be relevant, because it affects one's interpretation of the play. Although Shakespeare used anachronisms whenever they suited his purpose, a careless disregard of facts and logic was not typical of him. For example, both Hamlet and Horatio are students at Wittenberg. That this university was founded several hundred years after the death of the historical Hamlet is beside the point. What does seem important is that Wittenberg was the university of Martin Luther and a strong center of Protestantism. It is not unreasonable to assume, then, that Shakespeare wanted his audience to think of Denmark as a Protestant country (it was so in his day)—indeed that he wanted the entire drama to be viewed in contemporary perspective, a point that will be elaborated later in this chapter.

2. A Summary of the Play

The main lines of the plot of *Hamlet* are clear. Hamlet, Prince of Denmark and heir presumptive to the Danish throne, is grief-stricken and plunged into melancholy by the recent death of his father and the "o'erhasty" remarriage of his mother to her late husband's brother, who has succeeded to the throne. The ghost of the prince's father appears to him and reveals that he was murdered by his brother, who now occupies the throne and whom he describes as "incestuous" and "adulterate." Enjoining young Hamlet not to harm his mother, the ghost exhorts him to take revenge on the murderer. In order to ascertain beyond question the guilt of his uncle and subsequently to plot his revenge, Hamlet feigns madness. His sweetheart Ophelia and his former schoolfellows Rosencrantz and Guildenstern attempt to discover from him the secret of his "antic behavior" (Ophelia because her father, Polonius, has ordered her to do so, Rosencrantz and Guildenstern because the king has ordered them to do so). All are unsuccessful.

Before actually initiating his revenge, Hamlet wants to be sure it will hit the guilty person. To this end, he arranges for a company of traveling players to present a drama in the castle that will depict the murder of his father as the ghost has described it. When the king sees the crime reenacted, he cries out and rushes from the assembly. This action Hamlet takes to be positive proof of his uncle's guilt, and from this moment he awaits only the right opportunity to kill him. After the play, Hamlet visits his mother's apartment, where he mistakes Polonius for the King and kills him. The killing of Polonius drives Ophelia mad and also convinces the king that Hamlet is dangerous and should be gotten out of the way. He therefore sends Hamlet to England, accompanied by Rosencrantz and Guildenstern, ostensibly to collect tribute, but in reality to be murdered. However, Hamlet eludes this trap by substituting the names of his erstwhile schoolfellows on his own death warrant and escaping through the help of pirates. He reaches Denmark in time for the funeral of Ophelia, who has apparently drowned herself. Laertes, her brother, has returned from Paris vowing vengeance on Hamlet for the death of his father. The king helps Laertes by arranging a fencing match between the two young men and seeing to it that Laertes's weapon is naked and poisoned. To make doubly sure that Hamlet will not escape, the king also poisons a bowl of wine from which Hamlet will be sure to drink. During the match, Laertes wounds Hamlet, the rapiers change hands, and Hamlet wounds Laertes; the Queen drinks the poisoned wine; and Laertes confesses his part in the treachery to Hamlet, who then stabs the king to death. All the principals are thus dead, and young Fortinbras of Norway becomes king of Denmark.

3. Historical-Biographical Considerations

It will doubtless surprise many students to know that *Hamlet* is considered by some commentators to be topical and autobiographical in certain places. In view of Queen Elizabeth's advanced age and poor health—hence the precarious state of the succession to the British crown—Shakespeare's decision to mount a production of *Hamlet*, with its usurped throne and internally disordered state, comes as no surprise. (Edward Hubler has argued that *Hamlet* was probably written in 1600 [912, n.2].) There is some ground for thinking that Ophelia's famous characterization of Hamlet may be intended to suggest the Earl of Essex, formerly Elizabeth's favorite, who had incurred her severe displeasure and been tried for treason and executed:

> The courtier's, soldier's, scholar's, eye, tongue, sword
> The expectancy and rose of the fair state,
> The glass of fashion and the mould of form,
> The observed of all observers. . . . (III.i)

Also, something of Essex may be seen in Claudius's observation on Hamlet's madness and his popularity with the masses:

How dangerous it is that this man goes loose!
Yet must we not put the strong law on him:
He's loved of the distracted multitude,
Who like not in their judgment but their eyes;
And where 'tis so, the offender's scourge is weighed,
But never the offence. (IV.viii)

Yet another contemporary historical figure, the Lord Treasurer, Burghley, has been seen by some in the character of Polonius. Shakespeare may have heard his patron, the young Henry Wriothesley, Earl of Southampton, express contempt for Elizabeth's old Lord Treasurer; indeed, this was the way many of the gallants of Southampton's generation felt. Burghley possessed most of the shortcomings Shakespeare gave to Polonius; he was boring, meddling, and given to wise old adages and truisms. (He left a famous set of pious yet shrewd precepts for his son, Robert Cecil.) Moreover, he had an elaborate spy system that kept him informed about both friend and foe. One is reminded of Polonius's assigning Reynaldo to spy on Laertes in Paris (II.i). This side of Burghley's character was so well known that it might have been dangerous for Shakespeare to portray it on stage while the old man was alive (because Burghley had died in 1598, Shakespeare could with safety do so in this general way).

Other topical references include Shakespeare's opinion (II.ii) about the revival of the private theater, which would employ children and which would constitute a rival for the adult companies of the public theater, for which Shakespeare wrote. It is also reasonable to assume that Hamlet's instructions to the players (III.ii) contain Shakespeare's criticisms of contemporary acting, just as Polonius's description of the players' repertoire and abilities (II.ii) is Shakespeare's satire on dull people who profess preferences for rigidly classified genres. Scholars have also pointed out Shakespeare's treatment of other stock characters of the day: Osric, the Elizabethan dandy; Rosencrantz and Guildenstern, the boot-licking courtiers; Laertes and Fortinbras, the men of action; Horatio, the "true Roman" friend; and Ophelia, the courtly love heroine.

In looking at *Hamlet* the historical critic might be expected to ask, "What do we need to know about eleventh-century Danish court life or about Elizabethan England to understand this play?" Similar questions are more or less relevant to the traditional interpretive approach to any literary work, but they are particularly germane to analysis of *Hamlet*. For one thing, most contemporary American students, largely unacquainted with the conventions, let alone the subtleties, of monarchical succession, wonder (unless they are aided by notes) why Hamlet does not automatically succeed to the throne after the death of his father. He is not just the oldest son; he is the only son. Such students need to know that in Hamlet's day the Danish throne was an elective one. The royal council, composed of the most powerful nobles in the land, named the next king. The custom of the throne's descending to the oldest son of the late monarch had not yet crystallized into law.

As true as this may be in fact, however, J. Dover Wilson maintains that it is not necessary to know it for understanding *Hamlet*, because Shakespeare intended his audiences to think of the entire situation—characters, customs, and plot—as English, which he apparently did in most of his plays, even though they were set in other countries. Wilson's theory is based upon the assumption that an Elizabethan audience could have but little interest in the peculiarities of Danish government, whereas the problems of royal succession, usurpation, and potential revolution in a contemporary English context would be of paramount concern. He thus asserts that Shakespeare's audience conceived Hamlet to be the lawful heir to his father and Claudius to be a usurper and the usurpation to be one of the main factors in the play, important to both Hamlet and Claudius. Whether one accepts Wilson's theory or not, it is certain that Hamlet thought of Claudius as a usurper, for he describes him to Gertrude as

> A cutpurse of the empire and the rule,
> That from a shelf the precious diadem stole
> And put it in his pocket! (III.iv)

and to Horatio as one

> . . . that hath killed my king and whored my mother,
> Popped in between th' election and my hopes. . . . (V.ii)

This last speech suggests strongly that Hamlet certainly expected to succeed his father by election if not by primogeniture. Modern students are also likely to be confused by the charge of incest against the Queen. Although her second marriage to the brother of her deceased husband would not be considered incestuous today by many civil and religious codes, it was so considered in Shakespeare's day. Some dispensation or legal loophole must have accounted for the popular acceptance of Gertrude's marriage to Claudius. That Hamlet considered the union incestuous, however, cannot be emphasized too much, for it is this repugnant character of Gertrude's sin, perhaps more than any other factor, that plunges Hamlet into the melancholy of which he is victim.

And here it is necessary to know what "melancholy" was to Elizabethans and to what extent it is important in understanding the play. A. C. Bradley tells us that it meant to Elizabethans a condition of the mind characterized by nervous instability, rapid and extreme changes of feeling and mood, and the disposition to be for the time absorbed in a dominant feeling or mood, whether joyous or depressed. If Hamlet's actions and speeches are examined closely, they seem to indicate symptoms of this disease. He is by turns cynical, idealistic, hyperactive, lethargic, averse to evil, disgusted at his uncle's drunkenness and his mother's sensuality, and convinced that he is rotten with sin. To appreciate his apparent procrastination, his vacillating from action to contemplation, and the other superficially irreconcilable features in his conduct, readers need to realize that at least part of Hamlet's problem is that he is a victim of extreme melancholy. (For more detailed discussions of Hamlet's melancholy, see A. C. Bradley's *Shakespearean Tragedy,* J. Dover Wilson's *What Happens in "Hamlet,"* and Weston Babcock's *"Hamlet": A Tragedy of Errors.*)

One reason for the popularity of *Hamlet* with Elizabethan audiences was that it dealt with a theme they were familiar with and fascinated by—revenge. *Hamlet* is in the grand tradition of revenge tragedies and contains virtually every stock device observable in vastly inferior plays of this type. Thomas Kyd's *Spanish Tragedy* (ca. 1585) was the first successful English adaptation of the Latin tragedies of Seneca. The typical revenge tragedy began with a crime (or the recital of it); continued with an injunction by some agent (often a ghost) to the next of kin to avenge the crime; grew complicated by various impediments to the revenge, such as identifying the criminal and hitting upon the proper time, place, and mode of the revenge; and concluded with the death of the criminal, the avenger, and frequently all the principals in the drama.

One additional fact about revenge may be noted. When Claudius asks Laertes to what lengths he would go to avenge his father's death, Laertes answers that he would "cut [Hamlet's] throat i' th' church" (IV.vii). It is probably no accident that Laertes is so specific about the method by which he would willingly kill Hamlet. In Shakespeare's day it was popularly believed that repentance had to be vocal to be effective. By cutting Hamlet's throat, presumably before he could confess his sins, Laertes would deprive Hamlet of this technical channel of grace. Thus Laertes would destroy both Hamlet's soul and his body and would risk his own soul, a horrifying illustration of the measure of his hatred. Claudius's rejoinder

> No place indeed should murder sanctuarize;
> Revenge should have no bounds

indicates the desperate state of the king's soul. He is condoning murder in a church, traditionally a haven of refuge, protection, and legal immunity for murderers.

Elizabethan audiences were well acquainted with these conventions. They thought there was an etiquette, almost a ritual, about revenge; they believed that it was in fact a fine art and that it required a consummate artist to execute it.

4. Moral-Philosophical Considerations

Any discussion of *Hamlet* should acknowledge the enormous body of excellent commentary that sees the play as valuable primarily for its moral and philosophical insights. Little more can be done here than to summarize the most famous of such interpretations. They naturally center on the character of Hamlet. Some explain Hamlet as an idealist temperamentally unsuited for life in a world peopled by fallible creatures. He is therefore shattered when he discovers that some humans are so ambitious for a crown that they are willing to murder for it and that others are so highly sexed that they will violate not only the laws of decorum (for example, by remarrying within a month of a spouse's death) but also the civil and ecclesiastical laws against incest. He is further crushed when he thinks that his fiancée and his former schoolfellows are tools of his murderous uncle. Other critics see Hamlet's plight as that of the essentially moral and virtuous intellectual man, certainly aware of the gentlemanly code that demands satisfaction for a wrong, but too much the student of philosophy and the Christian religion to believe in the morality or the logic of revenge. Related to this is the view of Hamlet as a kind of transitional figure, torn between the demands and the values of the Middle Ages and those of the modern world. The opposed theory maintains that Hamlet *is* a man of action, thwarted by such practical obstacles as how to kill a king surrounded by a bodyguard. Many modern critics emphasize what they term Hamlet's psychoneurotic state, a condition that obviously derives from the moral complexities with which he is faced.

Hamlet fulfills the technical requirements of the revenge play as well as the salient requirements of a classical tragedy; that is, it shows a person of heroic proportions going down to defeat under circumstances too powerful for him to cope with. For most readers and audiences the question of Hamlet's tragic flaw will remain a moot one. But this will not keep them from recognizing the play as one of the most searching artistic treatments of the problems and conflicts that form so large a part of the human condition.

C. Traditional Approaches to
Adventures of Huckleberry Finn

There are few works of literature that lend themselves to so many interpretive analyses as *Huckleberry Finn*. Bernard De Voto has written that the novel contains "God's plenty"; in that verdict lies the key to the traditional critical approach. The phrase "God's plenty" was also applied by Dryden to Chaucer's *Canterbury Tales;* so we should remember those attributes of Chaucer's art that elicited such praise—narrative and descriptive power, keen knowledge of human nature, high comedy, biting satire, and lofty morality. All of these are also in *Huckleberry Finn.*

1. Dialect and Textual Matters

To Twain's good ear and appreciation of the dramatic value of dialect we owe not only authentic and subtle shadings of class, race, and personality, but also, as Lionel Trilling has said, a "classic prose" that moves with "simplicity, directness, lucidity, and grace" (xvii). T. S. Eliot called this an "innovation, a new discovery in the English language," an entire book written in the natural prose rhythms of conversation. This linguistic innovation is certainly one of the features to which Ernest Hemingway referred when he said that "all modern American literature comes from one book by Mark Twain called *Huckleberry Finn*" (22). If we agree with Hemingway, therefore, we can think of Twain as the "father of modern American literature."

Huckleberry Finn has an interesting textual history that space will allow us only to touch on here. Writing in a frontier dialect, Twain was trying, with what success we have just seen, to capture in both pronunciation and vocabulary the spirit of the times from the lips of contemporary people. Nevertheless, some of his editors (for example, Richard Watson Gilder of the *Century Magazine,* William Dean Howells, and especially Twain's wife Livvie) bowdlerized and prettified those passages they thought "too coarse or vulgar" for Victorian ears, in certain cases with Twain's full consent. It is a minor miracle that this censoring, though it has taken something from the verisimiltude of the novel, seems not to have harmed it materially. (Hamlin Hill and Walter Blair's *The Art of "Huckleberry Finn"* is an excellent succinct treatment of the textual history of this novel.)

2. The Genre and the Plot of the Novel

Huckleberry Finn is a novel—that is, an extended prose narrative dealing with characters within the framework of a plot. Such a work is usually fictitious, but both characters and situations or events may be drawn from real life. It may emphasize action or adventure (for example, *Treasure Island* or mystery stories); or it may concentrate on character delineation (that is, the way people grow or deteriorate or remain static in the happenings of life—*The Rise of Silas Lapham* or *Pride and Prejudice*); or it may illustrate a theme either aesthetically or propagandistically (*Wuthering Heights* or *Uncle Tom's Cabin*). It can, of course, do all three of these, as *Huckleberry Finn* does, a fact that accounts for the multiple levels of interpretation.

Huckleberry Finn is not only a novel; it is also a direct descendant of an important subgenre: the Spanish picaresque tale that arose in the sixteenth century as a reaction against the chivalric romance. In the latter type, pure and noble knights customarily rescued virtuous and beautiful heroines from enchanted castles guarded by fire-breathing dragons or wicked knights. In an attempt to debunk the artificiality and insipidity of such tales, Spanish writers of the day (notably the anonymous author of *Lazarillo de Tormes*) introduced into fiction as a central figure a kind of antihero, the picaro—a rogue or rascal of low birth who lived by his wits and his cunning rather than by exalted chivalric ideals. (Although not a pure picaro, Cervantes's Don Quixote is involved in a plot more rambling and episodic than unified and coherent.) Indeed, except for the fact that the picaro is *in* each of the multitude of adventures, all happening "on the road," the plot is negligible by modern standards. In these stories we simply move with his new type of hero from one wild and sensational experience to another, involving many pranks and much trenchant satire. Later treatments of the picaro have occasionally minimized and frequently eliminated his roguish or rascally traits. Dickens's picaros, for example, are usually model poor boys.

Many of the classics of world literature are much indebted to the picaresque tradition, among them René Le Sage's *Gil Blas,* Henry Fielding's *Tom Jones,* and Charles Dickens's *David Copperfield,* to mention only a few. *Huckleberry Finn* is an obvious example of the type. The protagonist is a thirteen- or fourteen-year-old boy living in the American antebellum South. He is a member by birth of the next-to-the-lowest stratum of Southern society, white trash—one who has a drunkard father who alternately abandons him and then returns to persecute him, but who has no mother, no roots, and no background or breeding in the conventionally accepted sense. He is the town bad boy who smokes, chews, plays hooky, and stays dirty, and whom two good ladies of St. Petersburg, Missouri, have elected to civilize.

The narrative moves onto "the road" when Huck, partly to escape the persecution of his drunken father and partly to evade the artificially imposed restrictions and demands of society, decides to accompany Jim, the slave of his benefactors, in his attempt to run for his freedom. The most immediate reason for Jim's deciding to run away is the fact that Miss Watson, his owner, has decided to sell him "down the river"—that is, into the Deep South, where instead of making a garden for nice old ladies or possibly being a house servant, he will surely become a field hand and work in the cane or cotton fields. These two, the teenaged urchin and the middle-aged slave, defy society, the law, and convention in a daring escape on a raft down the dangerous Mississippi River.

Continually in fear of being captured, Huck and Jim travel mostly at night. They board a steamboat that has run onto a snag in the river and has been abandoned; on it they find a gang of robbers and cutthroats, whom they manage to elude without detection. In a vacant house floating down the river they discover the body of a man shot in the back, who, Jim later reveals, is Huck's father. They become involved in a blood feud between two aristocratic pioneer families. They witness a cold-blooded murder and an attempted lynching on the streets of an Arkansas village. They acquire two disreputable traveling companions who force them to render menial service and to take part in burlesque Shakespearean performances, bogus revival meetings, and attempted swindles of orphans with newly inherited wealth. Finally, after some uneasy moments when Jim is captured, they learn that Jim has been freed by his owner, and Huck decides to head west— away from civilization.

3. Historical-Biographical Considerations

At the surface of narrative level, *Huckleberry Finn* is something of a thriller. The sensationalism may seem to make the story improbable, if not incredible, but we should consider its historical and cultural context. This was part of frontier America in the 1840s and 1850s, a violent and bloody time. It was the era of Jim Bowie and his murderous knife, of gunslingers like Jack Slade, of Indian fighters like Davy Crockett and Sam Houston. Certainly there is a touch of the frontier, of the South or the West, in the roughness, the cruelty, the lawlessness, and even the humor of *Huckleberry Finn*. Indeed, Mark Twain was very much in the tradition of such humorists of the Southwest as Thomas Bangs Thorpe and such professional comedians as Artemus Ward and Josh Billings; in various writings he employed dialect for comedy, burlesque, the tall tale, bombast, the frontier brag. *Huckleberry Finn*, of course, far transcends the examples of early American humor.

Furthermore, we know from Mark Twain's autobiographical writings and from scholarly studies of him, principally those of Bernard De Voto, A. B. Paine, and Dixon Wecter, that the most sensational happenings and colorful characters in *Huckleberry Finn* are based on actual events and persons Twain saw in Hannibal, Missouri, where he grew up, and in other towns up and down the Mississippi. For example, the shooting of Old Boggs by Colonel Sherburn is drawn from the killing of one "Uncle Sam" Smarr by William Owsley on the streets of Hannibal on January 24, 1845. The attempted lynching of Sherburn is also an echo of something that Mark Twain saw as a boy, for he declared in later life that he once "saw a brave gentleman deride and insult a [lynch] mob and drive it away." During the summer of 1847 Benson Blankenship, older brother of the prototype Huck, secretly aided a runaway slave by taking food to him at his hideout on an island across the river from Hannibal. Benson did this for several weeks and resolutely refused to be enticed into betraying the man for the reward offered for his capture. This is undoubtedly the historical source of Huck's loyalty to Jim that finally resulted in his electing to "go to Hell" in defiance of law, society, and religion rather than turn in his friend.

A point about Jim's escape that needs clarification is his attempt to attain his freedom by heading *south*. Actually, Cairo, Illinois, free territory and Jim's destination, is farther south on the river than St. Petersburg, Missouri, from which he is escaping. Thus when the fugitives miss Cairo in the fog and dark, they have lost their only opportunity to free Jim by escaping southward. Still another point is that if it had been Jim's object simply to get to *any* free territory, he might as easily have crossed the river to Illinois right at St. Petersburg, his home. But this was not his aim. Although a free state, Illinois had a law requiring its citizens to return runaway slaves. Jim therefore wanted particularly to get to Cairo, Illinois, a junction of the underground railroad system where he could have been helped on his way north and east on the Ohio River by abolitionists.

The obscene performance of the "Royal Nonesuch" in Bricksville, Arkansas, where the King prances about the stage on all fours as the "cameleopard," naked except for rings of paint, was based on some of the bawdier male entertainments of the old Southwest. This particular type featured a mythical phallic beast called the "Gyascutus." There were variations, of course, in the manner of presentation, but the antics of the King illustrate a common version. (Both Mark Twain and his brother Orion Clemens recorded performances of this type, Orion in an 1852 newspaper account of a Hannibal showing, Mark in a notebook entry made in 1865 while he was in Nevada.)

The detailed description of the Grangerford house with its implied yet hilarious assessment of the nineteenth-century culture may be traced to a chapter from *Life on the Mississippi* entitled "The House Beautiful." Here may be observed the conformity to the vogue of sentimentalism, patriotism, and piousness in literature and painting and the general garishness in furniture and knickknacks.

One pronounced theme in *Huckleberry Finn* that has its origin in Twain's personality is his almost fanatical hatred of aristocrats. Indeed, aristocracy was one of his chief targets. *A Connecticut Yankee in King Arthur's Court* is less veiled than *Huckleberry Finn* in its attack on the concept. But it was not only British aristocracy that Twain condemned; elsewhere he made his most vitriolic denunciations of the American Southern aristocrat. Though more subtle, *Huckleberry Finn* nevertheless is the more searching criticism of aristocracy. For one thing, aristocracy is hypocritical. Aristocrats are not paragons of true gentleness, graciousness, courtliness, and selflessness. They are trigger-happy, inordinately proud, implacable bullies. But perhaps Twain's antipathy to aristocracy, expressed in virtually all his works, came from the obvious misery caused to all involved, perpetrators as well as victims. The most significant expression of this in *Huckleberry Finn* is, of course, in the notion of race superiority. Clinging as they did to this myth, aristocrats—as Alex Haley has portrayed them in *Roots*—could justify any kind of treatment of blacks. They could separate families, as in the case of Jim and the Wilks slaves; they could load them with chains, forget to feed them, hunt them like animals, curse and cuff them, exploit their labor, even think of them as subhuman, and then rationalize the whole sordid history by affirming that the slaves ought to be grateful for any contact with civilization and Christianity.

Moreover, not only aristocrats but every section of white society subscribed to this fiction; thus a degenerate wretch like pap Finn could shoulder a free Negro college professor off the sidewalk and later deliver an antigovernment, racist tirade to Huck replete with the party line of the Know-Nothings, a semisecret, reactionary political group that flourished for a brief period in the 1850s. (Its chief tenet was hostility to foreign-born Americans and the Roman Catholic Church. It derived its name from the answer its oath-bound members made to any question about it, "I know nothing about it.") We thus sense the contempt Twain felt for Know-Nothingism when we hear its chief doctrines mouthed by a reprobate like pap Finn. (Indeed, it may be more than coincidental that Twain never capitalizes the word "pap" when Huck is referring to his father.)

Closely related to this indictment of aristocracy and racism and their concomitant evils are Twain's strictures on romanticism, which he thought largely responsible for the harmful myths and cultural horrors that beset the American South of his day. In particular, he blamed the novels of Sir Walter Scott and their idealization of a feudal society. In real life this becomes on the adult level the blood feud of the Grangerfords and Shepherdsons and on the juvenile level the imaginative high jinks of Tom Sawyer and his "robber gang" and his "rescue" of Jim.

There are many other examples of historical and biographical influences on the novel. Years spent as a steamboat pilot familiarized Mark Twain with every snag, sandbar, bend, or other landmark on the Mississippi, as well as with the more technical aspects of navigation—all of which add vivid authenticity to the novel. His vast knowledge of Negro superstitions was acquired from slaves in Hannibal, Missouri, and on the farm of his beloved uncle, John Quarles, prototype of Silas Phelps. Jim himself is modeled after Uncle Dan'l, a slave on the Quarles place. These superstitions and examples of folklore are not mere local color, devoid of rhyme or reason; but, as Daniel Hoffman has pointed out, they are "of signal importance in the thematic development of the book and in the growth toward maturity of its principal characters" (321). Huck was in real life Tom Blankenship, a boyhood chum of Twain's who possessed most of the traits Twain gave him as a fictional character. Although young Blankenship's real-life father was ornery enough, Twain modeled Huck's father on another Hannibal citizen, Jimmy Finn, the town drunk.

Like *The Canterbury Tales,* where Dryden found "God's plenty," *Huckleberry Finn* gives its readers a portrait gallery of the times. Scarcely a class is omitted. The aristocracy is represented by the Grangerfords, the Shepherdsons, and Colonel Sherburn. They are hardly Randolphs and Lees of tidewater Virginia, and their homes reveal that. The Grangerford parlor, for example, shows more of philistinism and puritanism than of genuine culture. These people are, nevertheless, portrayed as recognizable specimens of the traditional aristocrat, possessed of dignity, courage, devotion to principle, graciousness, desire to preserve ceremonious forms, and Calvinistic piety. Colonel Sherburn in particular illustrates another aspect of the traditional aristocrat—his contempt for the common man, which is reflected in his cold-blooded shooting of Old Boggs, his cavalier gesture of tossing the pistol on the ground afterward, and his single-handedly facing down the lynch mob.

Towns of any size in *Huckleberry Finn* contain the industrious, respectable, conforming bourgeoisie. In this class are the Widow Douglas and her old-maid sister Miss Watson, the Peter Wilks family, and Judge Thatcher. The Phelpses too, although they own slaves and operate a "one-horse cotton plantation," belong to this middle class. Mrs. Judith Loftus, whose canniness undoes Huck when he is disguised as a girl, is, according to De Voto, the best-drawn pioneer wife in any of the contemporary records. The host of anonymous but vivid minor characters reflects and improves upon the many eyewitness accounts. These minor characters include the ferryboat owner, the boatmen who fear smallpox as they hunt Jim, the raftsmen heard from a distance joking in the stillness of the night. The Bible Belt poor white, whether whittling and chewing and drawling on the storefront benches of an Arkansas village or caught up in the fervor of a camp meeting or joining his betters in some sort of mob action, is described with undeniable authenticity.

Criminals like the robbers and cutthroats on the *Walter Scott* and those inimitable confidence men, the King and the Duke, play their part. Pap Finn is surely among the earliest instances of Faulkner's Snopes types—filthy, impoverished, ignorant, disreputable, bigoted, thieving, pitifully sure of only one thing, his superiority as a white man. Then we observe the slaves themselves, convincing because they include not just stereotyped minstrel characters or "moonlight and magnolia good darkies," but interesting human beings, laughable, strong, honorable, trifling, dignified, superstitious, illiterate, wise, loving, pathetic, loyal, victimized. Most make only brief appearances, yet we feel that we have known a group of engaging, complex, and gifted people.

4. Moral-Philosophical Considerations

Important as are its historical and biographical aspects, the chief impact of *Huckleberry Finn* derives from its morality. This is, indeed, the *meaning* of the novel. All other aspects are subservient to this one. Man's inhumanity to man (as Huck says, "Human beings *can* be awful cruel to one another") is the major theme of this work, and it is exemplified in both calm and impassioned denunciation and satire. Almost all the major events and most of the minor ones are variations on this theme. The cruelty may be manifested in attempts to swindle young orphans out of their inheritance, to con village yokels with burlesque shows, to fleece religion-hungry frontier folk with camp meetings, or to tar and feather malefactors extralegally. Cruelty can and often does have even more serious consequences: for example, the brutal and senseless slaughter of the aristocratic Grangerfords and Shepherdsons and the murder of a harmless old windbag by another arrogant aristocrat.

The ray of hope that Mark Twain reveals is the relationship of Huck and Jim; Huck's ultimate salvation comes when of his own choice he rejects the values of the society of his time (he has all along had misgivings about them) and decides to treat Jim as a fellow human being. The irony is that Huck has made the right decision by scrapping the "right" reasons (that is, the logic of conventional theology) and by following his own conscience. He is probably too young to have intellectualized his decision and applied it to black people as a whole. Doubtless it applies only to Jim as an individual. But this is a tremendous advance for a boy of Huck's years. It is a lesson that is stubbornly resisted, reluctantly learned. But it is *the* lesson of *Huckleberry Finn*.

Huckleberry Finn is a living panorama of a country at a given time in history. It also provides insights, and it makes judgments that are no less valid in the larger sense today than they are about the period Mark Twain chronicled. This fidelity to life in character, action, speech, and setting; this personal testament; this encyclopedia of human nature; this most eloquent of all homilies—all of these are what cause this book to be not only a supreme artistic creation but also, in the words of Lionel Trilling, "one of the central documents of American culture" (6).

D. Traditional Approaches to "Young Goodman Brown"

"Young Goodman Brown," universally acclaimed as one of Hawthorne's best short stories, presents the student with not only several possible meanings but several rather ambiguous meanings. D. M. McKeithan lists the suggestions that have been advanced as "the theme" of the story: "the reality of sin, the pervasiveness of evil, the secret sin and hypocrisy of all persons, the hypocrisy of Puritanism, the results of doubt or disbelief, the devastating effects of moral scepticism, . . . the demoralizing effects of the discovery that all men are sinners and hypocrites" (93). Admittedly, these themes are not as diverse as they might at first appear. They are, with the possible exception of the one specifically mentioning Puritanism, quite closely related. But meaning is not restricted to theme, and there are other ambivalences in the story that make its meanings both rich and elusive. After taking into account some matters of text and genre, we shall look at "Young Goodman Brown" from our traditional perspectives.

1. The Text of the Story

Textually, "Young Goodman Brown," first published in 1835 in the *New England Magazine,* presents relatively few problems. Obsolete words in the story like "wot'st" (know), "Goody" (Goodwife, or Mrs.), and "Goodman" (Mr.) are defined in most desk dictionaries, and none of the other words has undergone radical semantic change. Nevertheless, as we have seen, although a literary work may have been written in a day when printing had reached a high degree of accuracy, a perfect text is by no means a foregone conclusion. With Hawthorne, as with other authors, scholars are constantly working on more accurate texts.

For example, the first edition of this handbook used a version of "Young Goodman Brown" that contained at least two substantive variants. About three-fourths of the way through the story the phrase "unconcerted wilderness" appeared. David Levin points out that nineteen years after Hawthorne's death, a version of the story edited by George P. Lathrop printed "unconcerted" for the first time: every version before then, including Hawthorne's last revision, had had "unconverted." In that same paragraph the first edition of this handbook printed "figure" as opposed to "apparition," the word that Levin tells us occurred in the first published versions of the story (346, n.8). Obviously, significant interpretive differences could hinge on which words are employed in these contexts.

2. The Genre and the Plot of the Story

"Young Goodman Brown" is a short story; that is, it is a relatively brief narrative of prose fiction (ranging in length from five hundred to twenty thousand words) characterized by considerably more unity and compression in all its parts than the novel—in theme, plot, structure, character, setting, and mood. In the story we are considering, the situation is this: one evening near sunset sometime in the late seventeenth century, Goodman Brown, a young man who has been married only three months, prepares to leave his home in Salem, Massachusetts, and his pretty young bride, Faith, to go into the forest and spend the night on some mission that he will not disclose other than to say that it must be performed between sunset and sunrise. Although Faith has strong forebodings about his journey and pleads with him to postpone it, Brown is adamant and sets off. His business is evil by his own admission; he does not state what it is specifically, but it becomes apparent to the reader that it involves attending a witches' Sabbath in the forest, a remarkable action in view of the picture of Brown, drawn early in the story, as a professing Christian who admonishes his wife to pray and who intends to lead an exemplary life after this one night.

The rising action begins when Brown, having left the village, enters the dark, gloomy, and probably haunted forest. He has not gone far before he meets the Devil in the form of a middle-aged, respectable-looking man with whom Brown has made a bargain to accompany on his journey. Perhaps the full realization of who his companion is and what the night may hold in store for him now dawns on Brown, for he makes an effort to return to Salem. It is at best a feeble attempt, however, for, though the Devil does not try to detain him, Brown continues walking with him deeper into the forest.

As they go, the Devil shocks Goodman Brown by telling him that his (Brown's) ancestors were religious bigots, cruel exploiters, and practitioners of the black art—in short, full-fledged servants of the Devil. Further, the young man is told that the very pillars of New England society, church, and state are witches (creatures actually in league with the Devil), lechers, blasphemers, and collaborators with the Devil. Indeed, he sees his childhood Sunday School teacher, now a witch, and overhears the voices of his minister and a deacon of his church as they ride past conversing about the diabolical communion service to which both they and he are going.

Clinging to the notion that he may still save himself from this breakup of his world, Goodman Brown attempts to pray, but stops when a cloud suddenly darkens the sky. A babel of voices seems to issue from the cloud, many recognizable to Brown as belonging to godly persons, among them his wife. After the cloud has passed, a pink ribbon such as Faith wears in her cap flutters to the ground. Upon seeing it, Goodman Brown is plunged into despair and hastens toward the witches' assembly. Once there, he is confronted with a congregation made up of the wicked and those whom Brown had always assumed to be righteous. As he is led to the altar to be received into this fellowship of the lost, he is joined by Faith. The climax of the story comes just before they receive the sacrament of baptism: Brown cries to his wife to look heavenward and save herself. In the next moment he finds himself alone.

The dénouement (resolution, unraveling) of the plot comes quickly. Returning the next morning to Salem, Goodman Brown is a changed man. He now doubts that anyone is good—his wife, his neighbors, the officials of church and state—and he remains in this state of cynicism until he dies.

The supernaturalism and horror of "Young Goodman Brown" mark the story as one variant of the Gothic tale, a type of ghost story originating formally in late eighteenth-century England and characterized by spirit-haunted habitations, diabolical villains, secret doors and passageways, terrifying and mysterious sounds and happenings, and the like. Obviously, "Young Goodman Brown" bears some resemblance to these artificial creations, the aesthetic value of most of which is negligible. What is much more significant is that here is a variation of the Faust legend, the story of a man who makes a bargain with the Devil (frequently the sale of his soul) in exchange for some desirable thing. In this instance Goodman Brown did not go nearly so far in the original indenture, but it was not necessary from the Devil's point of view. One glimpse of evil unmasked was enough to wither the soul of Brown forever.

3. Historical-Biographical Considerations

So much for textual matters, paraphrasable content, and genre. What kind of historical or biographical information do we need in order to feel the full impact of this story, aesthetically and intellectually? Obviously, some knowledge of Puritan New England is necessary. We can place the story in time easily, because Hawthorne mentions that it takes place in the days of King William (that is, William III, who reigned from 1688 to 1702). Other evidences of the time of the story are the references to persecution of the Quakers by Brown's grandfather (the 1660s) and King Philip's War (primarily a massacre of Indians by colonists [1675–1676]), in which Brown's father participated. Specific locales like Salem, Boston, Connecticut, and Rhode Island are mentioned, as are terms used in Puritan church organization and government, such as ministers, elders, meetinghouses, communion tables, saints (in the Protestant sense of *any* Christian), selectmen, and lecture days.

But it is not enough for us to visualize a sort of first Thanksgiving picture of Pilgrims with steeple-crowned hats, Bibles, and blunderbusses. For one thing, we need to know something of Puritan religion and theology. This means at least a slight knowledge of Calvinism, a main source of Puritan religious doctrine. A theology as extensive and complex as Calvinism and one that has been the subject of so many misconceptions cannot be described adequately in a handbook of this type. But at the risk of perpetuating some of these misconceptions, let us mention three or four tenets of Calvinism that will illuminate to some degree the story of Goodman Brown. Calvinism stresses the sovereignty of God—in goodness, power, and knowledge. Correspondingly, it emphasizes the helplessness and sinfulness of human beings, who have been since the Fall of Adam innately and totally depraved. Their only hope is in the grace of God, for God alone is powerful enough (sovereign enough) to save them. And the most notorious, if not the chief, doctrine is predestination, which includes the belief that God has, before their creation, selected certain people for eternal salvation, others for eternal damnation. Appearances are therefore misleading; an outwardly godly person might not be one of the elect. Thus it is paradoxical that Goodman Brown is so shocked to learn that there is evil among the apparently righteous, for this was one of the most strongly implied teachings of his church.

In making human beings conscious of their absolute reliance on God alone for salvation, Puritan clergymen dwelt long and hard on the pains of hell and the powerlessness of mere mortals to escape them. Brown mentions to the Devil that the voice of his pastor "would make me tremble both Sabbath day and lecture day." This was a typical reaction. In Calvinism, nobody could be sure of sinlessness. Introspection was mandatory. Christians had to search their hearts and minds constantly to purge themselves of sin. Goodman Brown is hardly expressing a Calvinistic concept when he speaks of clinging to his wife's skirts and following her to Heaven. Calvinists had to work out their own salvation in fear and trembling, and they were often in considerable doubt about the outcome. The conviction that sin was an ever-present reality that destroyed the unregenerate kept it before them all the time and made its existence an undoubted, well-nigh tangible fact. We must realize that aspects of the story like belief in witches and an incarnate Devil, which until the recent upsurge of interest in demonism and the occult world have struck modern readers as fantastic, were entirely credible to New Englanders of this period. Indeed, on one level, "Young Goodman Brown" may be read as an example of Satanism. Goody Cloyse and the Devil in the story even describe at length a concoction with which witches were popularly believed to have anointed themselves and a satanic worship attended by witches, devils, and lost souls.

It is a matter of historical record that a belief in witchcraft and the old pagan gods existed in Europe side by side with Christianity well into the modern era. The phenomenon has recurred in our own day, ballyhooed by the popular press as well as the electronic media. There was an analogous belief prevalent in Puritan New England. Clergymen, jurists, statesmen—educated people generally, as well as uneducated folk—were convinced that witches and witchcraft were realities. Cotton Mather, one of the most learned men of the period, attests eloquently to his own belief in these phenomena in *The Wonders of the Invisible World,* his account of the trials of several people executed for witchcraft. Some of the headings in the table of contents are instructive: "A True Narrative, collected by Deodat Lawson, related to Sundry Persons afflicted by Witchcraft, from the 19th of March to the 5th of April, 1692" and "The Second Case considered, viz. If one bewitched be cast down with the look or cast of the Eye of another Person, and after that recovered again by a Touch from the same Person, is not this an infallible Proof that the party accused and complained of is in Covenant with the Devil?"

Hawthorne's great-grandfather, John Hathorne (Nathaniel added the "w"), was one of the judges in the infamous Salem witch trials of 1692, during which many people were tortured, and nineteen hanged, and one crushed to death (a legal technicality was responsible for this special form of execution). Commentators have long pointed to "Young Goodman Brown," *The Scarlet Letter,* and many other Hawthorne stories to illustrate his obsession with the guilt of his Puritan forebears for their part in these crimes. In "The Custom House," his introduction to *The Scarlet Letter,* Hawthorne wrote of these ancestors who were persecutors of Quakers and witches and of his feeling that he was tainted by their crimes. The Devil testified that he helped young Goodman Brown's grandfather, a constable, lash a "Quaker woman . . . smartly through the streets of Salem," an episode undoubtedly related to Hawthorne's "Custom House" reference to his great-grandfather's "hard severity towards a woman of [the Quaker] sect."

Hawthorne's notebooks are also a source in interpreting his fiction. They certainly shed light on his preoccupation with the "unpardonable sin" and his particular definition of that sin. It is usually defined as blasphemy against the Holy Ghost, or continued conscious sin without repentance, or refusing to acknowledge the existence of God even though the Holy Spirit has actually proved it. The notebooks, however, and works of fiction like "Ethan Brand," "Young Goodman Brown," and *The Scarlet Letter* make it clear that for Hawthorne the Unpardonable Sin was to probe, intellectually and rationally, the human heart for depravity without tempering the search by a "human" or "democratic" sympathy. Specifically in the case of "Young Goodman Brown," Brown's obduracy of heart cuts him off from all, so that "his dying hour [is] gloom."

4. Moral-Philosophical Considerations

The terror and suspense in the Hawthorne story function as integral parts of the allegory that defines the story's theme. In allegory (a narrative containing a meaning beneath the surface one), there is usually a one-to-one relationship; that is, one idea or object in the narrative stands for only one idea or object allegorically. A story from the Old Testament illustrates this. The pharaoh of Egypt dreamed that seven fat cows were devoured by seven lean cows. Joseph interpreted this dream as meaning that seven years of plenty (good crops) would be followed by seven years of famine. "Young Goodman Brown" clearly functions on this level of allegory (while at times becoming richly symbolic). Brown is not just one Salem citizen of the late seventeenth century, but rather seems to typify humankind, to be in a sense Everyman, in that what he does and the reason he does it appear very familiar to most people, based on their knowledge of others and on honest appraisal of their own behavior.

For example, Goodman Brown, like most people, wants to experience evil—not perpetually, of course, for he is by and large a decent chap, a respectably married man, a member of a church—but he desires to "taste the forbidden fruit" ("have one last fling") before settling down to the business of being a solid citizen and attaining the good life. He feels that he can do this because he means to retain his religious faith, personified in his wife, who, to reinforce the allegory, is even named Faith. But in order to encounter evil, he must part with his Faith at least temporarily, something he is either willing or compelled to do. It is here that he makes his fatal mistake, for evil turns out to be not some abstraction nor something that can be played with for a while and then put down, but the very pillars of Goodman Brown's world—his ancestors, his earthly rulers, his spiritual overseers, and finally his Faith. In short, so overpowering are the fact and universality of evil in the world that Goodman Brown comes to doubt the existence of any good. By looking upon the very face of evil, he is transformed into a cynic and a misanthrope whose "dying hour was gloom."

Thomas E. Connolly has remarked that Goodman Brown has not *lost* his faith; he has *found* it (370–75). That is, Goodman Brown believes that he understands the significance of the Calvinistic teaching of the depravity of humans; this realization makes him doubt and dislike his fellows and in effect paralyzes his moral will so that he questions the motivation of every apparently virtuous act. But this is surely a strange conclusion for Brown to reach, for he has violated the cardinal tenets of Calvinism. If Calvinism stressed anything, it stressed the practical and spiritual folly of placing hope or reliance on human beings and their efforts, which by the very nature of things are bound to fail, whereas God alone never fails. Therefore all trust should be reposed in Him. It is just this teaching that Brown has not learned. On the practical plane, he cannot distinguish between appearance and reality. He takes things and people at face value. If a man *looks* respectable and godly, Brown assumes that he is. And if the man turns out to be a scoundrel, Brown's every standard crumbles. He is in a sense guilty of a kind of idolatry: human institutions in the forms of ministers, church officers, statesmen, and wives have been his god. When they are discredited, he has nothing else to place his trust in and thus becomes a cynic and a misanthrope.

Thus, rather than making a frontal attack on Calvinism, Hawthorne indicted certain reprehensible aspects of Puritanism: the widespread holier-than-thou attitude; the spiritual blindness that led many Puritans to mistake a pious front for genuine religion; the latent sensuality in the apparently austere and disciplined soul (the very capstone of hypocrisy, because sins of the flesh were particularly odious to Puritan orthodoxy).

It will perhaps be argued that Calvinism at its most intense, with its dim view of human nature, is quite likely to produce cynicism and misanthropy. But historically, if paradoxically, Calvinists have been dynamic and full of faith; they have been social and political reformers, educators, enterprisers in business, explorers, foes of tyranny. The religious furnace in which these souls were tempered, however, is too hot for Goodman Brown. He is of a weaker breed, and the sum of his experience with the hard realities of life is disillusion and defeat. He has lost his faith. Whether because his faith was false or because he wished for an objectively verifiable certainty that is the antithesis of faith, Hawthorne does not say. He does not even say whether the whole thing was a dream or reality. Actually, it does not matter. The result remains: faith has been destroyed and supplanted by total despair because Brown is neither a good Calvinist, a good Christian, nor, in the larger sense, a good man.

E. Traditional Approaches to "Everyday Use: for your grandmama"

This short story by Alice Walker is one of her most frequently anthologized. It was published in 1973, some nine years before she won the Pulitzer Prize for *The Color Purple*, which was subsequently made into a highly popular and much-discussed film. Like most of her work, this story deals with the lives of black people and the issues that affect them; Walker is particularly interested in the problems of black women and has written and spoken extensively about them.

1. The Plot of the Story

Situation: Two black women, a mother (whose name we infer is Johnson) and her daughter Maggie (who appears to be in her twenties) are sitting in the neatly swept front yard of the three-room, tin-roofed shack that is their home somewhere in the American South. It is sunny and hot, but they are in the shade of an elm tree waiting for the arrival of Dee, Maggie's brilliant and talented sister who left home for the freedom and opportunities of the city, possibly New York or Los Angeles. The time is in the 1970s, as suggested by the following facts: Dee has followed the example of some American blacks in adopting an African name to replace her original family name; she is traveling with a black man who has chosen an Arabic name, which the narrator is advised to pronounce "Hakim-a-barber"; and the narrator refers to a group of black Muslim cattle farmers in the neighborhood who have been harassed by local whites and have armed themselves for defense.

Generating Circumstance: The reader's curiosity is aroused when Wangero (Dee's new name) takes a condescending attitude toward her mother and sister because of their primitive living conditions and their apparent satisfaction with their underprivileged and politically unenlightened lives. They, on the other hand, are amazed if not amused at the unconventional appearance and behavior of their visitors. Maggie—homely, introverted, and less gifted intellectually than her sister—is intimidated by the latter's achievements.

Rising Action: While affecting to despise virtually everything in her old home, Wangero still wants to take things like the hand-carved churn and benches and the quilts as heirlooms or examples of "primitive" art, which can be shown to her acquaintances back in the city. Such artifacts would there become conversation pieces only; they would not have utility, nor would they generate significant feeling or emotion. In their proper humble setting, they are useful, revered, and considered beautiful. Because of her ingrained assertiveness and her formidable abilities, Wangero assumes she can bully her mother into giving her these "aesthetic creations," which are too good for "everyday use." Her mother allows her to confiscate the churn and its dasher but draws the line at the quilts, which she had promised to Maggie for a wedding present.

Climax: The climactic moment comes when the narrator snatches the quilts away from Wangero, and "dumps" them into the astounded Maggie's lap.

Dénouement: Wangero, followed by Hakim-a-barber, leaves in a huff, charging as she goes that her mother does not really understand their "heritage." The story closes with Maggie, happy in her newly discovered worth, and her mother, blissful with a dip of snuff, sitting in the yard quietly and contentedly, enjoying the end of the day.

2. Historical-Biographical Considerations

Alice Walker was born in Eatonton, Georgia, in 1944, ten years before the Supreme Court's landmark decision in *Brown vs. the Board of Topeka*, striking down segregation in schools. Because the South was slow to implement this decision, Walker and her five brothers and two sisters grew up in much the same racial environment as their parents, black sharecroppers, but not altogether typical. Her father, Willie Lee, and her mother, Minnie, were ambitious for their children, coveting education for them and wanting them to leave the South, where opportunities were limited. Despite the hard lot of blacks in the South of that day, Willie Lee had faith in much of the American system. He was among the very first black men to vote in his county in the 1930s after organizing a group of his fellow sharecroppers to seek their rights. He later became frustrated and disillusioned with the slowness of any real progress. These feelings and his poor health often resulted in his venting his anger and bitterness by beating his children. Alice, the youngest, seems to have received her full share of this harsh treatment.

Minnie, Walker's mother, was particularly outstanding as a role model for her children. Physically strong and strong-willed, she was a hard worker who managed to create beauty out of her limited surroundings by growing flowers, decorating the family cabin with flowers, quilting, and telling stories, at which she is reputed to have excelled.

Alice lost the sight of her right eye when she was only eight. A shot from a BB gun fired by one of her brothers accidentally hit her in this eye, blinding it and causing an unsightly white scar. Convinced that she was ugly by the way people stared at her face, she became shy and withdrawn. Six years later, when she was spending the summer in Boston with one of her brothers and his family—eventually all five brothers moved there—the scar was removed by a simple surgical procedure, which her brother and his wife paid for.

She returned home to Georgia, subsequently finished first in her high school class, and entered Spelman College in Atlanta, the nation's oldest college for black women. After two years at Spelman, she transferred to Sarah Lawrence College in New York, impelled undoubtedly by her increasing involvement with the civil rights movement and by Spelman's conservative educational and political philosophy. Her writing, which had started when she was still a child, increased in volume and quality under the tutelage of the distinguished poet Muriel Rukeyser and began to be recognized by prestigious prizes and fellowships.

Walker was deeply committed to the civil rights movement, working in voter registration and teaching black history in Mississippi in the 1970s. Other teaching appointments include Jackson (Mississippi) State, Tougaloo, the University of Massachusetts at Boston, the University of California at Berkeley in the 1980s, and Brandeis. When she left the South in 1974, she moved to Brooklyn and joined the editorial staff of the magazine *Ms.* Her controversial 1982 novel *The Color Purple* deals with the black experience as Walker has perceived and experienced it, especially the black woman's experience, wherein she finds black women to have been essentially victims, not only of racists but of men in general and black men in particular.

They have, of course, been physically brutalized, but equally important has been the attempt to stifle all aesthetic creativity in them. The ways in which this attempt has failed are depicted in *The Color Purple* and, less sensationally, in *In Search of Our Mothers' Gardens,* a collection of autobiographical and critical essays, some of which describe the folk art that black women created in their limited leisure and environment.

And, indeed, "Everyday Use" has pronounced biographical elements. The narrator is like Minnie Walker, Alice's mother, who, according to Janet Gray, was strong and hardworking and "did not regard gender as a barrier to any kind of labor" (521). The narrator describes herself in ruggedly masculine terms: "large, big-boned . . . rough man-working hands." She can perform typically male chores such as slaughtering, butchering, and dressing out hogs and calves. She boasts that she can work outdoors all day in subfreezing or scorching temperatures. Given these traits and accomplishments, it can come as something of a surprise to learn that the narrator has a refined and active aesthetic sensibility. She appreciates the material, the color, the artistry, and the history of the family quilts, which she regards as virtually sacred—but still to be used every day. Minnie Walker seems to have possessed similar characteristics. She worked all day in the fields with Alice's father, did her traditional female tasks in the evening, then exercised her enormous and widely recognized talents as a flower gardener and decorator with flowers.

It was in this way that Minnie made creativity an important part of everyday life and demonstrated that no form or material or setting was too humble or contemptible for its exhibition. Poor black women of an earlier day chose these unspectacular outlets for their artistic urges rather than submit to having them stifled altogether by constant and soul-numbing labor.

Other features of the story that contain biographical elements include the character Maggie, who in several ways reflects the young Alice Walker. For example, Maggie has "burn scars down her arms and legs" which she suffered in the fire that destroyed the family home some ten years before the time of the story. Her inordinate shyness and pitiful lack of self-esteem, manifested by her shuffling gait, downcast eyes, and nondescript figure, have their counterpart in Walker's embarrassment at her disfigurement from the loss of her eye and its negative impact on her schoolwork. Another but different side of Walker is discernible in Dee's sophistication and educational achievements. Like Walker, Dee delights in the beautiful handmade objects in her mother's home though, unlike Walker's, Dee's appreciation is trendy and superficial.

The exact historical setting of the story is not indicated, but a number of details point pretty clearly to a period covering part of the 1970s in the American South. For example, the narrator mentions a television show that unites aged parents long separated from children who have attained a high degree of success. She also refers to Johnny Carson, long-time host of the "Tonight Show," apparently at the zenith of his career. Dee and her traveling companion have chosen to use African or Muslim names rather than their birth names, which to them represent the names of their oppressors. They are also wearing hairstyles which they believe to be African or radically unconventional. The narrator also speaks of a group of industrious black stock farmers down the road, who have been the victims of harassment by their white racist neighbors. Many black entrepreneurs of this period converted to Islam and embarked on an austere course of economic and social self-determination. Another clue that the time is later than the 1960s is that the black stock farmers armed themselves with rifles to defend their property and lives, rather than calling upon local white law enforcement officers. That kind of action would have been uncommon even in the 1970s, so much so that the narrator said she "walked a mile and a half just to see the sight." It would have gratified her because she was a woman of an earlier generation, more apt to be intimidated by racial bullying (witness her rhetorical question and answer, "Who can even imagine me looking a strange white man in the eye? It seems to me I have always talked to them with one foot raised in flight"). This characteristic of the narrator, we might note, is decidedly not found in Minnie Walker, who according to Janet Gray "would explode at landlords" pressuring her to take her children out of school to work in the fields (521–22).

"Everyday Use" may profitably be read as a historical statement even though no specific years are actually mentioned. It describes, in addition to the human conflict which is its central business, a period and place where dramatic changes in racial relationships have taken place, where one young Southern black woman has rebelled against racism and chosen to express that rebellion by leaving her homeland and rejecting traditional and conventional standards and values. Her antagonists are her mother and sister, who have not rebelled and who, indeed, have found their own peace and satisfaction in the same locale of their historical oppression. It is not likely that Alice Walker, a strong civil rights activist, is advocating passivity in the face of racial injustice, but she does in this story pay a beautiful tribute to those like the narrator and Maggie who remained in their homes and prevailed by enduring and affirming the best in their troubled heritage.

3. Moral-Philosophical Considerations

It is obvious that racism, one of society's most troubling moral issues, underlies the actions in this story. It has unjustly reduced the narrator and Maggie to a low socioeconomic position and kept them there; it has bred an innate fear and mistrust of whites in the narrator, an otherwise strong, upright, and intelligent woman; it has alienated Dee, a bright and talented young woman, from whites to a degree that makes reconciliation unlikely; and along with its handmaiden, religious bigotry, it has impelled whites to engage in illegal and threatening action against hardworking black cattle raisers. And yet it is not the main moral or didactic point of the story. That point is Dee's misjudgment and mistreatment of her mother and sister, actions traceable to her ideological attitude that blinds her to their beauty and quiet heroism and the way these qualities have allowed them to know and respect themselves and their history in a way that Dee cannot understand. Like most dogmatists of whatever stripe, Dee is frequently obtuse. She assumes that her mother and sister have "chosen" to live in poverty in a racist community. She is too ashamed to bring her friends to her family's home, but she snaps numerous Polaroid pictures of the dilapidated shack, her "backward" family, even the cow wandering through the yard. Such pictures will not demonstrate tender or nostalgic feelings for the subjects but will serve some sort of political agenda. Dee is so arrogant and callous that she wants to appropriate for her own use even the few artifacts her mother and sister do possess that are simultaneously sacred and practically useful to them.

The narrator dominates the story, telling it from her point of view as both observer and participant. Though uneducated after the second grade and untraveled except in her dreams, she is a most remarkable woman, who demonstrates intelligence, sophistication, and a wry sense of humor in her narration. Her religion, a source of unalloyed joy to her as she worships, is also strength and guidance for tough living. Ideologues like Dee may think the church merely keeps her docile and uninvolved by its promises of "pie in the sky bye and bye." But it is an important part of black heritage, and it played a key role in the civil rights movement. It should also be noted here that it furnished part of the money for Dee's education. As far as the narrator is concerned, her religion has enabled her to rise above her oppressors without bitterness and without being obsessed by them. She feels no compulsion toward recrimination. In her dreams, Johnny Carson is "a smiling, gray, sporty man," who shakes her hand and compliments her on having a fine daughter like Dee. When thinking about the persons who poisoned some of the cattle belonging to her Black Muslim neighbors, the narrator simply calls them "white folks." They and the outrages of their kind, historic and contemporary, do not perpetually occupy her mind.

The narrator's dream of being reunited on the Johnny Carson show with Dee, the *Wunderkind* who has "made it" in the modern world, is an ironic inversion of what is about to take place. In her brief visit Dee does not find that her mother has shed a hundred pounds or used cosmetics to lighten the appearance of her skin or become a clever conversationalist. Nor does she pin an orchid on her and embrace her with tears of gratitude. After a generally unsatisfactory meeting, Dee leaves while lecturing her mother about not understanding her "heritage" and exhorting Maggie to reject her life-style—and, by implication, her mother—and to "make something of" herself.

The characters—the narrator and Maggie on one side, Dee and Hakim-a-barber on the other—represent two different points of view. The narrator depicts Dee and Hakim unsympathetically, satirically. They look odd. Dee, who always had style, looks like a sideshow: colors too loud and garish; dress too long (though the narrator concedes she likes its loose flowing quality); and excessive jewelry, jangling and gauche, unconventionally arranged (the narrator likens it to sheep and lizards). Hakim's hair is too long, and his chin whiskers look like a "kinky mule tail." The names these two have chosen appear ridiculous to the narrator through she is willing to learn them. She dashes cold water on Dee's claim that her given name is an oppressive white name by pointing out that she was named for her aunt and her grandmother.

When Hakim announces that he accepts some of the doctrines of the narrator's Muslim neighbors but that "farming and raising cattle is not my style," he implicitly criticizes the narrator, who has brained a bull calf with a sledgehammer and had the meat dressed out before nightfall. Dee's trendy pretensions to folk arts and crafts—which would have cruelly robbed her mother and sister of their most treasured possessions—reveal an even uglier aspect of character, one which the narrator thwarts with righteous indignation. Finally, Dee's condescension, self-aggrandizement, and arrogance, evidenced by her relentless "reading" to her "friends," her mother, and Maggie of material that was over their heads, prevent her from having a clue about her mother's and sister's feelings.

What the narrator reveals about herself and Maggie makes them very sympathetic characters. Early in the story, we admire the towering, matriarchal strength and wisdom of the narrator, her natural and keen ability to size up people, her dry wit, her refusal to become cynical and disillusioned about Dee or her own hard lot in life, her tenderness for the pitiful Maggie. Our hearts go out to Maggie, homely and less gifted than Dee, and thus cowed by her, scarred by the house fire in her childhood, and yet willing to relinquish her birthright of the family quilts to Dee, who could "appreciate" them. The moralist would maintain that readers may learn valuable lessons from both groups of characters, but the lessons are far from simple and clear-cut. It is too easy to reject Dee's militant individualism and pride with its implicit reverse racism and too easy to accept unquestioningly the narrator and Maggie's Christian stoicism and its suggested "Uncle Tom" attitude. It may be possible to reconcile these conflicting views of life.

There is certainly nothing in the traditional moral approach which insists on an all-or-nothing interpretive position.

· · ·

As we have seen in our discussions of these works, the traditional approach in literary interpretation is neither rigidly dogmatic nor unaesthetic. It is eclectic. And although it has its rationale in the methods discussed in this chapter, it does not eschew insights from any other critical approach; it nonetheless insists on its own fundamental validity. Those other critical approaches, however, do provide insights not stressed in the traditional, such as the appreciation of form, to which we now turn.

Quick Reference

Altick, Richard D. *The Art of Literary Research*. Rev. ed. New York: Norton, 1975.

Babcock, Weston. *"Hamlet": A Tragedy of Errors*. Lafayette, IN: Purdue University Press, 1961.

Bradley, A. C. *Shakespearean Tragedy*. London: Macmillan, 1914.

Cargill, Oscar. *Toward a Pluralistic Criticism*. Carbondale: Southern Illinois University Press, 1965.

Connolly, Thomas E. "Hawthorne's 'Young Goodman Brown': An Attack on Puritanic Calvinism." *American Literature* 28 (Nov. 1956): 370–75.

Crane, Ronald S. *A Collection of English Poems, 1660–1800*. New York: Harper, 1932.

Eliot, T. S. Introduction to *The Adventures of Huckleberry Finn*. London: Cresset, 1950. Reprinted in *Adventures of Huckleberry Finn*. 2nd ed. Ed. Sculley Bradley, Richard Croom Beatty, E. Hudson Long, and Thomas Cooley. New York: W. W. Norton, 1977.

Gray, Janet. "Alice Walker." In *American Writers: A Collection of Literary Biographies*. Supp. III, pt. 2. Ed. Lea Baechler and A. Walton Litz. New York: Scribner's, 1991.

Greetham, D. C. *Textual Scholarship: An Introduction*. Hamden, CT: Garland Publishing, 1994.

Hemingway, Ernest. *Green Hills of Africa*. New York: Scribner's, 1935.

Hill, Hamlin, and Walter Blair. *The Art of "Huckleberry Finn."* New York: Intext, 1962.

Hoffman, Daniel. *Form and Fable in American Fiction.* New York: Oxford University Press, 1961.

Housman, A. E. "The Application of Thought to Textual Criticism." In *Art and Error: Modern Textual Editing.* Ed. Ronald Gottesman and Scott Bennett. Bloomington: Indiana University Press, 1970.

Hoy, Cyrus, ed. *Hamlet.* New York: Norton (Critical Edition), 1963.

Hubler, Edward. Introduction to *Hamlet.* In *The Complete Signet Classic Shakespeare.* Ed. Sylvan Barnet. New York: Harcourt, 1972.

Levin, David. "Shadows of Doubt: Specter Evidence in Hawthorne's 'Young Goodman Brown.'" *American Literature* 34 (Nov. 1962): 344–52.

Lord, George de F. *Andrew Marvell, Complete Poetry.* New York: Random House (Modern), 1968.

Martz, Louis L. *The Anchor Anthology of Seventeenth-Century Verse.* Vol. 1. Garden City, NY: Doubleday, 1969.

McKeithan, D. M. "'Young Goodman Brown': An Interpretation." *Modern Language Notes* 67 (1952): 93–96.

Thorpe, James. *Principles of Textual Criticism.* San Marino, CA: The Huntington Library, 1972.

Trilling, Lionel. "Introduction." *The Adventures of Huckleberry Finn.* New York: Holt, 1948.

Walker, Alice. *In Search of Our Mothers' Gardens.* New York: Harcourt, 1983.

Wilson, J. Dover. *What Happens in "Hamlet."* London: Cambridge University Press, 1935.

3

The Formalistic Approach

I. READING A POEM: AN INTRODUCTION TO THE FORMALISTIC APPROACH

Here is the situation:

> The reader is to be presented with a short but complete poem. Its author and its era of composition are unknown. Its language, however, is English; it is not a translation.

Here is the poem:

> A slumber did my spirit seal;
>   I had no human fears;
> She seemed a thing that could not feel
>   The touch of earthly years.
>
> No motion has she now, no force;
>   She neither hears nor sees;
> Rolled round in earth's diurnal course,
>   With rocks, and stones, and trees.

The poem seems quite simple, easy to grasp and to understand. The speaker—a persona, not necessarily the poet—recalls a frame of mind sometime in the past, when "she" (the female figure) was so active and alive that the speaker (mother? father? lover?) could hardly comprehend any earthly touch to the living female figure. Now, in the present, the speaker tells the

reader or listener that the female is dead, but does so by circumlocution, or indirect statement. Only one word, "diurnal,"
should give even the mildest pause to most readers: it means
"daily." Monosyllabic words dominate the poem. The meter is
unvarying almost to the point of monotony—alternating soft
and strong syllables, usually four of each in the first, third, fifth,
and seventh lines; three of each in the other four lines. The
rhymes are equally regular and predictable. There is classic
restraint and regularity, a tight control.

There is also powerful emotional impact.

Whence comes that impact? Largely from the tightly stated
irony and paradox of the poem. The speaker has both gotten
what he or she desired and not gotten it: the expectations for
the female figure have been realized—and incontrovertibly
they have been demolished. Initially the speaker was confi-
dent in the eternal life of the female figure. What parent nur-
tures and enjoys a child while thinking thoughts of death
rather than life? What lover thinks constantly if at all that the
beloved will die, and prematurely at that? Life seems to ensure
continued life. This female figure would somehow transcend
earthly normalities, would not even age. The speaker was secure (slumbering) in that assumption. So we know from the
first stanza.

But there is a huge gap, and at once a leap beyond that gap,
between the first and second stanza. Something happened.
Somehow the child or woman died. She already has been
buried. The "slumber" of line one has become the eternal sleep
of death. The "seal" of the "spirit" has become the coffin seal
of the body. Even more poignantly, the life of the dynamic person in lines three and four, where sense perceptions of touching and feeling seem to be transmuted into ethereal or angelic
dimensions, is now the unfeeling death of one who has no energy, no vitality, no sense of hearing or seeing. She is no more
and no less than a rock or a stone or a tree fixed to the earth.
The final irony, that paradox, is that the once motion-filled person is still in motion—but not the vital motion of a human person; she now moves daily a huge distance, a full turn of the
earth itself, rotating with a motion not her own, but only that
of rocks and stones—gravestones—and rooted trees.

The essential structure, or form, of the poem is the irony that the speaker got precisely what he or she wanted—but hardly in the way anticipated—a structure that at a fairly obvious level contrasts by means of the two stanzas and resolves the paradox by their interaction. A closer look takes the reader beyond this now-evident contrast of two stanzas. The texture of the poem is enriched by the sleep imagery, the sleep of life becoming the sleep of death. The "slumber" of line 1 connotes rest and quiet, even that of a baby or young child. The sibilant sounds of "s" at first suggest that quiet contentment, but they appear throughout the poem, taking on the irony of the second stanza almost like mournful echoes of the first. "Spirit" and "seal" not only continue the sibilant quality but also in retrospect are ambiguous terms, for "spirit" suggests death as well as life, and "seal" suggests not only security but finality: the coffin and the grave. In the third line the word "thing" at first seems to be a noncommital, simply denotative word: perhaps the poet was not even able to think of a better word, and used a filler. But in retrospect the female figure now is indeed a "thing," like a rock or a stone, a mere thing—in truth, dust. Furthermore, "thing" contrasts with its bluntness of sound with the sibilant sounds of so much of the rest of the poem, and anticipates the alternating sounds of the last line, the "s" sounds alternating with the harder sounds of "r" and the consonant clusters "st" and "tr" in "rocks," "stones," and "trees."

Like the reference to sleep, the references to the senses ("feel," "touch") in the first stanza are expanded in the second: motion, or its lack, involves the muscles in kinetics and kinesthesia; hearing and seeing are explicitly mentioned. But in each of the three cases a negative word precedes the sense word—"no," "neither," "nor." Then in line 7, we meet the awesome reality of kinetic motion without kinesthesia. In "Rolled round" we have the forced motion of the inert body. In a striking change of metrics, we realize that the seeming monotony of the alternating soft and hard syllables is broken here by a spondee in place of the dominant iamb, and the spondee in turn is strengthened by the alliterating "r" and the consonance of the "d" at the end of each of the two words, echoed in the initial "d" of "diurnal." Once having noticed that pounding spondee, we might in retrospect reconsider the two uses of "no" in line five, for they can be read almost as strongly as the stressed syllables of the line, giving still greater impact to the negative effect of the whole statement. Finally, the contrast between lines 7 and 8 is devastating. If we lift the line totally from its context, we can hear almost an ebullient sound in the seventh line, a glorious sweeping rhythm, aided by the vowels or assonance in the middle several words: "Rolled round in earth's diurnal course." But that sweeping, soaring quality comes up against the finality and slowed pace of the heavily impeded line 8, where the punctuation and the three accented monosyllabic words join to give the impact of three strong chords at the end of the symphony.

· · ·

We have read a poem. Unless we know from other contexts, we still do not know the name of the author, the nationality, or the era of composition. We do not know who the speaker is, not even the sex of the speaker. We do not know if the poem concerns a real-life situation or a totally fictive one. We do not know whether the author took some similar real-life situation or incident that he or she then adapted and transmuted into a poem. We know only the poem itself, a short piece of richly textured literary art that bears up well under close analysis and resolves its tensions by means of irony and paradox, showing them not only in the contrast between two stanzas but also in seemingly minute details. We have read a poem and have analyzed it by using the formalistic approach to literature.

▪ II. THE PROCESS OF FORMALISTIC ANALYSIS: MAKING THE CLOSE READER

What we demonstrated in the preceding pages is a close reading in practice. The reading stands on its own. Others, perhaps many, have read the poem in much the same way. Indeed, perhaps most readers of the poem in the middle of the twentieth century would have read this poem in something of this way. That is so because the approach to the poem is what we call formalistic, an approach with a methodology, with a history, with practitioners, and with some detractors. Let us now learn more about this formalistic approach.

Obviously we are to be alert to "form." But to say that is just as obviously to beg the question "What is form?" And we cannot say simply that form is structure, or that structure is form, for that is to go in circles. So what are the ways to appreciate form?

Intensive reading begins with a sensitivity to the words of the text and all their denotative and connotative values and implications. An awareness of multiple meanings, even the etymologies of words as traced in dictionaries, will offer significant guidelines to what the work says. Usually adequate for most readers is one of the standard collegiate dictionaries. But one should also be aware of the vastly larger resources in unabridged dictionaries and especially the details and examples of historical changes in word meanings as recorded in the most recent edition of *The Oxford English Dictionary*. So first let us look at the words and the sentences in which we find them, and let us be alert.

But just as we begin to study closely the words and their meanings, almost simultaneously we must also begin to look for structural relationships and patterns—not just in the words and their relationships, but also in larger units. Form becomes much more than sentence patterns; it becomes the relationship of stanzas in a poem, or the interplay of an octave and a sestet in a sonnet. It becomes the tone or mood that the text builds, and possibly the shifting and alternating of moods. It becomes the sequence of plot elements, even episodes, in a narrative, or the juxtaposition of scenes in a play. It becomes the relationship between the teller of the narrative and the hearer, possibly the ambiguity of the teller's version of the story.

So let us assume that now we have some degree of knowledge of the words of the text, at least in their denotative senses. Let us also assume that we can mentally plot out the sequence of actions, or of sequences and shifting of what the words seem to be telling us. Now we can note that some of these words are deeply connotative also, or perhaps they name objects that have symbolic value, and as we probe the connotations and symbols they take on associations, or develop patterns that somehow have relevance within themselves and to other patterns. Images emerge as more and more important, perhaps insistently forcing themselves to the fore. We note that certain images, or colors, or references to time—a host of possibilities in our human experience—keep coming up. Some of these may contribute to the setting of the work, its actual place and time, or more subtly, its ambience. Bit by formal bit, we think we begin to see a theme emerging from the work.

None of this is happening in any set sequence. It is more like when we walk into a room new to us, crowded with people, furniture, art works, a fire in the hearth. How do we see things? How do our eyes move across the scene? What do we see first, what next?

In the printed text perhaps the next thing is an allusion that has caught our attention, a reference to a bit of history or mythology, or to another work of literature. Maybe a word has taken on more than one meaning, causing us to read the text at more than one level; or we suspect that there is irony developing in what we see, and we become suspicious that first impressions need modification. Or details of a narrative seem especially vivid or striking, but not yet clearly important as we move through the plot's complication—and then, suddenly perhaps, the narrative reaches a climactic point, and all details fall into place by the point in the narrative that we sometimes call the dénouement.

Then there is a sense of closure, a sense of fulfillment of the expectations that have been built up.

What did the author do by so arranging those words, those images and symbols, those details of plot and action? How did the author "achieve" this accomplishment? (We will return to the concept of "achieved content" later in this chapter.)

In retrospect, we can say that what the author did was to make us see that internal relationships gradually reveal a form, a principle by which all subordinate patterns can be accommodated and accounted for. When all the words, phrases, metaphors, images, and symbols are examined in terms of each other and of the whole, any literary text worth our efforts will display its own internal logic. When that logic has been established, the reader is very close to identifying the overall form of the work.

So now, in review, what must we do to make ourselves close readers in a formalistic way? Let this list remind us of what we saw in the poem at the beginning of this chapter, and what we shall look for in the works we will study in this chapter: structure, shape, interplay, interrelationships, denotations and connotations, contexts, images, symbols, repeated details, climax (rising action, falling action), dénouement, balances and tensions, rhythms and rhymes that catch our attention, sounds that do the same, the speaker's apparent voice, a single line— or even a word—set off all by itself. Whatever, in other words, contributes to the uniqueness of the work.

■ III. A BRIEF HISTORY OF FORMALISTIC CRITICISM

A. The Course of a Half Century

The formalistic approach, as we use the term in this book, emphasizes the manner of reading literature that was given its special dimensions and emphases by English and American critics in the first two-thirds of the twentieth century. To many, indeed to most, students of literature during that era, this approach came to be called the New Criticism.

In the last third of the century, the New Criticism came to be called by other names, not always favorable—and some epithets bordered on the vitriolic. At the least it has come to be called by many the *old* New Criticism, for even "newer" approaches have gained popularity and have had little or nothing in common with the old New Criticism. For that matter, the word *formalistic* needs some small qualification as well, for here it will be used more or less synonymously with the methodology of the New Critics, and it is not directly concerned with the Russian formalists, though the methodologies share some principles.

Regardless of shifting attitudes toward English and American formalist criticism (more about that shortly), we are quite content to sail against the winds of change and to assert that being a good reader of literature necessitates our reading closely and reading well. Reading well is what the New Critics helped us to do.

They taught us to look at the individual work of literary art as an organic form. They articulated the concept that in an organic form there is a consistency and an internal vitality that we should look for and appreciate. In doing so, we would appropriate the work to ourselves and make it part of our consciousness in the same way that we might when we study Mahler's *Ninth Symphony* or Michelangelo's *David*, or in the same way that the persona in Keats's ode studied the Grecian urn.

They taught us. But how new were the New Critics when they were called that by John Crowe Ransom in *The New Critics* in 1941? Actually—and this should come as no surprise—there were forebears of great note. The New Critics did not spring suddenly from Zeus's head. We should not be surprised at this because in a form of human endeavor so basic as the creation of literary art we can expect a continuity in the way that art is created or becomes art. Nor should we be surprised that criticism, the informed reading of that art, should have a continuity as well.

More specifically, we should not be surprised because one of the most salient considerations of the New Critics was emphasis on form, on the work of art as an object. Can we imagine any art—whether it be literary, musical, plastic, or dramatic, and regardless of its era, even our own, when formlessness is sometimes important—that does not have some sense of form? The form need not be geometric or physical or otherwise perceptible to the eye, and indeed often it is not, but it is there. To be sure, it might be most easily perceived at a physical level at first: the external and obvious shape of a statue, the geometric pattern of arches and of horizontal and vertical lines in a building, the four-line stanza of Sappho or the pattern of strophes in Pindar, or the careful physical shape of a sonnet, a sestina, or a haiku. The New Critics did not invent these obvious forms.

But they helped us to read better by reminding us of what was there eons earlier. Art entails form; form takes many forms.

So let us consider further some of the background elements of formalistic theory.

B. Backgrounds of Formalistic Theory

Classical art and aesthetics amply testify to a preoccupation with form. Plato exploits dialectic and shapes movement toward Socratic wisdom by his imagery, metaphor, dramatic scenes, characterization, setting, and tone. Aristotle's *Poetics* recommends an "orderly arrangement of parts" that form a beautiful whole or "organism." Horace admonishes the would-be poet: "In short, be your subject what it will, let it be simple and unified." And some awareness of formalism is at least implicit in many other classical, medieval, and Renaissance treatises on art or poetics.

But the Romantic movement in Europe in the late eighteenth and nineteenth centuries intensified speculations about form in literature. Samuel Taylor Coleridge (1772–1834) brought to England (and thus to America) the conception of a dynamic *imagination* as the shaping power and unifier of vision—a conception he had acquired from his studies of the German philosophical idealists: Kant, Hegel, Fichte, and Schelling. Such a conception encouraged discrimination between a poem and other forms of discourse by stressing the poem's power to elicit delight as a "whole" and "distinctive gratification from each component *part.*" In a *"legitimate* poem," Coleridge declared, the parts "mutually support and explain each other; all in their proportion harmonizing with, and supporting the purpose and known influences of metrical arrangement."

This interrelationship between the whole and the parts was manifested in a consistently recurring image among the Romantics—the image of growth, particularly of vegetation. Perhaps because of the Romantics' infatuation with nature, the analogy usually likened the internal life of a painting or poem to the quintessential unity of parts within a tree, flower, or plant: as the seed determines, so the organism develops and lives. In a letter to John Taylor (February 27, 1818) Keats wrote that one of his "axioms" was "That if Poetry comes not as naturally as the Leaves to a tree it had better not come at all." Shelley uses imagery of growth and of vegetation several times in his "Defence of Poetry." In talking of the relationship of sounds in poetry, he counsels against "the vanity of translation; it were as wise to cast a violet into a crucible that you might discover the formal principle of its colour and odour, as to seek to transfuse from one language into another the creations of a poet. The plant must spring again from its seed, or it will bear no flower. . . ." He calls the thoughts of the poet "the germs of the flower and the fruit of latest time," claiming, "All high poetry is infinite; it is as the first acorn, which contained all oaks potentially." And again of poetry,

> . . . this power arises from within, like the colour of a flower which fades and changes as it is developed. . . . The instinct and intuition of the poetical faculty is still more observable in the plastic and pictorial arts; a great statue or picture grows under the power of the artist as a child in the mother's womb. . . .

In America, Edgar Allan Poe (1809–1849), extending Coleridge's theory, asserted the excellence of short lyric poems and short tales because they can maintain and transmit a single, unitary effect more successfully than can long works like *Paradise Lost.* In "The Philosophy of Composition" Poe demonstrated how the parts of his "The Raven" allegedly developed from the single effect he desired. Poe also reprimanded certain contemporary poets like Henry Wadsworth Longfellow for committing what he called the "heresy of the didactic" by tacking on obtrusive (thus inorganic) moral lessons and accordingly violating the lyric effects of their poems.

Later in the nineteenth century and on into the twentieth, Henry James (1843–1916), in "The Art of Fiction" and the prefaces to his tales and novels, argued for fiction as a "fine art" and for the intricate, necessary interrelationships of parts and the whole:

> There are bad and good novels, as there are bad pictures and good pictures; but that is the only distinction in which I can see any meaning, and I can as little imagine speaking of a novel of character as I can imagine speaking of a picture of character. When one says picture one says of character, when one says novel one says of incident, and the terms seem to be transposed at will. What is character but the determination of incident? What is incident BUT the illustration of character? What is either a picture or a novel that is *not* of character? What else do we seek in it and find in it? It is an incident for a woman to stand up with her hand resting on a table and look at you in a certain way; or if it not be an incident, I think it will be hard to say what it is.

James implies the same interdependence and kinship for all other aspects of a work of fiction—setting, theme, scene and narrative, image and symbol. When the artist is attending to his craft, nothing that goes into the work will be wasted, and form will be present: "Form alone *takes,* and holds and preserves, substance—saves it from the welter of helpless verbiage that we swim in as in a sea of tasteless tepid pudding." When the work achieves "organic form," everything will count.

C. The New Criticism

Although there were antecedents from Plato through James, a systematic and methodological formalistic approach to literary criticism appeared only with the rise in the 1930s of what came to be called the New Criticism. Coming together originally at Vanderbilt University in the years following World War I, the New Critics included a teacher-scholar-poet, John Crowe Ransom, and several bright students—Allen Tate, Robert Penn Warren, and Cleanth Brooks. Associated at first in an informal group that discussed literature, they in time adopted the name of Fugitives and published an elegant literary magazine called *The Fugitive* in Nashville from 1922 to 1925. When the poetry and critical essays of T. S. Eliot came to their attention, they found sturdy reinforcement for ideas that were emerging from their study and writing of lyric poetry. Ideas thus shared and promoted included literature viewed as an organic tradition, the importance of strict attention to form, a conservatism related to classical values, the ideal of a society that encourages order and tradition, a preference for ritual, and the rigorous and analytical reading of literary texts. Eliot was particularly influential in his formulation of the objective correlative ("a set of objects, a situation, a chain of events which shall be the formula of [a] *particular* emotion; such that when the external facts are given, the emotion is immediately invoked"). Eliot was also influential in his endorsement of the English Metaphysical poets of the seventeenth century for their success in blending "states of mind and feeling" in a single "verbal equivalent." Such developments strengthened the emergent New Criticism, which by the 1950s had become the dominant critical system in such influential journals as *Sewanee Review, The Kenyon Review,* and *The Hudson Review* and in college and university English departments.

The New Critics sought precision and structural tightness in the literary work; they favored a style and tone that tended toward irony; they insisted on the presence within the work of everything necessary for its analysis; and they called for an end to a concern by critics and teachers of English with matters outside the work itself—the life of the author, the history of his times, or the social and economic implications of the literary work. In short, they turned the attention of teachers, students, critics, and readers to the essential matter: *what* the work says and *how* it says it as inseparable issues. To their great credit they influenced at least one generation of college students to become more careful and serious readers than they otherwise would have been.

Members and disciples of the group advanced their critical theory and techniques through a series of brilliant college textbooks on literary analysis: *Understanding Poetry* (1939) and *Understanding Fiction* (1943) by Brooks and Warren; *Understanding Drama* (1945) by Brooks and Robert B. Heilman; *The Art of Modern Fiction* by Ray B. West, Jr., and Robert W. Stallman; and *The House of Fiction* (1950) by Caroline Gordon and Allen Tate. After 1942, *The Explicator,* a monthly publication, published hundreds of short textual explications of great varieties of literary works; and prestigious literary journals and quarterlies still publish articles that show the continuing influence of the New Criticism.

But even as the formalistic approach of the New Critics was influencing readers, teachers, and students throughout the universities of the United States, well into the second half of the century, others were pointing to what they perceived to be deficiencies or worse in that approach. Frank Lentricchia in *After the New Criticism* (1980) offers a helpful overview of what was happening. He uses 1957 and the publication of three books that year to give one benchmark for the turn to other approaches and emphases. The three are Northrop Frye's *Anatomy of Criticism,* Cleanth Brooks and W. K. Wimsatt's *Literary Criticism: A Short History,* and Frank Kermode's *Romantic Image.* Coming hard upon Murray Krieger's *New Apologists for*

Poetry (1956), they seem to fulfill, Lentricchia says, Krieger's prediction "that the New Criticism had done all it could do for American literary critics . . ." (3). "By about 1957," Lentricchia says, "the moribund condition of the New Criticism and the literary needs it left unfulfilled placed us in a critical void. Even in the late 1940s, however, those triumphant times of the New Criticism, a theoretical opposition was already gathering strength" (4). Lentricchia goes on to cite a number of the works that show that gathering strength, and the reader is referred to his overview.

One article that he does not cite might earn a place here because it provides (witness its title) a kind of synopsis of the reaction setting in even as the vogue of the New Criticism was still gaining strength: "Cleanth Brooks; or the Bankruptcy of Critical Monism" by Ronald S. Crane, a neo-Aristotelian. Like others in the 1940s, Crane faults the reduction of pieces of literature to one or a few rhetorical devices that bring about a diminution of their potential. Whether it be irony or paradox or tension or texture: these, alone or together, do not a poem make.

However, it is not our present purpose to treat thoroughly the attack on or the divergence from the formalistic approach of the New Criticism. More of that can be seen in works such as those cited by Lentricchia and in the chapters that follow. Our present purpose is to show the enduring contribution of the formalistic approach, even as we call attention to some of its deficiencies.

▪ IV. CONSTANTS OF THE FORMALISTIC APPROACH: SOME KEY CONCEPTS, TERMS, AND DEVICES

We shall draw attention now to several of the constants of the formalistic approach, even though some may have been disparaged by the differing critical emphases of other writers. Keeping in mind the overview we gained from the analysis of "A Slumber Did My Spirit Seal" (we can now reveal that the poem is by William Wordsworth) and keeping in mind that these devices may recur in the analyses later in this chapter, let us look more carefully at these constants.

A. Form and Organic Form

We must, of course, begin with form. In systems of the past, the word *form* usually meant what we would call *external form.* Thus, when we identify a poem with fourteen lines of iambic pentameter, a conventional pattern of rhymes, and a conventional division into two parts as a sonnet, we are defining its external form. The same kind of description takes place when we talk about couplets, tercets, *ottava rima,* quatrains, Spenserian stanzas, blank verse, or even free verse. But the formalistic critic is only moderately interested in external forms (in fact, only when external form is related to the work's total form, when stanzaic or metrical pattern is integral to internal relationships, reverberations, patterns, and systems). The process of formalistic analysis is complete only when everything in the work has been accounted for in terms of its overall form.

Organic form is a particular concept important to the New Critics, inherited as we have noted from the English Romantics. In the Romantics, we find the emphasis on organicism not just in literary forms but in a broader, philosophical context, where the world itself is organic; objects within it are organisms that interact with each other in a larger organic universe. This notion may go so far as Wordsworthian pantheism, or what some thought to be pantheism, where a breeze in nature may awaken within the persona of the *Prelude* (in this case the poet himself) a "correspondent breeze" (1.35). Similarly there is the Romantic emphasis on the Aeolian lyre or harp, as in Coleridge's poem "The Eolian Harp," and the reference to the lyre in the imagery and symbolism of Shelley's "Ode to the West Wind," a notion that recurs in the second paragraph of Shelley's "Defence of Poetry." The vegetation imagery, mentioned earlier, is of course part of this organicism. Now the question for us is how this concept of organicism came into formalistic criticism of this century, especially among critics many of whom expressed no fondness for English Romanticism.

In the formalistic approach, the assumption is that a given literary experience takes a shape proper to itself, or at the least that the shape and the experience are functions of each other.

This may mean at a minimum that a precise metrical form couples with a complex of sounds in a line of verse to present one small bit of the experience (recall the treatment of the short lyric at the beginning of this chapter). Or it may mean that a generic form, like that of the sonnet, is used repeatedly in a sonnet cycle to show the interrelationship of thoughts to images, or problems to comment or solution. In such a case, even though the overt structure of the sonnet is repetitive, still the experience in any one Italian sonnet is structured across the octave and sestet or in the English form across the three quatrains and the concluding couplet. In a larger work, a full-length play or a novel might adopt much more complex and subtle forms to communicate the experience, such as the interrelationships of plot and subplot in Shakespeare's *Hamlet, Henry IV, Part 1,* or *The Tempest;* or in the complex stream of consciousness of Joyce's *Ulysses* or Faulkner's *Sound and the Fury.* Indeed, the fragmentation of story line and of time line in modern fiction and in some absurdist drama is a major formalistic device used not only to generate within the reader the sense of the immediacy and even the chaos of experience but also to present the philosophical notion of nonmeaning and nihilism. Thus we have the seeming paradox that in some cases the absence of form *is* the form, precisely.

Statements that follow discovery of form must embrace what Ransom called local texture and logical structure (347). The logical structure refers to the argument or the concept within the work; local texture comprises the particular details and devices of the work (for example, specific metaphors and images). However, such a dualistic view of a literary work has its dangers, for it might encourage the reduction of logical structure to précis or summary—what Brooks has called the "heresy of paraphrase." In *Understanding Poetry,* Brooks and Warren simply include "idea," along with rhythm and imagery, as a component of form: "the form of a poem is the organization of the material . . . for the creation of the total effect" (554). The emphasis, in any case, is upon accounting for all aspects of the work in seeking to name or define its form and effect. Mark Schorer pressed the distinction further between the critic's proper concentration on *form* and an improper total concern with *content only:* "Modern [i.e., formalistic] criticism has shown that to speak of content as such is not to speak of art at all, but of experience; and that it is only when we speak of the *achieved* content, the form, the work of art as a work of art, that we speak as critics. The difference between content, or experience, and achieved content, or art, is technique" ("Technique as Discovery" 67). He goes on to say that "technique is the only means [an author] has of discovering, exploring, developing his subject, of conveying its meaning, and, finally, of evaluating it."

B. Texture, Image, Symbol

As we turn more specifically to texture, we find that as with form and its potential to embody meaning, imagery and metaphor are an integral part of the work, especially in the poem. Once again, the formalistic critics—obviously—did not invent metaphor: Aristotle, very much a formalist, discussed metaphor in his *Poetics.* But the New Critics delighted in close analysis of imagery and metaphor, and they laid stress on a careful working out of imagery. The consistency of imagery in a lyric, whether it be a single dominant image throughout the poem or a pattern of multiple but related images, became for some an index to the quality of a given poem. Such consistency of imagery helped to create what John Crowe Ransom among others called texture. It was for such reasons that there was much interest in Metaphysical poetry and in the Metaphysical conceit. The interest was aided by publication of Herbert Grierson's collection *Metaphysical Lyrics and Poems of the Seventeenth Century* (1921). It was furthered by the attention of T. S. Eliot, Ransom, and Allen Tate. Critics praised the Metaphysical conceit because of its carefully worked out ("wrought") images that were elaborated over a number of lines, richly textured and endowed with a complexity of meanings, as in John Donne's "The Flea" or in the "stiff twin compasses" of his "Valediction: Forbidding Mourning." Donne's image of the "well-wrought urn" in "The Canonization" is cogent here, not only because of the working out of the image but also because the phrase gave Cleanth Brooks the title to one of his contributions to the rich library of New Criticism, *The Well-Wrought Urn* (1947). By way of contrast, a poem like

Shelley's "Lines: 'When the Lamp is Shattered'" was disparaged by formalist critics for its allegedly loose imagery; indeed, much of Shelley, along with other Romantics, was disparaged (but for a defense, see Pottle, 589–608).

When an image (or an incident or other discrete item) takes on meaning beyond its objective self, it moves into the realm of symbol. Here is a dilemma for some formalistic critics, those who espouse the autonomous and autotelic concept of a literary work so strenuously that anything outside it becomes a problem. Symbols may sometimes remain within the work, as it were; but it is the nature of symbols to have extensional possibilities, to open out to the world beyond the art object itself. When meaning and value outside the work of literature are the real purpose of the symbol, some formalistic critics may find fault with the work. On the other hand, such a restriction may well be one of the more limiting concerns of the New Critics (we recall Poe's denunciation of the didactic in favor of beauty), and we take the cautious position that even in a formalistic reading we must go sometimes beyond the pure aestheticism of the work in itself to the extended meaning of the work as suggested by its symbols. We have already said something of this sort when we alluded to the form of some modern novels or absurdist plays: form can embody theme, and theme transcends the individual work. Symbol is a way of using something integral to the work to reach beyond the work and engage the world of value outside the work. It might be an incident that takes on meaning, such as the apparent happenstance of events in a naturalistic writer like Thomas Hardy; it might be the conventional object or device—a crucifix, a color, a tree—that becomes symbolic of meanings within and without the poem, story, or play. When that happens, the formalistic approach must study such symbols as aspects of form, as exponents of meaning both within and without the work. Not to do so would be to turn the work too much within itself, making it overly centripetal. If a work is too centripetal because of the limiting notion that it should exist in and of and for itself alone, the work becomes an objet d'art, suitable for a shelf but in danger of losing the very life that makes it important to the reader. One must question this restriction, this reductionism, just as one questions Keats's Grecian urn as to whether beauty and truth are indeed the same, and as one questions Emerson's speaker in "The Rhodora," who said that "beauty is its own excuse for being."

C. Fallacies

Another formalistic term that has brought mixed responses is the intentional fallacy, along with its corollary the affective fallacy. In the intentional fallacy, we are told, the critic or the reader makes the mistake of not divorcing the literary work from any intention that the author might have had for the work. Instead, say Wimsatt and Beardsley in *The Verbal Icon* (1954), the work must give us from within itself any intention that might be garnered, and we must not go to the author for his or her intention: at the very least the author is not a reliable witness. Wimsatt and Beardsley review the arguments of some of the intentionists, and there are legitimate considerations on both sides of the question. For us a proper middle ground would be to take note of external evidence when it seems worthy, but to accept the caution that the work itself must first and always be seen as a work unto itself, having now left the author's care. Wimsatt and Beardsley also warned against the affective fallacy, wherein the work is judged by its effect on the reader or viewer, particularly its emotional effect. Again, however, those avoiding the reductionist tendency of formalistic criticism would note that no work of literary art can be divorced from the reader and therefore from the reader's response. For that matter, no less a critic than Aristotle gave us the concept of catharsis, the purging of the audience at a tragedy that cleanses the emotions. But we admit that the relationship is complex and the formalistic approach is correct in urging caution.

D. Point of View

Another device that a formalistic approach must heed is the point of view, which, like consistency of imagery, is generally considered a virtue in the work of literary art, for it preserves the internal form, the organic quality of the work. Conversely, a nonexistent point of view (that is, one in which several points of view are not clearly demarcated from each other) flaws the work, for the work then may go in several directions and therefore have no integrity: the center does not hold. Such a fragmentation may be avoided if we grant the narrator the privilege of knowing all, seeing all, from a perspective that in theological terms would have to be called divine. In the great epics and in most traditional novels of an earlier day, the omniscient narrator possessed that godlike quality and narrated from a third-person perspective.

But in more restricted points of view, the very form of the work is conditioned by the point of view to which the author limits the narrator. As Wayne Booth has reminded us, narrators may be either reliable (if they support the explicit or implicit moral norms of the author) or unreliable (if they do not). Thus Jake Barnes in *The Sun Also Rises* is a completely reliable narrator, for he is the very embodiment of what is often called the "Hemingway code"; on the other hand, the lawyer in Melville's *Bartleby the Scrivener* is unreliable in his early evaluations of himself because he is not involved with humanity. Whatever the point of view we encounter, it has to be recognized as a basic means of control over the area or scope of the action, the quality of the fictional world offered to the reader, and even the reactions of the reader.

In a first-person narration the author may condition the form even more. Thus a young boy named Huckleberry Finn, who narrates his own story, must not be allowed to know more than a young boy such as he would know. His view is limited to what he sees and reports. Nor does he understand all that he reports, not—at least—as a mature person devoid of cultural bias and prejudice might understand. In this first-person point of view, the narration is limited to that person's telling. If the author wishes to communicate anything beyond that to the reader, that wish becomes a challenge in technique, for the information must be reported naively by Huck Finn and interpreted maturely by the reader on the basis of what the author has Huck Finn say (again we must heed the admonitions about the intentional fallacy and the affective fallacy). In this sense Huck Finn is honest on the one hand, but an unreliable narrator on the other. To stretch the point a bit further, we may imagine a psychotic telling a story in a seemingly straightforward way—but the real story may be *about* the psychotic, and what he or she tells us at the obvious level may not have any credibility at all. In some circumstances the author may choose to have a shifting point of view to achieve different effects at different times (possibly this is what Chaucer the author did to Chaucer the pilgrim). Or there may be multiple points of view, as in Faulkner's *The Sound and the Fury*. Still another type is the point of view that would claim total objectivity—the scenic or dramatic: we read only the dialogue of characters, with no hints of a narrator to intrude any perspective other than what we get from the dialogue itself. All these points of view condition the form of literature, and a formalistic approach must study them for the reader to appreciate the fullness of the work.

E. The Speaker's Voice

Failure to note point of view as an aspect of form will result in a misreading or in an inadequate reading of the work. This challenge to the reader may be further illustrated by turning briefly to lyric poetry, where tone of voice is analogous to point of view. Although we do not usually think of point of view as an aspect of lyric poetry, the fact is that in a lyric there is a speaker—that is, a first-person situation. This immediately sets a context and a set of circumstances, for the speaker is doing something, somewhere. Possibly there is also a hearer, a second person (we readers only overhear the speaker), so that the hearer also conditions the experience. In Robert Browning's "Andrea del Sarto" it means much to know that Andrea is addressing a woman and that they are among his paintings at a certain time of day. Consequently it is even more important to know what Andrea feels about his inadequacy as a painter and as a man: his tone of voice, as much as details revealed to us, will largely reveal those feelings. Conversely, another painter, Fra Lippo Lippi in the poem of that name, responds ebulliently to his world and his confidence about his ability to capture and interpret it in his painting: his colloquial, jovial tone communicates this attitude. In Browning's "Porphyria's Lover" the reader will go totally astray if he does not understand that the lover is a madman—and that the beloved

though present has been murdered by him. In a more traditional love lyric or in one that describes a beautiful scene in nature, the speaker may reasonably be trusted to speak the truth.
But how does one interpret the speaker's voice in Donne's
"Song" ("Go and Catch a Falling Star")? What is the mixture of
genial satire, sardonicism, mere playfulness? The way the
reader hears the speaker will condition the poem, give it its
form, indeed may make the poem into poems by varying the
voice. So the formalist critic ends up with a problem: one poem,
or several? Perhaps, finally, there is only one, and that one is the
resolution of all the possibilities in one reality, a kind of super-
form that resolves and incorporates all the several forms.

F. Tension, Irony, Paradox

The resolution just mentioned is like the principle of the arch.
In an arch the way down is the way up: the arch stands because the force of gravity pulls the several stones down while
at the same time pushing them against the keystone. Gravity
therefore counteracts itself to keep the entire arch standing; for
that matter, the arch can carry great weight—just as a piece of
literature might.

This aspect of formalistic criticism might be called tension,
the resolution of opposites, often in irony and paradox. Coleridge enunciated at least part of this notion early on; the New
Critics laid great stress on the terminology, sometimes almost
to the exclusion of other elements. The basic terms—tension,
irony, paradox—are often nearly indistinguishable, so closely
do they work together. C. Hugh Holman and William Harmon
summarize tension as "A term introduced by Allen Tate,
meaning the integral unity that results from the successful
resolution of the conflicts of abstraction and concreteness, of
general and particular, of denotation and connotation. . . .
Good poetry, Tate asserts, is the 'full, organized body of all the
extension and intension that we can find in it" (473). Holman
and Harmon further note that "This concept has been widely
used by the New Critics, particularly of poetry as a pattern of
paradox or as a form of irony."

One could hardly find a better demonstration of the interrelationships of tension, irony, and paradox than what Robert

Penn Warren provided in "Pure and Impure Poetry." In making a case for impure poetry—poetry of "inclusiveness"—Warren not only analyzed the arguments of purists but also provided excellent analyses of poems and passages that include the impure and thereby prove themselves as poetry. Regularly the ironies and paradoxes—the tensions—are at the heart of the success of the items he studies. Near the conclusion of the essay he says:

> Can we make any generalizations about the nature of the poetic structure? First, it involves resistances, at various levels. There is the tension between the rhythm of the poem and the rhythm of speech . . . ; between the formality of the rhythm and the informality of the language; between the particular and the general, the concrete and the abstract; between the elements of even the simplest metaphor; between the beautiful and the ugly; between ideas . . . ; between the elements involved in irony . . . ; between prosaisms and poeticisms. . . .
>
> This list is not intended to be exhaustive; it is intended to be merely suggestive. But it may be taken to imply that the poet is like the jujitsu expert; he wins by utilizing the resistance of his opponent—the materials of the poem. In other words, a poem, to be good, must earn itself. It is a motion toward a point of rest, but if it is not a resisted motion, it is motion of no consequence. (27)

We may now turn to the formalistic approach in practice, applying some of its methods to the five literary works that we analyzed in chapter 2.

▪ V. THE FORMALISTIC APPROACH IN PRACTICE

A. Word, Image, and Theme: Space-Time Metaphors in "To His Coy Mistress"

August Strindberg, the Swedish novelist and playwright, said in the preface to *Miss Julie* that he "let people's minds work irregularly, as they do in real life." As a consequence, "The dialogue wanders, gathering in the opening scenes material which is later picked up, worked over, repeated, expounded and developed like the theme in a musical composition."

Tracing such thematic patterns in a literary composition assumes that significant literature does attempt to communicate, or at least to embody, meaningful experience in an aesthetically appealing form. This is not to say that literature merely sugarcoats a beneficial pill. Rather, in the creation of any given work, a literary artist has an idea, or an actual experience, or an imagined experience that he or she wishes to communicate or to embody. Consciously or otherwise, the artist then chooses a means of doing so, selecting or allowing the unconscious mind to present specific devices, and arranging them so that they can embody or communicate that experience. Once the author has created such a work for us, we readers must recreate the experience, in part by carefully tracing the motifs used to communicate it. If Strindberg has given us material in *Miss Julie* that he later picked up, worked over, and developed "like the theme in a musical composition," then our role is to seek out the indications of that theme. Bit by bit as we notice instances of a pattern, we work our way into the experience of the story, poem, or play. As we follow the hints of thematic statement, recognize similar but new images, or identify related symbols, we gradually come to live the experience inherent in the work. The evocative power of steadily repeated images and symbols makes the experience a part of our own consciousness and sensibility. Thus the image satisfies our senses, the pattern our instinctive desire for order, and the thematic statement our intellect and our moral sensibility.

Andrew Marvell's poem "To His Coy Mistress" presents us with a clear instance of how a particular set of images can open out to themes in the way just described. The opening line of the poem—"Had we but world enough and time"—introduces us to the space-time continuum. Rich in possibilities of verbal patterns, the motif is much more, for the structure of the poem depends on the subjunctive concept, the condition contrary to fact, which gives the whole poem its meaning: "Had we," the speaker says, knowing that they do not. From that point on, the hyperbole, the playfulness, the grim fear of annihilation are all based on the feeling of the speaker that he is bound by the dimensions of space and time.

Clearly, this poem is a proposition made by the eternal male to the eternal female. Just as clearly, and in a wholly different realm, the motif of space and time shows this poem to be a philosophical consideration of time, of eternity, of man's plea-sure (hedonism) and of salvation in an afterlife (traditional Christianity). In this way Marvell includes in one short poem the range between man's lust and man's philosophy.

On the other hand, we find that the words used to imply this range tend to be suggestive, to shift their meanings so as to demand that they be read at different levels at the same time. Let us begin with instances of the space motif. The space motif appears not only in obvious but also in veiled allusions. In the first section of the poem we find "world," "sit down," "which way/To walk," the suggested distance between "In-dian Ganges" and the Humber, the distance implicit in the allusions to the Flood and to the widespread Jews of the Dias-pora, "vaster than empires," the sense of spatial movement as the speaker's eyes move over the woman's body, and the hint of spatial relationship in "lower rate." The word "long" (line 4) refers to time, but has spatial meaning, too. Several other words ("before," "till," "go," "last") also have overlapping qualities, but perhaps we strain too far to consider them.

Space and time are clearly related in the magnificent image of the opening lines of the second stanza: "But at my back I al-ways hear / Time's winged chariot hurrying near." The next couplet provides "yonder," "before," "deserts," and, again, a phrase that suggests both space and time: "vast eternity." In the third stanza the word "sits" echoes the earlier use of the word, and several words suggest movement or action in space: "transpires," "sport," "birds of prey," "devour," "languish in slow-chapped power," "roll," "tear . . . /Thorough." The space motif climaxes in an image that again incorporates the time motif: the sun, by which the man measures time and which will not stand still in space, will be forced to run.

The time motif also appears in its own right, and not only by means of imagery. The word itself appears once in each stanza: near the beginning of stanzas 1 and 2 (lines 1 and 22), and in the third stanza as a central part of the lover's proposition (39). Clustering around this basic unifying motif are these phrases and allusions from the first stanza: the "long love's day," the specific time spans spent in adoring the woman's body and the vaster if less specific "before the Flood" and "Till the conver-

sion of the Jews," and the slow growth of "vegetable love" and
the two uses of "age" (lines 17 and 18). At the beginning of
stanza 2, the powerful image of time's winged chariot as it
moves across a desert includes the words "always" and "eternity." Other time words are "no more" and "long-preserved."
There is also the sense of elapsed time in the allusions to the
future decomposition of the lovers' bodies. The third stanza,
although it delays the use of the word "time," has for its first
syllable the forceful, imperative "now." The word appears
twice more in the stanza (lines 37 and 38). It is strengthened by
"instant," "at once," and "languish in [Time's] slow-chapped
power." The phrase "thorough the iron gates of life," though it
has more important meanings, also may suggest the passing
from temporal life into the not so certain eternity mentioned
earlier. The concluding couplet of the poem, as already shown,
combines space and time. Further, it may extend time backward to suggest Old Testament days and classic mythology:
Joshua stopped the sun so that the Israelites could win a battle,
and, even more pertinently, Zeus lengthened the night he
spent with Amphitryon's wife.

For the poem is also a love poem, both in its traditional context of the courtly love complaint and in the simple fact of its
subject matter: fearing that the afterlife may be a vast space
without time, the speaker looks for a means of enjoying whatever he can. This *carpe diem* theme is not uncommon, nor is the
theme of seduction. What gives the poem unusual power,
however, is the overbearing sense of a cold, calculated drive to
use the pleasures of sex to counterbalance the threats of empty
eternity. Thus a second major motif—after the space-time relationship—used to present the theme is the sexual motif.

We can follow this theme beginning with the title, which immediately sets up the situation. In the second line the word
"coyness" leads us into the poem itself; even the word "crime"
suggests the unconventional (though crime and conventional
morality are reversed in the context of the lover's address).
The motif gradually emerges, romantically at first, but more
frankly, even brutally, as the speaker continues. In the first
stanza the distant Ganges and the redness of rubies are romantic enough; the word "complain," in the sense of the courtly
lover's song, echoes the whole courtly tradition. The word

"love" appears twice before the courtly catalogue of the lady's beautiful body. The catalogue in turn builds to a climax with the increasing time spans and the veiled suggestiveness of "rest" and "part."

The second stanza, though it continues to be somewhat veiled, is less romantic, and becomes gruesome even while insisting upon sexual love. The lady's beauty will disappear in the marble vault. We may associate the word "marble" with the texture and loveliness of the living woman's skin, but here the lover stresses the time when that loveliness will be transferred to stone. The same type of transference of the lover's song, which finds no echoes in that vault, occurs in a veiled image of unrealized sexual union in life: worms will corrupt the woman in a way that the lover could not. "Quaint honor" is an ironic play on words to suggest the pudendum (*quaint* as in Middle English *queynte*; see Chaucer's "Miller's Tale"). The fires of lust will become ashes (with an implicit comparison to the coldness of marble), and the stanza closes with puns on "private" and "embrace."

The third stanza resumes the romantic imagery of the first ("youthful hue," "morning dew"), but it continues the bolder imagery of the second section. "Pore" is a somewhat unromantic allusion to the woman's body, and "instant fires" recalls the lust and ashes of the preceding stanza. "Sport" takes still a different tack, though it reminds us of the playfulness of the first stanza. After this line, the grimness of the second stanza is even more in evidence. The amorous birds are not turtledoves, but birds of prey, devouring time—and each other. Although the romantic or sentimental is present in the speaker's suggestion that they "roll all our strength and all / Our sweetness up into one ball," the emphasis on the rough and violent continues in the paradoxical "tear our pleasures with rough strife." Once the coy lady's virginity is torn away, the lover will have passed not through the pearly gates of eternity, but through the iron gates of life. Thus the lover's affirmation of life, compounded of despair and defiance, is produced by his suggestion that the birth canal of life and procreation is preferable to the empty vault and deserts of vast eternity. On the one hand, the instances of the sexual motif point to a degeneration from romantic convention in the first section to scarcely veiled explicitness in the last. But on the other hand, the speaker has proceeded from a question about the nature of eternity and the meaning of the space-time relationship in this world to an affirmation of what he suspects is one of the few realities left him. The very concreteness, the physicality of the sexual motif, provides an answer to the philosophical speculation about space, time, and eternity. Obviously different, the motifs just as obviously fuse to embody the theme of the poem.

There are other, lesser motifs that we could trace had we ourselves space enough and time, such as wings and birds, roundness, and minerals and other things of earth (rubies, marble, iron, ashes, and dust). Each of these serves as a means to greater insights into the poem.

In sum, a formalistic reading of "To His Coy Mistress" can originate in a study of images and metaphors—here, space-time images. It can then lead to complexes of other images—precious stones and marble vaults, chariots and rivers, worms and dust. Finally, it is the nature of a formalistic approach to lead us to see how images and metaphors form, shape, confect a consideration of philosophical themes—in this case a speculation on whether love and even existence itself can extend beyond the time we know, and, if they cannot, whether instant gratification is a sufficient response to the question raised.

B. The Dark, the Light, and the Pink: Ambiguity as Form in "Young Goodman Brown"

In short fiction, as in a poem, we can look for the telling word or phrase, the recurring or patterned imagery, the symbolic object or character, the hint of or clue to meaning greater than that of the action or plot alone. Because we can no more justify stopping with a mere summary of what happens outwardly in the story than we can with a mere prose paraphrase of a lyric poem's content, we must look for the key to a story's form in one or more devices or images or motifs that offer a pattern that leads us to larger implications. In short, we seek a point at which the structure of the story coincides with and illuminates its meaning.

As we approach a formalistic reading of Hawthorne's story, we should make another point or two of comparison and contrast. The lyric poem generally embraces a dramatic situation. That is, a speaker reacts to an experience, a feeling, an idea, or even a physical sensation. Only one voice is ordinarily present in the lyric poem, but in other literary genres there is usually a group of characters. In fiction the story is told by the author, by one of the characters in the story, or by someone who has heard of an episode. Unlike the novel, the other major fictional type, the short story is characteristically concerned with relatively few characters and with only one major situation, which achieves its climax and solution and thus quickly comes to an end. The short story is restricted in scope, like a news story, for example, but unlike the news story, the short story possesses balance and design—the polish and finish, the completeness that we associate with the work of art. A principle of unity operates throughout to give that single effect that Poe emphasized as necessary. In brief, like any other imaginative literary work, the short story possesses form.

Paradoxical as it may seem, we wish to suggest that ambiguity is a formal device in "Young Goodman Brown." One sure way to see this ambiguity is to trace the relationships between light and dark in the story, for the interplay of daylight and darkness, of town and (dark) forest, is important. For evidence of that importance the reader is urged to consult Richard Harter Fogle's classic study, *Hawthorne's Fiction: The Light and the Dark*. We shall not neglect the interplay of dark and light—indeed we assume it—but we wish to focus on another device of ambiguity.

In our formalistic reading of Marvell's "To His Coy Mistress" we stressed the recurrent pattern of words, images, and metaphors of space and time as a means of seeing the form that embodies meaning in that poem. In "Young Goodman Brown" we can start with a clearly emphasized image that almost immediately takes on symbolic qualities. That is the set of pink ribbons that belongs to Faith, young Brown's wife. Whatever she is (and much of the effect of the story centers on that "whatever"), the pink ribbons are her emblem as much as the scarlet letter is Hester Prynne's. They are mentioned three times in the first page or so of the story. Near the center of the story, a pink ribbon falls, or seems to fall, from a cloud that Goodman Brown sees, or thinks he sees, overhead. At the end of the story, when Faith eagerly greets her returning husband, she still wears her pink ribbons. Like the admixture of light and dark in the tale—as in much of Hawthorne—the ribbons are neither red nor white. They are somewhere between: they are ambiguity objectified. Clearly Hawthorne meant them to be suggestive, to be an index to one or more themes in the tale. But suggestive of what? Are they emblematic of love, of innocence, of good? Conversely, do they suggest evil, or hypocrisy, or the ambiguous and puzzling blend of good and evil? Are they symbolic of sex, of femininity, or of Christian faith? Should we even attempt to limit the meaning to one possibility? Would we be wise—or slovenly—to let the ribbons mean more than one thing in the story?

1. Virtues and Vices

Of this we can be sure: to follow this motif as it guides us to related symbols and patterns of relationships is to probe the complex interweaving of ideas within the story. Specifically, in the interpretation that follows we suggest that the mysterious pink ribbons are—at least among other things—an index to elements of theology. To see that relationship let us first consider the theological matrix of the story.

Because the Puritan setting of "Young Goodman Brown" is basic to the story, we can expect that some of its thematic patterns derive from traditional Christian concepts. For example, readers generally assume that Goodman Brown loses his faith—in Christ, in human beings, or in both. But the story is rich in ambiguities, and it is therefore not surprising that at least one reader has arrived at the opposite conclusion. Thomas E. Connolly has argued that the story is an attack on Calvinism, and that Faith (that is, faith) is not lost in the story. On the contrary, he says, Goodman Brown is confirmed in his faith, made aware of "its full and terrible significance." Either way—loss of faith or still firmer belief—we see the story in a theological context. Although we do not have to accept either of these views, we do not have to deny them either. Instead, let us accept the theological matrix within which both views exist. As a matter of fact, let us pursue this theological view by following the pattern of relationships of faith, hope, and love, and their opposed vices, in other words the form that this pattern creates in the mind of the reader.

We can assume that Hawthorne was familiar with some of the numerous passages from the Bible that bear upon the present interpretation. Twice in the first epistle to the Thessalonians, Saint Paul mentions the need for faith, hope, and love (1:3 and 5:8). In 1 Corinthians 13, after extolling love as the most abiding of the virtues, Paul concludes his eloquent description with this statement: "So there abide faith, hope, and love, these three; but the greatest of these is love." The author of the first epistle of Peter wrote, "But above all things have a constant mutual love among yourselves; for love covers a multitude of sins" (4:8). To these may be added the telling passages on love of God and neighbor (Matt. 22:36–40 and Rom. 13:9–10) and related passages on love (such as Col. 3:14 and 1 Tim. 1:5). Faith, hope, and love, we should note, have traditionally been called the theological virtues because they have God (*theos*) for their immediate object.

Quite possibly Hawthorne had some of these passages in mind, for it appears that he wove into the cloth of "Young Goodman Brown" a pattern of steady attention to these virtues. Surely he provided a clue for us when he chose Faith as the name for Goodman Brown's wife. Hawthorne thereby gave faith first place in the story, not necessarily because faith is the story's dominant theme (indeed, love may well be the dominant theme), but because faith is important in Puritan theology and because it is traditionally listed as the first of the three virtues. Allusions to faith could be made explicit in so many passages in the story and implicit in so many others that they would provide an evident pattern to suggest clearly the other two virtues. (Similarly, the epithet *goodman* could take on symbolic qualities and function almost as Brown's given name, not simply as something comparable to modern *mister*.)

An analysis of these passages, for example, shows not only explicit mentions of faith but also implicit allusions to the virtues of faith, hope, and love, and to their opposed vices, doubt, despair, and hatred. The first scene includes these: "And Faith, as the wife was aptly named"; "My love and my Faith"; "dost thou doubt me already . . . ?"; "he looked back and saw the head of Faith still peeping after him with a melancholy air"; "Poor little Faith!"; and "I'll cling to her skirts and follow her to heaven." Both Goodman Brown and the man he meets in the forest make similar allusions in the second scene, where we read: "Faith kept me back a while"; "We have been a race of honest men and good Christians"; "We are a people of prayer, and good works to boot" (a hint of the theological debate on faith and good works); "Well, then, to end the matter at once, there is my wife, Faith"; "that Faith should come to any harm"; and "why I should quit my dear Faith and go after [Goody Cloyse]." In the episode after the older man leaves Goodman Brown, we have these passages: "so purely and sweetly now, in the arms of Faith!"; "He looked up to the sky, doubting whether there really was a heaven above him"; "With heaven above and Faith below, I will yet stand firm against the devil!"; "a cloud," "confused and doubtful of voices," "he doubted"; " 'Faith!' shouted Goodman Brown, in a voice of agony and desperation"; and " 'My Faith is gone! . . . Come, devil. . . .' And, maddened with despair. . . ." The last scenes, the forest conclave and young Goodman Brown's return home, offer these: " 'But where is Faith?' thought Goodman Brown; and, as hope came"; "the wretched man beheld his Faith . . . before that unhallowed altar"; " 'Faith! Faith!' cried the husband, 'look up to heaven . . .' "; "the head of Faith . . . gazing anxiously"; "a distrustful, if not a desperate man"; "he shrank from the bosom of Faith . . . and turned away"; and "no hopeful verse . . . , for his dying hour was gloom."

2. Symbol or Allegory?
With these passages in mind, let us recall that there may be both symbolical and allegorical uses of the word "faith." Such ambivalence can complicate a reading of the story. If the tale is allegorical, for example, it may be that Goodman Brown gained his faith (that is, the belief that he is one of the elect) only three months before the action of the story, when he and Faith were married. The fall of the pink ribbon may be a sin or a fall, just as Adam's fall was the original sin, a lapse from grace. The allegory may further suggest that Goodman Brown shortly loses his new faith, for "he shrank from the bosom of

Faith." But allegory is difficult to maintain, often requiring a rigid one-to-one equivalence between the surface meaning and a "higher" meaning. Thus if Faith is faith, and Goodman Brown loses the latter, how do we explain that Faith remains with him and even outlives him? Strict allegory would require that she disappear, perhaps even vanish in that dark cloud from which the pink ribbon apparently falls. On the other hand, a pattern of symbolism centering on Faith is easier to handle, and may even be more rewarding by offering us more pervasive, more subtly interweaving ideas that, through their very ambiguity, suggest the difficulties of the theological questions in the story. Such a symbolic view also frees the story from a strict adherence to the Calvinistic concept of election and conviction in the faith, so that the story becomes more universally concerned with Goodman Brown as Everyman Brown.

3. Loss upon Loss

Whether we emphasize symbol or allegory, however, Goodman Brown must remain a character in his own right, one who progressively loses faith in his ultimate salvation, in his forebears as members of the elect or at least as "good" people, and in his wife and fellow townspeople as holy Christians. At a literal level, he does not lose Faith, for she greets him when he returns from the forest, she still wears her pink ribbons, she follows his corpse to the grave. Furthermore, she keeps her pledge to him, for it is *he* who shrinks from her. In other words, Brown has not completely lost Faith; rather he has lost faith, a theological key to heaven.

But when faith is lost, not all is lost, though it may very nearly be. Total loss comes later and gradually as Brown commits other sins. We can follow this emerging pattern when we recall that the loss of faith is closely allied to the loss of hope. We find that, in the story, despair (the vice opposed to hope) can be easily associated with doubt (the vice opposed to faith). For example, the two vices are nearly allied when Goodman Brown recognizes the pink ribbon: "'My Faith is gone!' cried he, after one stupefied moment. 'There is no good on earth; and sin is but a name. Come, devil; for to thee is this world given.' And, maddened with *despair,* so that he laughed loud and long, did Goodman Brown grasp his staff and set forth again . . ." (our italics).

Doubt, although surely opposed to belief, here leads to despair as much as to infidelity. Similarly, many passages that point to faith also point to hope. When Goodman Brown says, "'I'll follow her to heaven,'" he expresses hope as well as belief. When he says, "'With heaven above and Faith below,'" he hopes to "'stand firm against the devil.'" When he cries, "'Faith, look up to heaven,'" he utters what may be his last hope for salvation. Once again we see how motifs function in a formal structure. It is easy to touch the web at any one point and make it vibrate elsewhere.

Thus we must emphasize that Brown's hope is eroded by increasing doubt, the opposite of faith. We recall that the passages already quoted include the words "desperate," "despair," and "no hopeful verse." When Goodman Brown reenters the town, he has gone far toward a complete failure to trust in God. His thoughts and his actions when he sees the child talking to Goody Cloyse border on the desperate, both in the sense of despair and in the sense of frenzy. Later, we know that he has fully despaired, "for his dying hour was gloom."

"But the greatest of these is love," and "love covers a multitude of sins," the Scriptures insist. Goodman Brown sins against this virtue too, and as we follow these reiterations of the structural components we may well conclude that Hawthorne considered this sin the greatest sin in Brown's life. Sins against love of neighbor are important in other Hawthorne stories. It is a sin against love that Ethan Brand and Roger Chillingworth commit. It is a sin against love of which Rappaccini's daughter accuses Guasconti: "Farewell, Giovanni! Thy words of hatred are like lead within my heart; but they, too, will fall away as I ascend. Oh, was there not, from the first, more poison in thy nature than in mine?" In *The House of the Seven Gables*, it is love that finally overcomes the hate-engendered curse of seven generations.

In "Young Goodman Brown" perhaps the motif of love-hate is first suggested in the opening scene, when Goodman Brown refuses his wife's request that he remain: "'My love and my Faith,' replied young Goodman Brown, 'of all nights in the year, this one night must I tarry away from thee. . . . What, my sweet, pretty wife, dost thou doubt me already, and we but three months married?'" Significantly, the words "love" and "Faith" are used almost as synonyms. When the pink ribbons are mentioned in the next paragraph almost as an epithet ("Faith, with the pink ribbons"), they are emblematic of one virtue as much as the other. Later, Goodman Brown's love of others is diminished when he learns that he is of a family that has hated enough to lash the "Quaker woman so smartly through the streets of Salem" and "to set fire to an Indian village." Instead of being concerned for his own neighbor, he turns against Goody Cloyse, resigning her to the powers of darkness: "What if a wretched old woman do choose to go to the devil . . . ?" He turns against Faith and against God Himself when, after the pink ribbon has fallen from the cloud, he says, "'Come, devil; for to thee is this world given.'" To be sure, he still loves Faith enough at the forest conclave to call upon her yet to look to heaven; but next morning when she almost kisses her husband in front of the whole village, "Goodman Brown looked sternly and sadly into her face, and passed on without a greeting." By this time he is becoming guilty of the specific sin called rash judgment, for he rashly makes successive judgments on his neighbors. He shrinks from the blessing of "the good old minister," he disparages the prayers of old Deacon Gookin, he snatches a child away from the catechizing of "Goody Cloyse, that excellent old Christian." Thenceforth he stubbornly isolates himself from his fellow men and from his own wife. On the Sabbath day he questions their hymns and their sermons, at midnight he shrinks from his wife, at morning or eventide he scowls at family prayers. Having given his allegiance to the devil, he cannot fulfill the injunction of the second great commandment any more than he can fulfill that of the first. Unable to love himself, he is unable to love his neighbor.

"Faith, hope, and love: these three" he has lost, replacing them with their opposed vices, and the pink ribbons serve as emblems for them all and lead to a double pattern of virtues and vices. In "Young Goodman Brown" the motifs of faith, hope, and love, summed up in the pink ribbons, blend each into each. If the blend sometimes confuses us, like the alternating light and dark of the forest conclave, and more particularly like the mystery of the pink ribbons, it is perhaps no less than Hawthorne intended when he presented Goodman Brown's initiation into the knowledge of good evil, a knowledge that rapidly becomes confusion. For Goodman Brown it is a knowledge by which he seems to turn the very names and epithets of Goodman, Goody, and Gookin into variant spellings of "evil," just as Brown transmutes faith, hope and love into their opposed vices. For the reader the pink ribbons, like the balance of town and country, like the interplay of light and dark, remain in the mind an index to ambiguity, which is, paradoxically, as we have said, a formalistic device in the story.

C. Romance and Reality, Land and River:
The Journey as Repetitive Form in
Huckleberry Finn

In the preceding section, on formalistic qualities in "Young Goodman Brown," we noted that the short story is generally concerned with relatively few characters and with only one major situation. The short story achieves its climax and solution, and quickly concludes. The novel, however, contains more characters; and its plot, a number of episodes or situations. Its ampler space provides opportunity for creation of a world, with the consequent opportunity for the reader to be immersed in that world. But because the novel is ample, in comparison with a lyric poem or a short story, it offers a further challenge to its creator to give it its form. In fact, historically the formalistic approach in criticism has focused more on lyric poetry and short stories than on the novel. Nevertheless, the novel, too, is an art form, and a close reading will present one or more ways of seeing its form and how the author controls that form.

It will become clear as we approach the form of *Huckleberry Finn* that at one level its form can be simplistically diagrammed as a capital letter "I" lying on its side. At each end there is a block of chapters set on the land and in a world where Tom Sawyer can exist and even dominate. In the middle are chapters largely related to the river as Huck and Jim travel down that river; here realism, not a Tom Sawyer romanticism, dominates. Further, in the central portion there is a pattern of alternations between land and river. Taking the novel as a whole, then, there is a pattern of departures and returns.

But Twain was not limited to a pattern that can be charted, as it were, on graph paper. In a master stroke of the creative art, he chose Huck Finn himself as the point-of-view character. In doing so, Twain abandoned the simpler omniscient (or authorial) point of view that he had very successfully used in *The Adventures of Tom Sawyer* for a relatively sophisticated technique. He allowed the central character to relate his adventures in his own way—the point of view called first-person narrator. T. S. Eliot refers to the difference in points of view as indicative of the major qualitative distinction between *Tom Sawyer* and *Huckleberry Finn*: Tom's story is told by an adult looking at a boy and his gang; Huck's narrative requires that "we see the world through his eyes." Granted that Twain sometimes allows us to see beyond Huck's relatively simple narrative manner some dimensions of meaning not apparent to Huck, the point of view has been so contrived (and controlled) that we do not see anything that is not at least implicit in Huck's straightforward narration.

Several questions can be raised. What is the character of Huck like? How does his manner of telling his story control our responses to that story? Finally, how does this point of view assist us in perceiving the novel's form?

First, Huck is an objective narrator. He is objective about himself, even when that objectivity tends to reflect negatively upon himself. He is objective about the society he repeatedly confronts, even when, as he often fears, that society possesses virtues and sanctions to which he must ever remain a stranger. He is an outcast, he knows that he is an outcast, and he does not blame the society that has made and will keep him an outcast. He always assumes in his characteristic modesty that he must somehow be to blame for the estrangement. His deceptions, his evasions, his lapses from conventional respectability are always motivated by the requirements of a given situation; he is probably the first thoroughgoing, honest pragmatist in American fiction. When he lies or steals, he assumes that society is right and that he is simply depraved. He does not make excuses for himself, and his conscience is the stern voice of a pietistic, hypocritical backwoods society asserting itself within that sensitive and wistful psyche. We know that he is neither depraved nor dishonest, because we judge that society by the damning clues that emerge from the naive account of a boy about thirteen years old who has been forced to lie in order to get out of trouble but who never lies to himself or to his reader. In part, his lack of subtlety is a measure of his reliability as narrator: he has mastered neither the genteel speech of "respectable" folks nor their deceit, evasions of truth, and penchant for pious platitudes. He is always refreshingly himself, even when he is telling a tall tale or engaging in one of his ambitious masquerades to get out of a jam.

Thus the point of view Twain carefully establishes from the first words of the narrative offers a position from which the reader must consider the events of the narrative. That position never wavers from the trustworthy point of view of the hero-narrator's clear-eyed gaze. He becomes at once the medium and the norm for the story that unfolds. By him we can measure (although he never overtly does it himself) the hypocrisy of Miss Watson, perceive the cumulative contrast between Huck and the incorrigible Tom Sawyer, and finally judge the whole of society along the river. Eliot makes this important discrimination: "Huck has not imagination, in the sense in which Tom has it; he has, instead, vision. He sees the real world; and he does not judge it—he allows it to judge itself."

Huck's characteristic mode of speech is ironic and self-effacing. Although at times he can be proud of the success of his tall tales and masquerades, in the things that matter he is given to understatement. Of his return to "civilized" life with the Widow Douglas, he tersely confides, "Well, then, the old thing commenced again." Of the senseless horror with which the Grangerford-Shepherdson feud ends, Huck says with admirable restraint: "I ain't a-going to tell *all* that happened—it would make me sick again if I was to do that. I wished I hadn't ever come ashore that night to see such things. I ain't ever going to get shut of them—lots of times I dream about them." And in one of the most artfully conceived, understated, but eloquent endings in all fiction, Huck bids his reader and civilization goodbye simultaneously: "But I reckon I got to light out for the Territory ahead of the rest, because Aunt Sally she's going to adopt me and sivilize me, and I can't stand it. I been there before."

The movement of the novel likewise has an effect on the total shape of the work. The apparently aimless plot with its straight-forward sequence—what happened, what happened next, and then what happened after that, to paraphrase Gertrude Stein—is admirably suited to the personality of Huck as narrator. In the conventional romantic novel, of course, we expect to find a more or less complex central situation, in which two lovers come together by various stratagems of the novelist, have their difficulties, resolve their problems, and are destined to live hap-pily ever afterward. Even in such a classic novel as Jane Austen's *Pride and Prejudice,* the separate chapters and the pieces of the plot concern the manifestations, against the back-ground of early nineteenth-century English provincial life, of the many facets of Mr. Darcy's insuperable pride and Elizabeth Bennet's equally tenacious prejudice, but everything works to-ward the happy union of two very attractive young people.

In *Huckleberry Finn,* however, there is no real center to the plot as such. Instead we have what Kenneth Burke has called repetitive form: "the consistent maintaining of a principle under new guises . . . a restatement of the same thing in dif-ferent ways. . . . A succession of images, each of them regiv-ing the same lyric mood; a character repeating his identity, his 'number,' under changing situations; the sustaining of an attitude as in satire . . ." (125). The separate situations or episodes are loosely strung together by the presence of Huck and Jim as they make their way down the Mississippi River from St. Petersburg, while the river flows through all, becom-ing really a vast highway across backwoods America. In the separate episodes there are new characters who, after Huck moves on, usually do not reappear. There are new settings and always new situations. At the beginning, there are five chap-ters about the adventures of Huck and Tom and the gang in St. Petersburg; at the end, there are twelve chapters centering on the Phelps farm that chronicle the high jinks of the boys in try-ing to free Jim; in between, there are twenty-six chapters in which Huck and Jim pursue true freedom and in which Tom Sawyer does not appear. This large midsection of the book in-cludes such revealing experiences as Jim and Huck's encounter with the "house of death" (ch. 9); the dual masquerades before the perceptive Mrs. Judith Loftus (ch. 11); Huck's life with the Grangerfords (chs. 17 and 18); the performance of the Duke and Dauphin at Pokeville (ch. 20); the Arkansas premiere of Shakespeare and the shooting of Boggs by Colonel Sherburn (chs. 21 and 22); and, finally, the relatively lengthy involvement with the Wilks family (chs. 24–29).

Despite changes in settings and dramatis personae, the separate episodes share a cumulative role (their repetitive form): Huck learns bit by bit about the depravity that hides beneath respectability and piety. He learns gradually and unwillingly that society or civilization is vicious and predatory and that the individual has small chance to assert himself against a monolithic mass. Harmless as the sentimental tastes of the Grangerfords or their preference for the conventionally pretty may seem, Twain's superb sense for the objective correlative allows us to *realize* (without being *told*) that conventional piety and sentimentality hide depravity no more effectively than the high coloring of the chalk fruit compensates for the chips that expose the underlying chalk. Likewise, elaborate manners, love of tradition, and "cultivated" tastes for Graveyard School poetry and lugubrious drawings are merely genteel facades for barbarism and savagery. Mrs. Judith Loftus, probably the best-developed minor character in the entire novel, for all her sentimental response to the hackneyed story of a mistreated apprentice, sees the plight of the runaway slave merely in terms of the cash reward she and her husband may win. Even the Wilks girls, as charming as they seem to Huck, are easily taken in by the grossest sentimentality and pious clichés. A review of the several episodes discloses that, for all their apparent differences, they are really reenactments of the same insistent revelation: the mass of humanity is hopelessly depraved, and the genuinely honest individual is constantly being victimized, betrayed, and threatened.

The framework of the plot is, then, a journey—a journey from north to south, a journey from relative innocence to horrifying knowledge. Huck tends to see people for what they are, but he does not suspect the depths of evil and the pervasiveness of sheer meanness, of man's inhumanity to man, until he has completed his journey. The relative harmlessness of Miss Watson's lack of compassion and her devotion to the letter rather than the spirit of religious law or of Tom's incurable romanticism does not become really sinister until Huck reenters the seemingly good world at the Phelps farm, a world that is really the same as the "good" world of St. Petersburg— a connection that is stressed by the kinship of Aunt Sally and Aunt Polly. Into that world the values of Tom Sawyer are once more injected, but Huck discovers that he has endured too much on his journey down the river to become Tom's foil again.

Only the great, flowing river defines the lineaments of otherwise elusive freedom; that mighty force of nature opposes and offers the only possible escape from the blighting tyranny of towns and farm communities. The Mississippi is the novel's major symbol. It is the one place where a person does not need to lie to himself or to others. Its ceaseless flow mocks the static, stultifying society on its banks. There are lyrical passages in which Huck communicates, even with all his colloquial limitations, his feelings about the river, its symbolic functions, as in the image-packed description that follows the horrors of the Grangerford-Shepherdson carnage (ch. 19). In that memorable passage Huck extols the freedom and contemplation that the river encourages. In contrast to the oppressive places on land, the raft and the river promise release: "We said there warn't no home like a raft, after all. Other places do seem so cramped up and smothery, but a raft don't. You feel mighty free and easy and comfortable on a raft."

Like the river, Huck's narrative flows spontaneously and ever onward. Around each bend lies a possible new adventure; in the eddies, a lyrical interlude. But the river always carries Huck and Jim out of each adventure toward another uncertain try for freedom. That freedom is never really achieved is a major irony, but the book's structure parallels the river's flow. The separate adventures become infinite variations upon (repetitive forms of) the quest for freedom. That the final thwarting of freedom is perpetrated by the forces of St. Petersburg, of course, is no fault of the river or its promise of freedom; it simply seems that membership in humanity generates what we have elsewhere called the circular pattern of flight and captivity.

D. Dialectic as Form: The Trap Metaphor in *Hamlet*

1. The Trap Imagery

> My stronger guilt defeats my strong intent;
> And like a man to double business bound,
> I stand in pause where I shall first begin,
> And both neglect. (III.iii)

The words are not those of Hamlet. They are spoken by Claudius, as he tries to pray for forgiveness, even as he knows that he cannot give up those things for which he murdered his brother—his crown, his fulfilled ambition, and his wife. But the words may easily have been Hamlet's, for he too is by "double business bound." Indeed, much of the play centers on doubleness. In that doubleness lies the essence of what we mean by "dialectic" here—a confrontation of polarities. A consequence of that doubleness for many of the characters is that they are apparently caught in a trap—a key metaphor in the play—or, in another image, "Hoist with [their] own petard[s]" (III.iv).

Let us examine that metaphor of the trap, for it leads clearly to our seeing how dialectic provides form in *Hamlet*. Several times in the play, but in varying images, we find allusions to different kinds of entanglement. Polonius injudiciously uses the metaphor to warn Ophelia away from Hamlet's "holy vows of heaven," vows that he says are "springes to catch woodcocks" (I.iii). More significant is Hamlet's deliberate misnaming of "The Murder of Gonzago"; he calls it "The Mousetrap" (III.ii) because it is, as he says elsewhere, "the thing / Wherein I'll catch the conscience of the King" (II.ii). Claudius feels that he is trapped: "O limed soul, that, struggling to be free, / Art more engag'd" (III.iii). Hamlet, in the hands of plotters, finds himself "thus be-netted round with villainies" and one for whom Claudius has "Thrown out his angle [fish hook] for my proper life" (V.ii). The dying Laertes echoes his father's metaphor when he tells Osric that he is "as a woodcock to mine own springe" (V.ii). Here we have a pattern of trap images—springes, lime, nets, mousetraps, and angles or hooks.

Now traps are usually for animals, but we are dealing with human beings, persons who are trapped in their own dilemmas, in their own questions, in the very questioning of the universe.

2. The Cosmological Trap

Let us expand our formal approach to *Hamlet* by characterizing once again the world of the work. We need go no further than the first scene of act I to realize that it is a disturbed world, that a sense of mystery and deep anxiety preoccupies the soldiers of the watch. The ghost has appeared already and is expected to appear again. The guards instinctively assume that the apparition of the former king has more than passing import; and, in their troubled questions to Horatio about the mysterious preparations for war, the guards show how closely they regard the connection between the unnatural appearance of the dead king and the welfare of the state. The guards have no answers for the mystery, their uncertainty, or their premonitions; their quandary is mirrored in abundant questions and minimal answers—a rhetorical phenomenon that recurs throughout the play, even in the soliloquies of Hamlet; in other words, an instance of dialectic. The sense of cosmic implication in the special situation of Denmark emerges strongly in the exchange between Hamlet and his friends Rosencrantz and Guildenstern:

HAMLET. Denmark's a prison.

ROSENCRANTZ. Then is the world one.

HAMLET. A goodly one; in which there are many confines, wards, and dungeons, Denmark being the one o' th' worst. (II.ii)

These remarks recall the assertion of Marcellus as Hamlet and the ghost go offstage: "Something is rotten in the state of Denmark" (I.iv). Indeed, Hamlet acknowledges that the rottenness of Denmark pervades all of nature: ". . . this goodly frame the earth seems to me a sterile promontory; this most excellent canopy, the air, look you, this brave o'erhanging firmament, this majestical roof fretted with golden fire—why, it appeareth nothing to me but a foul and pestilent congregation of vapors" (II.ii). Much earlier, before his encounter with the ghost, Hamlet expressed his extreme pessimism at man's having to endure earthly existence within nature's unwholesome realm:

> How weary, stale, flat and unprofitable
> Seem to me all the uses of this world!
> Fie on't, ah, fie, 'tis an unweeded garden
> That grows to seed. Things rank and gross in nature
> Possess it merely. (I.ii)

As he speaks these lines, Hamlet apparently has no idea of the truth of his father's death but is dismayed over his mother's hasty marriage to the new king. He has discovered a seeming paradox in the nature of existence: the fair, in nature and humanity, inevitably submits to the dominion of the foul. His obsession with the paradox focuses his attention on Denmark as the model of nature and human frailty. Thus a pattern of increasing parallels between Denmark and the cosmos and between man and nature develops. Question and answer, dialogue and soliloquy, become a verbal unity of repeated words and phrases, looking forward to larger thematic assertion and backward to earlier adumbration.

The play constitutes a vast poem in which speculation about nature, human nature, the health of the state, and human destiny intensifies into a passionate dialectic. Mystery, riddle, enigma, and metaphysical question complicate the dialogue. Particularly in his soliloquies Hamlet confronts questions that have obsessed protagonists from Sophocles's Oedipus to Tom Stoppard's Rosencrantz and Guildenstern. What begins with the relatively simple questions of the soldiers of the watch in act I is magnified and complicated as the play moves on. Increasingly tenuous and rarified probes of the maddening gulf between reality and appearance proliferate. Moreover, the contrast between what the simple man cheerfully accepts at face value and what the thoughtful man is driven to question calls into doubt every surface of utterance, act, or thing. In the world of *Hamlet* the cosmic implications of myriad distinctions between "seem" and "be" confront us at every hand.

3. "Seeming" and "Being"

An index to form looms in the crucial qualitative differences between Hamlet's mode of speech and that of the other inhabitants of his strange world. Because Hamlet's utterances and manners are characteristically unconventional, the other major characters (except Horatio, of course) assume that he is mad or at least temporarily deranged. Conversely, because they *do* speak the simple, relatively safe language of ordinary existence, he assumes that they are hiding or twisting the truth. No one who easily settles for *seeming* is quite trustworthy to the man obsessed with the pursuit of *being*. Even the ghost's nature and origin (he may be a diabolical agent, after all) must be tentative for Hamlet until he can settle the validity of the ghost's revelations with the "play within the play." Even Ophelia must be treated as the possible tool of Claudius and Polonius. The presence of Rosencrantz and Guildenstern, not to mention their mission on the journey to England, arouses Hamlet's deepest suspicions. Only Horatio is exempt from distrust, and even to him Hamlet cannot divulge the full dimension of his subversion. Yet though Hamlet seems to speak only in riddle and to act solely with evasion, his utterances and acts always actually bespeak the full measure of his feelings and his increasingly single-minded absorption with his inevitable mission. The important qualification of his honesty lies in his full knowledge that others do not (or cannot) comprehend his real meanings and that others are hardly vitally concerned with deep truths about the state, mankind, or themselves.

For our purposes, of course, the important fact is that these contrasting levels of meaning and understanding achieve formal expression. When the king demands some explanation for his extraordinary melancholy, Hamlet replies, "I am too much in the sun" (I.ii). The reply thus establishes, although Claudius does not perceive it, Hamlet's judgment of and opposition to the easy acceptance of "things as they are." And when the queen tries to reconcile him to the inevitability of death in the natural scheme and asks, "Why seems it so particular with thee?" he responds with a revealing contrast between the seeming evidences of mourning and real woe—an unequivocal condemnation of the queen's apparently easy acceptance of his father's death as opposed to the vindication of his refusal to view that death as merely an occasion for ceremonial mourning duties. To the joint entreaty of Claudius and Gertrude that he remain in Denmark, he replies only to his mother: "I shall in all my best obey you, madam" (I.ii). But in thus disdaining to answer the king, he has promised really nothing to his mother, although she takes his reply for complete submission to the royal couple. Again we see that every statement of Hamlet is dialectic: that is, it tends toward double meaning—the superficial meaning of the world of Denmark and the subtler meaning for Hamlet and the reader.

As we have observed, Hamlet's overriding concern, even before he knows of the ghost's appearance, is the frustration of living in an imperfect world. He sees, wherever he looks, the pervasive blight in nature, especially human nature. Man, outwardly the acme of creation, is susceptible to "some vicious mole of nature," and no matter how virtuous he otherwise may be, the "dram of evil" or the "stamp of one defect" adulterates nobility (I.iv). Hamlet finds that "one may smile and smile, and be a villain" (I.v). To the uncomprehending Guildenstern, Hamlet emphasizes his basic concern with the strange puzzle of corrupted and corrupting man:

> What a piece of work is a man, how noble in reason, how infinite in faculties, in form and moving how express and admirable, in action how like an angel, in apprehension how like a god: the beauty of the world, the paragon of animals! And yet to me what is this quintessence of dust? Man delights not me— no, nor woman either, though by your smiling you seem to say so. (II.ii)

This preoccupation with the paradox of man, recurring as it does throughout the play, obviously takes precedence over the revenge ordered by the ghost. Instead of the ideal world Hamlet seeks, the real world that he finds is his father's death, his mother's remarriage, the defection of his supposed friends, and the fallen state of man. (The implications of the dangers inherent in this "man's" view of the world in *Hamlet* are explored in chapter 6.)

Reams have been written about Hamlet's reasons for the delay in carrying out his revenge; for our purpose, however, the delay is not particularly important, except insofar as it emphasizes Hamlet's greater obsession with the pervasive blight within the cosmos. From almost every bit of verbal evidence, he considers as paramount the larger role of investigator and punitive agent of all humankind: his verbal attack on the queen, his accidental murder of Polonius, his indignation about the state of the theater, his castigation of Ophelia, his delight in foiling Rosencrantz and Guildenstern and arranging their destruction, and his fight with Laertes over the grave of Ophelia. Hamlet, in living up to what he conceives to be a higher role than that of mere avenger, recurrently broods about his self-imposed mission, although he characteristically avoids naming it. In his warfare against bestiality, however, he asserts his allegiance to heaven-sent reason and its dictates:

> What is a man,
> If his chief good and market of his time
> Be but to sleep and feed? A beast, no more.
> Sure he that made us with such large discourse,
> Looking before and after, gave us not
> That capability and godlike reason
> To fust in us unused. Now, whether it be
> Bestial oblivion, or some craven scruple
> Of thinking too precisely on th'event—
> A thought which, quartered, hath but one part wisdom
> And ever three parts coward—I do not know
> Why yet I live to say, "This thing's to do,"
> Sith I have cause, and will, and strength, and means
> To do't. (IV.vi)

With some envy he regards the active competence of Fortinbras as opposed to his own "craven scruple / Of thinking too precisely on th'event" (that is, his obligation to act to avenge his father's death). In short, almost from his first appearance in the play, Hamlet, unlike Fortinbras, is overwhelmed that to him is given a vast and ambiguous task:

> The time is out of joint. O cursed spite
> That ever I was born to set it right! (I.v)

The time, like the place of Denmark, has been corrupted by men vulnerable to natural flaws. And once again Hamlet's statement offers formal reinforcement for the dialectic of the play—the opposition of two attitudes toward human experience that must achieve resolution or synthesis before the play's end.

To the ideal of setting things right, then, Hamlet gives his allegiance. The order he supports transcends the expediency of Polonius, the apostle of practicality, and of Claudius, the devotee of power and sexuality. Again and again we see Hamlet's visionary appraisal of an order so remote from the ken of most people that he appears at times inhuman in his refusal to be touched by the scales of ordinary joy or sorrow. He will set straight the political and social order by ferreting out bestiality, corruption (of state, marriage bed, or theater), trickery, and deceit. He is obsessed throughout the play by the "dusty death" to which all must come, and his speeches abound in images of sickness and death. But if he has finally gotten the king, along with his confederates, "Hoist with his own petard" (III.iv), Hamlet also brings himself, through his own trickery, deceit, perhaps even his own ambitions, to the fate of Yorick.

Thus does the play turn upon itself. It is no simple morality play. It begins in an atmosphere of mourning for the late king and apprehensions about the appearance of the ghost, and it ends in a scene littered with corpses. The noble prince, like his father before him, is, despite his best intentions, sullied by the "foul crimes done in my days of nature" (I.v). All men apparently are, as Laertes says of himself, "as a woodcock to mine own springe" (V.ii) (that is, like a fool caught in his own snare). And though all beauty and aspiration (a counterpoint theme) are reduced ultimately to a "quintessence of dust," it is in Hamlet's striving, however imperfectly and destructively, to bend the order of nature to a higher law that we must see the play's tragic assertion in the midst of an otherwise pervasive and unrelieved pessimism.

4. "Seeing" and "Knowing"

The design of the play can be perceived in part in the elaborate play upon the words "see" and "know" and their cognates. Whereas the deity can be understood as "Looking before and after" (IV.iv), the player king points out to his queen that there is a hiatus between what people intend and what they do:

"Our thoughts are ours, their ends none of our own" (III.ii). Forced by Hamlet to consider the difference between her two husbands, Gertrude cries out in anguish against having to see into her own motivations:

> O Hamlet, speak no more.
> Thou turn'st mine eyes into my very soul,
> And there I see such black and grained spots
> As will not leave their tinct. (III.iv)

But she does not see the ghost of her former husband, nor can she see the metaphysical implications of Hamlet's reason in madness. The blind eye sockets of Yorick's skull once saw their quota of experience, but most people in Denmark are quite content with the surface appearances of life and refuse even to consider the ends to which mortality brings everyone. The intricate weavings of images of sight thus become a kind of tragic algebra for the plight of a man who "seemed to find his way without his eyes" (II.i) and who found himself at last "placed to the view" of the "yet unknowing world" (V.ii).

The traveling players had acted out the crime of Denmark on another stage, but their play seemed to most of the audience only a diversion in a pageant of images designed to keep them from really knowing themselves or their fellows to be corrupted by nature and doomed at last to become "my Lady Worm's, chapless and knocked about the mazzard with a sexton's spade" (V.i). The contexts of these words assert a systematic enlargement of the play's tragic pronouncement of human ignorance in the midst of appearances. Formally, the play progresses from the relatively simple speculations of the soldiers of the watch to the sophisticated complexity of metaphysical inquiry. There may not be final answers to the questions Hamlet ponders, but the questions assume a formal order as their dimensions are structured by speech and action—in miniature, by the play within the play; in extension, by the tragedy itself.

Ophelia, in her madness, utters perhaps the key line of the play: "Lord, we know what we are, but we know not what we may be" (IV.v). Hamlet has earlier said that if the king reacts as expected to the play within the play, "I know my course" (II.ii); that is, he will spring the trap. But he is not sure of his course, nor does he even know himself—at least not until the final act. In the prison of the world and its myriad traps he can only pursue his destiny, which, as he realizes before the duel, inevitably leads to the grave. The contest between human aspiration and natural order in which Hamlet finds himself is all too unequal: idealism turns out to be a poor match for the prison walls of either Denmark or the grave.

E. Irony and Narrative Voice: A Formalistic Approach to "Everyday Use: for your grandmama"

The formalistic critic deals with irony and paradox, with ambiguity, with the tensions that result from multiple interactions within the organic form of the literary piece.

Reminded of these principles, we find that they abound in Alice Walker's "Everyday Use: for your grandmama." Indeed, the very title sets us going. "Everyday Use" seems easy enough, at first: it is a phrase used by Dee, the educated and supposedly sophisticated of the two sisters. But for her it is a term of disparagement about the use of the quilts; for her sister Maggie and for her mother the phrase suggests a worthy, daily use of the quilts. The quilts have different meanings for the members of the family.

And what are we to make of the subtitle, "for your grandmama"? Is it a dedication to a "real" grandmother, an actual specific person, about whom the author tells us nothing more in the text? If so, to whom does "your" refer? Or perhaps it is a kind of generic grandmother, a typical figure that compares with many women in the rural, predominantly African American culture that provides the setting of the story? Or is the subtitle not a dedication, but a recollection of the quilts' association with Maggie and Dee's grandmother? Someone who was there in fact, an everyday, dependable matriarchal figure? And the early pieces of the quilts were hers, "every day."

But the title is just the beginning of the interplay throughout this story.

At a fairly obvious level, what we earlier called "external form" is evident in "Everyday Use." Consider the sequence of events. The scene is set with the mother of the two sisters reporting the events to an unidentified and nonspeaking listener, or maybe just remembering what has happened, speaking ruminatively to herself. But in that report or reminiscence, she moves sequentially from the initial setting to the description of Maggie to the central episode—the visit by Dee and her friend, their meal and conversation together, the altercation between Dee and her mother about the quilts, the departure of the visitors, and the final lines about Maggie and her mother, just sitting there, "enjoying," as the day comes to a close. In this simple yet artfully structured way, the story has what Aristotle called for—an "orderly arrangement of parts." Neat, compact, controlled. A good external form.

However, there is an interesting discontinuity of sorts—a paradox—that might catch the reader's attention. Repeatedly, the mother notes her lack of sophistication and, specifically, her lack of education: "I never had an education myself. After second grade the school was closed down." She recalls that both her daughters have read to her—possibly a hint that she herself is illiterate, or almost so. On the other hand, the reader must soon note that the mother does not narrate as one without education would; nor does she speak in a less than standard dialect, although with a few colloquialisms, to be sure; nor is she at loss for words, whether as narrator or as speaker. In fact, she has a rich vocabulary, has a good sense of standard syntax, and is quite capable of turning a phrase or calling up a vivid image. Why, may we ask, is there this seeming discontinuity between what the narrator tells us about her lack of education and what she shows us? We have no reason to believe that she is an unreliable narrator. If she says that she has no education and if she may be illiterate, then quite possibly that is the factual truth.

But the actual telling of the episode, in the first person, seemingly belies the factual truth. Is it possible that she is telling herself the story, again, at some point in the time well beyond the original setting, when she is "free to sit here" (just as she said that she would be doing once Maggie was married and gone)? If so, then the telling is at the level not of monologue to an unidentified listener, but at the level of the mother's own mind, her own thought processes. And that is a significant point.

For the mother clearly is intelligent and rich in insight and understanding. She has a depth and wisdom (indeed even a sense of humor) that Dee cannot fathom.

That contrast between the lack of education and the real thought processes of the mother presents us with a remarkable "tension," not of a negative sort (though there is a psychological tension in the story that might be negative) but of the sort that the New Critics found important in the internal form of a piece of literary art. What the mother seems to be to daughter Dee is in fact belied by the thought processes, the articulate pattern of words and memories, that the mother in fact commands. The ironic discontinuity is at the heart of the story, so that "form" and "theme" become one.

Not surprisingly, this discontinuity compares with other tensions—which also resolve themselves into the organic form of the story—in "Everyday Use." In that complex we have at least part of the theme of the story, as form and content become complements of one another. For example, it is easy enough to see the overt conflict between the mother and Maggie on one side and Dee and Hakim-a-barber on the other. At a deeper level we see that there are cultural contrasts between them, richly shown in various symbolic details such as the butter churn, the furniture, and of course the quilts. But the contrast between the college-educated Dee and her mother and sister does resolve itself in what is a virtual thematic statement: the lived culture of the mother is richer and more vital than either Dee's college-oriented culture or what is represented by the "African" names assumed by Dee and her friend. That resolution comes in the forthright denial of the quilts to Dee and the giving of them to Maggie, just as in a less dramatic way the use of snuff amid a quiet setting concludes the story.

There are other contrasts also, filling out the form of the story and further adumbrating its themes. Names, for example, are clearly in this pattern. The mother's name—maiden or married is not clear—is Johnson, a simple, traditional name, appropriate enough for her sturdy personality. Her daughters' names and what they represent are a study in contrasts. "Maggie" is not much out of the ordinary and seemingly has no family "history," but it is Maggie who remembers some family name history: Dee says that Maggie has a "brain like an elephant's." On the other hand, "Dee" has been in the family for generations, with clear connections to individual forebears. But there is the rub, for Dee has rejected family history while claiming to want to preserve their "heritage." Rejecting her name, she has adopted a pseudotraditional name that her mother finds difficult to pronounce: "Ream it out again," she says. Of course, Dee's friend's name is even more difficult, and with a hint of disapproval the mother consciously plays upon his initial greeting ("Asalamalakim") as if it were his name, and later she reduces his name to "the barber." Clearly, names are not just incidentals in this story.

More might be said of a few other details that seem significant in the story, details that have some symbolic force. Some of these are the house fire and the building of the second house much like the first, the apparent confusion between Maggie and Dee's friend about the handshake, the recurrent "uhnnnh" that the mother associates with snakes and implicitly then with Dee's friend, and the interplay of the mother's dream of something like Johnny Carson's program and Dee's virtual dream world of assuming a different culture while claiming to preserve her original "heritage."

Finally a more positive word about Dee and her actions. Most of what has been said thus far about Dee seems satiric if not sardonic. But let us remember that we are seeing Dee through her mother's eyes. Earlier we noted that the mother is probably a reliable narrator at least insofar as she talks about her lack of education and other specific details of their family life. But is she totally reliable when she talks about Dee? After all, there is a contrast between two worlds here—one relatively unchanged from what it has been, one that reflects major changes in the society and economy. Dee is somewhat obtuse—but she has been to college, she has been in a different environment, she does suggest that Maggie "make something" of herself. And that is not all wrong. Perhaps that is the final irony, the lasting ambiguity, of the story.

▪ VI. LIMITATIONS OF THE FORMALISTIC APPROACH

By the 1950s, dissent was in the air. Still outraged by the award of the Bollingen Prize for Poetry to Ezra Pound in 1949, some voices thought they detected a pronounced elitism, if not more sinister rightist tendencies, in the New Critics, their disciples, and the poets to whom they had granted the favor of their attention. The details of this political argument need not compel our attention here. What does concern us is the realization that by 1955, some doubters were pointing to the formalistic critics' absorption with details, their greater success with intensive than with extensive criticism, their obvious preference for poets like Eliot and Yeats, and their lack of success with the novel and the drama (C. Hugh Holman, "The Defense of Art: Criticism Since 1930" 238–39).

Less general caveats have emphasized the restriction of formalistic criticism to a certain kind of literature simply because that kind proved itself especially amenable—lyric poetry generally but especially English poetry of the seventeenth century and the "modernist" poetry that stems from Pound and Eliot, and some virtually self-selecting fiction that significantly displays poetic textures (for example, *Moby-Dick* and *Ulysses*). New Critics tended to ignore or undervalue some poetry and other genres that do not easily respond to formalistic approaches (for example, the poetry of Wordsworth and Shelley, philosophical and didactic verse generally, and the essay). Apparently the problems increase whenever the language of the literary work tends to approach that of the philosopher, or even that of the critic himself. The formalistic approach sometimes seems to lapse into a treasure hunt for objective correlatives, conceits, the image, or ironic turns of phrase. It has not seemed to work particularly well for most American poetry written since 1950; as students often point out, it tends to overlook feeling and appears heartless and cold in its absorption with form.

Robert Langbaum pronounced the New Criticism "dead—dead of its very success." For, said he, "We are all New Critics nowadays, whether we like it or not, in that we cannot avoid discerning and appreciating wit in poetry, or reading with close attention to words, images, ironies, and so on" (11). There is more to criticism than "understanding the text, [which] is where criticism begins, not where it ends" (14). Langbaum believed that the New Criticism took us for a time outside the "main stream of criticism" (represented by Aristotle, Coleridge, and Arnold), and that we should return, with the tools of explication and analysis given us by the New Critics, to that mainstream. That is, instead of insisting upon literature's autonomy, we must resume relating it to life and ideas.

Still later, various charges were leveled against the New Critics, and a number of them will be noted in succeeding chapters.

Quick Reference

Booth, Wayne. *The Rhetoric of Fiction.* Chicago: University of Chicago Press, 1961.

Brooks, Cleanth, and Robert Penn Warren. *Understanding Poetry.* 3rd ed. New York: Holt, 1960.

Burke, Kenneth. *Counter-Statement.* Los Altos, CA: Hermes, 1953.

Connolly, Thomas E. "Hawthorne's 'Young Goodman Brown': An Attack on Puritanic Calvinism." *American Literature* 28 (Nov. 1956): 370–75.

Crane, Ronald S. "Cleanth Brooks; or the Bankruptcy of Critical Monism." *Modern Philology* 45 (1948): 226–45.

Eliot, T. S. Introduction to *The Adventures of Huckleberry Finn.* London: Cresset, 1950. Reprinted in *Adventures of Huckleberry Finn.* 2nd ed. Ed. Sculley Bradley, Richard Croom Beatty, E. Hudson Long, and Thomas Cooley. New York: W. W. Norton & Co., 1977.

Fogle, Richard Harter. *Hawthorne's Fiction: The Light and the Dark.* Norman: University of Oklahoma Press, 1952.

Holman, C. Hugh. "The Defense of Art: Criticism since 1930." In *The Development of American Literary Criticism.* Ed. Floyd Stovall: University of North Carolina Press, 1955.

Holman, C. Hugh, and William Harmon. *A Handbook to Literature.* 6th ed. New York: Macmillan, 1992.

Langbaum, Robert. *The Modern Spirit: Essays on the Continuity of Nineteenth- and Twentieth-Century Literature.* New York: Oxford University Press, 1970.

Lentricchia, Frank. *After the New Criticism.* Chicago: University of Chicago Press, 1980.

Pottle, Frederick A. "The Case of Shelley." *PMLA* 67 (1952): 589–608.

Ransom, John Crowe. *The World's Body.* New York: Scribner's, 1938.

Schorer, Mark. "Technique as Discovery." *The Hudson Review* 1 (spring 1948): 67–87.

Warren, Robert Penn. *Selected Essays of Robert Penn Warren.* New York: Random House (Vintage), 1966.

Wimsatt, W. K., and Monroe Beardsley. *The Verbal Icon: Studies in the Meaning of Poetry.* Lexington: University of Kentucky Press, 1954.

▪ 4 ▪

The Psychological Approach: Freud

▪ I. AIMS AND PRINCIPLES

Having discussed two of the basic approaches to literary understanding, the traditional and the formalistic, we now examine a third interpretive perspective, the psychological. Of all the critical approaches to literature, this has been one of the most controversial, the most abused, and—for many readers— the least appreciated. Yet, for all the difficulties involved in its proper application to interpretive analysis, the psychological approach can be fascinating and rewarding. Our purpose in this chapter is threefold: (1) to account briefly for the misunderstanding of psychological criticism; (2) to outline the psychological theory most commonly used as an interpretive tool by modern critics; and (3) to show by examples how readers may apply this mode of interpretation to enhance their understanding and appreciation of literature.

The idea of *enhancement* must be understood as a preface to our discussion. It is axiomatic that no single approach can exhaust the manifold interpretive possibilities of a worthwhile literary work; each approach has its own peculiar limitations. As we have already discovered, the limitations of the traditional approach lie in its tendency to overlook the structural intricacies of the work. The formalistic approach, on the other hand, often neglects historical and sociological contexts that may provide important insights into the meaning of the work.

In turn, the crucial limitation of the psychological approach is its aesthetic inadequacy: psychological interpretation can afford many profound clues toward solving a work's thematic and symbolic mysteries, but it can seldom account for the beautiful symmetry of a well-wrought poem or of a fictional masterpiece. Though the psychological approach is an excellent tool for reading beneath the lines, the interpretive craftsman must often use other tools, such as the traditional and the formalistic approaches, for a proper rendering of the lines themselves.

A. Abuses and Misunderstandings of the Psychological Approach

In the general sense of the word, there is nothing new about the psychological approach. As early as the fourth century B.C., Aristotle used it in setting forth his classic definition of tragedy as combining the emotions of pity and terror to produce catharsis. The "compleat gentleman" of the English Renaissance, Sir Philip Sidney, with his statements about the moral effects of poetry, was psychologizing literature, as were such romantic poets as Coleridge, Wordsworth, and Shelley with their theories of the imagination. In this sense, then, virtually every literary critic has been concerned at some time with the psychology of writing or responding to literature.

During the twentieth century, however, psychologcial criticism has come to be associated with a particular school of thought: the psychoanalytic theories of Sigmund Freud (1856–1939) and his followers. (The currently most significant of these followers, Jacques Lacan, will be discussed in chapter 6.) From this association have derived most of the abuses and misunderstandings of the modern psychological approach to literature. Abuses of the approach have resulted from an excess of enthusiasm, which has been manifested in several ways. First, the practitioners of the Freudian approach often push their critical theses too hard, forcing literature into a Procrustean bed of psychoanalytic theory at the expense of other relevant considerations (for example, the work's total thematic and aesthetic context). Second, the literary criticism of the psychoanalytic extremists has at times degenerated into a special occultism with its own mystique and jargon exclusively for the in-group. Third, many critics of the psychological school have been either literary scholars who have understood the principles of psychology imperfectly or professional psychologists who have had little feeling for literature as art: the former have abused Freudian insights through oversimplification and distortion; the latter have bruised our literary sensibilities.

These abuses have given rise to a widespread mistrust of the psychological approach as a tool for critical analysis. Conservative scholars and teachers of literature, often shocked by such terms as *anal eroticism, phallic symbol,* and *Oedipal complex,* and confused by the clinical diagnoses of literary problems (for example, the interpretation of Hamlet's character as a "severe case of hysteria on a cyclothymic basis"—that is, a manic-depressive psychosis), have rejected all psychological criticism, other than the commonsense type, as pretentious nonsense. By explaining a few of the principles of Freudian psychology that have been applied to literary interpretation and by providing some cautionary remarks, we hope to introduce the reader to a balanced critical perspective that will enable him or her to appreciate the instructive possibilities of the psychological approach while avoiding the pitfalls of either extremist attitude.

B. Freud's Theories

The foundation of Freud's contribution to modern psychology is his emphasis on the unconscious aspects of the human psyche. A brilliant creative genius, Freud provided convincing evidence, through his many carefully recorded case studies, that most of our actions are motivated by psychological forces over which we have very limited control. He demonstrated that, like the iceberg, the human mind is structured so that its great weight and density lie beneath the surface (below the level of consciousness). In "The Anatomy of the Mental Personality," Freud discriminates between the levels of conscious and unconscious mental activity:

> The oldest and best meaning of the word "unconscious" is the descriptive one; we call "unconscious" any mental process the existence of which we are obligated to assume—because, for instance, we infer it in some way from its effects—but of which we are not directly aware. . . . If we want to be more accurate, we should modify the statement by saying that we call a process "unconscious" when we have to assume that it was active *at a certain time,* although *at that time* we knew nothing about it. (99–100)

Freud further emphasizes the importance of the unconscious by pointing out that even the "most conscious processes are conscious for only a short period; quite soon they become *latent,* though they can easily become conscious again" (100). In view of this, Freud defines two kinds of unconscious:

> one which is transformed into conscious material easily and under conditions which frequently arise, and another in the case of which such a transformation is difficult, can only come about with a considerable expenditure of energy, or may never occur at all. . . . We call the unconscious which is only latent, and so can easily become conscious, the "preconscious," and keep the name "unconscious" for the other. (101)

That most of the individual's mental processes are unconscious is thus Freud's first major premise. The second (which has been rejected by a great many professional psychologists, including some of Freud's own disciples—for example, Carl Gustav Jung and Alfred Adler) is that all human behavior is motivated ultimately by what we would call sexuality. Freud designates the prime psychic force as libido, or sexual energy. His third major premise is that because of the powerful social taboos attached to certain sexual impulses, many of our desires and memories are repressed (that is, actively excluded from conscious awareness).

Starting from these three premises, we may examine several corollaries of Freudian theory. Principal among these is Freud's assignment of the mental processes to three psychic zones: the id, the ego, and the superego. An explanation of these zones may be illustrated with Freud's own diagram:

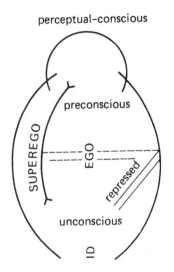

The diagram reveals immediately the vast portion of the mental apparatus that is not conscious. Furthermore, it helps to clarify the relationship between ego, id, and superego, as well as their collective relationship to the conscious and the unconscious. We should note that the id is entirely unconscious and that only a small portion of the ego and the superego is conscious. With this diagram as a guide, we may define the nature and functions of the three psychic zones.

✳ [1] The *id* is the reservoir of libido, the primary source of all psychic energy. It functions to fulfill the primordial life principle, which Freud considers to be the *pleasure principle*. Without consciousness or semblance of rational order, the id is characterized by a tremendous and amorphous vitality. Speaking metaphorically, Freud explains this "obscure inaccessible part of our personality" as "a chaos, a cauldron of seething excitement [with] no organization and no unified will, only an impulsion to obtain satisfaction for the instinctual needs, in accordance with the pleasure principle" (103–4). He further stresses that the "laws of logic—above all, the law of contradiction—do not hold for processes of the id. Contradictory impulses exist side by side without neutralizing each other or drawing apart. . . . Naturally, the id knows no values, no good and evil, no morality" (104–5).

The id is, in short, the source of all our aggressions and desires. It is lawless, asocial, and amoral. Its function is to gratify our instincts for pleasure without regard for social conventions, legal ethics, or moral restraint. Unchecked, it would lead us to any lengths—to destruction and even self-destruction—to satisfy its impulses for pleasure. Safety for the self and for others does not lie within the province of the id; its concern is purely for instinctual gratification, heedless of consequence. For centuries before Freud, this force was recognized in human nature but often attributed to supernatural and external rather than natural and internal forces: the id as defined by Freud is identical in many respects to the Devil as defined by theologians. Thus there is a certain psychological validity in the old saying that a rambunctious child (whose id has not yet been brought under control by ego and superego) is "full of the devil." We may also see in young children (and neurotic adults) certain uncontrolled impulses toward pleasure that often lead to excessive self-indulgence and even to self-injury.

✱ 2. In view of the id's dangerous potentialities, it is necessary that other psychic agencies protect the individual and society. The first of these regulating agencies, that which protects the individual, is the *ego*. This is the rational governing agent of the psyche. Though the ego lacks the strong vitality of the id, it regulates the instinctual drives of the id so that they may be released in nondestructive behavioral patterns. And though a large portion of the ego is unconscious, the ego nevertheless comprises what we ordinarily think of as the conscious mind. As Freud points out, "In popular language, we may say that the ego stands for reason and circumspection, while the id stands for the untamed passions." Whereas the id is governed solely by the pleasure principle, the ego is governed by the *reality principle*. Consequently, the ego serves as intermediary between the world within and the world without.

✱ 3. The other regulating agent, that which primarily functions to protect society, is the *superego*. Largely unconscious, the superego is the moral censoring agency, the repository of conscience and pride. It is, as Freud says in "The Anatomy of the Mental Personality," the "representative of all moral restrictions, the advocate of the impulse toward perfection, in short it is as much as we have been able to apprehend psychologically of what people call the 'higher' things in human life" (95). Acting either directly or through the ego, the superego serves to repress or inhibit the drives of the id, to block off and thrust back into the unconscious those impulses toward pleasure that society regards as unacceptable, such as overt aggression, sexual passions, and the Oedipal instinct. Freud attributes the development of the superego to the parental influence that manifests itself in terms of punishment for what society considers to be bad behavior and reward for what society considers good behavior. An overactive superego creates an unconscious sense of guilt (hence the familiar term *guilt complex* and the popular misconception that Freud advocated the relaxing of all moral inhibitions and social restraints). Whereas the id is dominated by the pleasure principle and the ego by the reality principle, the superego is dominated by the *morality principle.* We might say that the id would make us devils, that the superego would have us behave as angels (or, worse, as creatures of absolute social conformity), and that it remains for the ego to keep us healthy human beings by maintaining a balance between these two opposing forces. It was this balance that Freud advocated—not a complete removal of inhibiting factors.

One of the most instructive applications of this Freudian tripartition to literary criticism is the well-known essay "In Nomine Diaboli" by Henry A. Murray (435–52), a knowledgeable psychoanalyst and a sensitive literary critic as well. In analyzing Herman Melville's masterpiece *Moby-Dick* with the tools provided by Freud, Murray explains the White Whale as a symbolic embodiment of the strict conscience of New England Puritanism (that is, as a projection of Melville's own superego). Captain Ahab, the monomaniac who leads the crew of the *Pequod* to destruction through his insane compulsion to pursue and strike back at the creature who has injured him, is interpreted as the symbol of a rapacious and uncontrollable id. Starbuck, the sane Christian and first mate who struggles to mediate between the forces embodied in Moby-Dick and Ahab, symbolizes a balanced and sensible rationalism (that is, the ego).

Though many scholars are reluctant to accept Freud's tripartition of the human psyche, they have not reacted against this aspect of psychoanalytic criticism so strongly as against the application of his sexual theories to the symbolic interpretation of literature. Let us briefly examine the highlights of such theories. Perhaps the most controversial (and, to many persons, the most offensive) facet of psychoanalytic criticism is its tendency to interpret imagery in terms of sexuality. Following Freud's example in his interpretation of dreams, the psychoanalytic critic tends to see all concave images (ponds, flowers, cups or vases, caves, and hollows) as female or yonic symbols, and all images whose length exceeds their diameter (towers, mountain peaks, snakes, knives, lances, and swords) as male or phallic symbols. Perhaps even more objectionable to some is the interpretation of such activities as dancing, riding, and flying as symbols of sexual pleasure: for example, in *The Life and Works of Edgar Allan Poe: A Psycho-Analytic Interpretation*, Marie Bonaparte interprets the figure of Psyche in "Ulalume" as an ambivalent mother figure, both the longed-for mother and the mother as superego who shields her son from his incestuous instincts, concluding with the following startling observation: "Psyche's drooping, trailing wings in this poem symbolise in concrete form Poe's physical impotence. We know that flying, to all races, unconsciously symbolises the sex act, and that antiquity often represented the penis erect and winged." For the skeptical reader Bonaparte provides this explanation:

> Infinite are the symbols man has the capacity to create, as indeed, the dreams and religions of the savage and civilized well show. Every natural object may be utilised to this end yet, despite their multiple shapes, the objects and relations to which they attach are relatively few: these include the beings we loved first, such as mother, father, brothers or sisters and their bodies, but mainly our own bodies and genitals, and theirs. Almost all symbolism is sexual, in its widest sense, taking the word as the deeply-buried primal urge behind all expressions of love, from the cradle to the grave. (294)

Although such observations as these may have a sound psychoanalytic basis, their relevance to sound critical analysis has been questioned by many scholars. We may sympathize with their incredulousness when we encounter the Freudian essay that interprets even a seemingly innocent fairy tale like "Little

Red Riding Hood" as an allegory of the age-old conflict between male and female in which the plucky young virgin, whose red cap is a menstrual symbol, outwits the ruthless, sex-hungry "wolf" (Fromm 235–41).

Perhaps even more controversial than Freudian dream symbolism are Freud's theories concerning child psychology. Contrary to traditional beliefs, Freud found infancy and childhood a period of intense sexual experience, sexual in a sense much broader than is commonly attached to the term. During the first five years of life, the child passes through a series of phases in erotic development, each phase being characterized by emphasis on a particular *erogenous zone* (that is, a portion of the body in which sexual pleasure becomes localized). Freud indicated three such zones: the *oral,* the *anal,* and the *genital.* (Note that the uninitiated layman, unfamiliar with the breadth of Freud's term, generally restricts the meaning of "sexuality" to *"genital* sexuality.") These zones are associated not only with pleasure in stimulation but also with the gratification of our vital needs: eating, elimination, and reproduction. If for some reason the individual is frustrated in gratifying these needs during childhood, the adult personality may be warped accordingly (that is, development may be arrested or *fixated*). For example, adults who are compulsively fastidious may suffer, according to the psychoanalyst, from an anal fixation traceable to overly strict toilet training during early childhood. Likewise, compulsive cigarette smoking may be interpreted as a symptom of oral fixation traceable to premature weaning. Even among "normal" adults, sublimated responses occur when the individual is vicariously stimulated by images associated with one of the major erogenous zones. In his *Fiction and the Unconscious,* Simon O. Lesser suggests that the anal-erotic quality in *Robinson Crusoe* (manifested in the hero's scrupulous record keeping and orderliness) accounts at least partially for the unconscious appeal of Defoe's masterpiece (306).

According to Freud, the child reaches the stage of genital primacy around age five, at which time the Oedipus complex manifests itself. In simple terms, the Oedipus complex derives from the boy's unconscious rivalry with his father for the love of his mother. Freud borrowed the term from the classic Sophoclean tragedy in which the hero unwittingly murders his father and marries his mother. In *The Ego and the Id,* Freud describes the complex as follows:

> . . . the boy deals with his father by identifying himself with him. For a time these two relationships [the child's devotion to his mother and identification with his father] proceed side by side, until the boy's sexual wishes in regard to his mother become more intense and his father is perceived as an obstacle to them; from this the Oedipus complex originates. His identification with his father then takes on a hostile colouring and changes into a wish to get rid of his father in order to take his place with his mother. Henceforward his relation to his father is ambivalent; it seems as if the ambivalence inherent in the identification from the beginning had become manifest. An ambivalent attitude to his father and an object-relation of a solely affectionate kind to his mother make up the content of the simple positive Oedipus complex in a boy. (21–22)

Further ramifications of the Oedipus complex are a fear of castration and an identification of the father with strict authority in all forms; subsequent hostility to authority is therefore associated with the Oedipal ambivalence to which Freud refers. (The Oedipus complex figures strongly in Jacques Lacan's psychoanalytic theory [see chapter 6].) A story like Nathaniel Hawthorne's "My Kinsman, Major Molineux," for instance, has been interpreted by Lesser as essentially a symbolic rebellion against the father figure. And with this insight we may find meaning in the young hero's disturbing outburst of laughter as he watches the cruel tarring and feathering of his once-respected relative: the youth is expressing his unconscious joy in being released from parental authority. Now he is free, as the friendly stranger suggests, to make his own way in the adult world without the help (and restraint) of his kinsman.

▪ II. THE PSYCHOLOGICAL APPROACH IN PRACTICE

A. *Hamlet:* The Oedipus Complex

Although Freud himself made some applications of his theories to art and literature, it remained for an English disciple, the psychoanalyst Ernest Jones, to provide the first full-scale psychoanalytic treatment of a major literary work. Jones's *Hamlet and Oedipus,* originally published as an essay in *The American Journal of Psychology* in 1910, was later revised and enlarged.

Jones bases his argument on the thesis that Hamlet's much-debated delay in killing his uncle, Claudius, is to be explained in terms of internal rather than external circumstances and that the "play is mainly concerned with a hero's unavailing fight against what can only be called a disordered mind." In his carefully documented essay Jones builds a highly persuasive case history of Hamlet as a psychoneurotic who suffers from manic-depressive hysteria combined with an *abulia* (an inability to exercise willpower and come to decisions)—all of which may be traced to the hero's severely repressed Oedipal feelings. Jones points out that no really satisfying argument has ever been substantiated for the idea that Hamlet avenges his father's murder as quickly as practicable. Shakespeare makes Claudius's guilt as well as Hamlet's duty perfectly clear from the outset—if we are to trust the words of the ghost and the gloomy insights of the hero himself. The fact is, however, that Hamlet does not fulfill this duty until absolutely forced to do so by physical circumstances—and even then only after Gertrude, his mother, is dead. Jones also elucidates the strong misogyny that Hamlet displays throughout the play, especially as it is directed against Ophelia, and his almost physical revulsion to sex. All of this adds up to a classic example of the neurotically repressed Oedipus complex.

The ambivalence that typifies the child's attitude toward his father is dramatized in the characters of the ghost (the good, lovable father with whom the boy identifies) and Claudius (the hated father as tyrant and rival), both of whom are dramatic projections of the hero's own conscious-unconscious ambivalence toward the father figure. The ghost represents the conscious ideal of fatherhood, the image that is socially acceptable:

> See, what a grace was seated on this brow:
> Hyperion's curls, the front of Jove himself,
> An eye like Mars, to threaten and command,
> A station like the herald Mercury
> New-lighted on a heaven-kissing hill,

> A combination and a form indeed,
> Where every god did seem to set his seal,
> To give the world assurance of a man:
> This was your husband. (III.iv)

His view of Claudius, on the other hand, represents Hamlet's repressed hostility toward his father as a rival for his mother's affection. This new king-father is the symbolic perpetrator of the very deeds toward which the son is impelled by his own unconscious motives: murder of his father and incest with his mother. Hamlet cannot bring himself to kill Claudius because to do so he must, in a psychological sense, kill himself. His delay and frustration in trying to fulfill the ghost's demand for vengeance may therefore be explained by the fact that, as Jones puts it, the "thought of incest and parricide combined is too intolerable to be borne. One part of him tries to carry out the task, the other flinches inexorably from the thought of it" (78–79).

Norman N. Holland neatly summed up the reasons both for Hamlet's delay and also for our three-hundred-year delay in comprehending Hamlet's true motives:

> Now what do critics mean when they say that Hamlet cannot act because of his Oedipus complex? The argument is very simple, very elegant. One, people over the centuries have been unable to say why Hamlet delays in killing the man who murdered his father and married his mother. Two, psychoanalytic experience shows that every child wants to do just exactly that. Three, Hamlet delays because he cannot punish Claudius for doing what he himself wished to do as a child and, unconsciously, still wishes to do: he would be punishing himself. Four, the fact that this wish is unconscious explains why people could not explain Hamlet's delay. (158)

A corollary to the Oedipal problem in *Hamlet* is the pronounced misogyny in Hamlet's character. Because of his mother's abnormally sensual affection for her son, an affection that would have deeply marked Hamlet as a child with an Oedipal neurosis, he has in the course of his psychic development repressed his incestuous impulses so severely that this repression colors his attitude toward all women: "The total reaction culminates in the bitter misogyny of his outburst against Ophelia, who is devastated at having to bear a reaction so wholly out of proportion to her own offense and has no idea that in reviling her Hamlet is really expressing his bitter resentment against his mother" (Jones 96). The famous "Get thee to a nunnery" speech has even more sinister overtones than are generally recognized, explains Jones, when we understand the pathological degree of Hamlet's conditions and read "nunnery" as Elizabethan slang for brothel.

> The underlying theme relates ultimately to the splitting of the mother image which the infantile unconscious effects into two opposite pictures: one of a virginal Madonna, an inaccessible saint towards whom all sensual approaches are unthinkable, and the other of a sensual creature accessible to everyone. . . . When sexual repression is highly pronounced, as with Hamlet, then both types of women are felt to be hostile: the pure one out of resentment at her repulses, the sensual one out of the temptation she offers to plunge into guiltiness. Misogyny, as in the play, is the inevitable result. (97–98)

Although it has been attacked by the anti-Freudians and occasionally disparaged as "obsolete" by the neo-Freudians, Jones's critical tour de force has nevertheless attained the status of a modern classic. "Both as an important seminal work which led to a considerable re-examination of *Hamlet*, and as an example of a thorough and intelligent application of psychoanalysis to drama," writes Claudia C. Morrison, "Jones's essay stands as the single most important Freudian study of literature to appear in America . . ." (175).

B. Rebellion against the Father in *Huckleberry Finn*

Mark Twain's great novel has this in common with Shakespeare's masterpiece: both are concerned with the theme of rebellion—with a hostile treatment of the father figure. In both works the father figure is finally slain, and knowledge of his death brings a curious sense of relief—and release—for the reader. As we have seen, from the psychoanalytic viewpoint all rebellion is in essence a rejection of parental, especially paternal, authority. Sociologically speaking, Huck rebels against the unjust, inhumane restrictions of a society that condones slavery, hypocrisy, and cruelty. However, Mark Twain showed a remarkable pre-Freudian insight when he dramatized this theme of rebellion in the portrayal of Huck's detestable father as the lowest common denominator of social authority. The main plot of the novel is launched with Huck's escape from pap Finn ("pap," in keeping with the reductive treatment of this father figure, is not capitalized), a flight that coincides with Jim's escape from Miss Watson.

Symbolically, Huck and Jim, in order to gain freedom and to regain prelapsarian bliss (the happiness enjoyed by Adam before the Fall), must escape whatever is represented by Miss Watson and pap Finn (who reminds Huck of Adam all covered with mud—that is, Adam after the Fall). Despite their superficial and rather melodramatic differences, Miss Watson and pap Finn have much in common. They represent extremes of authority: authority at its most respectable and at its most contemptible. What is more, they both represent social and legal morality, again in the extremes of the social spectrum. Notwithstanding his obvious worthlessness, pap Finn is still Huck's sole guardian by law and holds near-absolute power over him, an authority condoned by society, just as Miss Watson has a similar power over Jim. In the light of such authority both Miss Watson and pap Finn may be said to represent the superego (for example, when Huck goes against his conscience by refusing to turn Jim in to the authorities, it is the letter to Miss Watson that he tears up). In this sense, then, it is to escape the oppressive tyranny and cruel restraints of the superego that Huck and Jim take flight on the river.

Huckleberry Finn cannot by any means be read as a psychological allegory, and it would be foolish to set up a strict one-to-one relationship of characters and events to ideas, particularly because Mark Twain wrote the book with no notion of Freudian concepts. But like most great writers, Twain knew human nature; and from the psychoanalytic perspective, a "linked analogy" can be seen between the structure of his novel and the Freudian structure of the human psyche. Water in any form is generally interpreted by the psychoanalysts as a female symbol, more specifically as a maternal symbol. From the superegoistic milieu of society Huck and Jim flee to the river, where they find freedom. Except when invaded by men, the river is characterized by a strange, fluid, dreamlike peacefulness; Huck's most lyrical comments are those describing the beauty of the river:

> Two or three days and nights went by; I reckon I might say they swum by, they slid along so quiet and smooth and lovely. . . . Not a sound anywheres—perfectly still—just like the whole world was asleep. . . . [Then] the nice breeze springs up, and comes fanning you from over there, so cool and fresh and sweet to smell on account of the woods and flowers; but sometimes not that way, because they've left dead fish laying around, gars and such, and they do get pretty rank. . . . [And] we would watch the lonesomeness of the river, and kind of lazy along, and by and by lazy off to sleep. . . . It's lovely to live on a raft. We had the sky up there, all speckled with stars, and we used to lay on our backs and look up at them, and discuss about whether they was made or only just happened. . . . Jim said the moon could 'a' *laid* them; well, that looked kind of reasonable, so I didn't say nothing against it, because I've seen a frog lay most as many, so of course it could be done. (ch. 19)

The foregoing passage is redolent with female-maternal imagery; it also suggests the dark, mysterious serenity associated with the prenatal state, as well as with death, in psychoanalytic interpretation. The tension between land and water may be seen as analogous to that between the conscious and the unconscious in Freudian theory. Lacking a real mother, Huck finds his symbolic mother in the river; in Freudian terms, he returns to the womb. From this matrix he undergoes a series of symbolic deaths and rebirths, punctuated structurally by the episodes on land. As James M. Cox (389–405) has pointed out, Huck's fake murder in escaping from pap Finn is crucial to our understanding the central informing pattern of death and rebirth: "Having killed himself, Huck is 'dead' throughout the entire journey down the river. He is indeed the man without identity who is reborn at almost every river bend, not because he desires a new role, but because he must re-create himself to elude the forces which close in on him from every side. The rebirth theme which began with pap's reform becomes the driving idea behind the entire action." Enhancing this pattern is the hermaphroditic figure of Jim, Huck's adopted friend and parent, whose blackness coincides with the darkness associated with death, the unconscious, and the maternal. (We are reminded of Whitman's celebration of death as the Dark Mother in such famous poems as "Out of the Cradle Endlessly Rocking" and "When Lilacs Last in the Dooryard Bloom'd.") Jim's qualities are more maternal than paternal. He possesses the gentleness, unquestioning loyalty, and loving kindness that we traditionally ascribe to the mother, in sharp contrast to the brutal authoritarianism of pap.

Viewed from a slightly different psychological angle, *Huckleberry Finn* is a story of the child as victim, embodying the betrayal-of-innocence theme that has become one of the chief motifs in American fiction. Philip Young has detected similarities between Huck's plight and that of the Hemingway hero. Young sees Huck as the wounded child, permanently scarred by traumas of death and violence; he has counted thirteen corpses in the novel and observes that virtually every major episode in the book ends with violence or death. Young makes explicit the causal relationship between the traumatic experiences suffered by Huck (and later by Hemingway's protagonists) and the growing preoccupation with death that dominates much modern literature:

> [Huck] is a wounded and damaged boy. He will never get over the terror he has seen and been through, is guilt-ridden and can't sleep at night for his thoughts. When he is able to sleep he is tortured with bad dreams. . . . This is a boy who has undergone an unhappy process of growing up, and has grown clean out of his creator's grasp. . . . Precisely as Clemens could never solve his own complications, save in the unmitigated but sophomoric pessimism of his last books, so he could not solve them for Huck, who had got too hot to handle and was dropped. What the man never realized was that in his journey by water he had been hinting at a solution all along: an excessive exposure to violence and death produced first a compulsive fascination with dying, and finally an ideal symbol for it. (200–201)

This ideal symbol is the dark river itself, which is suggestive of the Freudian death instinct, the unconscious instinct in all living things to return to the nonliving state and thereby achieve permanent surcease from the pain of living.

Our recognition of these symbolic implications does not, by any means, exhaust the interpretive potential of Twain's novel, nor does it preclude insights gained from other critical approaches. Such recognition should *enhance* our appreciation of the greatness of *Huckleberry Finn* by revealing that Mark Twain produced a masterwork that, intentionally or not, has appealed in a profound psychological way to many generations of readers. The Freudian reading—particularly in its focus on the death of the Father and the search for the Feminine—has enjoyed renewed attention from feminist psychoanalytic critics (see chapter 6, "Feminist Approaches").

C. "Young Goodman Brown": Id versus Superego

The theme of innocence betrayed is also central to Nathaniel Hawthorne's "Young Goodman Brown," the tale of the young bridegroom who leaves his wife Faith to spend a night with Satan in the forest. The events of that terrifying night are a classic traumatic experience for the youth. At the center of the dark wilderness he discovers a witches' Sabbath involving all the honored teachers, preachers, and friends of his village. The climax is reached when his own immaculate bride is brought forth to stand by his side and pledge eternal allegiance to the Fiend of Hell. Following this climactic moment in which the hero resists the diabolical urge to join the fraternity of evil, he wakes to find himself in the deserted forest wondering if what has happened was dream or reality. Regardless of the answer, he is a changed man. He returns in the morning to the village and to his Faith, but he is never at peace with himself again. Henceforth he can never hear the singing of a holy hymn without also hearing echoes of the anthem of sin from that terrible night in the forest. He shrinks even from the side of Faith. His dying hour is gloom, and no hopeful epitaph is engraved upon his tombstone.

Aside from the clearly intended allegorical meanings discussed elsewhere in this book, it is the story's underlying psychological implications that concern us here. We start with the assumption that, through symbolism and technique, "Young Goodman Brown" means more than it says. In this respect our task is one of extrapolation, an inferring of the unknown from the known. Our first premise is that Brown's journey is more than a physical one; it is a psychological one as well. To see what this journey means in psychological terms, we need to examine the setting, the time and place. Impelled by unmistakably libidinal force, the hero moves from the village of Salem into the forest. The village is a place of light and order, both social and spiritual order. Brown leaves Faith behind in the town at sunset and returns to Faith in the morning. The journey into the wilderness is taken in the night: "My journey . . . forth and back again," explains the young man to his wife, "must needs be done 'twixt now and sunrise." It is in the forest, a place of darkness and unknown terrors, that Brown meets the Devil. On one level, then, the village may be equated with consciousness, the forest with the dark recesses of the unconscious. But, more precisely, the village, as a place of social and moral order (and inhibition) is analogous to Freud's superego, conscience, the morally inhibiting agent of the psyche; the forest, as a place of wild, untamed passions and terrors, has the attributes of the Freudian id. As mediator between these opposing forces, Brown himself resembles the poor ego, which tries to effect a healthy balance and is shattered because it is unable to do so.

Why can't he reconcile these forces? Is his predicament that of all human beings, as is indicated by his common, nondistinctive surname? If so, are we all destined to die in gloom? Certainly, Hawthorne implies, we cannot remain always in the village, outside the forest. And sooner or later, we must all confront Satan. Let us examine this diabolical figure for a moment. When we first see him (after being prepared by Brown's expressed fear, "What if the devil himself should be at my very elbow!"), he is "seated at the foot of an old tree"—an allusion to the "old tree" of forbidden fruit and the knowledge of sin. He is described as "bearing a considerable resemblance" to the hero himself. He is, in short, Brown's own alter ego, the dramatic projection of a part of Brown's psyche, just as Faith is the projection of another part of his psyche. The staff Satan is carrying, similar to the maple stick he later gives to Brown, is like a "great black snake . . . a living serpent"—a standard Freudian symbol for the uncontrollable phallus. As he moves on through the forest, Brown encounters other figures, the most repected of his moral tutors: old Goody Cloyse, Deacon Gookin, and, at last, even Faith herself, her pink ribbon reflecting the ambiguity that Brown is unable to resolve, for pink is the mixture of white (for purity) and red (for passion). Thoroughly unnerved—then maddened—by disillusionment, Brown capitulates to the wild evil in this heart of darkness and becomes "himself the chief horror of the scene, [shrinking] not from its other horrors." That the whole lurid scene may be interpreted as the projection of Brown's formerly repressed impulses is indicated in Hawthorne's description of the transformed protagonist:

> In truth, all through the haunted forest there could be nothing more frightful than the figure of Goodman Brown. On he flew among the black pines, brandishing his staff with frenzied gestures, now giving vent to an inspiration of horrid blasphemy, and now shouting forth such laughter as set all the echoes of the forest laughing like demons around him. *The fiend in his own shape is less hideous than when he rages in the breast of man.* (our italics)

Though Hawthorne implies that Brown's problem is that of Everyman, he does not suggest that all humans share Brown's gloomy destiny. Like Freud, Hawthorne saw the dangers of an overactive suppression of libido and the consequent development of a tyrannous superego, though he thought of the problem in his own terms as an imbalance of head versus heart. Goodman Brown is the tragic victim of a society that has shut its eyes to the inevitable "naturalness" of sex as a part of humankind's physical and mental constitution, a society whose moral system would suppress too severely natural human impulses.

Among Puritans the word "nature" was virtually synonymous with "sin." In Hawthorne's *The Scarlet Letter*, little Pearl, illegitimate daughter of Hester Prynne and the Reverend Mr. Arthur Dimmesdale, is identified throughout as the "child of nature." In his speech to the General Court in 1645, Governor John Winthrop defined "natural liberty"—as distinguished from "civil liberty"—as a "liberty to do evil as well as good . . . the exercise and maintaining of [which] makes men grow more evil, and in time to be worse than brute beasts. . . ." Hawthorne, himself a descendant of Puritan witch hunters and a member of New England society, the moral standards of which had been strongly conditioned by its Puritan heritage, was obsessed with the nature of sin and with the psychological results of violating the taboos imposed by this system. Young Goodman Brown dramatizes the neurosis resulting from such a violation.

After his night in the forest he becomes a walking guilt complex, burdened with anxiety and doubt. Why? Because he has not been properly educated to confront the realities of the external world or of the inner world, because from the cradle on he has been indoctrinated with admonitions against tasting the forbidden fruit, and because sin and Satan have been inadvertently glamorized by prohibition, he has developed a morbid compulsion to taste of them. He is not necessarily evil; he is, like most young people, curious. But because of the severity of Puritan taboos about natural impulses, his curiosity has become an obsession. His dramatic reactions in the forest are typical of what happens in actual cases of extreme repression. Furthermore, the very nature of his wilderness fantasy substantiates Freud's theory that our repressed desires express themselves in our dreams, that dreams are symbolic forms of wish fulfillment. Hawthorne, writing more than a generation before Freud, was a keen enough psychologist to be aware of many of the same phenomena Freud was to systematize through clinical evidence.

D. *The Turn of the Screw:* The Consequences of Sexual Repression

Perhaps the most famous story dealing with the theme of sexual repression is Henry James's *Turn of the Screw*. One of the most celebrated ghost stories of our literature, this many-faceted gem has been the focus of critical controversy since 1924, when Edna Kenton published her Freudian analysis of the tale, "Henry James to the Ruminant Reader: The Turn of the Screw" (245–55). This interpretation was buttressed ten years later by the highly respected critic Edmund Wilson in "The Ambiguity of Henry James." It was exhaustively reinforced a generation later by Thomas M. Cranfill and Robert L. Clark, Jr., in *An Anatomy of "The Turn of the Screw."*

In *The Turn of the Screw* a young English governess takes a position as tutor and protectress of two beautiful children living in a magnificent old country mansion. The children's parents are dead, and their legal guardian is a debonair bachelor uncle who lives in London and does not want to be bothered with looking after his wards. He hires the young governess (the narrator of the story) with the proviso that she is to be in complete charge at Bly, his country estate, and that she will under no circumstances disturb him with appeals or complaints about her problems there. Though she is only twenty years old, she is to become governess of the estate as well as of the children, and the uncle is to be left alone, disburdened of worries about the welfare of his wards. The children, Miles and Flora, are two perfectly well-mannered youngsters with whom the governess immediately falls in love.

All seems to be well at Bly, except for the ugly mystery surrounding the relationship between the governess's predecessor, Miss Jessel, and the uncle's former valet, Peter Quint, both of whom are now dead. Also, there is the puzzling dismissal of little Miles from his school on the grounds that he "was an injury" to his fellow students. As best the governess can discover from rumor and from the scanty information given her by the housekeeper, Mrs. Grose, there had been "an affair" between Miss Jessel and Quint, carried on in the presence of the children, which had left some subtle mark of corruption on Miles and Flora. On several occasions after her arrival at Bly the governess sees the ghosts of Miss Jessel and Quint and deduces that they are somehow diabolically intent upon ensnaring the children's young souls. The actions of the children themselves, though superficially normal, suggest to the governess that her apprehensions are not without foundation. At the end of the narrative, little Flora turns against the governess and is taken off to the city by Mrs. Grose as a means, presumably, of preserving her from further corruption by Miss Jessel. The governess stays at Bly with Miles and fights for his soul against the apparition of Peter Quint. In this final climactic struggle the governess seems to triumph in driving off the evil spirit, but the little boy dies from the terrible ordeal of being dispossessed.

No brief summary can do justice to the complexities and the exquisite horror of James's tale; our primary concern here is with its interpretive possibilities. In his preface to volume 12 of the New York Edition of his collected works, James himself disavows all psychical implications in *The Turn of the Screw*, designating it as a pure and simple *amusette* intended "to catch those not easily caught (the 'fun' of the capture of the merely witless being ever but small), the jaded, the disillusioned, the fastidious"—a "Christmas-tide toy" designed "to rouse the dear old sacred terror."

Two questions may be asked about James's statements. Is he serious in disavowing a clinical intent? And does it really matter whether or not he intended the story to be no more than a simple *amusette*? The first question is unanswerable. We cannot be sure about his stated purpose; perhaps it, too, is designed to catch the literal-minded reader. To the second question we must answer a qualified no. In the strictest interpretive sense, James's conscious intentions are not directly relevant to our critical analysis of his story. Because the mind of the artist is structured essentially like other human minds and is therefore influenced by a welter of unconscious forces, the author may write more profoundly than he or she realizes. The important thing is not so much what writers intend as what we as careful, informed readers find in their works. The fact is, a very strong case can be made for the clinical implications in James's story.

In his essay on *The Turn of the Screw* (revised for *The Triple Thinkers*), Edmund Wilson pointed out that no one except the governess ever admits to seeing the ghosts of Peter Quint and Miss Jessel. We assume that the children see them, as we infer this from their curious behavior, but in truth we have only the governess's word. Mrs. Grose, the simple, illiterate housekeeper whose name signifies her down-to-earthness, never sees either ghost, despite several opportunities to do so. She, too, relies only upon the word of the highly sensitive governess.

What, then, is the significance of the ghosts, and why does only the young governess see them? To the psychoanalytic observer, the answer is fairly obvious. The governess is suffering from hallucinations, the result of a severe case of sexual repression; the ghosts are dramatic projections of her own unconscious sexual desires. As James's narrator informs us at the beginning of the story, she has been reared as the "youngest of several daughters of a poor country parson." We may therefore infer that, in such a sheltered, feminine world, her normal libidinous instincts have been powerfully inhibited, like those of Goodman Brown, by her parents and by a Victorian middle-class society even more repressive than the Puritan. She is admittedly infatuated with the children's uncle ("a gentleman, a bachelor in the prime of life, such a figure as had never risen, save in a dream or an old novel, before a fluttered, anxious girl out of a Hampshire vicarage"), and it is dressed in the uncle's clothing that the red-headed Peter Quint first appears. Not only this, but Peter Quint, whose very name is a metonymy of his libidinous function (his first and last names being vulgar terms for the male and female sexual organs), makes his first appearance on the tower, a phallic symbol, just as Miss Jessel first appears beside the lake, a female symbol. Wilson lends further support to his case by pointing out the pieces of wood with which little Flora is playing under the fascinated gaze of the governess at the time of Miss Jessel's initial appearance; the child is attempting to insert the mast of a toy ship into its appropriate hole. To sum up the Freudian case in Wilson's words:

> When we look back in the light of these hints, we are inclined to conclude from analogy that the story is primarily intended as a characterization of the governess: her somber and guilty visions and the way she behaves about them seem to present, from the moment we examine them from the obverse side of her narrative, an accurate and distressing picture of the poor country parson's daughter, with her English middle-class class-consciousness, her inability to admit to herself her natural sexual impulses and the relentless English "authority" which enables her to put over on inferiors even purposes which are totally deluded and not at all in the other people's best interests. . . . We find now that [this story] is a variation of one of [James's] familiar themes: the thwarted Anglo-Saxon spinster. . . . (*The Triple Thinkers* 95)

E. Death Wish in Poe's Fiction

Aside from Ernest Jones's *Hamlet and Oedipus* and Edmund Wilson's essay on *The Turn of the Screw,* one of the most widely known psychoanalytic studies of literature is Marie Bonaparte's *Life and Works of Edgar Allan Poe.* A pupil of Sigmund Freud, Bonaparte is, like Jones, one of those rare critics who have combined a thorough professional knowledge of psychoanalysis with a comparable grasp of her literary subject. For the uninitiated her book is as fantastic as it is fascinating. Her main thesis is that Poe's life and works are informed throughout by the Oedipal complex: hatred of father and psychopathic love of mother. The rejection of authority forms the core of Poe's critical writings; the mother fixation (the death wish or longing to return to the womb, manifested, for example, in his obsession with premature burial) is the matrix for Poe's poetry and fiction. Even his fatal weakness for drink is explained as a form of escape that enabled him to remain faithful to his dead mother, through a rigidly enforced chastity that was further ensured by alcoholic overindulgence. As Bonaparte writes,

> Ever since he was three, in fact, Poe had been doomed by fate to live in constant mourning. A fixation on a dead mother was to bar him forever from earthly love, and make him shun health and vitality in his loved ones. Forever faithful to the grave, his imagination had but two ways open before it: the heavens or the tomb according to whether he followed the "soul" or body of his lost one. . . .
>
> Thus, through his eternal fidelity to the dead mother, Poe, to all intents, became necrophilist. . . . Had [his necrophilia] been unrepressed, Poe would no doubt have been a criminal. (83)

Using such psychoanalytic theories as her foundation, Bonaparte proceeds to analyze work after work with a logical consistency that is as unsettling as it is monotonous. "The Cask of Amontillado" and "The Tell-Tale Heart" are seen as tales of revenge against the father. The wine vault in the former story is a symbol of the "interior of the woman's body . . . where the coveted, supreme intoxication dwells, [and] thus becomes the instrument of retribution. . . ." The victim in "The Tell-Tale

Heart" is likewise interpreted as a symbol of Poe's hated father, John Allan, and his horrible blind eye is a token of retributive castration. "The Fall of the House of Usher" is a psychoanalytic model of the Oedipal guilt complex. Madeline Usher, the vault in which she is prematurely interred, and the house itself are all, according to Freudian symbology, mother images. The weird tale of Ethelred, read to Roderick by the narrator and climaxed by the slaying of the dragon, is a reenactment of the slaying of the father to gain the mother-treasure.

F. Love and Death in Blake's "Sick Rose"

Though few writers lend themselves so readily as Poe to the psychoanalytic approach, a great deal of serious literature, if we accept Marie Bonaparte's premises, can be interpreted along the same basic lines established by Freud. The Romantic poets especially are susceptible to Freudian interpretations because, as F. L. Lucas has asserted, Romanticism is related to the unconscious—as opposed to Classicism, which, with its emphasis on restraint and order, is oriented toward the conscious, particularly the ego and superego.

A richly symbolic poem like William Blake's "Sick Rose" is exemplary:

> O Rose, thou art sick!
> The invisible worm,
> That flies in the night,
> In the howling storm,
>
> Has found out thy bed
> Of crimson joy;
> And his dark secret love
> Does thy life destroy.

From the Freudian perspective the sexual implications of Blake's imagery are readily discernible. The rose is a classic symbol of feminine beauty. But this beauty is being despoiled by some agent of masculine sexuality: the worm, symbol of death, of decay, and also of the phallus (worm = serpent = sexual instinct). Again, as in Poe's "Ulalume," we encounter flying as a symbol of sexual intercourse. Images of night, darkness, and howling storm suggest attributes of the unconscious or the id, as in the forest of "Young Goodman Brown." The second stanza sets forth in rather explicit images the idea of sensual destruction. In short, Blake's poem is a vaguely disturbing parable of the death instinct, which psychoanalysts affirm is closely conjoined with sexual passion. The sharp juxtaposition of "crimson joy" and "destroy" (coupled with "bed" and "his dark secret love") suggests that Eros, unmitigated by higher spiritual love, is the agent of evil as well of mortality.

G. Sexual Imagery in "To His Coy Mistress"

We see a similar juxtaposition in Andrew Marvell's "To His Coy Mistress," one of the most celebrated erotic poems in English literature. The speaker begins his proposition of love by stating an impossible condition: "Had we but world enough, and time,/This coyness, Lady, were no crime." Flattering his prospective mistress as "Lady," he proceeds to outline the "ideal" relationship of the two lovers:

> We would sit down and think which way
> To walk and pass our long love's day.
> • • • • • • • • • • • • • • • • • • •
> For, Lady, you deserve this state,
> Nor would I love at lower rate.

The speaker's argument in this first stanza achieves a fine sublimation. He has managed to refine his seductive motive of all its grossness, yet, ever so subtly, he has not swerved from his main purpose. His objective, despite the contradictory deceptiveness of "vegetable love" (a passion whose burning is so slow as to be imperceptible), is nevertheless the same: it is only a matter of time before the woman must capitulate to his blandishments.

But this "only" makes all the difference in the world, as he demonstrates in his second stanza, shifting dramatically from the allusive persuasion of the first stanza to the overt pressure of the second:

> But at my back I always hear
> Time's winged chariot hurrying near;
> And yonder all before us lie
> Deserts of vast eternity.

The flying chariot of Time (again we find the subtle implication of sexual union in the image of flying) is juxtaposed against an eternity of oblivion, just as the slow but sure fecundity of a vegetable love growing to the vastness of empires is contrasted with the barren deserts of death. After setting forth this prospect, the speaker dares to reveal precisely what all this means in terms of love:

> Thy beauty shall no more be found,
> Nor, in thy marble vault, shall sound
> My echoing song; then worms shall try
> That long preserved virginity,
> And your quaint honor turn to dust,
> And into ashes all my lust.

This statement, in even sharper contrast with the gentle cajolery of the first stanza, is brutal in its explicitness. The "marble vault" is a thinly disguised vaginal metaphor suggesting both rigor mortis and the fleshless pelvis of the skeleton. "My echoing song" and the sensual meanings of the lines following are extremely coarse (cf. "quaint" and James's "Quint" as yonic puns). From the eternal burning of a vegetable passion, in the face of reality, we see that all love must at last end in ashes—just as all chastity must end, the same as sexual profligacy, in dust. The speaker concludes this stanza with a devastating anticlimax:

> The grave's a fine and private place,
> But none, I think, do there embrace.

In the final stanza the speaker relaxes his harsh irony and appeals passionately to his reluctant sweetheart to seize the moment. Again, in contrast with both the vegetable metaphor of the first stanza and the frightening directness of the second stanza, he achieves a sublimation of sensual statement through the bold sincerity of his passion and through the brilliance of his imagery:

Now therefore, while the youthful hue
Sits on thy skin like morning dew,
And while thy willing soul transpires
At every pore with instant fires,
Now let us sport us while we may,
And now, like amorous birds of prey,
Rather at once our time devour
Than languish in his slow-chapped power.
Let us roll all our strength and all
Our sweetness up into one ball,
And tear our pleasures with rough strife
Thorough the iron gates of life:
Thus, though we cannot make our sun
Stand still, yet we will make him run.

Here, too, the sexual imagery is overt. The fire image, which smolders in stanza 1 and turns to ashes in stanza 2, explodes into passion in the concluding stanza. ("Fire, in the unconscious," says Marie Bonaparte, "is the classic symbol of urethral eroticism.") Furthermore, in contrast to the tone of Blake's "Sick Rose," here love-as-destruction is set forth rapturously. The poet conveys, instead of sinister corruption, a sense of desperate ecstasy. The eating-biting metaphor (oral eroticism in its primal form) is fused with the flying symbol in "amorous birds of prey" and set with metaphysical brilliance against the alternative of a slow, cannibalistic dissolution within the horrible maw of Time. In his last four lines the lover drives his message home with an orgasmic force through the use of harshly rhythmic spondees ("Thus, though" and "Stand still") and strongly suggestive puns ("make our sun" and "Make him run").

To read Marvell's great poem as nothing more than a glorification of sexual activity is, of course, a gross oversimplification. "To His Coy Mistress" is much more, as we have indicated in the preceding chapters and will elaborate in the following chapters. We agree with the formalistic critic that literature is autonomous, but we must also concur with critic Wayne Shumaker that it is "continuous with nonaesthetic life." As Simon O. Lesser has said, "Among [literary works] whose artistic authenticity cannot be questioned we give the highest place precisely to those works which ignore no aspect of man's nature, which confront the most disagreeable aspects of life deliberately and unflinchingly. . . ." Great literature has always dealt not merely with those aspects of the human mind that are pleasant and conscious but with the total human psyche, many facets of which are both unpleasant and unconscious. The enduring appeal of Marvell's poem, like that of the other works we have examined, derives from this kind of artistic and honest confrontation.

H. Morality over the Pleasure Principle in "Everyday Use"

"I will wait for her in the yard that Maggie and I made so clean and wavy yesterday afternoon," the narrator tells us in the opening sentence of Alice Walker's story. The "her" refers, of course, to the prodigal daughter who is about to make her first visit home since her transformation from old-fashioned "Dee" into the newly liberated "Wangero Leewanika Kemanjo."

We are told in the second paragraph of the story that Maggie is "ashamed of the burn scars down her arms and legs" and—even more revealingly—that " 'no' is a word the world never learned to say to her" sister.

In the next two paragraphs the narrator reveals her recurrent dream of being featured along with Dee on a major TV talk show like Johnny Carson's: "On TV mother and child embrace and smile into each other's faces. Sometimes the mother and father weep, the child wraps them in her arms and leans across the table to tell how she would not have made it without their help."

Thus far, we may see two symbolic components of Freudian theory at work in Walker's story: the superego and the id. At this point Maggie is clearly associated with two basic characteristics of the superego: order (the clean, neat yard) and guilt (shame over her appearance in social situations). As the story progresses, we will see an even more important identification of Maggie with the superego—but before that see Dee's affinity with the Freudian id.

As we pointed out earlier in this chapter, the id knows no moral or social restraints, being driven solely by the pleasure principle. This is Dee: " 'no' is a word the world never learned to say to her." Moreover, her entire life has been governed by the pleasure principle: "Dee wanted nice things. A yellow organdy dress to wear to her graduation from high school; black pumps to match a green suit she'd made from an old suit somebody gave me. She was determined to stare down any disaster in her efforts. . . . Hesitation was no part of her nature." Still further, the id is not only amoral but totally self-centered and asocial: "Mama, when did Dee ever *have* any friends?" Maggie remarks.

And what is the mother's role in our Freudian reading of this fine little drama? Early in her TV fantasy, as she sees herself emerging from "a dark and soft-seated limousine" and being greeted by a famous "smiling, gray, sporty man like Johnny Carson" before an applauding audience, she is clearly associating herself with Dee's pleasure principle: "Then we are on the stage and Dee is embracing me with tears in her eyes." But the pleasurable vision begins to grow dim in the next sentence: "She pins on my dress a large orchid, even though she has told me once that she thinks orchids are tacky flowers."

And she wakes from her tinsel dream of glory in the next paragraph: "In real life I am a large big-boned woman with rough, man-working hands" that can brain a bull-calf with one blow of a sledgehammer. In the fantasy, like Dee she dazzles the audience with her "quick and witty tongue"; in real life, she is slow, deliberate, and inarticulate. But she is not dim-witted; she is, in fact, a very rational human being—associated with the reality principle. In brief, she is representative of the ego, caught momentarily in precarious tension between the pleasure principle and the morality principle.

Naturally attracted to her pleasure-driven daughter, the narrator eagerly anticipates Dee's arrival—despite Maggie's open aversion to the meeting ("'Come back here,' I say. And she stops and tries to dig a well in the sand with her toe"). But her bright expectancy fades at the first glimpse of Dee's unctuously phallic companion, Hakim-a-barber. Her morally perceptive younger daughter sees him at once for what he is: "I hear Maggie suck in her breath. 'Uhnnnh,' is what it sounds like. Like when you see the wriggling end of a snake just in front of your foot on the road."

And with the fading of her false pleasure-vision comes the

increasing clarity of Mrs. Johnson's moral vision. Dee (a.k.a. "Wangero") wants it all and, given her own way, will have it all: "'This churn top is what I need. . . . And I want the dasher, too.'" (She will "'think of something artistic to do with the dasher'"!) Finally, uninhibited by ethical restraint or consideration for others, she will have the quilts made by Grandma Dee and promised to Maggie for her marriage to John Thomas. Lacking the aggressive intensity of the id, once-burned and still-scarred Maggie would acquiesce to her sister's libidinous will. But the mother, no longer dazzled by her false pleasure-dome, now turning her full attention from Dee to Maggie, has another vision more real as well as more moral: "Just like when I'm in church and the spirit of God touches me and I get happy and shout. I did something I never had done before: hugged Maggie to me, then dragged her on into the room, snatched the quilts out of Miss Wangero's hands and dumped them into Maggie's lap. . . . 'Take one or two of the others,' I said to Dee." For once, at least in Walker's well-wrought morality play, sweet reasonableness has prevailed over rampant self-interest—or, as a Freudian critic might put it, "Ego, bolstered by superego, has regulated the id."

▪ III. OTHER POSSIBILITIES AND LIMITATIONS OF THE PSYCHOLOGICAL APPROACH

This brings us to a final recapitulation and a few words of defense as well as of caution about the Freudian approach. First, in defense: incredibly farfetched as some psychoanalytic interpretations seem to many readers, such interpretations, handled by qualified critics, are not unsubstantiated in fact; they are based upon psychological insights often derived from and supported by actual case histories, and they are set forth in such works as those of Ernest Jones and Marie Bonaparte with remarkable cogency. They are—if we accept the basic premises of psychoanalysis—very difficult to refute. Furthermore, regardless of their factual validity, such theories have had a tremendous impact upon modern writing (in the works of such creative artists as James Joyce, Eugene O'Neill, Tennessee Williams, and Philip Roth, to mention only a few) and upon modern literary criticism (for example, in the essays of such major and diverse critics as Edmund Wilson, Lionel Trilling, F. L. Lucas, Frederick Hoffman, Sandra Gilbert, Hélène Cixous, and Julia Kristeva). It is therefore important that the serious student of literature be acquainted with psychoanalytic theory.

The danger is that the serious student may become theory-ridden, forgetting that Freud's is not the only approach to literary analysis. To see a great work of fiction or a great poem primarily as a psychological case study is often to miss its wider significance and perhaps even the essential aesthetic experience it should provide. A number of great works, despite the claims of the more zealous Freudians and post-Freudians, do not lend themselves readily, if at all, to the psychoanalytic approach, and even those that do cannot be studied exclusively from the psychological perspective. Literary interpretation and psychoanalysis are two distinct fields, and though they may be closely associated, they can in no sense be regarded as parts of one discipline. The literary critic who views the masterpiece solely through the lens of Freud is liable to see art through a glass darkly. However, those readers who reject psychoanalysis as neurotic nonsense deprive themselves of a valuable tool in understanding not only literature but human nature and their individual selves as well.

Quick Reference

Bonaparte, Marie. *The Life and Works of Edgar Allan Poe: A Psycho-Analytic Interpretation.* London: Imago, 1949.

Cox, James M. "Remarks on the Sad Initiation of Huckleberry Finn." *Sewanee Review* 62 (1954): 389–405.

Cranfill, Thomas M., and Robert L. Clark, Jr. *An Anatomy of "The Turn of the Screw."* Austin: University of Texas Press, 1965.

Freud, Sigmund. "The Anatomy of the Mental Personality." *New Introductory Lectures on Psychoanalysis.* New York: Norton, 1964.

————. *The Ego and the Id.* New York: Norton, 1962.

Fromm, Erich. *The Forgotten Language.* New York: Grove, 1957.

Holland, Norman N. *The Shakespearean Imagination.* Bloomington: Indiana University Press, 1968.

Jones, Ernest. *Hamlet and Oedipus.* Garden City, NY: Doubleday (Anchor), 1949.

Kenton, Edna. "Henry James to the Ruminant Reader: The Turn of the Screw." *The Arts* 6 (1924): 245–55.

Lesser, Simon O. *Fiction and the Unconscious.* Boston: Beacon Press, 1957.

Morrison, Claudia C. *Freud and the Critic.* Chapel Hill: University of North Carolina Press, 1968.

Murray, Henry A. "In Nomine Diaboli." *New England Quarterly* 24 (1951): 435–52.

Shumaker, Wayne. *Literature and the Irrational.* Englewood Cliffs, NJ: Prentice-Hall, 1960.

Wilson, Edmund. "The Ambiguity of Henry James." *Hound and Horn* 7 (1934): 385–406. Revised for *The Triple Thinkers.* New York: Oxford University Press, 1948.

Young, Phillip. *Ernest Hemingway.* NewYork: Holt, 1952.

⬛ 5 ⬛

Mythological and Archetypal Approaches

⬛ I. DEFINITIONS AND MISCONCEPTIONS

In *The Masks of God,* Joseph Campbell recounts a curious phenomenon of animal behavior. Newly hatched chickens, bits of eggshells still clinging to their tails, will dart for cover when a hawk flies overhead; yet they remain unaffected by other birds. Furthermore, a wooden model of a hawk, drawn forward along a wire above their coop, will send them scurrying (if the model is pulled backward, however, there is no response). "Whence," Campbell asks, "this abrupt seizure by an image to which there is no counterpart in the chicken's world? Living gulls and ducks, herons and pigeons, leave it cold; but *the work of art strikes some very deep chord!*" (31; our italics).

Campbell's hinted analogy, though only roughly approximate, will serve nonetheless as an instructive introduction to the mythological approach to literature. For it is with the relationship of literary art to "some very deep chord" in human nature that mythological criticism deals. The myth critic is concerned to seek out those mysterious elements that inform certain literary works and that elicit, with almost uncanny force, dramatic and universal human reactions. The myth critic wishes to discover how certain works of literature, usually those that have become, or promise to become, "classics," image a kind of reality to which readers give perennial response—while other works, seemingly as well constructed, and even some forms of reality, leave them cold. Speaking figuratively, the myth critic studies in depth the "wooden hawks" of great literature: the so-called archetypes or archetypal patterns that the writer has drawn forward along the tensed structural wires of his or her masterpiece and that vibrate in such a way that a sympathetic resonance is set off deep within the reader.

An obviously close connection exists between mythological criticism and the psychological approach discussed in chapter 4: both are concerned with the motives that underlie human behavior. Between the two approaches are differences of degree and of affinities. Psychology tends to be experimental and diagnostic; it is closely related to biological science. Mythology tends to be speculative and philosophical; its affinities are with religion, anthropology, and cultural history. Such generalizations, of course, risk oversimplification; for instance, a great psychologist like Sigmund Freud ranged far beyond experimental and clinical study into the realms of myth, and his distinguished sometime protégé, Carl Gustav Jung, became one of the foremost mythologists of our time. Even so, the two approaches are distinct, and mythology is wider in its scope than psychology. For example, what psychoanalysis attempts to disclose about the individual personality, the study of myths reveals about the mind and character of a people. And just as dreams reflect the unconscious desires and anxieties of the individual, so myths are the symbolic projections of a people's hopes, values, fears, and aspirations.

According to the common misconception and misuse of the term, myths are merely primitive fictions, illusions, or opinions based upon false reasoning. Actually, mythology encompasses more than grade school stories about the Greek and Roman deities or clever fables invented for the amusement of children (or the harassment of students in college literature courses). It may be true that myths do not meet our current standards of factual reality, but then neither does any great literature. Instead, they both reflect a more profound reality. As Mark Schorer says in *William Blake: The Politics of Vision*, "Myth is fundamental, the dramatic representation of our deepest instinctual life, of a primary awareness of man in the universe, capable of many configurations, upon which all particular opinions and attitudes depend" (29). According to Alan W. Watts, "Myth is to be defined as a complex of stories—some no doubt fact, and some fantasy—which, for various reasons, human beings regard as demonstrations of the inner meaning of the universe and of human life" (7).

Myths are by nature collective and communal; they bind a tribe or a nation together in common psychological and spiritual activities. In *The Language of Poetry*, edited by Allen Tate, Philip Wheelwright explains, "Myth is the expression of a profound sense of togetherness of feeling and of action and of wholeness of living" (11). Moreover, like Melville's famous white whale (itself an archetypal image), myth is ubiquitous in time as well as place. It is a dynamic factor everywhere in human society; it transcends time, uniting the past (traditional modes of belief) with the present (current values) and reaching toward the future (spiritual and cultural aspirations).

▪ II. SOME EXAMPLES OF ARCHETYPES

Having established the significance of myth, we need to examine its relationship to archetypes and archetypal patterns. Although every people has its own distinctive mythology that may be reflected in legend, folklore, and ideology—although, in other words, myths take their specific shapes from the cultural environments in which they grow—myth is, in the general sense, universal. Furthermore, similar motifs or themes may be found among many different mythologies, and certain images that recur in the myths of peoples widely separated in time and place tend to have a common meaning or, more accurately, tend to elicit comparable psychological responses and to serve similar cultural functions. Such motifs and images are called *archetypes*. Stated simply, archetypes are universal symbols. As Philip Wheelwright explains in *Metaphor and Reality*, such symbols are

> those which carry the same or very similar meanings for a large portion, if not all, of mankind. It is a discoverable fact that certain symbols, such as the sky father and earth mother, light, blood, up-down, the axis of a wheel, and others, recur again and again in cultures so remote from one another in space and

time that there is no likelihood of any historical influence and causal connection among them. (111)

Examples of these archetypes and the symbolic meanings with which they tend to be widely associated follow (it should be noted that these meanings may vary significantly from one context to another):

A. Images

1. Water: the mystery of creation; birth-death-resurrection; purification and redemption; fertility and growth.
   According to Jung, water is also the commonest symbol for the unconscious.
   a. The sea: the mother of all life; spiritual mystery and infinity; death and rebirth; timelessness and eternity; the unconscious.
   b. Rivers: death and rebirth (baptism); the flowing of time into eternity; transitional phases of the life cycle; incarnations of deities.

2. Sun (fire and sky are closely related): creative energy; law in nature; consciousness (thinking, enlightenment, wisdom, spiritual vision); father principle (moon and earth tend to be associated with female or mother principle); passage of time and life.
   a. Rising sun: birth; creation; enlightenment.
   b. Setting sun: death.

3. Colors
   a. Red: blood, sacrifice, violent passion; disorder.
   b. Green: growth; sensation; hope; fertility; in negative context may be associated with death and decay.
   c. Blue: usually highly positive, associated with truth, religious feeling, security, spiritual purity (the color of the Great Mother or Holy Mother).
   d. Black (darkness): chaos, mystery, the unknown; death; primal wisdom; the unconscious; evil; melancholy.
   e. White: highly multivalent, signifying, in its positive aspects, light, purity, innocence, and timelessness; in its negative aspects, death, terror, the supernatural, and the

blinding truth of an inscrutable cosmic mystery (see, for instance, Herman Melville's chapter "The Whiteness of the Whale" in *Moby-Dick*).

4. Circle (sphere): wholeness, unity.

    a. Mandala (a geometric figure based upon the squaring of a circle around a unifying center; see the accompanying illustration of the classic Shri-Yantra mandala): the desire for spiritual unity and psychic integration. Note that in its classic Asian forms the mandala juxtaposes the triangle, the square, and the circle with their numerical equivalents of three, four, and seven.

    b. Egg (oval): the mystery of life and the forces of generation.

    c. Yang-yin: a Chinese symbol (below) representing the union of the opposite forces of the yang (masculine principle, light, activity, the conscious mind) and the yin (female principle, darkness, passivity, the unconscious).

d. Ouroboros: the ancient symbol of the snake biting its own tail, signifying the eternal cycle of life, primordial unconsciousness, the unity of opposing forces (cf. yang-yin).

5. Serpent (snake, worm): symbol of energy and pure force (cf. libido); evil, corruption, sensuality; destruction; mystery; wisdom; the unconscious.

6. Numbers:
   a. Three: light; spiritual awareness and unity (cf. the Holy Trinity); the male principle.
   b. Four: associated with the circle, life cycle, four seasons; female principle, earth, nature; four elements (earth, air, fire, water)
   c. Seven: the most potent of all symbolic numbers—signifying the union of *three* and *four,* the completion of a cycle, perfect order.

7. The archetypal woman (Great Mother—the mysteries of life, death, transformation):
   a. The Good Mother (positive aspects of the Earth Mother): associated with the life principle, birth, warmth, nourishment, protection, fertility, growth, abundance (for example, Demeter, Ceres).
   b. The Terrible Mother (including the negative aspects of the Earth Mother): the witch, sorceress, siren, whore, femme fatale—associated with sensuality, sexual orgies, fear, danger, darkness, dismemberment, emasculation, death; the unconscious in its terrifying aspects.
   c. The Soul Mate: the Sophia figure, Holy Mother, the princess or "beautiful lady"—incarnation of inspiration and spiritual fulfillment (cf. the Jungian anima).

8. The Wise Old Man (savior, redeemer, guru): personification of the spiritual principle, representing "knowledge, reflection, insight, wisdom, cleverness, and intuition on the one hand, and on the other, moral qualities such as goodwill and readiness to help, which make his 'spiritual' character sufficiently plain. . . . Apart from his cleverness, wisdom, and insight, the old man . . . is also notable for his moral qualities; what is more, he even tests the moral qualities of others and makes gifts dependent on

this test. . . . The old man always appears when the hero is in a hopeless and desperate situation from which only profound reflection or a lucky idea . . . can extricate him. But since, for internal and external reasons, the hero cannot accomplish this himself, the knowledge needed to compensate the deficiency comes in the form of a personified thought, i.e., in the shape of this sagacious and helpful old man" (Jung, *The Archetypes and the Collective Unconscious* 217ff.).

9. The Trickster (joker, jester, clown, fool, fraud, prankster, picaro [rogue], poltergeist, confidence man ["con man"], medicine man [shaman], magician [sleight-of-hand artist], "Spirit Mercurius" [shape-shifter], *simia dei* ["the ape of God"], witch: The trickster appears to be the opposite of the wise old man because of his close affinity with the shadow archetype (for "shadow," see III. B.1 below); however, we should mention that he has a positive side and may even serve a healing function through his transformative influence. Jung remarks that "He is a forerunner of the saviour, and, like him, God, man, and animal at once. He is both subhuman and superhuman, a bestial and divine being . . . " (*Archetypes* 263). Jane Wheelwright's definition is particularly instructive: "Image of the archetype of mischievousness, unexpectedness, disorder, amorality, the trickster is an archetypal shadow figure that represents a primordial, dawning consciousness. Compensating for rigid or overly righteous collective attitudes, it functions collectively as a cathartic safety valve for pent-up social pressures, a reminder of humankind's primitive origins and the fallibility of its institutions" (286). Jeanne Rosier Smith points out that myths, "as they appear in literature, can be read as part of an effort for human and cultural survival. The trickster's role as survivor and transformer, creating order from chaos, accounts for the figure's universal appeal and its centrality to the mythology and folklore of so many cultures" (3). While the trickster archetype has appeared in cultures throughout the world from time immemorial, he (or, in some cases, she) is particularly notable in African American and American In-

dian cultures (see our discussion of *Huckleberry Finn* in chapter 7).

10. Garden: paradise; innocence; unspoiled beauty (especially feminine); fertility.

11. Tree: "In its most general sense, the symbolism of the tree denotes life of the cosmos: its consistence, growth, proliferation, generative and regenerative processes. It stands for inexhaustible life, and is therefore equivalent to a symbol of immortality" (Cirlot 328; cf. the depiction of the cross of redemption as the tree of life in Christian iconography).

12. Desert: spiritual aridity; death; nihilism, hopelessness.

These examples are by no means exhaustive, but represent some of the more common archetypal images that the reader is likely to encounter in literature. The images we have listed do not necessarily function as archetypes every time they appear in a literary work. The discreet critic interprets them as such only if the total context of the work logically supports an archetypal reading.

B. Archetypal Motifs or Patterns

1. Creation: perhaps the most fundamental of all archetypal motifs—virtually every mythology is built on some account of how the cosmos, nature, and humankind were brought into existence by some supernatural Being or beings.

2. Immortality: another fundamental archetype, generally taking one of two basic narrative forms:
   a. Escape from time: "return to paradise," the state of perfect, timeless bliss enjoyed by man and woman before their tragic Fall into corruption and mortality.
   b. Mystical submersion into cyclical time: the theme of endless death and regeneration—human beings achieve a kind of immortality by submitting to the vast, mysterious rhythm of Nature's eternal cycle, particularly the cycle of the seasons.

3. Hero archetypes (archetypes of transformation and re-demption):

   a. The quest: the hero (savior, deliverer) undertakes some long journey during which he or she must perform impossible tasks, battle with monsters, solve unanswerable riddles, and overcome insurmountable obstacles in order to save the kingdom.

   b. Initiation: the hero undergoes a series of excruciating ordeals in passing from ignorance and immaturity to social and spiritual adulthood, that is, in achieving maturity and becoming a full-fledged member of his or her social group. The initiation most commonly consists of three distinct phases: (1) separation, (2) transformation, and (3) return. Like the quest, this is a variation of the death-and-rebirth archetype.

   c. The sacrificial scapegoat: the hero, with whom the welfare of the tribe or nation is identified, must die to atone for the people's sins and restore the land to fruitfulness.

C. Archetypes as Genres

Finally, in addition to appearing as images and motifs, archetypes may be found in even more complex combinations as genres or types of literature that conform with the major phases of the seasonal cycle. Northrop Frye, in his *Anatomy of Criticism*, indicates the correspondent genres for the four seasons as follows:

1. The mythos of spring: comedy

2. The mythos of summer: romance

3. The mythos of fall: tragedy

4. The mythos of winter: irony

With brilliant audacity Frye identifies myth with literature, asserting that myth is a "structural organizing principle of literary form" (341) and that an archetype is essentially an "element of one's literary experience" (365). And in *The Stubborn Structure* he claims that "mythology as a whole provides a kind of diagram or blueprint of what literature as a whole is all about, an imaginative survey of the human situation from the beginning to the end, from the height to the depth, of what is imaginatively conceivable" (102).

▪ III. MYTH CRITICISM IN PRACTICE

Frye's contribution leads us directly into the mythological approach to literary analysis. As our discussion of mythology has shown, the task of the myth critic is a special one. Unlike the traditional critic, who relies heavily on history and the biography of the writer, the myth critic is interested more in prehistory and the biographies of the gods. Unlike the formalistic critic, who concentrates on the shape and symmetry of the work itself, the myth critic probes for the inner spirit which gives that form its vitality and its enduring appeal. And, unlike the Freudian critic, who is prone to look on the artifact as the product of some sexual neurosis, the myth critic sees the work holistically, as the manifestation of vitalizing, integrative forces arising from the depths of humankind's collective psyche.

Despite the special importance of the myth critic's contribution, this approach is, for several reasons, poorly understood. In the first place, only during the twentieth century did the proper interpretive tools become available through the development of such disciplines as anthropology, psychology, and cultural history. Second, many scholars and teachers of literature have remained skeptical of myth criticism because of its tendencies toward the cultic and the occult. Finally, there has been a discouraging confusion over concepts and definitions among the myth initiates themselves, which has caused many would-be myth critics to turn their energies to more clearly defined approaches such as the traditional or formalistic. In carefully picking our way through this maze, we can discover at least three separate though not necessarily exclusive disciplines, each of which has figured prominently in the development of myth criticism. In the following pages we examine these in roughly chronological order, noting how each may be applied to critical analysis.

A. Anthropology and Its Uses

The rapid advancement of modern anthropology since the end of the nineteenth century has been the most important single influence on the growth of myth criticism. Shortly after the turn of the century this influence was revealed in a series of important studies published by the Cambridge Hellenists, a group of British scholars who applied recent anthropological discoveries to the understanding of Greek classics in terms of mythic and ritualistic origins. Noteworthy contributions by members of this group include *Anthropology and the Classics*, a symposium edited by R. R. Marett; Jane Harrison's *Themis*; Gilbert Murray's *Euripides and His Age*; and F. M. Cornford's *Origin of Attic Comedy*. But by far the most significant member of the British school was Sir James G. Frazer, whose monumental *The Golden Bough* has exerted an enormous influence on twentieth-century literature, not merely on the critics but also on such creative writers as James Joyce, Thomas Mann, and T. S. Eliot. Frazer's work, a comparative study of the primitive origins of religion in magic, ritual, and myth, was first published in two volumes in 1890, later expanded to twelve volumes, and then published in a one-volume abridged edition in 1922. Frazer's main contribution was to demonstrate the "essential similarity of man's chief wants everywhere and at all times," particularly as these wants were reflected throughout ancient mythologies. He explains, for example, in the abridged edition, that

> [u]nder the names of Osiris, Tammuz, Adonis, and Attis, the peoples of Egypt and Western Asia represented the yearly decay and revival of life, especially vegetable life, which they personified as a god who annually died and rose again from the dead. In name and detail the rites varied from place to place: in substance they were the same. (325)

The central motif with which Frazer deals is the archetype of crucifixion and resurrection, specifically the myths describing the "killing of the divine king." Among many primitive peoples it was believed that the ruler was a divine or semidivine being whose life was identified with the life cycle in nature and in human existence. Because of this identification, the safety of the people and even of the world was felt to depend upon the life of the god-king. A vigorous, healthy ruler would ensure natural and human productivity; on the other hand, a sick or maimed king would bring blight and disease to the land and its people. Frazer points out that if

the course of nature is dependent on the man-god's life, what catastrophes may not be expected from the gradual enfeeblement of his powers and their final extinction in death? There is only one way of averting these dangers. The man-god must be killed as soon as he shows symptoms that his powers are beginning to fail, and his soul must be transferred to a vigorous successor before it has been seriously impaired by threatened decay. (265)

Among some peoples the kings were put to death at regular intervals to ensure the welfare of the tribe; later, however, substitute figures were killed in place of the kings themselves, or the sacrifices became purely symbolic rather than literal.

Corollary to the rite of sacrifice was the scapegoat archetype. This motif centered in the belief that, by transferring the corruptions of the tribe to a sacred animal or person, then by killing (and in some instances eating) this scapegoat, the tribe could achieve the cleansing and atonement thought necessary for natural and spiritual rebirth. Pointing out that food and children are the primary needs for human survival, Frazer emphasizes that the rites of blood sacrifice and purification were considered by ancient peoples as a magical guarantee of rejuvenation, an assurance of life, both vegetable and human. If such customs strike us as incredibly primitive, we need only to recognize their vestiges in our own civilized world—for example, the irrational satisfaction that some people gain by the persecution of such minority groups as blacks and Jews as scapegoats, or the more wholesome feelings of renewal derived from our New Year's festivities and resolutions, the homely tradition of spring-cleaning, our celebration of Easter and even the Eucharist. Modern writers themselves have employed the scapegoat motif with striking relevance—for example, Shirley Jackson's "The Lottery."

The insights of Frazer and the Cambridge Hellenists have

been extremely helpful in myth criticism, especially in the mythological approach to drama. Many scholars theorize that tragedy originated from the primitive rites we have described. The tragedies of Sophocles and Aeschylus, for example, were written to be played during the festival of Dionysos, annual vegetation ceremonies during which the ancient Greeks celebrated the deaths of the winter-kings and the rebirths of the gods of spring and renewed life.

Sophocles's *Oedipus* is an excellent example of the fusion of myth and literature. Sophocles produced a great play, but the plot of *Oedipus* was not his invention. It was a well-known mythic narrative long before he immortalized it as tragic drama. Both the myth and the play contain a number of familiar archetypes, as a brief summary of the plot indicates. The king and queen of ancient Thebes, Laius and Jocasta, are told in a prophecy that their newborn son, after he has grown up, will murder his father and marry his mother. To prevent this catastrophe, the king orders one of his men to pierce the infant's heels and abandon him to die in the wilderness. But the child is saved by a shepherd and taken to Corinth, where he is reared as the son of King Polybus and Queen Merope, who lead the boy to believe that they are his real parents. After reaching maturity and hearing of a prophecy that he is destined to commit patricide and incest, Oedipus flees from Corinth to Thebes. On his journey he meets an old man and his servants, quarrels with them and kills them. Before entering Thebes he encounters the Sphinx (who holds the city under a spell), solves her riddle, and frees the city; his reward is the hand of the widowed Queen Jocasta. He then rules a prosperous Thebes for many years, fathering four children by Jocasta. At last, however, a blight falls upon his kingdom because Laius's slayer has gone unpunished. Oedipus starts an intensive investigation to find the culprit—only to discover ultimately that he himself is the guilty one, that the old man whom he had killed on his journey to Thebes was Laius, his real father. Overwhelmed by this revelation, Oedipus blinds himself with brooches taken from his dead mother-wife, who has hanged herself, and goes into exile. Following his sacrificial punishment, Thebes is restored to health and abundance.

Even in this bare summary we may discern at least two archetypal motifs: (1) In the quest motif, Oedipus, as the hero, undertakes a journey during which he encounters the Sphinx, a supernatural monster with the body of a lion and the head of a woman; by answering her riddle, he delivers the kingdom and marries the queen. (2) In the king-as-sacrificial-scapegoat motif, the welfare of the state, both human and natural (Thebes is stricken by both plague and drought), is bound up with the personal fate of the ruler; only after Oedipus has offered himself up as a scapegoat is the land redeemed.

Considering that Sophocles wrote his tragedy expressly for a ritual occasion, we are hardly surprised that *Oedipus* reflects certain facets of the fertility myths described by Frazer. More remarkable, and more instructive for the student interested in myth criticism, is the revelation of similar facets in the great tragedy written by Shakespeare two thousand years later.

1. The Sacrificial Hero: Hamlet

One of the first modern scholars to point out these similarities was Gilbert Murray. In his "Hamlet and Orestes," delivered as a lecture in 1914 and subsequently published in *The Classical Tradition in Poetry*, Murray indicated a number of parallels between the mythic elements of Shakespeare's play and those in *Oedipus* and in the *Agamemnon* of Aeschylus. The heroes of all three works derive from the *Golden Bough* kings; they are all haunted, sacrificial figures. Furthermore, as with the Greek tragedies, the story of Hamlet was not the playwright's invention but was drawn from legend. As literary historians tell us, the old Scandinavian story of Amlehtus or Amlet, Prince of Jutland, was recorded as early as the twelfth century by Saxo Grammaticus in his *History of the Danes*. Murray cites an even earlier passing reference to the prototypal Hamlet in a Scandinavian poem composed in about A.D. 980. Giorgio de Santillana and Hertha von Dechend in *Hamlet's Mill* have traced this archetypal character back through the legendary Icelandic Amlodhi to Oriental mythology. It is therefore evident that the core of Shakespeare's play is mythic. In Murray's words,

> The things that thrill and amaze us in *Hamlet* . . . are not any historical particulars about mediaeval Elsinore . . . but things belonging to the old stories and the old magic rites, which

stirred and thrilled our forefathers five and six thousand years ago; set them dancing all night on the hills, tearing beasts and men in pieces, and giving up their own bodies to a ghastly death, in hope thereby to keep the green world from dying and to be the saviours of their own people. (236)

By the time Sophocles and Aeschylus were producing their tragedies for Athenian audiences, such sacrifices were no longer performed literally but were acted out symbolically on stage; yet their mythic significance was the same. Indeed, their significance was very similar in the case of Shakespeare's audiences. The Elizabethans were a myth-minded and symbol-receptive people. There was no need for Shakespeare to interpret for his audience: they *felt* the mythic content of his plays. And though myth may smolder only feebly in the present-day audience, we still respond, despite our intellectual sophistication, to the archetypes in *Hamlet*.

Such critics as Murray and Francis Fergusson have provided clues to many of Hamlet's archetypal mysteries. In *The Idea of Theater*, Fergusson discloses point by point how the scenes in Shakespeare's play follow the same ritual pattern as those in Greek tragedy, specifically in *Oedipus*; he indicates that

in both plays a royal sufferer is associated with pollution, in its very sources, of an entire social order. Both plays open with an invocation for the well-being of the endangered body politic. In both, the destiny of the individual and of society are closely intertwined; and in both the suffering of the royal victim seems to be necessary before purgation and renewal can be achieved. (118)

To appreciate how closely the moral norms in Shakespeare's play are related to those of ancient vegetation myths, we need only to note how often images of disease and corruption are used to symbolize the evil that has blighted Hamlet's Denmark. The following statement from Philip Wheelwright's *The Burning Fountain*, explaining the organic source of good and evil, is directly relevant to the moral vision in *Hamlet*, particularly to the implications of Claudius's crime and its disastrous consequences. From the natural or organic standpoint,

Good is life, vitality, propagation, health; evil is death, impotence, disease. Of these several terms *health* and *disease* are the most important and comprehensive. Death is but an interim evil; it occurs periodically, but there is the assurance of new life ever springing up to take its place. The normal cycle of life and death is a healthy cycle, and the purpose of the major seasonal festivals (for example, the Festival of Dionysos) was at least as much to celebrate joyfully the turning wheel of great creative Nature as to achieve magical effects. Disease and blight, however, interrupt the cycle; they are the real destroyers; and health is the good most highly to be prized. (197)

Wheelwright continues by pointing out that because murder (not to be confused with ritual sacrifice) does violence to both the natural cycle of life and the social organism, the murderer is symbolically diseased. Furthermore, when the victim is a member of the murderer's own family, an even more compact organism than the tribe or the political state, the disease is especially virulent.

We should mention one other myth that relates closely to the meaning of *Hamlet,* the myth of divine appointment. This was the belief, strongly fostered by such Tudor monarchs as Henry VII, Henry VIII, and Elizabeth I, that not only had the Tudors been divinely appointed to bring order and happiness out of civil strife but also any attempt to break this divine ordinance (for example, by insurrection or assassination) would result in social, political, and natural chaos. We see this Tudor myth reflected in several of Shakespeare's plays (for example, in *Richard III, Macbeth,* and *King Lear*) where interference with the order of divine succession or appointment results in both political and natural chaos, and where a deformed, corrupt, or weak monarch epitomizes a diseased political state. This national myth is, quite obviously, central in *Hamlet.*

The relevance of myth to *Hamlet* should now be apparent. The play's thematic heart is the ancient, archetypal mystery of the life cycle itself. Its pulse is the same tragic rhythm that moved Sophocles's audience at the festival of Dionysos and moves us today through forces that transcend our conscious processes. Through the insights provided us by anthropological scholars, however, we may perceive the essential archetypal pattern of Shakespeare's tragedy. Hamlet's Denmark is a diseased and rotten state because Claudius's "foul and most unnatural murder" of his king-brother has subverted the divinely ordained laws of nature and of kingly succession. The disruption is intensified by the blood kinship between victim and murderer. Claudius, whom the ghost identifies as "The Serpent," bears the primal blood curse of Cain. And because the state is identified with its ruler, Denmark shares and suffers also from his blood guilt. Its natural cycle interrupted, the nation is threatened by chaos: civil strife within and war without. As Hamlet exclaims, "The time is out of joint; O cursed spite,/That ever I was born to set it right!"

Hamlet's role in the drama is that of the prince-hero who, to deliver his nation from the blight that has fallen upon it, must not only avenge his father's murder but also offer himself up as a royal scapegoat. As a member of the royal family, Hamlet is infected with the regicidal virus even though he is personally innocent. We might say, using another metaphor from pathology, that Claudius's murderous cancer has metastasized so that the royal court and even the nation itself is threatened with fatal deterioration. Hamlet's task is to seek out the source of this malady and to eliminate it. Only after a thorough purgation can Denmark be restored to a state of wholesome balance. Hamlet's reluctance to accept the role of cathartic agent is a principal reason for his procrastination in killing Claudius, an act that may well involve his self-destruction. He is a reluctant but dutiful scapegoat, and he realizes ultimately that there can be no substitute victim in this sacrificial rite—hence his decision to accept Laertes's challenge to a dueling match that he suspects has been fixed by Claudius. The bloody climax of the tragedy is therefore not merely spectacular melodrama but an essential element in the archetypal pattern of sacrifice-atonement-catharsis. Not only must all those die who have been infected by the evil contagion (Claudius, Gertrude, Polonius, Rosencrantz and Guildenstern—even Ophelia and Laertes), but the prince-hero himself must suffer "crucifixion" before Denmark can be purged and reborn under the healthy new regime of Fortinbras.

Enhancing the motif of the sacrificial scapegoat is Hamlet's long and difficult spiritual journey—his initiation, as it were—

from innocent, carefree youth (he has been a university student) through a series of painful ordeals to sadder, but wiser, maturity. His is a long night's journey of the soul, and Shakespeare employs archetypal imagery to convey this thematic motif: *Hamlet* is an autumnal, nighttime play dominated by images of darkness and blood, and the hero appropriately wears black, the archetypal color of melancholy. The superficial object of his dark quest is to solve the riddle of his father's death. On a deeper level, his quest leads him down the labyrinthine ways of the human mystery, the mystery of human life and destiny. (Observe how consistently his soliloquies turn toward the puzzles of life and of self.) As with the riddle of the Sphinx, the enigmatic answer is "man," the clue to which is given in Polonius's glib admonition, "To thine own self be true." In this sense, then, Hamlet's quest is the quest undertaken by all of us who would gain that rare and elusive philosopher's stone, self-knowledge.

2. Archetypes of Time and Immortality: "To His Coy Mistress"

Even though the mythological approach lends itself more readily to the interpretation of drama and the novel than to shorter literary forms such as the lyric poem, it is not uncommon to find elements of myth in these shorter works. In fact, mythopoeic poets like William Blake, William Butler Yeats, and T. S. Eliot carefully structured many of their works on myth. Even those poets who are not self-appointed mythmakers often employ images and motifs that, intentionally or not, function as archetypes. Andrew Marvell's "To His Coy Mistress" seems to fit into this latter category.

Because of its strongly suggestive (and suggested) sensuality and its apparently cynical theme, "To His Coy Mistress" is sometimes dismissed as an immature if not immoral love poem. But to see the poem as little more than a clever proposition is to miss its greatness. No literary work survives because it is merely clever, or merely well written. It must partake somehow of the universal and, in doing so, may contain elements of the archetypal. Let us examine "To His Coy Mistress" with an eye to its archetypal content.

Superficially a love poem, "To His Coy Mistress" is, in a

deeper sense, a poem about time. As such, it is concerned with immortality, a fundamental motif in myth. In the first two stanzas we encounter an inversion or rejection of traditional conceptions of human immortality. Stanza 1 is an ironic presentation of the "escape from time" to some paradisal state in which lovers may dally for an eternity. But such a state of perfect, eternal bliss is a foolish delusion, as the speaker suggests in his subjunctive "Had we . . ." and in his description of love as some kind of monstrous vegetable growing slowly to an infinite size in the archetypal garden. Stanza 2 presents, in dramatic contrast, the desert archetype in terms of another kind of time, naturalistic time. This is the time governed by the inexorable laws of nature (note the sun archetype imaged in "Time's winged chariot"), the laws of decay, death, and physical extinction. Stanza 2 is as extreme in its philosophical realism as the first stanza is in its impracticable idealization.

The concluding stanza, radically altered in tone, presents a third kind of time, an escape into cyclical time and thereby a chance for immortality. Again we encounter the sun archetype, but this is the sun of "soul" and of "instant fires"—images not of death but of life and creative energy, which are fused with the sphere ("Let us roll all our strength and all/Our sweetness up into one ball"), the archetype of primal wholeness and fulfillment. In *Myth and Reality*, Mircea Eliade indicates that one of the most widespread motifs in immortality myths is the *regressus ad uterum* (a "return to the origin" of creation or to the symbolic womb of life) and that this return is considered to be symbolically feasible by some philosophers (for example, the Chinese Taoists) through alchemical fire:

> During the fusion of metals the Taoist alchemist tries to bring about in his own body the union of the two cosmological principles, Heaven and Earth, in order to reproduce the primordial chaotic situation that existed before the Creation. This primordial situation . . . corresponds both to the egg (that is, the archetypal sphere) or the embryo and to the paradisal and innocent state of the uncreated World. (83–84)

We are not suggesting that Marvell was familiar with Taoist philosophy or that he was consciously aware of immortality archetypes. However, in representing the age-old dilemma of time and immortality, Marvell employed a cluster of images charged with mythic significance. His poet-lover seems to offer the alchemy of love as a way of defeating the laws of naturalistic time; love is a means of participating in, even intensifying, the mysterious rhythms of nature's eternal cycle. If life is to be judged, as some philosophers have suggested, not by duration but by intensity, then Marvell's lovers, at least during the act of love, will achieve a kind of immortality by "devouring" time or by transcending the laws of clock time ("Time's winged chariot"). And if this alchemical transmutation requires a fire hot enough to melt them into one primordial ball, then it is perhaps also hot enough to melt the sun itself and "make him run." Thus we see that the overt sexuality of Marvell's poem is, in a mythic sense, suggestive of a profound metaphysical insight, an insight that continues to fascinate those philosophers and scientists who would penetrate the mysteries of time and eternity.

B. Jungian Psychology and Its Archetypal Insights

The second major influence on mythological criticism is the work of C. G. Jung, the great psychologist-philosopher and onetime student of Freud who broke with the master because of what he regarded as a too-narrow approach to psychoanalysis. Jung believed libido (psychic energy) to be more than sexual; also, he considered Freudian theories too negative because of Freud's emphasis on the neurotic rather than the healthy aspects of the psyche.

Jung's primary contribution to myth criticism is his theory of racial memory and archetypes. In developing this concept, Jung expanded Freud's theories of the personal unconscious, asserting that beneath this is a primeval, collective unconscious shared in the psychic inheritance of all members of the human family. As Jung himself explains in *The Structure and Dynamics of the Psyche*,

> If it were possible to personify the unconscious, we might think of it as a collective human being combining the characteristics of both sexes, transcending youth and age, birth and death,

and, from having at its command a human experience of one or two million years, practically immortal. If such a being existed, it would be exalted over all temporal change; the present would mean neither more nor less to it than any year in the hundredth millennium before Christ; it would be a dreamer of age-old dreams and, owing to its immeasurable experience, an incomparable prognosticator. It would have lived countless times over again the life of the individual, the family, the tribe, and the nation, and it would possess a living sense of the rhythm of growth, flowering, and decay. (349–50)

Just as certain instincts are inherited by the lower animals (for example, the instinct of the baby chicken to run from a hawk's shadow), so more complex psychic predispositions are inherited by human beings. Jung believed, contrary to eighteenth-century Lockean psychology, that "Mind is not born as a *tabula rasa* [a clean slate]. Like the body, it has its pre-established individual definiteness; namely, forms of behaviour. They become manifest in the ever-recurring patterns of psychic functioning" (*Psyche and Symbol* xv). Therefore what Jung called "myth-forming" structural elements are ever present in the unconscious psyche; he refers to the manifestations of these elements as "motifs," "primordial images," or "archetypes."

Jung was also careful to explain that archetypes are not inherited ideas or patterns of thought, but rather that they are predispositions to respond in similar ways to certain stimuli: "In reality they belong to the realm of activities of the instincts and in that sense they represent inherited forms of psychic behaviour" (xvi). In *Psychological Reflections*, he maintained that these psychic instincts "are older than historical man, . . . have been ingrained in him from earliest times, and, eternally living, outlasting all generations, still make up the groundwork of the human psyche. It is only possible to live the fullest life when we are in harmony with these symbols; wisdom is a return to them" (42).

In stressing that archetypes are actually "inherited forms," Jung also went further than most of the anthropologists, who tended to see these forms as social phenomena passed down from one generation to the next through various sacred rites rather than through the structure of the psyche itself. Furthermore, in *The Archetypes and the Collective Unconscious*, he theorized that myths do not derive from external factors such as the seasonal or solar cycle but are, in truth, the projections of innate psychic phenomena:

> All the mythologized processes of nature, such as summer and winter, the phases of the moon, the rainy seasons, and so forth, are in no sense allegories of these objective occurrences; rather they are symbolic expressions of the inner, unconscious drama of the psyche which becomes accessible to man's consciousness by way of projection—that is, mirrored in the events of nature. (6)

In other words, myths are the means by which archetypes, essentially unconscious forms, become manifest and articulate to the conscious mind. Jung indicated further that archetypes reveal themselves in the dreams of individuals, so that we might say that dreams are "personalized myths" and myths are "depersonalized dreams."

Jung detected an intimate relationship between dreams, myths, and art in that all three serve as media through which archetypes become accessible to consciousness. The great artist, as Jung observes in *Modern Man in Search of a Soul*, is a person who possesses the "primordial vision," a special sensitivity to archetypal patterns and a gift for speaking in primordial images that enable him or her to transmit experiences of the "inner world" through art. Considering the nature of the artist's raw materials, Jung suggests it is only logical that the artist "will resort to mythology in order to give his experience its most fitting expression." This is not to say that the artist gets materials secondhand: "The primordial experience is the source of his creativeness; it cannot be fathomed, and therefore requires mythological imagery to give it form" (164).

Although Jung himself wrote relatively little that could be called literary criticism, what he did write leaves no doubt that he believed literature, and art in general, to be a vital ingredient in human civilization. Most important, his theories have expanded the horizons of literary interpretation for those critics concerned to use the tools of the mythological approach and for psychological critics who have felt too tightly constricted by Freudian theory.

1. *Some Special Archetypes: Shadow, Persona, and Anima*

In *The Archetypes and the Collective Unconscious,* Jung discusses at length many of the archetypal patterns that we have already examined (for example, water, colors, rebirth). In this way, although his emphasis is psychological rather than anthropological, a good deal of his work overlaps that of Frazer and the others. But, as we have already indicated, Jung is not merely a derivative or secondary figure; he is a major influence in the growth of myth criticism. For one thing, he provided some of the favorite terminology now current among myth critics. The term "archetype" itself, though not coined by Jung, enjoys its present widespread usage among the myth critics primarily because of his influence. Also, like Freud, he was a pioneer whose brilliant flashes of insight have helped to light our way in exploring the darker recesses of the human mind.

One major contribution is Jung's theory of *individuation* as related to those archetypes designated as the *shadow,* the *persona,* and the *anima.* Individuation is a psychological growing up, the process of discovering those aspects of one's self that make one an individual different from other members of the species. It is essentially a process of recognition—that is, as one matures, the individual must consciously recognize the various aspects, unfavorable as well as favorable, of one's total self. This self-recognition requires extraordinary courage and honesty but is absolutely essential if one is to become a well-balanced individual. Jung theorizes that neuroses are the results of the person's failure to confront and accept some archetypal component of the unconscious. Instead of assimilating this unconscious element into their consciousness, neurotic individuals persist in projecting it upon some other person or object. In Jung's words, projection is an "unconscious, automatic process whereby a content that is unconscious to the subject transfers itself to an object, so that it seems to belong to that object. The projection ceases the moment it becomes conscious, that is to say when it is seen as belonging to the subject" (*Archetypes* 60). In layman's terms, the habit of projection is reflected in the attitude that "everybody is out of step but me" or "I'm the only honest person in the crowd." It is a commonplace that we can project our own unconscious faults and weaknesses on others much more easily than we can accept them as part of our own nature.

The shadow, the persona, and the anima are structural components of the psyche that human beings have inherited, just as the chicken has inherited his built-in response to the hawk. We encounter the symbolic projections of these archetypes throughout the myths and the literatures of humankind. In melodrama, such as the television or Hollywood western, the persona, the anima, and the shadow are projected respectively in the characters of the hero, the heroine, and the villain. The shadow is the darker side of our unconscious self, the inferior and less pleasing aspects of the personality, which we wish to suppress. "Taking it in its deepest sense," writes Jung in *Psychological Reflections*, "the shadow is the invisible saurian [reptilian] tail that man still drags behind him" (217). The most common variant of this archetype, when projected, is the Devil, who, in Jung's words, represents the "dangerous aspect of the unrecognized dark half of the personality" (*Two Essays* 94). In literature we see symbolic representations of this archetype in such figures as Shakespeare's Iago, Milton's Satan, Goethe's Mephistopheles, and Conrad's Kurtz.

The anima is perhaps the most complex of Jung's archetypes. It is the "soul-image," the spirit of a man's élan vital, his life force or vital energy. In the sense of "soul," says Jung, anima is the "living thing in man, that which lives of itself and causes life. . . . Were it not for the leaping and twinkling of the soul, man would rot away in his greatest passion, idleness" (*Archetypes* 26–27). Jung gives the anima a feminine designation in the male psyche, pointing out that the "anima-image is usually projected upon women" (in the female psyche this archetype is called the *animus*). In this sense, anima is the contrasexual part of a man's psyche, the image of the opposite sex that he carries in both his personal and his collective unconscious. As an old German proverb puts it, "Every man has his own Eve within him"—in other words, the human psyche is bisexual, though the psychological characteristics of the opposite sex in each of us are generally unconscious, revealing themselves only in dreams or in projections on someone in our environment. The phenomenon of love, especially love at first sight, may be explained at least in part by Jung's theory of the anima: we tend to be attracted to members of the opposite sex who mirror the characteristics of our own inner selves. In literature, Jung regards such figures as Helen of Troy, Dante's Beatrice, Milton's Eve, and H. Rider Haggard's She as personifications of the anima. Following his theory, we might say that any female figure who is invested with unusual significance or power is likely to be a symbol of the anima. (Examples for the animus come less readily to Jung; like Freud, he tended to describe features of the male psyche more than those of the female, even though both analysts' patients were nearly all women.) One other function of the anima is noteworthy here. The anima is a kind of mediator between the ego (the conscious will or thinking self) and the unconscious or inner world of the male individual. This function will be somewhat clearer if we compare the anima with the persona.

The persona is the obverse of the anima in that it mediates between our ego and the external world. Speaking metaphorically, let us say that the ego is a coin. The image on one side is the anima; on the other side, the persona. The persona is the actor's mask that we show to the world—it is our social personality, a personality that is sometimes quite different from our true self. Jung, in discussing this social mask, explains that, to achieve psychological maturity, the individual must have a flexible, viable persona that can be brought into harmonious relationship with the other components of his or her psychic makeup. He states, furthermore, that a persona that is too artificial or rigid results in such symptoms of neurotic disturbance as irritability and melancholy.

2. "Young Goodman Brown": A Failure of Individuation

The literary relevance of Jung's theory of shadow, anima, and persona may be seen in an analysis of Hawthorne's story "Young Goodman Brown." In the first place, Brown's persona is both false and inflexible. It is the social mask of a God-fearing, prayerful, self-righteous Puritan—the persona of a good man with all its pietistic connotations. Brown considers himself both the good Christian and the good husband married to a "blessed angel on earth." In truth, however, he is much less the good man than the bad boy. His behavior from start to finish is that of the adolescent male. His desertion of his wife, for example, is motivated by his juvenile compulsion to have one last fling as a moral Peeping Tom. His failure to recognize himself (and his own base motives) when he confronts Satan—his shadow—is merely another indication of his spiritual immaturity.

Just as his persona has proved inadequate in mediating between Brown's ego and the external world, so his anima fails in relating to his inner world. It is only fitting that his soul-image or anima should be named Faith. His trouble is that he sees Faith not as a true wifely companion but as a mother (Jung points out that, during childhood, anima is usually projected on the mother), as is revealed when he thinks that he will "cling to her skirts and follow her to heaven." In other words, if a young man's Faith has the qualities of the Good Mother, then he might expect to be occasionally indulged in his juvenile escapades. But mature faith, like marriage, is a covenant that binds both parties mutually to uphold its sacred vows. If one party breaks this covenant, as Goodman Brown does, he must face the unpleasant consequences: at worst, separation and divorce; at best, suspicion (perhaps Faith herself has been unfaithful), loss of harmony, trust, and peace of mind. It is the latter consequences that Brown has to face. Even then, he still behaves like a child. Instead of admitting to his error and working maturely for a reconciliation, he sulks.

In clinical terms, young Goodman Brown suffers from a failure of personality integration. He has been stunted in his psychological growth (individuation) because he is unable to confront his shadow, recognize it as a part of his own psyche, and assimilate it into his consciousness. He persists, instead, in projecting the shadow image: first, in the form of the Devil; then on the members of his community (Goody Cloyse, Deacon Gookin, and others); and, finally on Faith herself (his anima), so that ultimately, in his eyes, the whole world is one of shadow, or gloom. As Jung explains in *Psyche and Symbol*, the results of such projections are often disastrous for the individual:

> The effect of projection is to isolate the subject from his environment, since instead of a real relation to it there is now only an il-

lusory one. Projections change the world into the replica of one's own unknown face. . . . The resultant [malaise is in] turn explained by projection as the malevolence of the environment, and by means of this vicious circle the isolation is intensified. The more projections interpose themselves between the subject and the environment, the harder it becomes for the ego to see through its illusions. [Note Goodman Brown's inability to distinguish between reality and his illusory dream in the forest.]

It is often tragic to see how blatantly a man bungles his own life and the lives of others yet remains totally incapable of seeing how much the whole tragedy originates in himself, and how he continually feeds it and keeps it going. Not *consciously*, of course—for consciously he is engaged in bewailing and cursing a *faithless* [our italics] world that recedes further and further into the distance. Rather, it is an unconscious factor which spins the illusions that veil his world. And what is being spun is a cocoon, which in the end will completely envelop him. (9)

Jung could hardly have diagnosed Goodman Brown's malady more accurately had he been directing these comments squarely at Hawthorne's story. That he was generalizing adds impact to his theory as well as to Hawthorne's moral insight.

3. Syntheses of Jung and Anthropology

As we can see from our interpretation of "Young Goodman Brown," the application of Jungian theory to literary analysis is likely to be closer to the psychological than to the mythological approach. We should therefore realize that most of the myth critics who use Jung's insights also use the materials of anthropology. A classic example of this kind of mythological eclecticism is Maud Bodkin's *Archetypal Patterns in Poetry*, first published in 1934 and now recognized as the pioneer work of archetypal criticism. Bodkin acknowledges her debt to Gilbert Murray and the anthropological scholars, as well as to Jung. She then proceeds to trace several major archetypal patterns through the great literature of Western civilization (for example, rebirth in Coleridge's "Rime of the Ancient Mariner"; heaven-hell in Coleridge's "Kubla Khan," Dante's *Divine Comedy*, and Milton's *Paradise Lost*; the image of woman as reflected in Homer's Thetis, Euripides's Phaedra, and Milton's

Eve). The same kind of critical synthesis may be found in subsequent mythological studies like Northrop Frye's *Anatomy of Criticism*, in which literary criticism, with the support of insights provided by anthropology and Jungian psychology, promises to become a new "social science."

One of the best of these myth studies is James Baird's *Ishmael: A Study of the Symbolic Mode in Primitivism*. Baird's approach derives not only from Jung and the anthropologists but also from such philosophers as Susanne Langer and Mircea Eliade. Though he ranges far beyond the works of Herman Melville, Baird's primary objective is to find an archetypal key to the multilayered meanings of *Moby-Dick* (which, incidentally, Jung considered "the greatest American novel"). He finds this key in primitive mythology, specifically in the myths of Polynesia to which young Melville had been exposed during his two years of sea duty in the South Pacific. (Melville's early success as a writer was largely due to his notoriety as the man who had lived for a month among the cannibals of Taipi.) Melville's literary primitivism is authentic, unlike the sentimental primitivism of such writers as Rousseau, says Baird, because he had absorbed certain Asian archetypes or "life symbols" and then transformed these creatively into "autotypes" (that is, individualized personal symbols).

The most instructive illustration of this creative fusion of archetype and autotype is Moby-Dick, Melville's infamous white whale. Baird points out that, throughout Asian mythology, the "great fish" recurs as a symbol of divine creation and life; in Hinduism, for example, the whale is an avatar (divine incarnation) of Vishnu, the "Preserver contained in the all being of Brahma." (We might also note that Christ was associated with fish and fishermen in Christian tradition.) Furthermore, Baird explains that *whiteness* is the archetype of the all-encompassing, inscrutable deity, the "white sign of the God of all being who has borne such Oriental names as Bhagavat, Brahma—the God of endless contradiction." Melville combined these two archetypes, the great fish or whale and whiteness, in fashioning his own unique symbol (autotype), Moby-Dick. Baird's reading of this symbol is substantiated by Melville's remarks about the contrarieties of the color white (terror, mystery, purity) in his chapter "The Whiteness of the

Whale," as well as by the mysterious elusiveness and awesome power with which he invests Moby-Dick. Moby-Dick is therefore, in Baird's words, a "nonambiguous ambiguity." Ahab, the monster of intellect, destroys himself and his crew because he would "strike through the mask" in his insane compulsion to understand the eternal and unfathomable mystery of creation. Ishmael alone is saved because, through the wholesome influence of Queequeg, a Polynesian prince, he has acquired the primitive mode of accepting this divine mystery without question or hostility.

C. Myth Criticism and the American Dream: Huckleberry Finn as the American Adam

In addition to anthropology and Jungian psychology, a third influence has been prominent in myth criticism, especially in the interpretation of American literature. This influence derives not only from those already mentioned but also from a historical focus upon the informing myths of our culture. It is apparent in that cluster of indigenous myths called "the American Dream" and subsequently in an intensified effort by literary scholars to analyze those elements that constitute the peculiarly American character of our literature. The results of such analysis indicate that the major works produced by American writers possess a certain distinctiveness and this distinctiveness can largely be attributed to the influence, both positive and negative, of the American Dream.

The central facet of this myth cluster is the Myth of Edenic Possibilities, which reflects the hope of creating a second paradise, not in the next world and not outside time, but in the bright New World of the American continent. From the time of its settlement by Europeans, America was seen as a land of boundless opportunity, a place where human beings, after centuries of poverty, misery, and corruption, could have a second chance to actually fulfill their mythic yearnings for a return to paradise. As early as 1654 Captain Edward Johnson announced to the Old-World-weary people of England that America was "the place":

> All you the people of Christ that are here Oppressed, Imprisoned and scurrilously derided, gather yourselves together,

your Wifes and little ones, and answer to your several Names as you shall be shipped for His service, in the Westerne World, and more especially for planting the united Colonies of new England. . . . Know this is the place where the Lord will create a new Heaven, and a new Earth in new Churches, and a new Commonwealth together.

Fredric I. Carpenter, in *American Literature and the Dream*, points out that although the Edenic dream itself was "as old as the mind of man," the idea that "this is the place" was uniquely American:

Earlier versions had placed it in Eden or in Heaven, in Atlantis or in Utopia; but always in some country of the imagination. Then the discovery of the new world gave substance to the old myth, and suggested the realization of it on actual earth. America became "the place" where the religious prophecies of Isaiah and the Republican ideals of Plato [and even the mythic longings of primitive man, we might add] might be realized. (6)

The themes of moral regeneration and bright expectations, which derive from this Edenic myth, form a major thread in the fabric of American literature, from J. Hector St. John Crèvecoeur's *Letters from an American Farmer* through the works of Emerson, Thoreau, and Whitman to such modern writers as Hart Crane and Thomas Wolfe.

Closely related to the Myth of Edenic Possibilities is the concept of the American Adam, the mythic New World hero. In *The American Adam*, R. W. B. Lewis describes the type: "a radically new personality, the hero of the new adventure: an individual emancipated from history, happily bereft of ancestry, untouched and undefiled by the usual inheritances of family and race; an individual standing alone, self-reliant and self-propelling, ready to confront whatever awaited him with the aid of his own unique and inherent resources" (5). One of the early literary characterizations of this Adamic hero is James Fenimore Cooper's Natty Bumppo, the central figure of the Leatherstocking saga. With his moral purity and social innocence, Natty is an explicit version of Adam before the Fall. He is a child of the wilderness, forever in flight before the corrupting influences of civilization—and from the moral compromises of Eve (Cooper never allows his hero to marry). He is also, as we might guess, the literary great-grandfather of the Western hero. Like the hero of Owen Wister's *The Virginian* and Matt Dillon of television's "Gunsmoke," he is clean-living, straight-shooting, and celibate. In his civilized version, the American Adam is the central figure of another corollary myth of the American Dream: the dream of success. The hero in the dream of success is that popular figure epitomized in Horatio Alger's stories and subsequently treated in the novels of William Dean Howells, Jack London, Theodore Dreiser, and F. Scott Fitzgerald: the self-made man who, through luck, pluck, and all the Ben Franklin virtues, rises from abject poverty to high social estate.

More complex, and therefore more interesting, than this uncorrupted Adam is the American hero during and after the Fall. It is with this aspect of the dream rather than with the adamant innocence of a Leatherstocking that our best writers have most often concerned themselves. The symbolic loss of Edenic innocence and the painful initiation into an awareness of evil constitutes a second major pattern in American literature from the works of Hawthorne and Melville through Mark Twain and Henry James to Ernest Hemingway and William Faulkner to Stephen King. This is the darker thread in our literary fabric, which, contrasting as it does with the myth of bright expectancy, lends depth and richness to the overall design; it also reminds us of the disturbing proximity of dream and nightmare. From this standpoint, then, we may recall Hawthorne's young Goodman Brown as a representative figure—the prototypal American hero haunted by the obsession with guilt and original sin that is a somber but essential part of America's Puritan heritage.

The English novelist D. H. Lawrence was first among the modern critics to perceive the "dark suspense" latent in the American Dream. As early as 1923 he pointed out the essential paradox of the American character in his *Studies in Classic American Literature*, a book whose cantankerous brilliance has only lately come to be fully appreciated by literary scholars. "America has never been easy," he wrote, "and is not easy today. Americans have always been at a certain tension. Their liberty is a thing of sheer will, sheer tension: a liberty of THOU SHALT NOT. And it has been so from the first. The land of

THOU SHALT NOT" (5). Lawrence saw Americans as a people frantically determined to slough off the old skin of European tradition and evil, but constricted even more tightly by their New World heritage of Puritan conscience and inhibition. He pointed out the evidence of this "certain tension" in the writings of such classic American authors as Cooper, Poe, Hawthorne, and Melville. Though Lawrence is certainly not the only source of such insights, much of myth criticism of American literature—notably such works as Leslie Fiedler's *End to Innocence, Love and Death in the American Novel,* and *No! in Thunder*—reflects his brilliantly provocative influence.

Huck Finn epitomizes the archetype of the American Adam. *Huckleberry Finn* is one of the half dozen most significant works in American literature. Many critics rank it among the masterpieces of world literature, and not a few consider it to be the Great American Novel. The reasons for this high esteem may be traced directly to the mythological implications of Twain's book: more than any other novel in our literature, *Huckleberry Finn* embodies myth that is both universal and national. The extent of its mythic content is such that we cannot hope to grasp it all in this chapter; we can, however, indicate a few of those elements that have helped to give the novel its enduring appeal.

First, *Huckleberry Finn* is informed by several archetypal patterns encountered throughout world literature:

1. *The Quest:* Like Don Quixote, Huck is a wanderer, separated from his culture, idealistically in search of one more substantial than that embraced by the hypocritical, materialistic society he has rejected.

2. *Water Symbolism:* The great Mississippi River, like the Nile and the Ganges, is invested with sacred attributes. As T. S. Eliot has written in "The Dry Salvages," the river is a "strong brown god" (line 2); it is an archetypal symbol of the mystery of life and creation—birth, the flowing of time into eternity, and rebirth. (Note, for example, Huck's several symbolic deaths, his various disguises and new identities as he returns to the shore from the river; also note the mystical lyricism with which he describes the river's majes-

tic beauty.) The river is also a kind of paradise, the "Great Good Place," as opposed to the shore, where Huck encounters hellish corruption and cruelty. It is, finally, an agent of purification and of divine justice.

3. *Shadow Archetype:* Huck's pap, with his sinister repulsiveness, is a classic representation of the devil figure designated by Jung as the shadow.

4. *Trickster:* Huck—as well as those notorious "con men," the King and the Duke—exemplifies this archetypal figure. Also see chapter 7.

5. *Wise Old Man:* In contrast to pap Finn, the terrible father, Jim exemplifies the Jungian concept of the wise old man who provides spiritual guidance and moral wisdom for the young hero.

6. *Archetypal Women*
   a. The Good Mother: the Widow Douglas, Mrs. Loftus, Aunt Sally Phelps.
   b. The Terrible Mother: Miss Watson, who becomes the Good Mother at the end of the novel.
   c. The Soul-Mate: Sophia Grangerford, Mary Jane Wilks.

7. *Initiation:* Huck undergoes a series of painful experiences in passing from ignorance and innocence into spiritual maturity; he comes of age—is morally reborn—when he decides to go to hell rather than turn Jim in to the authorities.

In addition to these universal archetypes, *Huckleberry Finn* contains a mythology that is distinctively American. Huck himself is the symbolic American hero; he epitomizes conglomerate paradoxes that make up the American character. He has all the glibness and practical acuity that we admire in our businesspeople and politicians; he is truly a self-made youth, free from the materialism and morality-by-formula of the Horatio Alger hero. He possesses the simple modesty, the quickness, the daring and the guts, the stamina and the physical skill that we idolize in our athletes. He is both ingenious and ingenuous. He is mentally sharp, but not intellectual. He also displays the ingratiating capacity for buffoonery that we so dearly love in our public entertainers. Yet, with all these extraverted virtues, Huck is also a sensitive, conscience-burdened loner troubled by man's inhumanity to man and by his own occasional callousness to Jim's feelings. Notwithstanding his generally realistic outlook and his practical bent, he is a moral idealist, far ahead of his age in his sense of human decency, and at times, a mystic and a daydreamer (or, more accurately, a night dreamer) who is uncommonly sensitive to the presence of a divine beauty in nature. He is, finally, the good bad boy whom Americans have always idolized in one form or another. And, though he is exposed to as much evil in human nature as young Goodman Brown had seen, Huck is saved from Brown's pessimistic gloom by his sense of humor and, what is more crucial, by his sense of humanity.

D. "Everyday Use": The Great [Grand]Mother

With the possible exceptions of such masterpieces as Jack London's "Samuel" and Sherwood Anderson's "Death in the Woods," no modern short story more clearly dramatizes the archetypal female as Great Mother than does Alice Walker's brilliant *tour de force*, which is perhaps the major reason that this little gem has achieved classic status in less than a generation since its original publication.

If Walker's theme is only hinted at in her title, it is made explicit in her dedication: "*for your grandmama.*" In brief, "Everyday Use" and all that title connotes is not simply a tribute to the author's—or any *one* person's—grandmama: it is a celebration for *your*—indeed, for all humanity's—Great (or, if you prefer, *Grand*) Mother.

In this story, the archetypal woman manifests herself as both Good Mother and Earth Mother. As she informs us at the outset, her *earthen* yard is "not just a yard . . . but an extended *living* room" (our italics). True to her nature, the Good Mother is appropriately associated with the life principle. She is also an androgynous figure, combining the natural strengths of female and male. "In real life," she says, "I am a large, big-boned woman with rough, man-working hands. In the winter I wear flannel nightgowns to bed and overalls during the day. I can kill and clean a hog as mercilessly as a man."

Further in keeping with her archetypal nature, the Good Mother is associated with such life-enhancing virtues as warmth, nourishment, growth, and protection. With a modicum of formal education (she can scarcely read), she has maintained her farm and brought two children into maturity—even despite such catastrophes as the burning of her old house and the scarring of her younger daughter. Now, as the story opens, it is her function to preserve the natural order of things, including tradition and her family heritage. The central symbol in the story is a nice combination of metonymy and symbol— the quilts, associated with warmth and signifying the family heritage:

> They had been pieced by Grandma Dee and then Big Dee and me had hung them on the quilt frames on the front porch and quilted them. . . . In both of them were scraps of dresses Grandma Dee had worn fifty and more years ago. Bits and pieces of Grandpa Jarrell's paisley shirts. And one teeny faded blue piece, about the size of a penny matchbox, that was from Great Grandpa Ezra's uniform that he wore in the Civil War.

For the Good Mother, hers is always a living heritage, a vital tradition of "everyday use." Dee, the daughter and antagonist, has broken that tradition.

> "What happened to 'Dee'?" I wanted to know.
> "She's dead," Wangero said. "I couldn't bear it any longer, being named after the people who oppress me."

For Wangero Leewanika Kemanjo (a.k.a. "Dee"), on the contrary, tradition is an essentially *useless* thing, heritage something inert to be framed and hung on the wall as mere ornament, as artificial and pretentious as her new name and her new prince consort "Hakim-a-barber."

But, touched by "the spirit of God," this mother righteously defends the natural order, protecting her precious "everyday" from the specious order of the "new day." Maggie, blessed child with scarred hands but unscarred spirit, will marry John Thomas, with mossy teeth and earnest face. The family heritage will be hers to maintain. The quilts, emblems of this heritage—like Nature and the Good Mother herself—will not merely endure but prevail. "This was Maggie's portion. This was the way she knew God to work."

▪ IV. LIMITATIONS OF MYTH CRITICISM

It should be apparent from the foregoing illustrations that myth criticism offers some unusual opportunities for the enhancement of our literary appreciation and understanding. No other critical approach possesses quite the same combination of breadth and depth. As we have seen, an application of myth criticism takes us far beyond the historical and aesthetic realms of literary study—back to the beginning of humankind's oldest rituals and beliefs and deep into our own individual hearts. Because of the vastness and the complexity of mythology, a field of study whose mysteries anthropologists and psychologists are still working to penetrate, our brief introduction can give the reader only a surperficial and fragmentary overview. But we hope we have given interested students a glimpse of new vistas and that they will explore myth on their own.

We should point out some of the inherent limitations of the mythological approach. As with the psychological approach, the reader must take care that enthusiasm for a new-found interpretive key does not tempt him or her to discard other valuable critical instruments or to try to open all literary doors with this single key. Just as Freudian critics sometimes lose sight of a great work's aesthetic values in their passion for sexual symbolism, so myth critics tend to forget that literature is more than a vehicle for archetypes and ritual patterns. In other words, they run the risk of being distracted from the aesthetic experience of the work itself. They forget that literature is, above all else, art. As we have indicated before, the discreet critic will apply such extrinsic perspectives as the mythological and psychological only as far as they enhance the experience of the art form, and only as far as the structure and potential meaning of the work consistently support such approaches.

Quick Reference

Baird, James. *Ishmael: A Study of the Symbolic Mode in Primitivism.* New York: Harper, 1960.

Bodkin, Maud. *Archetypal Patterns in Poetry: Psychological Studies of Imagination.* New York: Vintage, 1958.

Campbell, Joseph. *The Masks of God: Primitive Mythology.* New York: Viking, 1959.

Carpenter, Fredric I. *American Literature and the Dream.* New York: Philosophical Library, 1955.

Cirlot, J. E. *A Dictionary of Symbols.* Trans. Jack Sage. New York: Philosophical Library, 1962.

Cornford, F. M. *Origin of Attic Comedy.* London: Arnold, 1914.

Eliade, Mircea. *Myth and Reality.* New York: Harper, 1963.

Fergusson, Francis. *The Idea of Theater.* Princeton, NJ: Princeton University Press, 1949.

Fiedler, Leslie. *End to Innocence.* Boston: Beacon Press, 1955.

———. *Love and Death in the American Novel.* New York: Criterion, 1960.

———. *No! in Thunder.* Boston: Beacon Press, 1960.

Frazer, James G. *The Golden Bough.* Abridged ed. New York: Macmillan, 1922.

Frye, Northrop. *Anatomy of Criticism.* Princeton, NJ: Princeton University Press, 1957.

———. *The Stubborn Structure.* Ithaca, NY: Cornell University Press, 1970.

Harrison, Jane. *Themis.* London: Cambridge University Press, 1912.

Jung, C. G. *The Archetypes and the Collective Unconscious.* 2nd ed. Princeton, NJ: Princeton University Press, 1968.

———. *Modern Man in Search of a Soul.* New York: Harcourt, n.d.; first published in 1933.

———. *Psyche and Symbol.* Garden City, NY: Doubleday, 1958.

———. *Psychological Reflections.* New York: Harper, 1961.

———. *The Structure and Dynamics of the Psyche.* 2nd ed. Princeton, NJ: Princeton University Press, 1969.

———. *Two Essays on Analytical Psychology.* 2nd ed. Princeton, NJ: Princeton University Press, 1966.

Lawrence, D. H. *Studies in Classic American Literature.* New York: Viking, 1964.

Lewis, R. W. B. *The American Adam.* Chicago: University of Chicago Press, 1955.

Marett, R. R., ed. *Anthropology and the Classics.* New York: Oxford University Press, 1908.

Murray, Gilbert. *The Classical Tradition in Poetry.* Cambridge, MA: Harvard University Press, 1927.

———. *Euripides and His Age.* New York: Holt, 1913.

de Santillana, Giorgio, and Hertha von Dechend. *Hamlet's Mill.* Boston: Gambit, 1969.

Schorer, Mark. *William Blake: The Politics of Vision.* New York: Holt, 1946.

Smith, Jeanne Rosier. *Writing Tricksters: Mythic Gambols in American Ethnic Literature.* Berkeley: University of California Press, 1997.

Sugg, Richard P., ed. *Jungian Literary Criticism.* Evanston, IL: Northwestern University Press, 1992.

Tate, Allen, ed. *The Language of Poetry.* New York: Russell, 1960.

Watts, Alan W. *Myth and Ritual in Christianity.* New York: Vanguard Press, 1954.

Wheelwright, Jane. *Death of a Woman.* New York: St. Martin's Press, 1981.

Wheelwright, Philip. *The Burning Fountain.* Bloomington: Indiana University Press, 1954.

———. *Metaphor and Reality.* Bloomington: Indiana University Press, 1962.

■ 6 ■

Feminist Approaches

■ I. FEMINISM AND FEMINIST LITERARY CRITICISM: DEFINITIONS

"I myself have never been able to find out precisely what feminism is," British author and critic Rebecca West remarks, "I only know that other people call me a feminist whenever I express sentiments that differentiate me from a doormat or prostitute" (219). Indeed, feminism and feminist literary criticism are often defined as a matter of what is absent rather than what is present. Unlike the other approaches we have examined, feminist literary criticism is often a political attack upon other modes of criticism and theory, and its social orientation moves beyond traditional literary criticism. In its diversity feminism is concerned with the marginalization of all women: that is, with their being relegated to a secondary position. Most feminists believe that our culture is a patriarchal culture: that is, one organized in favor of the interests of men. Feminist literary critics try to explain how power imbalances due to gender in a given culture are reflected in or challenged by literary texts.

Adrienne Rich, a contemporary American poet, describes feminism as "the place where in the most natural, organic way subjectivity and politics have to come together" (in Gelpi and Gelpi 114). This critical stance allows feminism to protest the exclusion of women from the literary canon, to focus upon the personal (such as diary literature), to exhibit a powerful political orientation (as in the work of Marxist feminists), and to redefine literary theory itself (in its concern with the psychosexual aspects of language). Feminist literary criticism is not, as critic Toril Moi observes, "just another interesting critical approach" like "a concern for sea-imagery or metaphors of war in medieval poetry" (204). In short, feminism represents one of the most important social, economic, and aesthetic revolutions of modern times.

Feminist critics see the very act of speaking—of *having* a language—as a focus for studying women writers, so often silenced in the past. Tillie Olsen demands to hear women's voices in her 1978 work *Silences*, a study of the impediments to creativity encountered by women, citing those "mute inglorious Miltons: those whose working hours are all struggle for existence; the barely educated; the illiterate; women. Their silence is the silence of the centuries as to how life was, is, for most of humanity." Silences result from "'circumstances' of being born into the wrong class, race or sex, being denied education, becoming numbed by economic struggle, muzzled by censorship or distracted or impeded by the demands of nurturing." But women's use of silence can also be "resistance to the dominant discourse" (Fishkin and Hedges, *Listening to Silences* 5). Examples might be Emily Dickinson's "slant truth" or inner dialogues of such "quiet" characters as Charlotte Brontë's Jane Eyre or Virginia Woolf's Mrs. Ramsay and Lily Briscoe.

Feminists examine the experiences of women from all races and classes and cultures, including, for example, African American, Latina, Asian American, American Indian, lesbian, handicapped, elderly, and Third World subjects. Annette Kolodny aptly describes this richness as a "playful pluralism," for it exhibits liberal tolerance, interdisciplinary links, and an insistence on connecting art to the diversities of life (161).

Despite their diversity, feminist critics generally agree that their goals are to expose patriarchal premises and resulting prejudices, to promote discovery and reevaluation of literature by women, and to examine social, cultural, and psychosexual contexts of literature and literary criticism. Feminist critics therefore study sexual, social, and political issues once thought to be "outside" the study of literature.

▪ II. HISTORICAL OVERVIEW AND MAJOR THEMES IN FEMINIST CRITICISM

Elaine Showalter, one of the leading feminist critics in the United States, has identified three historical phases of women's literary development: the "feminine" phase (1840–80), during which women writers imitated the dominant tradition; the "feminist" phase (1880–1920), during which women advocated minority rights and protested; and the "female" phase (1920–present), during which dependency on opposition—that is, on uncovering misogyny in male texts—is being replaced by a rediscovery of women's texts and women. Showalter attacks traditional literary history that reduces female writers to only a few who are "accepted." She describes a women's tradition in literature that is an "imaginative continuum [of] certain patterns, themes, problems, and images from generation to generation" (11).

Notwithstanding the contributions of such outstanding female authors as George Eliot, Mary Wollstonecraft, Virginia Woolf, Rebecca West, and Charlotte Perkins Gilman, in Showalter's context feminist literary criticism has mostly developed since the beginning of the contemporary women's movement, with Simone de Beauvoir, Kate Millett, and Betty Friedan. These critics examined the female "self" as a cultural idea promulgated by male authors, and their analyses of literature and culture concentrated on how male fears and anxieties were portrayed through female characters. They saw texts as models of power. De Beauvoir asked, What is woman? How is she constructed differently from men? Answer: She is constructed differently *by* men (see *The Second Sex*). The thesis that men write about women to find out more about men has had lasting implications. De Beauvoir established the fundamental issues of modern feminism by arguing that *man* defines the human, not woman. Friedan demystified the dominant image of the happy American suburban housewife and mother (*The Feminine Mystique*). Her book appeared amidst new women's organizations, manifestos, protests, and publications that called for an end to sex discrimination and enforcement of equal rights. An author of many articles in publications such as *Good Housekeeping*, Friedan also analyzed reductive images of women in American magazines. Millett's *Sexual Politics* was the first widely read work of feminist literary criticism. Millett's focus, unlike Friedan's, was a critique of ideology. Distinguishing between sex as biologically determined and gender as a psychological concept that refers to culturally acquired sexual identity, Millett wrote that "the essence of politics is power," and that the most fundamental and pervasive concept of power in our society is male dominance (25). She saw literature as a record of the collective consciousness of patriarchy; her reading of D. H. Lawrence, Norman Mailer, Henry Miller, and Jean Genet offered a powerful challenge to traditional social values of capitalism, violence against women, crude sexuality, and male power in general, while it also assaulted the reigning formalism in literary criticism of her day. As a "resisting reader" who focused on patterns of dominance and submission, Millett found that these writers distort female characters by associating them with deviance. As she observed, the "interior colonization" of women by men is "sturdier than any form of segregation, and more rigorous than class stratification, more uniform, certainly more enduring" (24–25).

Elaine Showalter identifies four models of difference: biological, linguistic, psychoanalytic, and cultural. The *biological model* is the most extreme; if the text somehow mirrors the body, this can reduce women merely *to* bodies. Yet Showalter praises frankness with regard to the body in female poets and finds in their intimate and confessional tone a rebuke to those women who continue to write "outside" the female body, as though it did not exist. Showalter's *linguistic model* of difference posits women speaking men's language as a foreign tongue; purging language of "sexism" is not going far enough. If women continue to speak as men do when they enter discourse, whatever they say will be alienated. Yet advocates of this position admit that there is no separate "female" language and no evidence to suggest that the sexes are programmed to develop structurally different languages. Showalter's *psychoanalytic model* identifies gender difference as the basis of the psyche, focusing on the relation of gender to the artistic process. It stresses feminine difference as the free play of meaning outside the need for closure. Showalter's most important contribution has been to describe the *cultural model* that places feminist concerns in social contexts, acknowledging class, racial, national, and historical differences and determinants among women, but offering a collective experience that unites women over time and space—a "binding force" ("Feminist Criticism in the Wilderness" 186–88, 193, 196–202).

With these general distinctions in mind, in the following pages we preface our analysis of literary works by looking at the most significant movements in feminist criticism, combining the diverse approaches listed above into four main types currently most pervasive in feminist criticism: gender studies, Marxist studies, psychoanalytic studies, and minority studies. In all these areas, there has been a general shift from a negative attack on male writing about women and a shift towards positive delineation of women's redefinition of their identity in their own writing. Such "gynocentric" criticism concentrates on female creativity, stylistics, themes, images, careers, and literary traditions. This new emphasis began with the rediscovery of neglected or forgotten female writers and has grown into the attempt to redefine gender in literary studies.

▪ III. FOUR SIGNIFICANT CURRENT PRACTICES

A. Gender Studies

Gender determines everything, some say, including language; as Elizabeth Abel has argued, "sexuality and textuality both depend on difference" (173). Yet while some feminists stress gender differences, others believe that the entire concept of female difference is what has caused female oppression; they wish to move beyond "difference" altogether.

Because of this second emphasis, gender critics have broadened definitions. Male critics who wish to pursue feminist studies often do so under the umbrella term of gender studies, and in gay studies critics often approach their subject through the topic of gender. Both of these groups are less interested in a writer's or reader's biological sex than in certain qualities of masculinity and femininity.

While some would argue that writing is writing and cannot be categorized as masculine or feminine, feminist critics disagree. In moving away from formalism, feminist critics alert their readers to underlying patriarchal assumptions. Maggie Humm responds to arguments against this position by noting that in literary studies male critics are seen to be "unaligned," while "a feminist is seen as a case of special pleading." Male criticism, not feminism, she claims, is ideologically blind to the implications of gender (12–13).

In criticism and in literature, feminist critics identify sex-related writing strategies, including matters of subject, vocabulary, syntax, style, imagery, narrative structure, characterization, and genre preference. For example, the novel is often described as a female genre; feminists debate whether the female preference for the novel is based on its realism or on its subjectivity, and whether there is a distinction to be made between these notions. In general, while male writers seem more interested in closure, female writers often respond with open endings. Feminine logic in writing is often associational, male logic sequential—that is, goal-oriented. Male objectivity is challenged by feminine subjectivity. This list of contrasts could go on, but of course exceptions are everywhere.

By studying women's writing as a gender issue, we are led to ask the general question, What is to be valued? Is diary literature or the Gothic romance automatically less worthy than the "realistic" novel or the "high modernist" poem? Do female writers value diversity merely for its own sake? Do they attack men and valorize women excessively? The male tradition seemingly would have it so. But the last few years have seen an unprecedented challenge to traditional thinking, with greater attention paid to such suppressed or devalued artistic genres as women's letters and journals.

In the past, descriptions of prose in masculine terms (that is, praising someone's prose as "virile") were taken as the norm; today, applying a term like *virile* might be intended to describe the *limitations* of a work. Feminist critic Myra Jehlen is aware that many traditional critics regard such talk of gender, class, and race as threatening to diminish literature. But she counters that such reading actually complicates meaning by refusing to reduce the complexities of sexual and other interactions to a false common denominator. Jehlen believes that with authors who seem unconscious of gender as an issue in their work we must make an effort to read *for* it instead: ". . . literary criticism involves action as much as reflection, and reading for gender makes the deed explicit." As women escape the masculine "norms" of society, men also benefit: "men, . . . upon ceasing to be mankind, become, precisely, men" ("Gender" 263–65, 273).

B. Marxist Feminism

Marxist feminist criticism focuses on the relation between reading and social realities. Certainly the establishment of feminist women's studies programs, bookstores, libraries, political action committees, film boards, and community groups attests to the crucial connection between theory and reality offered by feminism. Unlike some other intellectual strategies, feminism acts on ideas. Karl Marx argued that all historical and social developments are determined by forms of economic production. Marxist feminists attack the prevailing capitalistic system of the West, which they view as sexually as well as economically exploitative. Marxist feminists thus combine study of class with that of gender. In Marxist feminism personal identity is not seen as separate from cultural identity. Since Marxists emphasize historical and economic contexts of literary discourse, they often direct attention toward the conditions of production of literary texts—that is, the economics of publishing and distributing texts.

Marxists are often attacked for undervaluing or misunderstanding the nature of quality in art. For them literary value is not a transcendent property, but something conditioned by social beliefs and needs. What is "good" art for many Marxists is simply what people in a given society agree upon as good. This view has been criticized as failing to account for aesthetics or for artistic genius.

Lillian Robinson responds to such criticisms with a counterattack on formalism. Form, style, and history are not independent of content, ideology, or politics, she asserts, and formalism serves ruling-class interests, connecting it to the systematic exclusion of women, nonwhites, and the working class. Feminist criticism, she contends, "is criticism with a cause, engaged criticism. . . . It must be ideological and moral criticism; it must be revolutionary" (3). Such assertions characterize feminism as committed criticism that combines the unsentimental with the unapologetically personal and insists upon the *matter* rather than the *manner* of a text.

C. Psychoanalytic Feminism

Many feminists have been attracted to the psychoanalytic approach. In America, psychoanalytic criticism has tended to be practical and not particularly terminology-ridden. Sandra Gilbert and Susan Gubar examine female images in the works of Jane Austen, Mary Shelley, Charlotte and Emily Brontë, and George Eliot. They address such topics as mothering, living within enclosures, doubling of characters and of the self, women's diseases, and feminized landscapes, and they make the interesting argument that female writers often identify themselves with the literary characters they detest. Gilbert and Gubar point out how the monster/madwoman figure represents aspects of the author's self-image—like the angel/heroine figure—as well as elements of the author's antipatriarchal strategies. They describe a feminine utopia in which wholeness rather than "otherness" would prevail as a definition of identity.

The most innovative and far-reaching use of psychoanalytic theories for feminist criticism is among the French. Elaine Showalter has observed that "English feminist criticism, essentially Marxist, stresses oppression; French feminist criticism, essentially psychoanalytic, stresses repression; American feminist criticism, essentially textual, stresses expression"; all three, however, have become gynocentric, searching for terminology to rescue the feminine from being a synonym for inferiority ("Feminist Criticism in the Wilderness" 186). While French critics who practice what they call *l'écriture féminine* uphold the power of the psychological category of the feminine, they dismiss the actual sex of an author as unimportant (following their deconstructive attack upon the author or self as a meaningful term in discussion). The French feminists see feminism in its binary oppositions as a male cultural notion left over from the past. They also reject the idea that art is mimetic or representational, for images in art are merely tropes, or effects of language.

From the Freudian revisionist Jacques Lacan comes the notion of the Imaginary, a pre-Oedipal stage in which the child has not yet differentiated himself or herself from the mother and has accordingly not yet learned language. The Oedipal crisis marks the entrance of the child into a world of symbolic order (language) in which everything is separate, including conscious and unconscious, self and other, words and actions. This transition also marks entry into a world ruled by the "Law of the Father" where "isms" or rules confine us; Lacan calls it the phallocentric or phallogocentric universe (by which he connects maleness to the power of the word he believes men control—"phallus" and "logos"). The Imaginary is the realm of the feminine and the vital source of language that will later be tamed and codified by the Laws of the Father.

The relevance of Freud and Lacan for French feminism arises from their treatment of language. Lacan describes the unconscious as structured like a language; like language its power arises from the sense of openness and play of meaning. When we "read" language we may identify gaps in what is signified as evidence of the unconscious, for language is a mixture of fixed meanings and metaphors. "Femininity" is then a "language" of the unconscious that destabilizes sexual categories. Thus *écriture féminine* disrupts the unities of Western discourse, pointing to its silences. French feminists speak of "exploding" the sign rather than interpreting signs. French feminists who follow Lacan, particularly Hélène Cixous, propose a utopian place, a primeval female space which is free of symbolic order, sex roles, otherness, and the Law of the Father and in which the self is still linked with what Cixous calls the Voice of the Mother. This place, with its Voice, is the source of all feminine writing, Cixous contends; to gain access to it is to find a source of immeasurable feminine power.

Julia Kristeva furnishes the most psychoanalytically based version of French feminism in *Desire in Language* and other works. She describes a Mother-centered realm of expression as the *semiotic* as opposed to the *symbolic* Law of the Father. Like Lacan, in her mind the prior semiotic realm of the Feminine is present in symbolic discourse as absence or contradiction, and great writers are those who offer the reader the greatest amount of disruption of the nameable. Like Cixous and Luce

Irigaray, Kristeva opposes phallocentrism with images derived from women's corporeal experiences. Such psychoanalytic theory thus attempts, as does Marxist feminist theory, to connect the personal with the social.

One can easily see why Freud's accounts of his female patients' first-person narratives of their fantasies and diseases figure so strongly in Lacan's work and in feminist psychological commentary: before such maladies as Freud addresses could be treated medically, they first had to be voiced subjectively. Freud stressed the textual nature of psychoanalytic cases, and he read his patients much as readers read literary texts. Thus, maneuvers such as bringing a subtext to light are similar in literary criticism and psychoanalysis, for the goal of both is understanding rather than repression. What Kristeva and the other French psychoanalytic feminists contribute to this comparison is the notion that such therapy is not locked into the individual psyche but is a quality of all language and experience.

But Kristeva's later work moves away from strictly psychoanalytic theorizing toward an embrace of motherhood as the model for psychic health. "Stabat Mater," her prose poem meditation on her own experience with maternity accompanied by a hypertext essay on the cult of the Virgin Mary, understands motherhood as, like language, a separation accompanied by a joining of signification. Kristeva makes the succinct observations that "A mother is a continuous separation, a division of the very flesh." The experience of giving birth paradoxically "wounds but increases" with "the calm of another life, the life of that other who wends his way while I remain henceforth like a framework" (*The Kristeva Reader* 178). As Suzanne Clark remarks, Kristeva "advocates a notion of cultural and personal identity which recognizes that the strangeness of the other is a strangeness within. At the level of the state, this implies the acceptance of foreigners. At the level of the individual, this implies the recognition of the unconscious. Identity, then, must be seen as provisional rather than exclusive, constructed as an effect of the heterogeneous processes of discourses." Clark recognizes in Kristeva's personal and political thought a "relational, collaborative view of rhetoric" (306–16). This collaborative view is perhaps best stated in Kristeva's essay, "Women's

Time," in which she characterizes the future of feminism as one with a utopian vision that "many voices are always speaking, and that each individual can have many voices" (Bizzell and Herteberg 1229–31).

With a different set of psychoanalytic concerns, feminism and cultural studies converge in film theory. Following the important work of British film critic Laura Mulvey, it is no longer possible to think of literature as only dried ink on a page, since many of her ideas about film have been transferred to literary analyses. Her notion is that films can compel the female viewer to participate in her own humiliation, for the technical and psychological organization of the classic Hollywood film is based on voyeurism and fetishism, the only pleasure available being the classic male one of looking at women's bodies.

Using examples from Alfred Hitchcock's films and others, Mulvey's essay "Visual Pleasure and Narrative Cinema" examines the ways that male ambivalence toward the image of woman makes viewers choose among devaluing, punishing, or saving the guilty female, or turning her into a pedestal figure or fetish (303–14). These extremes leave little place for the female viewer. According to Mulvey, woman is the image in film, while man is the bearer of the look, or voyeur: "In a world ordered by sexual imbalance pleasure in looking has been split," and the "male gaze projects its phantasy onto the female figure, which is styled accordingly" (304, 309). The pleasure in cinema, then, is about male domination.

One other type of psychological approach, myth criticism, has its own history and methodology (see chapter 5), but several feminist writers have adopted its perspectives and transformed them for the purposes of feminist criticism. Notable among these is Annis Pratt. Although she criticizes Jung for his lack of discussion of the female psyche, she offers intriguing connections between feminism and Jungian archetypal criticism, as in *Archetypal Patterns in Women's Fiction* and "The New Feminist Criticism." Feminist myth critics tend to center their discussion on the Great Mother and other early female images and goddesses, viewing these figures as the radical others that can offer hope against the patriarchal repression of women. Especially popular are figures of Medusa, Cassandra, Arachne, and Isis.

In *The Lost Tradition: Mothers and Daughters in Literature* (ed. Davidson and Broner), prominent feminist myth critics, including Annis Pratt and Adrienne Rich, define myth as the key critical genre for women. Criticizing Northrop Frye and others for ignoring gender in their scientific classification of myths and archetypes, these writers direct our attention to actual practices of diverse ethnic groups. Since most myths are constructed and studied by men, there are some difficult issues concerning women's representation in myths; thus the need is even greater for women's creation of their own myths. Many of these new feminist myth critics reject the Greco-Roman tradition as hegemonic and instead seek pre-Greek myths, such as those of Isis, and diverse, lesser known cultural myths in different parts of the world, such as those of American Indian legend. Rich conforms to these general strategies, but focuses on the ways mothers are portrayed in mythology and literature. Rich argues, like Kristeva, that motherhood is *the* feminine status. She distinguishes between the fact of motherhood and the institution a patriarchal culture makes of it, finding that society's oppression of women comes precisely from its need to romanticize (and in a certain sense avoid facing) the terrible and wonderful mythic powers of the mother. Feminist Jungians have returned to the power of the narrative as a means of conducting psychological counseling, examining the "literary" features of a subject's story with renewed interest.

Myth can also help ethnic groups, especially oppressed minorities, reorganize and reorient themselves within a dominant culture. Myth manages to bring together private and public experiences in forms that can be as direct or as masked as the situation demands. It especially appeals to women because of their identification with nature, as in the vegetation-goddess archetypes such as Ceres or Diana-Selene-Hecate. Even the most destructive women in mythology, such as Medea, can be analyzed to show their attraction for modern women, their power of resistance; it is well-documented that in many cultures, when matriarchal societies were replaced with patriarchal ones, the previously venerated goddesses were turned by the new culture into witches, seductresses, or fools. Studying these transformations once again reveals the powers of the goddesses. Yet myth criticism has been attacked as too homogenizing, promoting a false universality of identity. In the next section, we will see how such a concern is central to all contemporary feminism.

D. Minority Feminist Criticism

Within the feminist minority there are still other significant minorities, the most prominent being black and lesbian feminists. While it is true that many black and lesbian feminists include each other in analyses of the problems of either group, and certainly feminism in general has allied itself with diverse arguments against racism, xenophobia, and homophobia, it may seem to violate their most fundamental ideas to address them in a single section, since they have strongly protested both their marginalization in society and their often unwanted groupings with other minorities. But they have become a widespread pairing among the subgroups of feminist critics; they are the most vocal and successful of feminist minorities. Our treatment of their similar concerns is meant to suggest issues that confront other minorities as well.

Blacks and lesbians have been violently attacked in all manner of ways in Western literature and culture in general; thus for them, the personal is even more political than for other women. Their work, both artistic and critical, tends to use irony as a primary literary device to focus on their self-definition—their "coming out"—for they often reject classic literary tradition as oppressive. Not only do they find many other critics to be racist and/or misogynist, but they accuse other feminist critics of developing their ideas only in reference to white, upper-middle-class women who oftentimes practice feminism only in order to become part of the patriarchal power structure. That is, the majority of feminists want to be counted as men and share in the bounties of the dominant society, such as equal wages, child care, or other accepted social rights. Black and lesbian feminists thus argue that most women have more in common with men than with each other. Lesbians and women of color have been "written out" of literature and history more than white heterosexual women. The need to create a new set of traditions helps explain the strong lesbian contingent in the civil rights movement, as well as vigorous publishing of black lesbians. Maggie Humm has suggested that "the central motifs of Black and lesbian criticism need to become pivotal to feminist criticism rather than the other way around" (106). This statement has many implications.

During the 1960s interest in black culture grew, as the inclusion of black writers in syllabi and anthologies attests. In the 1970s and 1980s this was followed by the emergence of black feminist critics. Criticism and theory have been barely able to keep up with the explosion of interest in black writers. Things have happened so quickly that even the term *black feminist* is problematic. When referring to black feminists in the United States in particular or in the New World in general, the preferred usage is *African American*; we use *black* here to include black feminists elsewhere as well. And then there are those black female writers who reject the term *feminist*; among them is Alice Walker, one of the most successful black female authors and critics. Speaking as a woman of color, Walker writes that she has replaced *feminist* with *womanist*, remarking that a womanist does not turn her back on the men of her community (*In Search of Our Mothers' Gardens: Womanist Prose*). She identifies black female creativity in earlier generations through folk art, including quilting, music, and gardening. Black writers such as Walker look to figures like Zora Neale Hurston (1906–60), Harlem Renaissance writer and folklorist, who insisted upon the connection between the telling of folktales and other communal pursuits of black women and the creation of a body of black womanist literature. Hurston's unusual career, including her folktale collection *Mules and Men* (1935) and her feminist novel *Their Eyes Were Watching God* (1937), inspired Walker to emulate her conjoining of racial community and individual expression.

Approaches by other black women feminists are quite varied. Seeking out the autobiographies of black women, especially in slave narratives, has been important to many. Challenges to traditional criticism have included new bibliographies of neglected or suppressed works, recovery of figures such as the mammy or tragic mulatta, and an interdisciplinary approach that organizes music, painting, literature, autobiography, and literary criticism in radically new ways. Audre Lorde asks us to seek "the Black mother in each of us": that is, to rely on "intuitive" language rather than analysis and to see African culture's emphasis upon the mother-bond as an alternative to white patriarchal culture's way of thinking (*A Sister Outside*). Black feminist critics attack white culture's preference for black male protest writing (such as the works of Richard Wright and Ralph Ellison) over black women's works. Black feminists believe the issues that concern black female writers and characters should be expanded and given a greater place in literary criticism in general. In this sense they tend to be engaged in a variant of the feminist critique described by Showalter—namely, the attack on male-centered literary values—but they are also celebrating the portrayal of black women as complex selves (see Bell, *The Afro-American Novel and Its Tradition* 242–43).

In *Inspiring Influences: Tradition, Revision, and Afro-American Women's Novels*, Michael Awkward makes an important general distinction between the ways black female writers influence each other and the way male writers do. Awkward points out that black female writers carry out their relationships as mothers, daughters, sisters, and aunts rather than as sons vying with fathers. The competitive attitude among male authors seems inappropriate to female writers in general and to black female writers in particular. This places them in contrast to Western literary tradition in general, in which Oedipal battles among men—to say things not another way but a *better* way—characterize influence. In her four-volume autobiography Maya Angelou is an excellent example of a black feminist writer who speaks for and in turn inspires many other women. As she traces her childhood rape by her mother's boyfriend, her ensuing withdrawal from the world, her time as a prostitute and the lover of a drug addict and thief, and her eventual escape from misery, she connects her personal nightmares with larger social issues. From *I Know Why the Caged Bird Sings* (1970) to *The Heart of a Woman* (1981), Angelou works with the tropes of African American women's violation and betrayal by men, guilt at their own perceived betrayals of their race, the life of the single mother, their sense of displacement, their experimenting with cultural identities, and the continuing process of self-discovery. Angelou's message becomes a celebration of black people—and of black women in particular.

Like black feminists, lesbian feminists attempt to show how criticism can be redefined to work in a positive manner for all feminists, but especially for lesbians. Lesbian critics sometimes counter their marginalization by considering lesbianism a privileged stance and a testament to the primacy of women. Terms such as "alterity," "woman-centeredness," and "difference" take on new and more sharply defined meanings when used by lesbian critics. Lesbianism has been a stumbling block for many other feminists, and lesbian feminists have at times attempted to exclude heterosexual women. Some lesbians define lesbianism as the norm of female experience, seeing heterosexuality as abnormal for women. Others go even further and argue that only lesbians can offer an adequate feminist analysis. Such views can lead other feminists to reject lesbian feminism. But for the most part lesbian feminists have tried to be inclusive and have offered other feminists new techniques, such as, for example, the rejection of the traditional critical essay form in favor of a more creative and unbounded style.

In *Sexual Practice, Textual Theory: Lesbian Cultural Criticism*, Julia Penelope and Susan J. Wolfe try to define what does and does not constitute a lesbian and what is and what is not lesbian criticism. The authors believe that the postmodern questioning of identity has denied the category of lesbian. They accuse Michel Foucault, for example, of "an obtuseness and ingenuousness" in his *History of Sexuality* that marginalizes women and ignores lesbians. Lesbian writers imagine a world in which males are no longer central, and they do not wish to be categorized with all other feminists but rather preserve their sense of difference. Bonnie Zimmerman believes that an overly inclusive definition of lesbians will only blur the distinctions between lesbian relationships and nonlesbian female friendships. She describes "lesbianism" as a kind of relationship in which two women's strongest feelings and affections are directed toward each other. There may be sexual contact or it may be entirely absent, but the preference of the women is to spend their time together and to share most aspects of their lives with each other. She focuses upon Mary Wollstonecraft, Mary Wortley Montagu, Sarah Orne Jewett, Emily Dickinson, and others who have long been heroines of lesbian writers ("What Never Has Been" 34, 38–39).

Lesbian critics reject the notion of a unified text, much as do the French feminists; accordingly, they investigate mirror images, secret codes, dreams, and stories of identity; they are drawn to neologisms, unconventional grammar, and other experimental techniques. Again, like most other feminists, they stress ambiguity and open endings of stories, and they seek double meanings. Lesbian critics offer new genres as well as new views of such accepted genres as the *Bildungsroman*, the Gothic tale, or the utopian tale. They are particularly drawn to experimental lesbian writers such as Radclyffe Hall, Colette, Virginia Woolf, Djuna Barnes, Gertrude Stein, Ivy Compton-Burnett, and May Sarton.

▪ IV. THE FUTURE OF FEMINIST LITERARY STUDIES: SOME PROBLEMS AND LIMITATIONS

Feminism has caused a major reorientation of values in literary studies and elsewhere in Western culture, and it will continue to challenge long-held beliefs and practices. It is a vigorous, growing, diverse school of thought, and it has thus far managed to use its internal conflicts to further its dynamic growth. But it has not been popular in all quarters. It has been attacked by those who are suspicious of its social values and who fear its politicizing of artistic value. Though it is no longer acceptable to display sexist values in the academy or workplace, hostility to feminists persists, to say nothing of the denigration of female writers. And some problems within feminist criticism remain to be solved.

First, many women who think of themselves as feminists are somehow not considered feminist "enough" by more radical feminists, and this often leads women in the first group to reject feminism as a field of study altogether. Older women in particular often feel that they are being judged and found wanting by their younger and more theoretically inclined "sisters." These women complain that to be allowed to do as one pleases and think as one pleases, not adopting a rigid party line, should be the goal of feminism.

Many female critics also feel that feminist literary criticism has become too theoretical and too radical entirely and has lost sight of both its social roots and its application to reading texts.

Myra Jehlen has criticized the separatism of feminist criticism and theory. In "Archimedes and the Paradox of Feminist Criticism," she reaffirms the autonomy of the work of art and urges us to remember that art can contain good ideas as well as bad ones, but that this does not determine literary value. She believes that we should ask the questions of a work of art that it asks us to ask, and not others. Other feminist critics such as Elaine Showalter and Annette Kolodny have criticized feminism's growing bifurcation of literary scholarship and political action.

Jehlen's call to formalism is echoed by female critics who do not think of themselves primarily as feminists, as well as by male critics of many different types. When one has proclaimed that "all art is political," one ought to wonder exactly what one has said. Is it like saying, "All human activity has to do with sex" or "All human endeavors are based on the opposable thumb"? The reductiveness of some feminist theory, like that of Marxist theory, is a nagging problem that has not been adequately addressed. As has often been noted, radical movements do not like compromise, and this tendency has both strengthened feminism and cost it supporters. Also, some feel that the issue of art as a matter of aesthetics versus art as a political statement is not a question about women's rights, but about the entire nature of literary criticism—that is, there is something in art that transcends the particulars of a historical time and place.

Helen Vendler's criticisms of feminism's political biases caused a storm of protests from feminist critics, particularly Sandra Gilbert and Susan Gubar. The debate centers on formalism versus political meaning. Vendler seems to have little to complain of in feminist political theory in general, but in feminist literary criticism she finds much that is lacking. She criticizes early feminist critics for looking at women in male novels in a naive fashion, treating the characters as real people and predictably not finding them portrayed correctly. She also finds fruitless the attempt of later feminist critics to discover a distinctively female way of writing or a women's language. She finds that "feminism's unacknowledged problem, visible from its inception, has been its ascription of special virtue to women. In its most sentimental form, feminism assumes that men, as a class, are base and women are moral; in its angry version, that men are oppressors and women the oppressed." But she argues that it is the possession of power that determines who is oppressed; if feminism is to succeed, she says, it must de-idealize women "to the extent that truth is preferable to cant" (19–22).

Another problem is what to do with male feminist critics. Unlike male practitioners of the other approaches described in this handbook, males who perform feminist criticism can have a hard time of it. Many feminists believe that no man can possibly read or write or teach as a feminist; some even feel that men should be barred from teaching as feminists. Maggie Humm argues that no man can read as a feminist because at any time he can escape into patriarchy; the extent of "difference," she feels, is "infinite" (13–14). Toril Moi states that in practice "the would-be male feminist critic ought to ask himself whether he as a male is really doing feminism a service in our present situation by muscling in on the one cultural and intellectual space women have created for themselves within 'his' male-dominated discipline" (208). But many well-known male critics have read and taught as feminist critics, including Houston A. Baker, Jr., Paul Lauter, Wayne C. Booth, Jonathan Culler, Terry Eagleton, and Robert Scholes, and there will undoubtedly be more male students and critics who find the issues raised by feminism to be the issues they want to study.

Feminism continues to flourish in its many forms, and it will continue to offer society and literary studies a fruitful and exciting set of intellectual problems. Most feminists do not want to abolish male values; instead, they wish to do away with such gender-typed categories altogether.

Today we now find, for reasons which are not clear, many young women who have benefited from the social gains of feminists for women, yet who refuse to use the term "feminist" to describe themselves. We even hear of a "backlash" against feminism among women. Perhaps the key to feminism's continuing usefulness as a self-description will lie in its willingness or unwillingness to grow with the times and not only lead the way to reforms but adapt itself to the changing needs of women and men. Feminism, as a catalyst for so much of postmodern literary and cultural studies, will find itself transformed by its own creations.

▨ V. FIVE FEMINIST APPROACHES

A. The Marble Vault: The Mistress in "To His Coy Mistress"

Addressing himself to a coy or putatively unwilling woman, the speaker in Andrew Marvell's poem pleads for sex using the logical argument that since they have not "world enough, and time" to delay pleasure, the couple should proceed with haste. But the poem's supposed logic and its borrowing from traditional love poetry only thinly veil darker psychosexual matters. What is most arresting about the address is not its John Donne-like argumentation but its shocking attack on the female body.

The woman in "To His Coy Mistress" not only is unwilling to accept the speaker, but is obviously quite intelligent; otherwise, he would not bother with such vaulting metaphysics. Yet the speaker seeks to frighten her into sexual compliance. This is most clear in his violent and grotesque descriptions of her body.

Her body is indeed the focus, not his nor theirs together. Following a series of exotic settings and references to times past and present, the speaker offers the traditional adoration of the various parts of her body, effectively dismembering her identity into discrete sexual objects, including her eyes, her forehead, her breasts, "the rest," and "every part," culminating in a wish for her to "show" her heart. This last image moves in the direction of more invasive maneuvers toward her body.

The woman's body is next compared to a "marble vault," and this important image occurs in the center of the poem. The speaker's problem is that despite the woman's charms, her vault is coldly closed to him. He deftly uses this refusal as a means to forward his assault on the woman, however, since the word vault (tomb) points toward her death. He clinches the attack with the next image, the most horrifying one in the poem. If she refuses him, "then worms shall try/That long preserved virginity."

Returning to more traditional overtures, the speaker praises her "youthful hue" and dewy skin, from which, through "every pore," he urges her "willing soul" to catch fire. These pores are more openings into her body, and the connection with the earlier openings and the penetrating worms belies the surface innocence of this set of images. The violence directed at the woman is expanded and redirected toward the couple as "amorous birds of prey" who may "devour" time, not "languish in his slow-chapped power." The closing vision of how they will "tear our pleasures with rough strife/Thorough the iron gates of life" returns to the language of assault on the female body. All in all, the woman is subject to being "devoured" by her amorous admirer and by time itself.

Written in the context of the Renaissance poetic tradition of equating the female body with a fortress that must be assaulted, and phrased in terms of the seventeenth century's fondness for morbid and grotesque Metaphysical imagery, the poem powerfully depicts the secondary status of the female body. Indeed, when the speaker notes that she will find herself in her grave one day, he does not describe the moldering away of his body in the vault as he does hers, though he does imagine his lust turned to ashes. He fails to note where he will be, almost as though he will not pay the penalties she will.

But it is a mistake to see "To His Coy Mistress" as belittling women in a simplistic way; indeed, just as it is today, women's marginality in a male-dominated world can indicate not their helplessness, but their pent-up power. The woman addressed is goddesslike: capricious and cruel, she is one who must be complained to and served. Both the speaker's flattery and his verbal attacks mask his fear of her. To him the feminine is enclosed and unattainable—tomblike as well as womblike. The speaker's gracefulness of proposition, through the courtly love tradition, gives way to crude imagery as the woman's power is exercised in continued refusal (it is evident that she has *already* said no to him). The feminine is thus portrayed as a *negative* state: that is, she does not assent; she is not in the poem; her final decision is not stated. It is a poem about power, and the power may be with the silent female, with the vault or womb, the negative space of the feminine.

As distinct from his speaker, Marvell offers a portrayal of

male and female roles of his day that celebrates their various positions while sharply indicating their limitations. It is a positive and negative evaluation. On the one hand, it is a poem about youth and passion for life, both intellectual and physical, both male and female. It gives us a picture of the lives of sophisticated people during the time, people who enjoy sex for pleasure and who are not above making jokes and having fun arguing about it. No mention is made of procreation in the poem, nor of marriage, nor really of love. It is about sex. The poem is so sophisticated that instead of merely restating the courtly love tradition, it parodies it. Yet on the other hand, as the male speaker satirizes the lady's coyness, he is even more satirizing himself and his peevish fear of the feminine as expressed in his imagistic attempts to scare her into sex with him. The repellent quality of his images of women—like a bad dream—haunts us long after his artful invention and his own coy sense of humor fade.

B. Frailty, Thy Name Is Hamlet:
Hamlet and Women

The hero of *Hamlet* is afflicted, as we pointed out in chapter 4, with the world's most famous Oedipus complex, surpassing that even of the namesake of the complex. The death of his father and the hasty remarriage of his mother to his uncle so threaten Hamlet's ego that he finds himself splintered, driven to action even as he resists action with doubts and delays. He is a son who must act against his "parents," Gertrude and Claudius, in order to avenge his image of his real father as well as to alleviate his own psychic injury, which could be described as a symbolic castration. But because his conflict is driven by two irreconcilable father-images, Hamlet directs his fury toward his mother—and, to a lesser degree, toward his beloved Ophelia—even as he attempts to act against the father(s). Hamlet's irresolvable tension between his two fathers becomes a male-female conflict that is likewise unannealed. Though a feminist reading of the play has some things in common with what we discussed in our earlier chapter, the assumptions and conclusions are very different. The feminist reading that follows is based upon Hamlet's loathing of his mother and of all feminine subjects as well. His hatred of women turns inward and destroys him.

In the play's father-son conflicts as well as in its depiction of a clash between genders, women in the play generate various dualities. Hamlet contends with a woman's body, his mother's, and he in turn has been acted upon by that body. That Hamlet sees sexuality as evil is manifested in his revulsion at Claudius, his disgust at his mother, and his cruel denunciation of Ophelia, and also in his own self-loathing at being born out of *that* body. His most thoroughgoing hatred is occasioned by the conflicting sexual feelings that threaten him from his own unconscious.

The world of *Hamlet* is riven by power struggles within and without Elsinore Castle, and the play's psychological themes are made more powerful by their contact with the other major thematic pattern in the play, that of politics. As Shakespeare was writing *Hamlet*, perhaps the advancing age of Queen Elizabeth I and the precariousness of the succession—always with the accompanying danger of war at home and abroad— were elements in the dramatist's conjoining a man's relations with women with his relation to political power. The play gives us a picture of the role of women in Elizabethan society, from the way Ophelia must obey her father without question, to the dangers maidens might expect to encounter from young men, to the inappropriateness of Queen Gertrude's sexual desire. Admittedly, cultural roles of the women of the court, as in this play, are not applicable to women of all classes in Elizabethan times or in our own, but what women stand for psychologically and sexually in *Hamlet* has universal significance.

The emphasis upon family relationships from the beginning of the play is accompanied by an emphasis upon political matters. The night from which the ghost initially emerges is identified in female terms, compounding the fear of unrest in general with fear of the feminine: the ghost lies in the "womb of earth" (I.i) and walks in an unwholesome night in which a "witch has power to charm" (I.i), banished only by a male figure, the crowing "cock." Claudius has taken as his wife "our sometime sister, now our queen" albeit with "a defeated joy,/With an auspicious, and a dropping eye,/With mirth in funeral, and with dirge in marriage" (I.ii).

The father-son images in Claudius's description of matters between Denmark and Norway are followed by Claudius's fatherly behavior to young Laertes and then by the first appearance of Hamlet in the play. Hamlet's first words are directed to his mother in response to an address by Claudius; when Claudius gets as far as calling Hamlet "my son," Hamlet's aside, "A little more than kin, and less than kind" (I.ii), illustrates the personal and political conflicts that have arisen. Gertrude pleads with Hamlet to stop mourning his father, and Claudius asks Hamlet to think of him as a father, but, ignoring Claudius, Hamlet replies only to his mother.

What follows is the first of his many soul-searching monologues. When Hamlet thinks of himself he thinks first of "this too too sallied flesh" (for which alternate readings have offered "sullied" and "solid" for "sallied"), which he would destroy had "the Everlasting not fix'd/His canon 'gainst self-slaughter." If his flesh is sullied, his mother's is polluted: in the monologue he blames his mother's "frailty" for exchanging "Hyperion" for a "satyr." She is "unrighteous" and beastlike in her lust, even incestuous (I.ii). He is interrupted from his thoughts by the news that guards have sighted his father, and he is eager for the night to come so that the foul deeds of the past may rise.

Hamlet's meditation on his mother's faults and his later assault on her are keys to understanding his torment, but while many critics have been content to go through the play seeing Gertrude through her son's eyes, feminist critic Carolyn Heilbrun provided an important revision of Gertrude. Instead of a "well-meaning but shallow" Gertrude, Heilbrun describes through feminist analysis of Gertrude's own words a Queen whose speech is quite pointed "and a little courageous" rather than hollow and uninformed. Gertrude time and time again expresses herself well. She is solicitous of Hamlet, asking him to sit near her to give him a sense of belonging to the court, and her speech to Laertes upon Ophelia's death is a model of decorum and sensitivity, one instance in which her usual directness would not be appropriate. If there is one quality that characterizes all of Gertrude's speeches, it is her "ability to see reality clearly, and to express it," Heilbrun says, even when turned upon herself. As Hamlet rails against her and even violently seizes her in act III, despite her fear—"Thou wilt not murder me?" (III.iv)—she betrays no knowledge of the murder and asks Hamlet "What have I done, that thou dar'st wag thy tongue/In noise so rude against me?" (III.iv). Hamlet denounces her sexual passion, and she responds: "O Hamlet, speak no more!/ Thou turn'st mine eyes into my very soul,/And there I see such black and grained spots/As will not leave their tinct" (III.iv). She knows lust is her sin, and she admits it. But this is very different from being an accomplice to murder. She thinks Hamlet mad, and promises she will not betray him, and she does not. In the end, Heilbrun sums up Gertrude: ". . . if she is lustful, [she] is also intelligent, penetrating, and gifted" (*Hamlet's Mother and Other Women* 1–17).

Let us contrast the distorted image of the Mother that Hamlet projects upon Gertrude with Gertrude's own evident dimension as a character. Their relationship is most significant for a feminist reading, since Gertrude is the ground upon which all the battles of the play are fought; hers is the contested body and hers is the female psyche configured and reconfigured by her son, husbands, and courtiers. Gertrude as woman is the source of all the conflicts in the play, but she herself is apparently not willingly engaged in any of them.

When the ghost of Hamlet's father addresses Gertrude's sin—"O Hamlet, what a falling-off was there/From me"—he argues that she has married because of her lust (I.v). He identifies his own body with the temple and the city ("And in the porches of my ears did pour/The leprous distillment"), while describing his wife's body as thorny vegetation. But the ghost warns Hamlet against taking revenge on his mother: "Leave her to Heaven" (I.v). Following the Ghost's lead, throughout the play such negative images of women are associated with unwholesome characters, even as Ophelia's innocence serves as an ironic (but hopeless) contrast. For example, there are the crude sex jokes of Rosencrantz and Guildenstern, who characterize first the earth and then Fortune as whores. And when Laertes warns Ophelia about Hamlet's intentions, she jibes him about his own behavior toward women; more to the point, Polonius pays Reynaldo to spy on Laertes to see whether he is whoring. This fact helps establish Ophelia as reliable as against the actions of her hypocritical brother and father. Thus, we know she is the better judge of Hamlet's strange behavior—he truly is disturbed in his seeming disgust for her—than Polonius, who puts it down merely to lovesickness. Gertrude knows what is wrong with her son: "I doubt it is no other but the main,/His father's death and our o'erhasty marriage" (II.ii).

When a troupe of players comes to the castle, Hamlet asks one of them to repeat Aeneas's speech to Dido, an appropriate male-versus-female scene in that Aeneas abandons Dido in order to pursue his political destiny. The "strumpet" Fortune is referred to again, but the most important image of a woman offered in Hamlet's conversation with the players is the mention of Hecuba, wife of King Priam, who, unlike Hamlet's mother, mourns for her children rather than they for her. Hamlet thinks of his own genuine grief in response to the players' delineation of Hecuba's, and calls himself a "whore" and "drab" who must only "unpack" his heart with words—acting, that is, instead of taking action (II.ii).

The Queen's half-hearted questions evince her growing despair with her son's behavior. Continuing the whore image, Claudius in an aside compares his own pious playacting to a "harlot's cheek, beautied with plast'ring art" (III.i), but when the Queen is accused of whoredom she does not appear whorish, only sad.

These doubts about truth in kingship and in love are followed by Hamlet's famous musing on suicide in his "To be, or not to be" speech (III.i), a speech ended by the entrance of Ophelia, whom Hamlet addresses as "nymph" and whom he asks to pray for him. But as they speak he begins to berate her violently; this is the first time he has fully revealed his emotions to another person. His demands to know whether she is "honest and fair" escalate into his shouting at her, "Get thee to a nunnery" (*nunnery* being Elizabethan slang for brothel), and his words recall the advice against young men she has heard from Polonius and Laertes. He ends by accusing her and all women of making monsters of men. Hamlet never voices his anger to Claudius, only to Gertrude and Ophelia.

"Heavenly powers, restore him!" Ophelia sadly prays after he has departed: "O, what a noble mind is here o'erthrown!" Hamlet was the model for manhood, "Th' expectation and rose of the fair state,/The glass of fashion and the mould of form." Ophelia's punning on "the fair state" to mean women as well as his polity effectively yokes together the feminine and the male political power that denies it. Perhaps Hamlet is falling prey to the denial of his own "feminine" traits—gentleness, a forgiving heart, stability—caught as he is in the personal and political throes of male ego struggles. Ophelia too is co-opted by what women represent when she characterizes herself as "of ladies most deject and wretched,/That suck'd the honey of his music vows" (III.i). But her reason, her love, and her faith demonstrate her value.

Later, in the play-within-the-play, the poison used to kill the King is described as "Hecat's ban thrice blasted, thrice infected" (III.ii). The witch Hecat (Hecate) is a dark feminine image from Greek mythology, while both "blasted" and "infected" are words that refer to venereal disease, like the "sullied" with which Hamlet earlier described himself and like the terms used to describe whores. This imagery expresses what has been driving everyone: the "sin" of sexuality.

We sense that the scene between Hamlet and his mother is that which has been put off so long, but in typically misdirected anger Hamlet murders the foolish Polonius instead of taking direct action and confronting himself. He begs his mother to repent of her marriage. Fittingly, when Laertes learns of his father's murder, the images in which he expresses his frustrated desire to revenge him are those of whoredom: "That drop of blood that's calm proclaims me bastard,/Cries cuckold to my father, brands the harlot/Even here between the chaste unsmirched brow/Of my true mother" (IV.v). Following Hamlet's failure the feminine is again perceived as negative by the males, and this in contrast to Ophelia's pitiful grief, and her mock dirge for all women: "Good night, ladies, good night. Sweet ladies, good night, good night" (IV.v).

The final act begins with Hamlet and Laertes fighting in Ophelia's newly dug grave, after which Hamlet confesses his love for her, a question that has been left hanging until now. Perhaps Ophelia's death has awakened him to his true nature as a lover of women instead of a victim of them. Laertes, now described as the gentleman's model instead of Hamlet, has taken Hamlet's masculine, provoking, revenge-seeking place.

They fight, and each is wounded with the poisoned sword of the father-king, Claudius. The Queen drinks a poisoned cup. She says she "carouses" to Hamlet's "fortune" and urges him on. She calls, "Here, Hamlet, take my napkin, and rub thy brows," just as a proud and loving mother would do: perhaps she has been healed as well (V.ii). Dying, Hamlet forces Claudius to drink from the cup. But it is all too late, even for revenge, and it is left to Horatio to tell Hamlet's story. Hamlet and the two women he loved join his two fathers and Laertes in death. Political stability is restored by Fortinbras with a manly flourish. The crisis of sons and fathers is over, and the world of male political power is renewed, but the problem of the feminine realm remains unsolved.

C. Men, Women, and the Loss of Faith in "Young Goodman Brown"

From a feminist point of view, Nathaniel Hawthorne was unusual for his time in that his portraits of women go against the prevailing literary sexism of his day. Despite his comment that he was tired of competing with the "mob of scribbling women" writing romance novels, he generally used women not just as symbols of wholeness and goodness, as they are often pictured, but as possessing knowledge that approaches that of the author and narrator. Hawthorne also treated women with more realism and depth than did most other writers, especially male writers. This became an important legacy to other writers, particularly Henry James and William Faulkner, who also portray women as powerful moral agents.

Hawthorne's most interesting women characters are Hester Prynne and Pearl of *The Scarlet Letter*, Zenobia of *The Blithedale Romance*, Hepzibah Pyncheon of *The House of the Seven Gables*, Miriam of *The Marble Faun*, Georgiana Aylmer of "The Birthmark," and Beatrice Rappaccini of "Rappaccini's Daughter." All these women engage in conflict with the men in their lives and all of them have the sympathy—to varying degrees—of the author. Hester is Hawthorne's greatest creation of a character, male or female, and from the lips of the magnificent Zenobia, Hawthorne gives us as eloquent a speech on women's rights as was ever penned.

However, Faith Brown of "Young Goodman Brown" is not a three-dimensional character. With her allegorical name and small role in the story, readers might be likely to overlook her significance. But, in fact, the story centers on her—more specifically, on her husband's rejection of her. The tale is a psychosexual parable of the rejection of the feminine in favor of the father-figure symbolized by the Devil. Good and evil are thus engendered qualities in the story. Hawthorne's sympathies are with the woman and not with the misconstrued masculinity of the rigid Brown, whose failure is his rejection of his wife's sexuality in favor of some unstated allure in the forest. What he finds there is a frightening masculine figure who actually resembles his own father. Rejecting the feminine, Brown gives up his adult sexuality in favor of a regression to powerlessness at the mercy of a Terrible Father.

The sexual aspect of Brown's mission is indicated in the repeated mentions of the women who will be present at the witch meeting, from Goody Cloyse and the governor's wife to the most spent of prostitutes. It is important that Brown learned his religion from Goody Cloyse, and that when he wonders whether he is hurting Faith by continuing his wilderness journey, the Devil produces Goody Cloyse to make Brown suspect women. Goody Cloyse says she is attending the ceremony to see a man, while the men on horseback Brown overhears seem to be drawn there to see the women whom they expect. Sex is certainly at the heart of things: the Devil's snaky staff is an appropriate phallic symbol, and the ritual itself turns out to be a black mass. But the general tone is far from a celebration of male and female sexuality; women are victimized in this story. Significantly, the Devil mentions his having helped Brown's grandfather persecute Quaker women in Salem.

Women are seen by Brown as either innocents or temptresses, from Martha Carrier, a "rampant hag" who "had received the devil's promise to be queen of hell" to the seemingly unspotted maidens who crowd around the evil altar. To Brown, sex with women is alluring but deadly, and this is reinforced by the juxtaposition of the bloody basin and Brown's paleness at the altar of unholy communion. When he sees his wife at the altar, he sees her only as a "polluted wretch."

Of course, in the end, Brown is the one polluted; as the narrator tells us, he is the most "frightful" figure in the forest, and he returns home to rebuke and frighten his wife. We are told that his "hoary corpse" is carried to his grave followed by his wife and his children and grandchildren, and instead of shuddering at his gloomy death, one shudders instead to think that Faith and her children lived all those empty years with his blighted self, a failed husband and father.

D. Women and "Sivilization" in *Huckleberry Finn*

When Huck Finn dresses as a girl, "Sarah Mary Williams," and tries to get information from the clever housewife, Mrs. Judith Loftus, in chapter 11 of *Huckleberry Finn*, is Twain reminding female readers that they are not persons who could enjoy Huck's male adventuring, or is he illustrating the close connection between Huck's willingness to cross gender lines and his later freedom to cross racial lines? The novel's overall theme of the individual versus the community uses the feminine in very important ways. In one sense, the feminine has been described as what Huck is running away from—"sivilization." But on the other hand, the novel's satire so often suggests what Twain demonstrates elsewhere in his portraits of women—including those of Roxy in *Pudd'nhead Wilson*, Eve in her "Autobiography," and his beloved Joan of Arc—what is *not* in community that ought to be. The treatment of gender is important in what is preeminently the boy's book of its day.

Several critics have produced important studies of Twain and the feminine, including Shelley Fisher Fishkin, who notes how scholars have seen women as "bad for Twain" and Twain as "bad for women." Biographers such as Van Wyck Brooks and Justin Kaplan felt that Twain's wife, Olivia Langdon Clemens, emasculated his authorial power and artistic integrity with her conventionality, and even Twain's early admirers, such as William Dean Howells and Bernard De Voto, complained of the thinness of his female characters. Fishkin urges a "more nuanced, complex perspective" on the subject. She sees women as key to his creative process, including his wife, and notes his largely female audience. Twain's work was and is an important force for shaping writing by women, including that of Gertrude Stein, Tillie Olsen, and Toni Morrison (53–54, 67–69).

A more radical stance is that of Laura Skandera-Trombley, who argues that critics have severely underemphasized the influence of women on Twain's life and works, merely blaming them for certain problems. Twain existed within a sort of "charmed circle" of women who read drafts, heard passages read aloud, offered commentary, and even acted as editors. They were, according to Skandera-Trombley, no less than his source of creative energy; they were "collaborators," and the sentimental romance novels they read were an inspiration to him. She sees Olivia as the single most important relationship in his life. And Twain was also influenced by several other women who were "dynamic, intelligent, and unapologetic as well as committed feminists," such to his daughter Susy, whose untimely death effectively produced "personal and creative dysfunction" in him (59, 131, 168).

The most positive figure in the story, the slave Jim, is a happily married man who in the end is to be reunited with his wife and family. Jim's tenderness is the book's most feminine quality, and with the exception of Jim, it is almost entirely absent in the men Huck encounters. In his function as servant (making fires, washing pots, showing hospitality to guests), Jim enacts a mother's role, a moral touchstone, according to Paulette Wasserstein (31–33). Yet, as Nancy Walker notes, though the virtues Huck begins to develop—"honesty, compassion, a sense of duty"—are "defined in the novel as female virtues," his sex requires that he ultimately emulate men, see women as "other," and in the end, run from the "sivilizing" presence of women, unable to distinguish between society's false concept of virtue and true morality (488).

But whether Huck truly attains an understanding of the feminine or not, the novel could be viewed as a quest for contact with the feminine through its challenges to gender identities as well as race. The archetypal male adventure story and American *Bildungsroman*, *Huckleberry Finn* may be better understood not as a flight from "sivilization" and all it represents—including feminine propriety—but rather as a flight from masculine authority to seek out alternatives. Instead of undergoing a *rite de passage* to prepare him for manhood in the traditional sense, Huck may be searching on the flowing river for an archetype of the mother. Certainly some of the novel's most characteristic and memorable scenes take place on the river.

We noted earlier that Judith Loftus casts all categorization of male and female roles into question. But Twain himself also seems confused in the episode about the lines between maleness and femaleness. Mrs. Loftus is quite schooled in the *appearance* of gender; after Huck is found out, her list of how women do things as opposed to how men do them demonstrates not the absoluteness of gender but its existence as merely interpretable and alterable behavior. For example, Mrs. Loftus tells Huck that "when you set out to thread a needle, don't hold the thread still and fetch the needle up to it; hold the needle still and poke the thread at it—that's the way a woman most always does; but a man always does it t'other way." Yet in chapter 13 of *The Prince and the Pauper*, Twain has Miles Hendon do it exactly opposite: "He did as men have always done, and probably always will do, to the end of time— held the needle still, and tried to thrust the thread through the eye, which is the opposite of a woman's way." That Twain seems unsure of women's or men's true ways indicates his ambivalence about the social role of the feminine.

One gets the feeling that Mrs. Loftus is bored and that she likes the diversion of Huck. She is anything but the arid disciplinarian Miss Watson; she is more akin to the kind Widow Douglas. But Mrs. Loftus is more. In this scene, the combination of her sagacity, kindness, and willingness to playact seems to set the stage for Huck's own lies and performances throughout the novel in the various disguises he dons to protect himself and Jim. The notion that femininity *is* a role is important to Huck's learning about role playing by people in society in general, and it points toward the arbitrariness of the role assigned to blacks in the South.

The Judith Loftus episode is one of the most important uses of the feminine in the novel, but the role of women continues to be fundamental throughout. Their representation is paradoxical: on the one hand, they represent in their "sivilizing" roles the conventionality of society, the very conventionality from which Huck and Jim are attempting to escape. Most are reduced to titles: "Widow," "Miss," "Aunt," and "Sister," instead of full names. On the other hand, implicit in many of these characterizations is also the principle of union, nurture, and moral stability imaged by femininity and maternity.

A brief look at other female characters bears out both these assertions. Huck's own mother is barely mentioned, but when she is it is to oppose her to pap's antipathy to any values Huck might develop. Pap invades the Widow's home to insist that Huck stop going to school because "Your mother couldn't read, and she couldn't write, nuther, before she died. None of the family couldn't before they died. I can't; and you're a-swelling yourself up like this." Huck notes that he didn't want to go to school before, but "I reckoned I'd go now to spite pap," even though he is "thrashed" by his father for doing so.

The Widow Douglas, kind and motherly but ultimately ineffectual, is the one from whom Huck runs and the one whom he reveres. She seems, like Aunt Polly, to understand and love children, and she encourages him to develop a conscience: "She said she warn't ashamed of me." Huck thus finds himself torn between his desire to draw near to the Widow and his rebellion against the enforced identity Miss Watson wishes to foist upon him. Miss Watson represents a balance to the Widow. Though she is also a reformer like the Widow, she is the worst of "sivilization": hypocritical, self-righteous, repressed. And yet she frees Jim in the end. One wonders if she too comes to rebel against the male authority figures she reveres in her town and in her Bible.

In Huck's lies about his family, there is almost always a dead mother and a threatened sister or female family friend (such as "Miss Hooker"—a name Twain took from his wife's close friend, Alice Hooker Day, niece of Henry Ward Beecher). Foolish though she is, when Aunt Sally Phelps mothers Huck he says he feels "mean" and ashamed of his bad behavior; indeed, the comedy of the last chapters depends almost entirely on her exaggerated reactions to the boys' pranks. One wonders just how much she really does know is going on. Yet when she wants to adopt and "sivilize" Huck, he heads for the Territory. Aunt Sally is accompanied by her stereotyped, bumbling husband (both are figures of frontier humor) and her know-it-all-friend, Sister Hotchkiss, who in chapter 41 provides comic relief from the suspenseful last events of the story. A final mother figure is Aunt Polly, who appears like a *dea ex machina*; she is severe to the boys, but tender to a fault in her concern for Tom. Aunt Sally and Miss Watson might be seen as representing two ends of the spectrum: Aunt Sally is hopelessly inept at reform, while Miss Watson fails because she is harsh; the ideal middle, as Nancy Walker has suggested, is the Widow Douglas with her loving discipline. She teaches Huck how to care for others, evidenced in his concern for Jim's "essential humanity" (Nancy Walker 496).

Younger women figure importantly as well. Emmeline Grangerford represents a shallow, anemic romanticism; her "art" of poetry is heavily satirized. All her sorrow is wasted on her insubstantial self. Yet she also points toward important characterizations of women at the time, such as the cults of hysteria and idleness, reminding one of Edgar Allan Poe's female characters or the heroine of Charlotte Perkins Gilman's "The Yellow Wallpaper." She also reveals in her gloomy paintings a realistic sense of the climate of darkness around her as the murderous feuds are enacted year after year. Sophia Grangerford is a welcome contrast, a beautiful and courageous young woman, the eternal bride. Through her friendship with Huck she is able to escape her fear-ridden world. The "Harelip" whom Huck meets at the Wilks house is a humorous interlude between dangers: she wryly sees through Huck's ridiculous lies—made to impress her—about life in England. Sober, serious-minded, and shrewd, despite her unveiling of Huck she does not attack him. Mary Jane Wilks is like Sophia, but wiser and calmer, and like the Harelip, only more attractive. And, as Mark Altschuler has noted in "Motherless Child," she is especially appealing to Huck because she "embodies mother, victim, and orphan—the three most powerful images for Huck." Her "unearned nurturing" is a key to his ultimate moral development; she is the only mother-figure in the text he does not reject—we are even led to wonder if he will take up prayer again under Mary Jane's influence. Her friendship with Huck allows him to save her and her family from the evil manipulations of the King and the Duke. Huck seems to respect this more verbal and down-to-earth version of Sophia more than any other woman in the book, or any other character except Jim, for that matter. One pictures Mary Jane Wilks growing up into a woman like the Widow, for she brings out Huck's maleness in a positive way that allows both himself and others to grow and maintain human dignity. That he does not ultimately mature—at least within the novel—is not her fault, but is a larger statement about the "ineffectuality of women in his society" (Nancy Walker 499).

Though *Huckleberry Finn* does seem to want to turn women into mothers, keep sex out of the picture, use women for the most part as symbols of undesirable cultural conventionality, and defeat women in the end, its variety of female nurturers does offer an enriching view of women throughout its chapters. After all, Huck Finn is not the only one who journeys downriver; we must remember that the redoubtable Aunt Polly travels many hundreds of miles to see to the safety of her Tom and, by chance, to that of America's most famous orphan.

E. "In Real Life": Recovering the Feminine Past in "Everyday Use"

Whose story is this? "For your grandmama." For your mama, sister, daughter, friend. For *you*, girl, no matter where you are or who you are—for *you*. Are you scarred and scared Maggie, afraid to be anything more? Are you Dee, with your college-educated fear of the past and grandiose design for the future? Are you the mother of these sisters, whose rough work "does not show on television," but who knows when something hits her on the top of the head "just like when I'm in church"? Are your hands quick with the needle, piecing Lone Star and Walk Around the Mountain with scraps of old dresses? Or maybe Afroed and art-historied and aware? Or, perhaps, are you living in "real life," finally finding that quick tongue to give voice to your heritage and then sit with it "just enjoying"?

"Everyday Use" is about the everyday lives of black women past and present, encircled by family and culture. Its quilt is an emblem of American women's culture itself, an object of communal harmony made by women out of their well-worn clothes. The quilt warms and protects our bodies; it is passed down like mother's wisdom from generation to generation; its designs mirror the most everyday but most profound concerns of all women—marriage, family, love. Like much women's art it is decentered, nonhierarchical, intimate. It is a product of bonding—daughter/mother, woman/woman, domestic/aesthetic, etc. As Barbara Christian aptly notes, "Walker is drawn to the integral and economical process of quilt making as a model for her own craft"; it helps her answer the writer's question, "From whence do I come?" (*Black Feminist Criticism* 85).

Walker identifies the quilt as one of the traditional art forms of African American women, along with gospel singing and gardening, that "kept alive" the creativity of the black woman "century after century." These women, the "the mule[s] of the world," were in fact "Creators, who lived lives of spiritual waste, because they were so rich in spirituality" (*In Search of Our Mothers' Gardens* 233). Like Virginia Woolf in *A Room of One's Own*, Walker searches for her literary foremothers, noting that "we have constantly looked high, when we should have looked low." In her poem "Women" Walker praises the "Headragged Generals" of her mother's generation, who, through their manual labor, "battered down/Doors" for their children "To discover books" while ". . . they knew what we/Must know/Without knowing a page/Of it/Themselves" (*Revolutionary Petunias* 5).

In "Everyday Use," Walker's concept of heritage is in part articulated in response to the black power movements of the 1960s, particularly the cultural nationalism that many African Americans felt during that time, with its emphasis upon the appreciation of the African cultural past. According to Christian, Walker's feminism, also born in the 1960s, articulates this response and critiques the short-sightedness of radicals who would have seen the narrator as "that supposedly backward Southern ancestor the cultural nationalists of the North probably visited during the summers of their youth and probably considered behind the times." Walker "gives voice to an entire maternal ancestry often silenced by the political rhetoric of the period." It is her way of "breaking silences and stereotypes about her grandmothers', mothers', sisters' lives" (Introduction to *"Everyday Use": Alice Walker* 10–11).

In a 1973 interview with Mary Helen Washington, as reported by Barbara Christian, Walker identifies three cycles of black women she would explore in her writings, characters who Walker felt were missing from contemporary writing. First are those "who were cruelly exploited, spirits and bodies mutilated, relegated to the most narrow and confining lives, sometimes driven to madness"—as is clear in the portraits of women in her novel *The Third Life of Grange Copeland* (1970) and in the short stories of *In Love and Trouble* (1973), which contains "Everyday Use." The women of Walker's second cycle are those who are not so much physically but psychically abused as a result of wanting desperately to participate in mainstream American life, the most poignant example being her fellow writer Hurston. Those in the third cycle are black women who gain a new consciousness of what Christian terms "their right to be themselves and to shape the world," as seen in the heroines of *Meridian* (1976) and in *The Color Purple*, as well as in a second collection of short stories, *You Can't Keep a Good Woman Down* (1981) (Introduction to *"Everyday Use"*: *Alice Walker* 3–7).

"Everyday Use" contains examples of all three cycles. Maggie does not know her own worth; her mother says she walks like "a lame animal, perhaps a dog run over by some careless person rich enough to own a car." Dee inhabits the second cycle; though she appears not to want to assimilate into white society, she does not appreciate her own heritage until it has become fashionable to do so. Though her mother applauds Dee's strength of self, she is saddened by her denigration of her own people's past. The mother prefigures the women of Walker's third cycle in her self-reliance but simultaneous connectedness to her past. As an older woman, she is in a position in her little "community" to pass along her wisdom to the woman of the first cycle, Maggie, and perhaps also even to Dee, and in so doing she becomes a fresh, modern, believable character, as Christian notes. The mother's sudden snatching away of the quilts from Dee and presentation of them to Maggie demonstrates a rejection of stereotypes (Introduction to *"Everyday Use"*: *Alice Walker* 9, 12).

In "Everyday Use" Walker makes a conscious choice to portray women. The only men in the story are dead, absent, or unnamed (we never do find out what Dee's boyfriend's real name is). Houston A. Baker, Jr., and Charlotte Pierce-Baker see Maggie as "the arisen goddess of Walker's story; she is the sacred figure who bears the scarifications of experience and knows how to convert patches into robustly patterned and beautifully quilted wholes" (in *"Everyday Use": Alice Walker* "Patches" 162), connecting Maggie's hidden powers with those of African goddesses of creativity and generation. Maggie's humility and sense of beauty cast her as the innocent in the story, and her quiet femininity is upheld in the end when her mother takes her side against her sister. She will marry John Thomas and live with him, her quilts, and presumably the children begotten in their bed, and she will become an adult woman with her own life and traditions, but she would not have passed the point of fearing life without her mother's help. Walker, herself scarred in a childhood accident to her eye, presents Maggie with great pity and tenderness, but in the end shows how she has started to overcome her deficiencies.

Dee, who tells her mother that she just "doesn't understand," comes off for most readers as the one who doesn't understand. Dee's bossiness and her flashes of hypocrisy put off readers; there is also the hint that she set the house on fire on purpose and is responsible for Maggie's handicap. At the least Dee is pretentious and selfish. But we must also see Dee as an example of what most of the girls who grew up with her could only dream of: she is the feminist's ideal—a woman who makes a success of herself despite overwhelming odds. She has managed to move to the city, get an education, and get a good job. She is politically involved and active. She is the future. Walker's own feelings toward Dee must be mixed, as with Maggie, for Dee is based upon Walker's sister Molly, the subject of the bittersweet poem, "For My Sister Molly Who In the Fifties." In an interview Walker says of her sister, "When she came to visit us in Georgia it was—at first—like having Christmas with us all during her vacation. She loved to read and tell stories; she taught me African songs and dances; she cooked fanciful dishes that looked like anything but plain old sharecropper food. I loved her so much it came as a great shock—and a shock I don't expect to recover from—to learn that she was ashamed of us. We were so poor, so dusty, and sunburnt. We talked wrong. We didn't know how to dress, or use the right eating utensils. And so, she drifted away, and I did not understand it" (O'Brien, "Interview with Alice Walker," in Christian, 79–80). The narrator says Dee "washed us in a river of make-believe, burned us with a lot of knowledge we didn't necessarily need to know. Pressed us to her with the serious way she read, to shove us away at just the moment, like dimwits, we seemed about to understand."

At the end of "Everyday Use," Dee has accepted the *things* passed on as her heritage but not the *spirit* that Maggie has accepted. She has allowed heritage to become, as Christian points out, an "abstraction rather than a living idea," and hence subordinated people to artifacts, elevated culture above community (*"Everyday Use": Alice Walker* 130). Dee is defeated, but to assert only that is to miss the deeper point of the story, which attempts to redefine black feminism in terms that will reconcile Dee's effort with Maggie's traditionalism: their mother is the bridge that connects past and future. She is a typical example of Walker's Southern black female character who insists upon challenging conventions, "on her right to be herself" (*"Everyday Use": Alice Walker* 7). She brings to mind Walker's refusal to use the term *feminist* and her insistence on using *womanist* instead. As an epigraph to *In Search of Our Mothers' Gardens*, Walker gives four definitions of the term "womanist." First, it is "a black feminist or feminist of color" derived from "womanish," a black folk expression of mothers to female children who are "outrageous, audacious, or wilful," who want to know more than is good for them, who want to be grown up (too soon). Second, the term can refer to "a woman who loves other women, sexually and/or nonsexually," who "appreciates and prefers women's culture, . . . women's emotional flexibility, . . . and women's strength." Third, the womanist "Loves music. Loves dance. Loves the moon. *Loves* the Spirit. Loves love and food and roundness. Loves struggle. *Loves* the Folk. Loves herself. *Regardless.*" And, finally, "Womanist is to feminist as purple is to lavender."

• • •

As is evident from the foregoing, feminist criticism has affinities with a number of other critical approaches, especially with cultural studies, as we shall see in the next chapter.

Quick Reference

Abel, Elizabeth. "Editor's Introduction." *Critical Inquiry* 8 (1981): 173–78.

Altschuler, Mark. "Motherless Child: Huck Finn and a Theory of Moral Development." *American Literary Realism* 22, no. 1 (fall 1989): 31–41.

Awkward, Michael. *Inspiring Influences: Tradition, Revision, and Afro-American Women's Novels.* New York: Columbia University Press, 1989.

Baker, Houston A., Jr. *Workings of the Spirit: The Poetics of Afro-American Women's Writing.* Chicago: University of Chicago Press, 1991.

Baker, Houston A., Jr., and Charlotte Pierce-Baker. "Patches: Quilts and Community in Alice Walker's 'Everyday Use.'" In *"Everyday Use": Alice Walker.* New Brunswick, NJ: Rutgers University Press, 1994.

Barrett, Michele. *Women's Oppression Today: Problems in Marxist Feminist Analysis.* London: Verso Editions, 1980.

de Beauvoir, Simone. *The Second Sex.* 1949. Reprint, Harmondsworth, England: Penguin, 1972.

Bell, Bernard W. *The Afro-American Novel and Its Tradition.* Amherst: University of Massachusetts Press, 1987.

Bizzell, Patricia, and Bruce Herteberg. "Julia Kristeva and 'Women's Time.'" In *The Rhetorical Tradition: Readings from Classical Times to the Present.* Boston: St. Martin's Press (Bedford), 1990.

Chodorow, Nancy. *The Reproduction of Mothering: Psychoanalysis and the Sociology of Gender.* Berkeley: University of California Press, 1978.

Christian, Barbara. *Black Feminist Criticism.* New York: Pergamon Press, 1985.

———, ed. *"Everyday Use": Alice Walker.* New Brunswick, NJ: Rutgers University Press, 1994.

Cixous, Hélène. "The Character of 'Character.'" *New Literary History* 52 (1974): 383–402.

———. "The Laugh of the Medusa." *Signs* 1, no. 4 (1976): 875–93.

Clark, Suzanne. "Julia Kristeva: Rhetoric and the Woman as Stranger." *Reclaiming Rhetorica: Women in the Rhetorical Tradition.* Ed. Andrea Lunsford. Pittsburgh: University of Pittsburg Press, 1995.

Cruikshank, Margaret. *Lesbian Studies: Present and Future.* New York: Feminist Press, 1982.

Daly, Mary. *Gyn/Ecology*. Boston: Beacon Press, 1978.

Davidson, Cathy M., and E. M. Broner, eds. *The Lost Tradition: Mothers and Daughters in Literature*. New York: Ungar, 1980.

DeVeau, Alexis. *Black Women Writers at Work*. Ed. Claudia Tate. New York: Continuum, 1983.

Faderman, Lillian. *Surpassing the Love of Men: Romantic Friendship and Love between Women from the Renaissance to the Present*. New York: William Morrow & Co., 1981.

Felski, Rita. *Beyond Feminist Literature and Social Change*. Cambridge, MA: Harvard University Press, 1990.

Fishkin, Shelley Fisher. "Mark Twain and Women." In *The Cambridge Companion to Mark Twain*. Ed. Forrest G. Robinson. Cambridge: Cambridge University Press, 1995.

Fishkin, Shelley Fisher, and Elaine Hedges, eds. *Listening to Silences: New Essays in Feminist Criticism*. Oxford: Oxford University Press, 1994.

Friedan, Betty. *The Feminine Mystique*. 1963. Reprint, Harmondsworth, England: Penguin, 1982.

Gelpi, Barbara C., and Albert Gelpi, eds. *Adrienne Rich's Poetry*. New York: Norton, 1975.

Gilbert, Sandra, and Susan Gubar. *No Man's Land: The Place of the Woman Writer in the Twentieth Century*. 2 vols. New Haven: Yale University Press, 1988.

―――. *The Madwoman in the Attic*. New Haven: Yale University Press, 1979.

Greer, Germaine. *The Female Eunuch*. London: Paladin, 1971.

Hansen, Karen, and Ilene J. Philipson, eds. *Women, Class and the Feminist Imagination: A Socialist-Feminist Reader*. Philadelphia: Temple University Press, 1990.

Heilbrun, Carolyn. *Hamlet's Mother and Other Women*. New York: Columbia University Press, 1990.

―――. *Toward a Recognition of Androgyny*. New York: Columbia University Press, 1990.

Humm, Maggie. *Feminist Criticism: Women as Contemporary Critics*. Brighton, England: Harvester, 1986.

Irigaray, Luce. *Speculum of the Other Woman*. Trans. Gillian C. Gill. Ithaca, NY: Cornell University Press, 1985.

―――. "When Our Lips Speak Together." *Signs* 6, no. 1 (1980): 69–79.

Jehlen, Myra. "Archimedes and the Paradox of Feminist Criticism." *Signs* 6, no. 2 (1981): 575–601.

———. "Gender." In *Critical Terms for Literary Study*. Ed. Frank Lentricchia and Thomas McLaughlin. Chicago: University of Chicago Press, 1990.

Kolodny, Annette. "Dancing through the Minefield: Some Observations on the Theory, Practice, and Politics of a Feminist Literary Criticism." In *The New Feminist Criticism: Essays on Women, Literature and Theory*. Ed. Elaine Showalter. New York: Pantheon Books, 1985.

Kristeva, Julia. *Desire in Language: A Semiotic Approach to Literature and Art*. New York: Columbia University Press, 1980.

———. *The Kristeva Reader*. Ed. Toril Moi. New York: Columbia University Press, 1986.

Leitch, Vincent. *American Literary Criticism from the Thirties to the Eighties*. New York: Columbia University Press, 1988.

Lorde, Audre. *A Sister Outsider*. New York: Crossing Press, 1984.

McLaughlin, Andree Nicola. "A Renaissance of the Spirit: Black Women Remaking the Universe." In *Wild Women in the Whirlwind: Afra-American Culture and the Contemporary Literary Renaissance*. Ed. Joanne M. Braxton and A. N. McLaughlin. New Brunswick: Rutgers University Press, 1990.

Millett, Kate. *Sexual Politics*. 1970. Reprint, London: Virago, 1977.

Moers, Ellen. *Literary Women*. Garden City, NY: Doubleday, 1976.

Moi, Toril. "Feminist Literary Criticism." In *Modern Literary Theory: A Comparative Introduction*. 2nd ed. Ed. Ann Jefferson. Lanham, MD: Barnes Imports, 1987.

Mulvey, Laura. *Movies and Methods: An Anthology*. Vol. 2. Ed. Bill Nichols. Berkeley: University of California Press, 1985.

Penelope, Julia, and Susan J. Wolfe. *Sexual Practice, Textual Theory: Lesbian Cultural Criticism*. Cambridge, England: Blackwell, 1993.

Pratt, Annis. *Archetypal Patterns in Women's Fiction*. Brighton, England: Harvester, 1982.

———. "The New Feminist Criticism: Exploring the History of the New Space." In *Beyond Intellectual Sexism: A New Woman, A New Reality*. Ed. Joan I. Roberts. New York: David McKay, 1976.

Robinson, Lillian. *Sex, Class, and Culture*. Bloomington: Indiana University Press, 1978.

Ruthven, K. K. *Feminist Literary Studies: An Introduction*. Cambridge: Cambridge University Press, 1984.

Showalter, Elaine. "Feminist Criticism in the Wilderness." *Critical Inquiry* 8 (1981): 181–205.

———. *A Literature of Their Own: British Women Novelists from Brontë to Lessing*. Princeton, NJ: Princeton University Press, 1977.

Skandera-Trombley, Laura. *Mark Twain in the Company of Women*. Philadelphia: University of Pennsylvania Press, 1994.

Smith, Barbara. *Toward a Black Feminist Literary Criticism*. New York: Out and Out Books, 1977.

Vendler, Helen. "Feminism and Literature." *New York Review of Books* 31 May 1990.

Walker, Alice. *In Search of Our Mothers' Gardens: Womanist Prose*. London: Women's Press, 1984.

———. *Revolutionary Petunias and Other Poems*. San Diego: Harcourt, 1973.

Walker, Nancy. "Reformers and Young Maidens: Women and Virtue in *Adventures of Huckleberry Finn*." In *One Hundred Years of "Huckleberry Finn": The Boy, His Book, and American Culture*. Ed. Robert Sattlemeyer and J. Donald Crowley. Columbia: University of Missouri Press, 1985.

Wasserstein, Paulette. "Twain's *Huckleberry Finn*." *Explicator* (fall 1987): 31–33.

West, Rebecca. *The Young Rebecca*. Ed. Jane Marcus. London: Virago, 1982.

Zimmerman, Bonnie. "What Never Has Been: An Overview of Lesbian Feminist Criticism." In *Sexual Practice, Textual Theory: Lesbian Cultural Criticism*. Ed. Julia Penelope and Susan J. Wolfe. Cambridge, England: Blackwell, 1993.

· 7 ·

Cultural Studies

■ I. WHAT IS "CULTURAL STUDIES"?

A college class on the American novel is reading Alice Walker's *The Color Purple*. The professor identifies African literary and cultural sources and describes some of the effects of the multilayered narrative structure, moving on to a brief review of the book's feminist framework and its critique of contemporary American gender and racial attitudes. Students and professor discuss these issues briefly, analyzing some key passages in the text.

A student raises her hand and notes that the Steven Spielberg film version drew angry responses from many African American viewers. The discussion takes off: Did Alice Walker "betray" African Americans with her harsh depiction of African American men? Did Spielberg enhance this feature of the book or play it down? Are whites "fairly" portrayed? Another hand goes up: "Is Walker promoting lesbianism?" "Spielberg *really* played that down!" the professor replies.

A contentious voice in the back of the room interjects: "Well, I just want to know what a serious film is doing with Oprah Winfrey in it." With the professor's guidance, class members respond to the question, examining the interrelationships between race, gender, popular culture, the media, and literature. They ask about the conventions—both historical and contemporary—that operate within novels, on "The Oprah Winfrey

239

Show," and in Hollywood films. They conclude by trying to identify the most important conventions Walker employs in constructing individual characters and their communities in *The Color Purple.*

This class is practicing "cultural studies."

It is hard to define cultural studies mostly because the word "culture" is notoriously hard to pin down, according to cultural critic Raymond Williams. Unlike most of the other approaches discussed in this volume, cultural studies is not really a discrete "approach" at all, but rather a set of practices. As Patrick Brantlinger points out, cultural studies is not "a tightly coherent, unified movement with a fixed agenda," but a "loosely coherent group of tendencies, issues, and questions" (ix). Arising amidst the turmoils of the 1960s, cultural studies is composed of elements of Marxism, new historicism, feminism, gender studies, anthropology, studies of race and ethnicity, film theory, sociology, urban studies, public policy studies, popular culture studies, and postcolonial studies: those fields that focus on social and cultural forces that either create community or cause division and alienation.

Practiced in such widely varied journals as *Critical Inquiry, Cultural Studies, Diacritics, Discourse, Feminist Studies, Media, Culture and Society, Representations, Signs, Social Text,* and *Works and Days,* cultural studies involves scrutinizing a cultural phenomenon—Italian opera, Latino *telenovelas,* nineteenth-century British novels by women, the architectural styles of prisons, body piercing—and drawing conclusions about the changes in that phenomenon over a period of time. As one can see from these examples, cultural studies is not necessarily about literature or even "art." But cultural studies approaches generally share four goals.

1. *Cultural studies transcends the confines of a particular discipline such as literary criticism or history.* In their introduction to *Cultural Studies,* Lawrence Grossberg, Cary Nelson, and Paula Treichler emphasize that the intellectual promise of cultural studies lies in its attempts to "cut across diverse social and political interests and address many of the struggles within the current scene." Methodology might involve textual analysis, semiotics, deconstruction, ethnography, interviews, linguistic analysis, and psychoanalysis (1–3). According to cultural stud-

ies practitioners, intellectual works cannot and should not stop at the borders of single texts, historical problems, or disciplines; the critic's own connections to what is analyzed are actually part of the analysis.

2. *Cultural studies is politically engaged.* Cultural critics see themselves as "oppositional" to the power structures of society; they question inequalities within power structures, including the classroom, and seek to restructure relationships among dominant and subordinated cultures. Because meaning and individual subjectivity are culturally *constructed*, they can thus be *re*-constructed. Cultural studies, taken to an extreme, denies the autonomy of the individual, whether an actual person or a work of literature. This constitutes a rebuttal of the humanist "Great Man" or "Great Book" approach and moves aesthetics and culture from the ideal realms of taste and sensibility into the arena of a whole society's everyday life, of its common "constructions."

3. *Cultural studies denies the separation of "high" and "low" or elite and popular culture.* All forms of cultural production need to be studied in relation to other cultural practices. Cultural studies is committed to examining the entire range of a society's beliefs, institutions, and communicative practices, including arts. This might mean studying the poetry of Ezra Pound alongside rapping in Central Park. Popular culture has long been studied in universities, but not with the kind of intensity and elevated analysis it now receives. Cultural studies is seen by some as a route to bringing the university back into contact with the public with a "counter"-disciplinary breaking down of intellectual barriers.

4. *Cultural studies analyzes not only the cultural work that is produced but also the means of production.* Marxist critics have long recognized the importance of such paraliterary questions as these: Who supports a given artist? Who publishes his or her books, and how are these books distributed? Who buys books, and how are they marketed? A well-known analysis of production is Janice Radway's landmark study of the American romance novel and its readers (*Reading the Romance: Women, Patriarchy and Popular Literature*), which demonstrates the textual effects of the mass-market publishing industry's decisions about which books will minimize its financial risks. Another

significant contribution is the volume *Reading in America: Literature and Social History*, edited by Cathy N. Davidson, which includes essays on literacy and gender in colonial New England; urban magazine audiences in eighteenth-century New York City; the impact on reading of such technical innovations as better eyeglasses, electric lights, and trains; the Book-of-the-Month Club; and how writers and texts go through fluctuations of popularity and canonicity. These studies help us realize that literature does not occur in a space separate from most of the other concerns of our lives.

Cultural studies thus joins *subjectivity*—that is, culture in relation to individual lives—with *engagement*, a direct approach to attacking class inequities in society. Though cultural studies practitioners deny "humanism" or "the humanities" as valid categories, they strive for what they call "social reason," which often strongly resembles (humanist) democratic ideals.

What difference does a cultural studies approach make for the student? Gerald Graff and James Phelan observe that "It is a common prediction that the culture of the next century will put a premium on people's ability to deal productively with conflict and cultural difference. Learning by controversy is sound training for citizenship in that future" (v). They advise: "If you have felt alienated from traditional, impersonal academic criticism, your alienation may be reduced by the recent insistence that we all read from particular 'subject positions' and perspectives rather than as objective minds contemplating universal values" (11). And to the question, "Why study critical controversies?" they note that today a student can go from one class in which the value of Western culture is never questioned to another class during the next hour in which the notion that Western culture is hopelessly compromised by racism, sexism, and imperialism is equally beyond question: ". . . constructing a conversation for yourself out of such different courses can be the most exciting part of your education" (8).

Defenders of tradition and advocates of cultural studies are waging what are sometimes called the "culture wars" of the academy. On the one hand are offered impassioned defenses of the notion of humanism as a foundation—since the time of the ancient Greeks—of Western civilization and modern democratic values. On the other hand, as Marxist theorist Terry Eagleton believes, the current "crisis" in the humanities can be seen as a result of the failure of the humanities; this "body of discourses" about "imperishable" values sometimes negates those very values in its practices (Foreword to *Social Figures*).

One of the most challenging features of the culture wars is the assault on traditional categories of gender and sexuality. Along with all other absolutes, these have been replaced with ambivalence, ambiguity, and multiplicity of identities. We saw in chapter 6 that feminism has not only redefined femininity but also given rise to the entire field of gender studies. This has meant that, following Michel Foucault, cultural critics see sexuality as disengaged from gender and from the binary opposition male/female. We also looked at the ideas of some lesbian feminist critics. But the greatest controversies have arisen from the arguments of critics focusing upon gay male aesthetics. We have only to think of the outcry that followed the exhibition of the late Robert Mapplethorpe's photographs in the early 1990s to recognize how intense cultural conflicts in the arts can be when they involve male homosexuality, a controversy that rages within classrooms as well as the halls of Congress.

In *Epistemology of the Closet*, Eve Kosofsky Sedgwick deconstructs the pathology of the homosexual and sees sexuality itself as "an array of acts, expectations, narratives, pleasures, identity-formations, and knowledges . . ." (22–27, 29). Using Sedgwick as a starting point, a number of critics calling themselves practitioners of "queer theory" have rejected the notion of a unitary sexual identity and linked the instability of sexuality to the ineffability of desire. "Queer theory" is not a theory *of* anything but a practice that aspires to create publics that "can afford sex and intimacy in sustained, unchastening ways," according to Lauren Berlant and Michael Warner, editors of a special issue of *PMLA* devoted to queer theory. A "queer public" includes self-identified gays, lesbians, bisexuals, and the transgendered. At the same time, this "public" has "different understandings of membership at different times." The word *queer* was chosen for its shock value and "wrenching sense of recontextualization" (343–45).

With a commitment only to pleasure, "queer" rejects the En-

244 • A Handbook of Critical Approaches to Literature

lightenment notion of progressive social change, not unlike
the aesthetes of the "art for art's sake" movement in late
nineteenth- and early twentieth-century Britain. Desire is "the
unruly and uncontainable excess that accompanies the production of meaning," Donald Morton states; it is "the excess
produced at the moment of the human subject's entry into the
codes and conventions of culture." As such, desire is an autonomous entity outside history, "uncapturable" and "inex-
pressible." Morton sees queer theory's roots in the anarchic
skepticism of Nietzsche and even as an analogue to "the decentered, Internetted, normless society" of the 1990s (370–71,
373–77). Queer commentary has produced significant analyses
of "the costs of closure and the pleasure of unruly subplots;
vernacular idioms and private knowledge; voicing strategies;
gossip; elision and euphemism; jokes; identification and other
readerly relations to texts and discourse" (Berlant and Warner
345–49). Critics such as Alan Sinfield have provided startling
new readings of Shakespeare and other dramatists, while
other readers have returned to gay writers such as Walt Whitman with better clues to sexual codes embedded in the text
and a better sense of the role desire plays in the text.

It is ironic that the weaknesses of cultural studies lie in its
defining strengths, particularly its emphasis on diversity of
approach and subject matter. Cultural studies can become
merely an intellectual smorgasbord in which a critic blithely
combines fascinating texts and objects in response to other
texts and objects without adequately researching and explaining what makes a "culture" in the first place. That is, cultural
studies is not always accompanied by the kind of "hard" research that historians do to establish "culture." Oftentimes cultural critics posit the existence of a culture solely on the basis
of only a few literary sources and a handful of anecdotes. And
many opponents of cultural studies feel that if everything is
"culturally constructed" and not authored or treated by *individual* sensibilities—that is, human beings—and if there is no
realm of truth to which we can appeal, be it religious, philosophical, psychological, or otherwise, then the world as well as
the shelf of great literature can suddenly seem quite empty.
But like all approaches to literature, cultural studies has much
to offer when it is not taken as the *only* means of understand-

ing ourselves and our art. After brief discussion of three prevailing cultural studies approaches, we shall turn to the five works to be viewed through the many lenses of cultural studies.

■ II. THREE WAYS TO STUDY CULTURE

A. British Cultural Materialism

Key to the development of what would later become cultural studies, usually referred to as "cultural materialism" in Britain, Matthew Arnold and his contemporary intellectuals worked to redefine the "givens" of British culture. Edward Burnett Tylor was an anthropologist whose pioneering study, *Primitive Culture* (1871), begins, "Culture or civilization, taken in its widest ethnographic sense, is that complex whole which includes knowledge, belief, art, morals, law, custom, and any other capabilities and habits acquired by man as a member of society" (1). Claude Lévi-Strauss, an important Continental influence on British thinkers, was similarly moved to assign "culture" to primitives (see *The Raw and the Cooked*), and eventually reformist Marxists such as Raymond Williams would attribute "culture" to the working class as well as the elite, arguing that culture is "ordinary." As Williams memorably states: "There are no masses; there are only ways of seeing [other] people as masses" (*Culture and Society* 300).

Thus in Britain two trajectories developed for "culture." One led back to the past and the feudal hierarchies that ordered community: culture in its sacred function as preserver of the past against the present. The second led toward the future, a socialist utopia that would annul the distinction between labor and leisure and make transformation, not fixity, the rule. As noted in *The Johns Hopkins Guide to Literary Theory and Criticism*, British cultural materialism features a leftist political orientation "critical of the aestheticism, formalism, antihistoricism, and apoliticism common among the dominant postwar methods of academic literary criticism" (Groden and Kriezwirth, eds. 180).

Cultural materialism as we know it today began in the 1950s in Britain in the work of F. R. Leavis, which was heavily influ-

enced by Arnold. Leavis sought to use the educational system to distribute literary knowledge and appreciation more
widely; Leavisites promoted the "great tradition" of Shakespeare and Milton in order to improve the moral sensibilities
of readers. The threat to this project was mass culture.
Raymond Williams and Simon Hoggart, two theorists from
working-class backgrounds who responded ambivalently to
Leavisism, applauded the richness of canonical texts but
found that they tended to erase the communal forms of life
that surrounded them. With the aid of Marxist thinkers such as
Theodor Adorno, Max Horkheimer, and Antonio Gramsci, the
notion of cultural "hegemony" became current: the term refers
to relations of domination which are not always visible as
such. Williams characterizes hegemony as "a sense of reality
for most people . . . beyond which it is very difficult for
most members of the society to move" (*Marxism and Literature*
110).

Based on the work of Louis Althusser and Jacques Lacan, a
structuralist form of thinking emerged that identified individuals as constructs of an ideology necessary if the state and
capitalism are to reproduce themselves without fear of revolution. Identifying with such an ideology makes people feel
strong, for, as Lacan's psychoanalytic theory argues, people
see themselves mirrored in the dominant ideology and act to
"take the father's place" out of "fear of castration" or anxieties
that true independence can never be attained. Its lure is always
imaginary (During 5–6). According to Althusser, ideologies are
"misrecognitions" that act upon people through a process
which escapes them. But historical materialism such as Karl
Marx's allows people to recognize the workings of ideology,
what Frederic Jameson called the "political unconscious"
(Althusser, *For Marx* 233; see also Jameson, *The Political Unconscious*).

The semiotics—or study of language as "signs"—of Roland
Barthes and others arose as a method that would allow culture
to be "read" with the same kind of critical acumen that it takes
to read literature. English critics were led to "read" the "sign"
as ideological or hegemonic and uncover "maps of meaning"
within their codes. Meaning became the site of class struggle.
As the Russian Formalist Mikhail Bakhtin and his colleagues

also argued, meaning is dialogically produced within that struggle, at once conflictual and communal, individual and social.

"Polysemy"—or shifting meaning—helped critics see how cultural products may be combined with new elements to produce different effects in different settings. Feminism was especially important in helping cultural materialists recognize seemingly "disinterested" thought as in fact shaped by power structures such as patriarchy. The relations of power between elite and popular forms have been most provocatively studied by the French anthropologist Pierre Bourdieu, whose contribution to British thought was his notion of "symbolic capital": for example, in many cultures a family name is "the most valuable form of accumulation" in society. Those with material capital must also build and exhibit symbolic capital, such as art, in order to maintain control over labor and over their material goods (179–80, 188–89, 196). For example, images of India circulated during the colonial rule of the British raj by writers like Rudyard Kipling, which seem innocent, reveal an entrenched argument for the superiority of the white "race" over Asians; but race itself was not the issue for the British, Bourdieu would say: it was money.

B. The New Historicism

"Laputa"—"The whore." What did Jonathan Swift mean when he gave that name to the flying island in the third voyage of *Gulliver's Travels*? It is a question that has tantalized readers—and professional critics—since the eighteenth century. The science-fiction aspect of that island can still captivate us—but why "the whore?" There may be an answer, and the new historicism may be a way of finding it. More about that later in this section.

"If the 1970s could be called the Age of Deconstruction," Joseph Litvak writes, "some hypothetical survey of late twentieth-century criticism might well characterize the 1980s as marking the Return to History, or perhaps the Recovery of the Referent" (120). As Frederic Jameson insists, "Always historicize!" This is a slogan, he believes, "imperative for all dialectical thought" (9). As a return to historical scholarship, the volatile practice of new historicism concerns itself with extraliterary matters, including letters, diaries, films, paintings, medical treatises, etc. It looks for an opposing tension in a text, then for an opposing tension related in history. New historicists seek "surprising coincidences" (an example of which we present at the end of this section) that may cross generic, historical, and cultural lines previously maintained, highlighting unsuspected lending and borrowing of metaphor, ceremony, dance, dress, or popular culture (Veeser xii).

New historicism arises out of a diverse set of practices that are not in themselves new: as Carolyn Porter has observed, "'the turn toward history' has been in evidence for some time." She credits the emergence of American studies, women's studies, and Afro-American studies programs on college and university campuses as an important sign of the changing nature of literary criticism (743–49).

Like cultural studies, the new historicism is difficult to define; as H. Aram Veeser notes, "It brackets together literature, ethnography, anthropology, art history, and other disciplines and sciences" in such a way that "its politics, its novelty, its historicality, [and] its relationship to other prevailing ideologies all remain open questions" (xi). New historicists have resisted identifying their approaches with a single methodology, for they believe that as history and culture must be described as constantly changing constructions made by variously interested men and women, so new historicists must contain what Forrest G. Robinson identifies as "a principled flexibility, a sharp eye to the distortion in all perspectives, a cultivated pleasure in the discovery of doubleness and subversion" (104).

Forrest Robinson and many others identify Stephen Greenblatt, a Renaissance scholar and founding editor of the journal *Representations*, as the leader of the new historicism. Greenblatt's English Institute essay, "Improvisation and Power," along with a series of path-breaking articles and Modern Language Association sessions, inspired other early new historicists such as Louis Montrose, Walter Benn Michaels, and Catherine Gallagher. Greenblatt himself offered the term "new historicism" in his introduction to a special issue of the journal *Genre*, though it seems to have been coined by another critic in Renaissance studies (McCanles 77–87). Greenblatt names the major influences on his own practice as Foucalt, Jameson, and Jean-François Lyotard, all of whom raise the question of art and society as related institutionalized practices. Greenblatt notes that as Jameson blames capitalism for perpetrating a false distinction between the public and the private, and as Lyotard argues that capitalism has forced a false integration of these worlds, new historicism exists between these two poles in an attempt to work with the "apparently contradictory historical effects of capitalism" without insisting upon an inflexible historical and economic theory (Veeser 1–6; see also Robinson 104).

New historicism has, according to Veeser, "struck down the doctrine of noninterference that forbade humanists to intrude on questions of politics, power, indeed on all matters that deeply affect people's practical lives—matters best left, prevailing wisdom went, to experts who could be trusted to preserve order and stability in 'our' global and intellectual domains" (ix). This crossing of boundaries has threatened opponents of new historicism who warn that if "we"—critics—cross over into "their" territory, then "they"—historians, psychologists, economists—may very well threaten "our" territory and obscure what has been thought of previously as the special, protected practice of literary criticism. This counterattack has best been voiced by Edward Pechter, who seems to be concerned mostly about the Marxist influences on the new historicism, a "new politicization" of literary studies (292–303). Yet, as Veeser responds, just as the new historicism is an attack on naive formalism, it is also "as much a reaction against Marxism as a continuation of it" (xi). Catherine Gallagher supports this view when she argues that good criticism should embody no particular political values but should always be open to the most stringent sort of debate on all topics (37–48).

Despite new historicists' wish to dissociate themselves from simple identification with Marxism, new historicism frequently uses terminology from the marketplace: "exchange," "negotiation," "circulation" of ideas are often described. As Veeser notes, it is the "moment of exchange" that fascinates new historicists, since social values are said to be reflective of "symbolic capital" that may be presented in a literary text: "the critic's role is to dismantle the dichotomy of the economic and the non-economic, to show that the most purportedly dis-interested and self-sacrificing practices, including art, aim to maximize material or symbolic profit" (xiv). As Greenblatt puts it, "contemporary theory must situate itself . . . not out-side interpretation, but in the hidden places of negotiation and exchange" ("Towards a Poetics of Culture" 13).

Porter has contrasted new historicism to old historicism; the latter tries "to periodize [history] by reference to world views magisterially unfolding as a series of tableaux in a film called Progress," as though all Elizabethans, for example, held views in common. The new historicism rejects these tableaux in favor of ordering history only through the interplay of forms of Power (765). Yet some new historicists such as Douglas Bruster are reevaluating "old" historicism, arguing that "only by adapt-ing the rich traditions of historicist and historical-formalist criti-cism are we likely to get Shakespeare's own relations to history right" (2). This sort of constant attention to dualism, dynamism, dialogism—to *relationship*—makes new historicism exciting.

Let us conclude this section with a brief example of a new historicist reading of a well-known text. In "The Flying Island and Female Anatomy: Gynaecology and Power in *Gulliver's Travels*" (60–76), Susan Bruce offers a reading of book three of *Gulliver's Travels*, "A Voyage to Laputa," that makes some new sense of that mysterious book. It has always been difficult to answer the inevitable question from students acquainted with Spanish: "Why does Swift name the flying island 'Laputa,' which in Spanish means 'the whore'?" In her article Bruce ties together some events of the year 1727, soon after *Gulliver's Travels* was published, including eighteenth-century gender is-sues, the relationship between midwives and physicians, and a famous scandal involving a "monstrous birth."

Bruce begins by describing a four-volume commentary on *Gulliver's Travels* published in 1727 by one Corolini di Marco, in which the author offers a dry account of his observations on Swift's work until he gets to the episode in book four, "A Voy-age to the Houyhnhnms," in which Gulliver catches rabbits for food. At that point, di Marco loses control of his rhetoric and launches into a tirade:

> But here I must observe to you, Mr. Dean, en passant, that Mr. Gulliver's Rabbits were wild Coneys, not tame Gutless ones,

such as the consummate native effronterie of St. André has paulmed upon the publick to be generated in the Body of the Woman at Godalming in Surrey. St. André having, by I know not what kind of fatality, insinuated himself among the foreigners, obtained the post of Anatomist-Royal.

Di Marco was referring to a notorious scandal involving the royal physician, St. André, and the so-called "rabbet-woman" of Surrey, Mary Toft, who managed to convince various members of the medical profession in 1727 that she had given birth to a number of rabbits, which she had actually inserted into her vagina and then "labored" to produce. Bruce asks why di Marco should have felt it necessary to include this reference, and by researching records of Mary Toft's famous trial and the ultimate ruin of St. André, she connects this event with the literary depiction of the female body in *Gulliver's Travels* and elsewhere.

Bruce describes the trend toward the education of midwives and the medical profession's desire to stamp them out. Examining books published for literate midwives during the period and quoting testimony from Mary Toft's trial allow Bruce to describe the hostility not only toward the midwife that collaborated with Toft in the hoax, but toward women in general. Bruce then connects the male establishment's outrage at the female power expressed in the hoax to Gulliver's observations on women in *Gulliver's Travels*, particularly his nauseating descriptions of the female body, such as his descriptions of the queen of Brobdingnag at table or of a giant tumor on a Brobdingnagian woman's breast into which he imagines crawling. The implication is that under the male gaze, the magnification of the female body leads not to enhanced appreciation but rather to horror and disgust. But Bruce connects Gulliver's anxious fascination for what is in the body to the anxieties of his age involving the rise of science.

Turning to book three, Bruce brings her insights to bear on the floating island of Laputa, which she describes as a gigantic trope of the female body. A circular island with a round chasm in its center, through which the astronomers of the island descend to the domelike structure of the "Flandona Gagnole," or "astronomer's cave," Laputa has at its center a giant lodestone on which the movement of the island depends. Bruce compares the floating physical structure of Laputa to the uterus and vagina, noting that Gulliver and the Laputians are able to enter this cavity at will and by doing so control not only the movements of the lodestone but also of their entire society. As Bruce notes, "It is this which engenders the name of the island: in a paradigmatic instance of misogyny, the achievement of male control over female body itself renders that body the whore: *la puta*" (71).

Yet, as Bruce goes on to observe, eventually the attempted control over the female body that drives Laputa becomes its undoing, for the more the men of the island try to restrict their women from traveling below to Balnibarbi (where the women are described as having sexual adventures with Balnibarbian men), the more male impotence threatens Laputian society. One recalls that Gulliver notes the men's ineffectuality in several ways, from the descriptions of the "Flappers" that must slap them out of their scientific reveries in order to make them speak, to the way Gulliver tells us the women have "Abundance of Vivacity; they condemn their Husbands, and are exceedingly fond of Strangers. . . . But the vexation is, that they act with too much Ease and Security, for the Husband is always so rapt in Speculation, that the Mistress and Lover may proceed to the greatest Familiarities before his Face, if he be but provided with Paper and implements, and without his *Flapper* by his side." Bruce connects the "doomed attempt of various types of science to control the woman's body" (72) to the debate about language in book three (such as the "Engine for Improving Speculative Knowledge" that produces only broken sentences) and the demand of the women and the commoners to be allowed "to speak with their Tongues, after the Manner of their Forefathers."

Thus in "A Voyage to Laputa" the attempt to bring the female body under control clashes with the realization that such control would have to include control over the discourse produced by that body. The female body, Swift implies, cannot be so managed because no one has discovered a way of controlling female discourse or sexual desire. Di Marco's anxiety over the Mary Toft episode indicates that the most confusing and least understood section of the most canonized satire of the age "is directly connected to a crux of debate over female power taking place in this period, a power which revolved around a woman's control over her own body and her power over, or in relation to, discourse." One final historical note: a pamphlet published in 1727 was purportedly written by "Lemuel Gulliver, Surgeon and Anatomist to the Kings of Lilliput and Blefuscu, and Fellow of the Academy of Sciences in Balnibarbi." It is entitled: *The Anatomist Dissected: or the Man-Midwife finally brought to Bed*. Its subject is Mary Toft, the "rabbet-woman."

Such an innovative and illuminating approach as Bruce's makes clear the potential of the new historicism. As Porter argues, once we are freed from "History," from the stasis of "world views" or controlling ideologies in criticism, we may take the opportunity to "approach literary texts as agents as well as effects of cultural change, as participating in a cultural conversation rather than merely re-presenting the conclusion reached in that conversation, as if it could have reached no other. . . . [F]urthermore, we ought to be able to produce a criticism that would make significant strides toward understanding 'language in history: that full field'" (782).

C. American Multiculturalism

In 1966, the year the first edition of this *Handbook* was published, race riots erupted in Cleveland, Chicago, Milwaukee, Atlanta, San Francisco, and other American cities; the previous year the Watts riots had drawn worldwide attention; and the following year's "long, hot summer" saw more violent insurrections in Newark, New York, Detroit, and many other places. The very television screens seemed ablaze. In 1966 the Black Panther Party was founded; James Meredith, the first African American to enroll at the University of Mississippi, was shot by a white segregationist; black State Representative Julian Bond was denied his seat in the Georgia House of Representatives. Murders and attacks on civil rights activists followed the march on Selma, Alabama, and President Lyndon Johnson's signing of the Voting Rights Act. In 1966 nearly all African American students in the South attended segregated schools, and discrimination was largely unquestioned in most industries—despite the Civil Rights Act of 1964 (Cowan and Maguire 248–52).

Interracial marriage was still illegal in many parts of the United States in 1966, though the following year the United States Supreme Court struck down all state laws against miscegenation. Thirty years later, interracial marriage had increased dramatically. By 1993, of all new marriages by blacks, 12.1 percent were to white partners, up from 2.6 percent in 1976 (*The New York Times*, 4 July 1996, A10). According to the 1990 U.S. Census, 2 million children under 18 identified themselves as "multiracial." Evolving identities of non-European racial and ethnic groups have challenged the very notion of "race" in the United States: "race" has increasingly been seen by historians and social scientists as a construct invented largely to assign social status and privilege. Unlike sex, for which there are X and Y chromosomes, race has no genetic markers. In fact, a 1972 Harvard study by the geneticist Richard Lewontin found that most genetic differences were within racial groups, not between them (*The New York Times*, 20 July 1996, A1, A7). In another century, if interracial trends continue, Americans will be puzzled by such notions as "race discrimination," since children of multiracial backgrounds could very well be the norm rather than the exception. Yet today race is a feature of American life riven with powerful contradictions and ambiguities; it is arguably both the greatest source of social conflict and the richest source of cultural development in America.

Henry Louis Gates, Jr., one of the most prominent African American literary critics, uses the word "race" in quotation marks. It "pretends to be an objective term of classification," but it is a "dangerous trope . . . of ultimate, irreducible difference between cultures, linguistic groups, or adherents of specific belief systems which—more often than not—also have fundamentally opposed economic interests." Without biological criteria "race" is dangerous because it is arbitrary: "Yet we carelessly use language in such a way as to *will* this sense of *natural* difference into our formulations. To do so is to engage in a pernicious act of language, one which exacerbates the complex problem of cultural or ethnic difference, rather than to assuage or redress it," Gates observes (*"Race," Writing and Difference* 4–5).

Like "race," the term "multiculturalism" is full of paradoxes—for example, the interracial marriage phenomenon itself. Why, one wonders, is this happening at a time when so many politicians and civil rights leaders are speaking of heightened racial polarization in American society? One answer is that racism is diminishing in America, but another is that its effects have been worse than has been recognized: one reason interracial marriages are up is that society has utterly failed to deal with the problems that beset black men, 32 percent of whom aged 20 to 29—their prime marrying age—are in prison or on parole, while in contrast the number of black women attending colleges is greatly outpacing the number of black men. More and more black women are saying they have no choice but to marry outside their race (*The New York Times*, 4 July 1996, A10). And there are disagreements about whether a "multiracial" category should be added to census forms alongside the existing racial designations; some, especially those who are multiracial, believe this would reflect the reality of their existence, while others, mostly civil rights advocates, fear that denying race will dilute identity and reduce federal affirmative action benefits.

Multicultural questions pervade art and literature: Which "cultures" are to be canonized? Who decides? What constitutes a "culture"? Does it have to be ethnic, or could gays and lesbians be considered "cultures"? What does "we" mean? And who are "they"—"the other"? Should "multicultural" or "ethnic" texts be incorporated into the mainstream, or should the existing "we" even think in terms of a "mainstream"? Does celebrating "the other" actually reaffirm a structure of center/margin, that is, of a mainstream culture that "admits" for special study marginalized cultures within it? These ambiguities demonstrate that complacency about ethnic or cultural politics is unrealistic and undesirable.

Cultural studies in the United States engages a transplanted British model and its hybrid American forms against longstanding models practiced in U.S. ethnic studies. As Leon Botstein puts it, "tradition is an evolving reality." Students must read Aeschylus, Dante, Shakespeare, "because what Shakespeare and Dante and the so-called Great Books are all about is penetrating through details to what's really essential about the common experience of being a member of this species." But at the same time, while every American should read Thucydides on the subject of being a member of seafaring, democratic, global power, he or she should also read Bernal Diaz's account of the conquest of Mexico: "Every American should understand Mexico from the point of view of the observers of the conquest and of the history before the conquest. . . . [And] [n]o American should graduate from college without a framework of knowledge that includes at least some construct of Asian history, of Latin-American history, of African history" (Sill 35). The values that built the concept and practice of "democracy" around the world, and particularly in the United States, are the same that encourage tolerance, multiple views, and an evolving tradition of response to changes in the make-up of the citizenry and its needs.

1. African American Writers
African American writers are the minority literary tradition most familiar to literary criticism in the United States, from eighteenth-century poems by slaves such as Phillis Wheatley to the experimental novels of Toni Morrison. In *Shadow and Act* Ralph Ellison remarks that any "viable theory of Negro American culture obligates us to fashion a more adequate theory of American culture as a whole" (253).

What can a focus on black literature do for the college classroom? Robert Hemenway, biographer of Zora Neale Hurston, believes that in addition to the commitment to egalitarian principles, there are practical benefits as well: it can release the classroom from "its aura of privilege—no small benefit for a student population that from now to the end of the century will be increasingly from the working class and increasingly black" (66–67).

African American writing displays a folkloric conception of humankind; an ambivalent consciousness arising from bicultural identity; irony, parody, and sometimes bitter comedy in negotiating this ambivalence; attacks on white cultural superiority; and a focus on survival, including language games like "jiving," "sounding" (direct insult), "signifying" (profane goading through word play), "playing the dozens" (explicit sexual insult of someone's parent, especially mother), and rapping. These practices symbolically characterize "the group's attempt to humanize the world" in order to survive, according to Ralph Ellison (in Bernard Bell, *The Afro-American Novel and Its Tradition* xvi, 19). Ellison points to evidence of a willingness to trust experience and one's own definition of reality, rather than allow one's masters "to define these crucial matters." Folklore was what "black people had before they knew there was such a thing as art" (173). In reviewing the primary features of African American writing, Bernard Bell turns to history:

> Traditional white American values emanate from a providential vision of history and of Euro-Americans as a chosen people, a vision that sanctions their individual and collective freedom in the pursuit of property, profit, and happiness. Radical Protestantism, Constitutional democracy, and industrial capitalism are the white American trinity of values. In contrast, black American values emanate from a cyclical, Judeo-Christian vision of history and of African-Americans as a disinherited, colonized people, a vision that sanctions their resilience of spirit and pursuit of social justice.

As Bell stresses, no other ethnic or cultural group in America has shared anything like the experience of American blacks: Africa, the transatlantic or Middle Passage, slavery, Southern plantation traditions, emancipation, Reconstruction, post-Reconstruction, Northern migration, urbanization, and racism (5). Thus questions about whether "ethnic" writing is merely "propaganda" ring hollow in some ears.

Out of painfully convoluted cultural origins evolved African American literature. It may be divided into the following periods: Colonial and Early American (1773–1860), Antebellum (1860–1865), Post-War and Reconstruction (1865–1900), Pre-World War I (1900–1917), the Harlem Renaissance (1918–1937), Naturalism and Modernism (1937–1960), and Contemporary (1960–present). The most important Colonial work is Phillis Wheatley's volume *Poems on Various Subjects, Religious and Moral* (1773), the first book of poems published by an African American. One of Wheatley's most poignant verses is her "To S. M., a Young African Painter, on Seeing his Works," which praises the paintings but laments that their "calm and serene" moments will only be available after death, since, by implication, they will not be fully appreciated or available in the painter's own time:

> But when these shades of time are chas'd away,
> And darkness ends in everlasting day,
> On what seraphic pinions shall we move,
> And view the landscapes in the realms above?
> There shall thy tongue in heav'nly murmurs flow,
> And there thy muse with heav'nly transport glow. . . .
> For nobler themes demand a nobler strain,
> Purer language on th' ethereal plain.

Other antebellum figures include Harriet E. Wilson, whose *Our Nig; or Sketches from the Life of a Free Black, in a Two-Story White House, North* (1859), is the first novel written by an African American woman; Linda Brent, author of *Incidents in the Life of a Slave Girl* (1860); and Elizabeth Keckley, Mary Todd Lincoln's dressmaker and author of *Behind the Scenes, or Thirty years a Slave and four Years in the White House* (1868). After the Civil War came the rise of social realism among African American writers, with works such as Frances Ellen Watkins Harper's *Iola Leroy; or, Shadows Uplifted* (1892), stressing the moral duty of mulattos to repress the urge to "pass" for white. Charles W. Chesnutt's *The Conjure Woman, and Other Stories* (1899) and *The Wife of His Youth and Other Stories of the Color Line* (1899), along with Paul Laurence Dunbar's *The Strength of Gideon and Other Stories* (1900) and *The Sport of the Gods* (1902), made extensive use of dialect.

Following Chesnutt and Dunbar, the turn of the century saw a shift from transforming folk culture into "high" culture back to validation of the moral authority, spiritual wisdom, and aesthetic quality of folk culture itself. There evolved a powerful dynamic between naturalism and romanticism in black writing, especially among male writers, that opposed a deterministic view of social life with a sense of black Americans' own moral responsibility and freewill. Perhaps most significant in this period was James Weldon Johnson's *Autobiography of an Ex-Colored Man* (1912), published anonymously, and at first believed to be nonfiction. It offers a panoramic view of black society as well as the mulatto hero's psychology of social ambivalence.

The Harlem Renaissance was a tremendous upsurge of interest in black culture and especially primitivism that occasioned another return to the folkloristic sources of African American writing. The so-called "New Negro" celebrated and affirmed black culture and reexamined sources in Africa. Nathan Eugene "Jean" Toomer combined African spiritualism and Christianity with the modern psychological experimentalist mode in his *Cane* (1923), a black *Künstlerroman*. Other important figures included Langston Hughes (1902–67), Zora Neale Hurston (1891–1960), and Countee Cullen (1903–46).

Hurston, a novelist, short story writer, playwright, and folklorist, had a most influential and controversial career, though the extent of her influence and the complexities of its conflicts did not become fully apparent until she was rediscovered by Alice Walker in the 1980s. Since then, her works have received concentrated attention, including *Mules and Men* (1935), a folklore collection; and *Their Eyes Were Watching God* (1937), her most popular novel. She was controversial in her day partly because of her tendency to enrage her white patrons and black artist colleagues alike with her self-dramatizing and her critical views of received mythologies. Her complexity arose from her dual identity as artist and anthropologist (she studied with Franz Boas at Columbia University), but her unwavering belief in the beauty of African American language and culture in its own right and in its own words have made her a touchstone in black literature. She simple refused to "clean up" or compromise the realism of the Southern rural world she wrote about, where her love of the natural and the unvarnished comes through in descriptions of characters as well as of the environment.

African American writing entered the literary mainstream with the advent of the literary naturalists and their social protest novels in the 1940s. Spurred by the Depression, sociological studies of urbanization, and socialism, writers such as Richard Wright directly, angrily attacked white American society as racial violence erupted in American cities in response to the Civil Rights movement. Wright found hope for reform in Communism and expressed his radical views in such works as *Native Son* (1938) and *Black Boy* (1945). His anti-hero in *Native*

Son, Bigger Thomas, is the archetypal "Bad Nigger" feared by whites: a rebel in a mindless, exploitive society, Bigger becomes a psychopathic killer.

It was not until the 1950s that African American literature truly began to attract mainstream readers, when the writer known as America's most distinguished black author, if one of its least prolific, emerged. Ralph Ellison did not stop writing after his masterpiece, *Invisible Man*, was published in 1949, but many people believe he did because he published very little afterward. Like many of his predecessors, Ellison was influenced by African traditions of the Trickster, as well as by jazz, blues, "signifying," and political activism. But he was also heavily influenced by European and American writers, including Conrad, Joyce, Eliot, Dostoyevsky, James, and Faulkner, whom he discusses extensively in his preface to *Invisible Man*. This novel is a spiritual and physical odyssey by a young black man who moves forward in time and north in direction, but whose effort is largely to reclaim and come to terms with his past and the past of his people.

The 1960s brought "Black Power" as one of its many rebellions. The "Black Arts" movement was seen as an avenue for reordering the western cultural aesthetic, proposing a separate symbology and new traditions; major figures were LeRoi Jones, Chuck Berry, B. B. King, Aretha Franklin, Stevie Wonder, and Jimi Hendrix, and these were accompanied by a new wave of black faces in other media. The important literary figures of this time shade into the contemporary era, including Margaret Abigail Walker, Toni Morrison, Alice Walker, Ernest Gaines, John Edgar Wideman, and Ishmael Reed, among many others. As Morrison's masterpiece of magical realism, *Beloved*, especially shows, protagonists in these writers' works face the unthinkable results of race hatred in America and emerge from their trials with a new sense of self-ownership.

2. Latina/o Writers

Hispanic. Mexican American. Puerto Rican. Cuban American. Chicano. Or maybe Olmec, Aztec, Maya, Toltec, Inca. Which name or names to use?

We shall use the term "Latina/o" to designate a general sense of ethnicity; it broadly symbolizes the ethnic diversity of the Spanish–speaking populations of the United States. Mexican Americans are the largest and most influential of Latina/o ethnicities in the United States.

Though there is no one culture or group in the United States that can be described as "Latina/o," the diversity of Spanish-speaking peoples, including Mexican Americans, Puerto Ricans, Central and South Americans, Native Americans, Africans, and Europeans, with different religions, skin colors, class identifications, political beliefs, and especially differing views of what it means to be "Latina/o," has contributed meaningfully to American cultural life. The history of the indigenous cultures of the New World is punctuated by conquest by other Indian groups; by European countries such as Spain, Portugal, and England; and by the United States. Over time, there emerged a new culture, a *mestizo* (mixed blood) culture of the New World that brings into question all "borders," whether between nations or between individuals. The term "American" does not refer to the United States alone, but to a number of ethnic groups within its borders.

Indeed, the problem of borders provides the controlling metaphor in the study of Latina/o culture. In her *Borderlands/ La Frontera: The New Mestiza*, Gloria Anzaldúa demonstrates that Latina/os live *between*: between two countries, two languages, two cultures, as she also makes clear in her well-known poem, "To Live in the Borderlands Means You." But as borders between nations have become more permeable, so too has movement between cultures and languages. One encounters a phenomenon called "code switching." Speakers move back and forth from Spanish to English (sometimes called "Spanglish" in border towns), and linguists note when and why certain words are uttered in one language or the other. Often, words that have to do with outside institutions or authorities are in English, while words that refer to family, church, or emotional, "inside" lives are in Spanish. Liminality, or "between-ness," is characteristic of postmodern experience, but has special connotations for Latina/os. A sense of living between cultures but not being entirely at home in either is especially strong for newly arrived immigrants, but also for long-time residents of the border.

The Chicano movement (1965–75), for example, resulted in a

flowering of portrayals of ethnic experience. The key ingredient in Chicano writing is an autobiographical focus, but the two best-known performers in this genre are also two of the most problematic "Chicanos." Oscar Zeta Acosta, author of *The Autobiography of a Brown Buffalo* (1972) and *The Revolt of the Cockroach People* (1973), is often left out of the canon of Chicano literature for being too Americanized and "not Chicano enough." Richard Rodriguez's *Hunger of Memory* (1981) is probably the best-known Mexican American narrative. Rodriguez eloquently traces his boyhood and his education, arguing that it was necessary and right for him to become "mainstreamed," that to do otherwise would have been to fail. But Rodriguez has been attacked by Chicano critics, mostly for his opposition to bilingual education and his self-conscious position as an academic intellectual—what Rodriguez himself sees as the product of being a "scholarship boy" (Paredes 281–95).

Though some Chicanas were among the early writers of the movement, until the 1970s it was the male authors who were recognized. Chicanas attempt to redefine the traditional Mexican cultural myths and archetypes that have rigidly defined gender in the past, for their past differs from that of their men; they face more than racial discrimination. Chicanas focus on redeeming their relationships with men—particularly abusive relationships—rescuing women from marginalization, and liberating themselves sexually. Poetry and the autobiographical essay are important genres (Rebolledo and Rivera 25–31).

Three cultural archetypes are central to Chicana identity: La Malinche, La Virgen de Guadalupe, and La Llorona, and together they offer a full range of Chicana themes and concerns. Malinche is the name given to the Indian woman who became Cortés's aide and lover following his conquest of Mexico and his settlement in Veracruz. Sold into slavery by her parents, she was eventually given to Cortés. She bore him a son, but he later married a Spanish noblewoman. Malinche's name has been synonymous with betrayal and treachery, since she is looked upon as partly responsible for the downfall of her people. But Chicana feminists have attempted to revise the prevailing view of Malinche by pointing to her victimization by the patriarchies in which she lived and by recognizing her as the mother of the new *mestizo* race (Madison 11). The Virgin of

Guadalupe is the most widespread religious figure in Mexico and the Southwest, appearing almost everywhere, from icons in churches to good luck candles, calendars, and charms dangling from taxicab rearview mirrors. She is the indigenous brown goddess of Mexico: mother, protector, nurturer. She is a descendant of Tonantzin, the Indian Earth Mother and Aztec goddess of fertility, on whose horned moon she stands. When the Spanish introduced the Virgin Mary to Mexico, Tonantzin was then identified with Guadalupe. Guadalupe, like Malinche, is revered as the mother of the *mestizo* race, but she is seen as loyal to her people and as the essence of virtue, self-sacrifice, and humility (Madison 12). This "Queen of Mexico" is regarded as the patron saint of the Americas and of unborn children. She appears in a blue robe flecked with stars, and she stands in front of a great burst of light symbolizing her Son. Like the Virgin of Guadalupe, La Llorona's origins are both Spanish and Indian. She is said to have been an Indian woman who, upon discovering her husband's infidelity, murdered their children and was condemned to an eternity of penance and sorrow. According to legend, she wanders through the night weeping and crying out for her children. Like the other representations, she stands for the extremes of purity and guilt the European tradition and Indian traditions ascribe to motherhood, but as Chicanas retell their own stories and recast their archetypes, tabooed figures take on rather different appearances (Madison 12). "Chicanas are Malinches all," write Rebolledo and Rivera, "for they, too, are translators" (33).

3. American Indian Literature

In predominantly oral cultures, storytelling passes on religious beliefs, moral values, political codes, ethics, and practical lessons of everyday life. For American Indians, stories are a source of strength in the face of centuries of silencing by European Americans.

Again, a word on names: "Native American" seems to be the term preferred by academics, who feel that the term "Indian" is always a misnomer for the inhabitants of the Western Hemisphere, and is furthermore a stereotype—as in "cowboys and Indians" or "Indian giver"—that helped whites wrest a continent from the hands of the native peoples. And yet

"American Indian" is the term often preferred by Indians over "Native American" (Velie, Introduction to *American Indian Literature: An Anthology* 3); this is also demonstrated in the names of such organizations as the American Indian Movement (AIM) and the Association for the Study of American Indian Literature (ASAIL). The best terms to use are the tribal names of the hundreds of separate cultures and independent nations, with their differing languages, beliefs, and customs, that are confusingly lumped together as "Indian." Like most Europeans, who identify themselves first as Spaniards, Dutch, or English, and only secondarily as "European," American Indians think of themselves first as tribal members.

At the time of the "discovery" of the "New World," many millions of people lived in the Western Hemisphere. When Columbus landed, thousands of independent tribes spoke hundreds of different languages from various language groups, some of which were as different from each other as English is different from Chinese. Another misconception is that Indian tribes were merely "primitive"; in fact, they had more stringent taboos against casual sex and divorce than many more technologically advanced peoples. Their cultures were generally stable before the advent of whites, spiritually oriented, harmonious, and with complex worldviews. However, it would be an error to romanticize the Indians; they were, according to Alan R. Velie, "heavily conformist, warlike, chauvinistic, and sexist." They were not the "sylvan pacifists" used by some "as a stick to beat white America" (Velie, *American Indian Literature: An Anthology* 3–5).

Two kinds of Indian literature have evolved as fields of study. *Traditional* literature includes tales, songs, and oratory that have existed on this continent for centuries, composed in tribal languages and performed for a tribal audience, such as the widely studied Winnebago Trickster cycle. Today, traditional literature is usually composed in English. *Mainstream* literature refers to works by Indians written in English in one of the standard American genres, such as poetry, the novel, or autobiography. Traditional literature was and is primarily oral. Because Indians did not have a written literature, many whites have surmised that they did not have a literature (but, as Velie pointedly notes, that would mean that the Greeks of *The Iliad*

and *The Odyssey* didn't have one either). Far from the stereotype of the mute and stoic Indian, Indians have always been
highly verbal people who created the first American literature
(Velie, *American Indian Literature: An Anthology* 9). Sadly, of
course, every year more of the traditional memory dies out.

It is not easy to translate from Cherokee, for example, into
English: the contextual frames do not translate, nor does the
oral/performative/sacred function of American Indian "literature." Compounding these difficulties, Indians do not traditionally separate "literature" from everyday life as a special
category to be enjoyed only by a leisured, educated elite. All
members of the tribe listen to the songs and chants, and there
is no distinction between "high" and "low" culture. The tribe's
myths and stories are designed to educate the young about
tribal beliefs, cure illnesses, ensure victory in battle, or secure
the fertility of the fields. It is *practical* (Velie, *American Indian
Literature: An Anthology* 7). For Americans trained in the idea
that "art" inhabits an "aesthetic" sphere, these concepts are
hard to understand, let alone translate.

Samson Occom, a Mohegan schoolmaster, wrote the first
work published by an American Indian (1772). Subsequent
writers of the nineteenth and early twentieth centuries, such as
William Apess, Luther Standing Bear, Yellow Bird (John Rollin
Ridge), Simon Pokagnon, Charles Eastman, Alexander Posey,
Sara Winnemucca Hopkins, D'Arcy McNickle, and Mourning
Dove (Humishuma), dealt with issues of native rights, the du-
plicities of the U.S. government and military, education of Indians, racial ambivalence, myths of native creation, trickster
humor, and themes of tribal constancy in the face of devasta-
tion—for survival and the retention of what Gerald Vizenor
calls "tragic wisdom" (5–6). Of particular interest to later generations was Gertrude Bonnin, also known as Zitkala-Ša, a
Dakota Sioux, who compiled a collection of trickster tales from
her girlhood, which she called *Old Indian Legends* (1901). Today
these stories are widely reprinted in anthologies. They were
followed by her *American Indian Stories* (1921), an account of
her experiences at a white boarding school.

It was not really until the 1960s that the American reading
public became aware of works by American Indian writers, especially after the publication of Kiowa writer M. Scott Moma-

day's *House Made of Dawn* (1968), which won the Pulitzer Prize in 1969, and his memoir, *The Way to Rainy Mountain* (1969), beginning a modern renaissance of American Indian fiction and poetry. Momaday was a student of Yvor Winters at Stanford University and represents one of the literary critical categories Winters was fond of using, "post-Symbolist," which described a writer who worked with a rejection of logical organization in favor of an associational organization based on reverie. Momaday's poem "Angle of Geese" is about death and the inadequacy of language to cope; it begins with a discussion of the death of a friend's child and jumps symbolistically to the killing of a goose on a childhood hunting trip, making a general statement about death itself. After Momaday, James Welch, Leslie Marmon Silko, Louise Erdrich, Paula Gunn Allen, Simon Ortiz, Joy Harjo, and others appeared as major literary figures both in fiction and poetry (the tendency of Indian writers is to do both), making little known but historically vital regions of the country speak of their own Indian myths and realities.

Louise Erdrich avoids romanticizing Indians, but presents their history in a starkly realistic and grotesque style. Her masterpiece is *Love Medicine* (1984), and she has gone on to continue her contemporary epic of whites and Indians in North Dakota with *The Beet Queen* (1986) and *Tracks* (1988). Her characters—the families of the Kashpaws, Morrisseys, Lamartines, and Lazarres—are venal, libidinous, and grotesque. But through the seven narrators of *Love Medicine* emerges a unified story of community. Erdrich seeks to educate readers about Indian history and to replace white-authored histories with her multivoiced versions. Paula Gunn Allen and Simon Ortiz warn readers of the psychic dangers to Indians and whites in the modern technological world in such collections as Gunn's *Shadow Country* (1982) and Ortiz's *Going for the Rain* (1976). In *She Had Some Horses*, Creek Joy Harjo employs lyrical, "traditional" Indian cadences to tell "the fantastic and terrible story of our survival" and the joy of carrying it forward. Her verse cries out with the voice of the dispossessed, which she frames through metaphors of the body and the southwestern landscape.

The tendency in the past was to see Indians as mere victims, ignoring Indians' successes. Today, however, Indian history and literature courses, while they examine events like the massacres carried out by the U.S. Cavalry upon Indians, do not stress only the negative chapters of Indian history. Our misperceptions lead us where we do not suspect. Even in Oklahoma, where it is considered a matter of pride to claim Indian ancestry, and where every Oklahoman knows of the Trail of Tears from the East on which thousands of Cherokees died, there is still a curious invisibility to Indian history and ethnicity. Remarking on this, Velie points out, "It is a curious phenomenon that however prominent a black person becomes he or she is always black, but when Indians become successful, somehow they lose their identity. Almost all Americans have heard of Will Rogers; how many of them know he was Cherokee?" (6).

4. Asian American Writers

Asian American literature is written by persons of Asian descent in the United States, not necessarily citizens, a status denied to Asian immigrants by law until the 1940s and 1950s. Asian American writers address the experience of living in a society that perceives them as alien, what Edward Said has called "Orientalism," or the the rejection of Asian culture accompanied by exoticizing it. Asian American writers include Chinese, Japanese, Korean, Filipino, Vietnamese, Malaysian, Melanesian, Polynesian, Hindu, Pakistani, and many other peoples of Asia, the Indian Subcontinent, and the Pacific Rim. These many cultures present a bewildering display of differences; they do not share common social structures, religious beliefs, skin colors, or languages—and thus the category to which they are assigned as "Asian American" is more artificial than "American Indian." Furthermore, some Asian American writers are new arrivals in the United States, while others have been residents for many years, and sometimes their forebears for generations. But all write in the English language, expressing their different stories of assimilating to the American experience.

Asian American literature can be said to have begun around the turn of the twentieth century, primarily with autobiographies, but it also included novels, short stories, drama, and poetry. Two important autobiographical forms emerged from early Chinese American writers: "paper son" stories and "confessions." Paper son stories were carefully fabricated for Chinese immigrant men to make the authorities believe that their New World sponsors were really their fathers, when in fact they were not. These tales had to provide each man with the same details of their fictitious village life together. Personal confessions were made by Chinese American women rescued by missionaries from prostitution in California's mining towns and migrant labor camps. As Stephen Sumida points out, teaching English to these women was part of the missionaries' campaign to convert the "heathen" (402). We might add to this list of "texts" created by Asian American "authors" the self-descriptions written by "picture brides" from Asian countries seeking American husbands.

Asian American autobiography clearly inherits these descriptive strategies, as Maxine Hong Kingston's *The Woman Warrior: Memoirs of a Girlhood Among Ghosts* (1976) illustrates. This well-known book at first inspired confusion in the Chinese American literary community: was it a critique of its narrator or an unapologetic statement about what it means to grow up as a Chinese American woman? The fact that it was sold as nonfiction tended to support the latter notion, despite Kingston's disclaimers.

Chinese American women make up the largest and most influential group of Asian American writers. Ironically, given the silencing of Asian women—as witnessed by foot-binding, slavery, and ritual suicide—they have managed to produce an astonishing array of literary works, far outdistancing the male writers. Of course, working-class women hardly had the leisure to write. Most of the few Chinese American women authors were daughters of diplomats and scholars or those schooled in Western mission schools (Ling 219, 221, 225).

Chinese American literary history can be said to begin with two Eurasian sisters, Edith and Winnifred Eaton, who emigrated with their parents to the United States. Edith Eaton's stories were published under the title *Mrs. Spring Fragrance* (1912) and present Chinese as fully developed, three-dimensional people. Winnifred Eaton chose to write "Japanese" novels of a highly sentimentalized and romantic nature, filled with moonlit bamboo groves, cherry blossoms, and doll-like women in delicate kimonos (Ling 223). Another family of sisters were popular writers just before World War II: Adet, Anor, and Memei Lin, whose best-known work was their reminiscence *Dawn Over Chunking* (1941), a firsthand experience of war written by a seventeen-year-old, a fourteen-year-old, and a ten-year-old, portraying without flinching the horrifying sights of war: rotting corpses, burning houses, abandoned children. Anor Lin later took the name Lin Tay-yi and wrote her best work, *War Tide* (1943), an experimental novel that renders in surrealistic detail the invasion of Hangchow by the Japanese Army.

Jade Snow Wong's female *Bildungsroman* entitled *Fifth Chinese Daughter* strikes a very different tone with its classic tale of the American dream. The narrator is tormented by a child in the school yard who maliciously calls her "Chinky, Chinky, Chinaman." But she does not react, for she is simply astonished by his behavior: "Jade Snow thought that he was tiresome and ignorant. Everybody knew that the Chinese people had a superior culture. Her ancestors had created a great art heritage and had made inventions important to world civilization. . . . She had often heard Chinese people discuss the foreigners and their strange ways, but she would never have thought of running after one of them and screaming with pointed finger, 'Hair on your chest!'" (68). Jade Snow's parents come to accept their daughter and the Americanness she masters.

Among contemporary Chinese American writers, the work of Amy Tan is perhaps best known. Her *Joy Luck Club* traces a group of four Chinese immigrant women's lives and relations with their daughters through several years of development. The women and their daughters live in San Francisco, where the mothers still meet in the "Joy Luck Club" they formed in 1949 to play mah-jongg and to tell each other their stories of life in China; their daughters' vignettes alternate with the mothers' as the novel proceeds, and both the conflicts between the generations and the problems they share are built up in this modern tragicomedy. That the novel was made into a successful Hollywood film, won numerous awards, and stayed on the 1989 *New York Times* bestseller list for nine months is evidence of the growing popularity of Asian American literature.

III. Cultural Studies in Practice

A. Two Characters in *Hamlet*: Marginalization with a Vengeance

In several instances earlier in this chapter we noted the cultural and new historical emphases on power relationships. For example, we noted that cultural critics assume "oppositional" roles in terms of power structures, wherever they might be found. Veeser, we pointed out, credited the new historicists with dealing with "questions of politics, power, indeed on all matters that deeply affect people's practical lives" (ix). And of course there are the large emphases on power in the matter of Jonathan Swift's Laputa, as previously noted.

Let us now approach Shakespeare's *Hamlet* with a view to seeing power in its cultural context.

Shortly after the play within the play, Claudius is talking privately with Rosencrantz and Guildenstern, Hamlet's fellow students from Wittenberg (III.iii). In response to Claudius's plan to send Hamlet to England, Rosencrantz delivers a speech that—if read out of context—is both an excellent set of metaphors (almost in the shape of a sonnet) and a summation of the Elizabethan concept of the role and power of kingship:

> The singular and peculiar life is bound
> With all the strength and armor of the mind
> To keep itself from noyance, but much more
> That spirit upon whose weal depends and rests
> The lives of many. The cease of majesty
> Dies not alone, but like a gulf doth draw
> What's near it with it. It is a massy wheel
> Fixed on the summit of the highest mount,
> To whose huge spokes ten thousand lesser things
> Are mortised and adjoined; which, when it falls,
> Each small annexment, petty consequence,
> Attends the boisterous ruin. Never alone
> Did the King sigh but with a general groan.
>
> (III.iii)

Taken alone, the passage is a thoughtful and imagistically successful passage, worthy of a wise and accomplished statesman.

But how many readers and viewers of the play would rank this passage among the best-known lines of the play—with Hamlet's soliloquies, for instance, or with the King's effort to pray, or even with the aphorisms addressed by Polonius to his son Laertes? We venture to say that the passage, intrinsically good if one looks at it alone, is simply not well known.

Why?

Attention to the context and to the speaker gives the answer. Guildenstern had just agreed that he and Rosencrantz would do the King's bidding. The agreement is only a reaffirmation of what they had told the King when he first received them at court (II.ii). Both speeches are wholly in character, for Rosencrantz and Guildenstern are among the jellyfish of Shakespeare's characters. Easy it is to forget which of the two speaks which lines—indeed easy it is to forget most of their lines altogether. The two are distinctly plot-driven: empty of personality, sycophantic in a sniveling way, eager to curry favor with power even if it means spying on their erstwhile friend. Weakly they admit, without much skill at denial, that they "were sent for" (II.ii). Even less successfully they try to play on Hamlet's metaphorical "pipe," to know his "stops," when they are forced to admit that they could not even handle the literal musical instrument that Hamlet shows them (III.ii). Still later these nonentities meet their destined "non-beingness," as it were, when Hamlet, who can play the pipe so much more efficiently, substitutes their names in the death warrant intended for him.

If ever we wished to study two characters who are marginalized, then let us look upon Rosencrantz and Guildenstern.

The meanings of their names hardly match what seems to be the essence of their characters. Murray J. Levith, for example, has written that "Rosencrantz and Guildenstern are from the Dutch-German: literally, 'garland of roses' and 'golden star.' Although of religious origin, both names together sound sing-song and odd to English ears. Their jingling gives them a lightness, and blurs the individuality of the characters they label" (50).

Lightness to be sure. Harley Granville-Barker once wrote in an offhand way of the reaction these two roles call up for actors. Commenting on Solanio and Salarino from *The Merchant of Venice*, he noted that their roles are "cursed by actors as the two worst bores in the whole Shakespearean canon; not excepting, even those other twin brethren in nonentity, Rosencrantz and Guildenstern" (from *Prefaces to Shakespeare*).

Obvious too is the fact that the two would not fit the social level or have the level of influence of those whom Harold Jenkins reports as historical persons bearing these names: "These splendidly resounding names, by contrast with the unlocalized classical ones, are evidently chosen as particularly Danish. Both were common among the most influential Danish families, and they are often found together" (422). He cites various appearances of the names among Danish nobles, and even notes the appearance of the names as Wittenberg students around 1590 (422).

No, these details do not seem to fit the personalities and general vacuity of Shakespeare's two incompetents. So let us look elsewhere for what these two characters tell us. Let us review what they do, and what is done to them. Simply, they have been students at Wittenberg. They return to Denmark, apparently at the direct request of Claudius (II.ii). They try to pry from Hamlet some of his inner thoughts, especially of ambition and frustration about the crown (II.ii). Hamlet foils them. They crumble before his own questioning. As noted above, Claudius later sends them on an embassy with Hamlet, carrying a letter to the King of England that would have Hamlet summarily executed. Though they may not have known the contents of that "grand commission," Hamlet's suspicion of them is enough for him to contemplate their future—and to "trust them as adders fanged":

> They must sweep my way,
> And marshal me to knavery. Let it work,
> For 'tis the sport to have the engineer
> Hoist with his own petard. And 't shall go hard
> But I will delve one yard below their mines
> And blow them to the moon: Oh, 'tis most sweet
> When in one line two crafts directly meet.
>
> (III.iv)

In a moment of utmost trickery on his own part, Hamlet blithely substitutes a forged document bearing their names rather than his as the ones to be "put to sudden death,/Not shriving time allowed" (V.ii). When Horatio responds laconically with "So Guildenstern and Rosencrantz go to 't," Hamlet is unmoved:

> Why, man, they did make love to this employment.
> They are not near my conscience. Their defeat
> Does by their own insinuation grow.
> 'Tis dangerous when the baser nature comes
> Between the pass and fell incensèd points.
> Of mighty opposites.

And with that Shakespeare—as well as Hamlet—is done with these two characters. "They are not near [Hamlet's] conscience."

Again, why? For one thing, Hamlet may well see himself as righting the moral order, not as a murderer, and much has been said on that matter. But let us take note of another dimension: the implications for power. Clearly Hamlet makes reference in the lines just noted to the "mighty opposites" represented by himself and Claudius. Clearly, too, the ones of "baser nature" who "[made] love to this employment" do not matter much in this struggle between powerful antagonists. They are pawns for Claudius first, for Hamlet second. It is almost as if Hamlet had tried before the sea voyage to warn them of their insignificant state; he calls Rosencrantz a sponge, provoking this exchange:

HAMLET: . . . Besides, to be demanded of a sponge! What replication should be made by the son of a king?

ROSENCRANTZ: Take you me for a sponge, my lord?

HAMLET: Aye, sir, that soaks up the King's countenance, his rewards, his authorities. But such officers do the King best service in the end. He keeps them, like an ape, in the corner of his jaw, first mouthed, to be last swallowed. When he needs what you have gleaned, it is but squeezing you and, sponge, you shall be dry again.

So they are pawns, or sponges, or monkey food: the message of power keeps coming through. Thus, they do not merit a pang of conscience. True, there may be some room for believing that at first they intended only good for their erstwhile schoolfellow (see, for example, Bertram Joseph, *Conscience and the King* 76). But their more constant motive is to please the king, the power that has brought them here. Their fate, however, is to displease mightily the prince, who will undermine them and "hoist [them] with [their] own petard."

For such is power in the world of kings and princes. Nor is it merely a literary construct. England had known the effects of such power off and on for centuries. Whether it was the deposing and later execution of Richard II, or the crimes alleged of Richard III, or the beheading of a Thomas More or of a wife or two, or the much more recent actions in and around the court of Elizabeth: in all these cases, power served policy. Witness especially the fate of the second Earl of Essex, whose attempt at rebellion led to his own execution in 1601, and even more especially the execution of Elizabeth's relative, Mary Queen of Scots, who had been imprisoned by Elizabeth for years before Elizabeth signed the death warrant. A generation later, another king, Charles I, would also be beheaded. With historical actions such as these, we can understand why Shakespeare's work incorporates power struggles. (For instances of power relative to the "other" during Elizabeth's time, and for a discussion of Elizabeth's actions relative to Essex and Mary Queen of Scots, see the essay by Steven Mullaney, "Brothers and Others, or the Art of Alienation," 67–89.)

Claudius was aware of power, clearly, when he observed of Hamlet's apparent madness that "Madness in great ones must not unwatched go" (III.i). With equal truth Rosencrantz and Guildenstern might have observed that power in great ones must not go unwatched.

To say, then, that the mighty struggle between powerful antagonists is the stuff of this play is hardly original. But our emphasis in the present reading is that one can gain a further insight into the play, and indeed into Shakespeare's culture, by thinking not about kings and princes but about the lesser persons caught up in the massive oppositions.

It is instructive to note that the reality of power reflective of Shakespeare's time might in another time and in another culture reflect a radically different worldview. Let us enrich our response to *Hamlet* by looking at a related cultural and philosophical manifestation from the twentieth century. In the twentieth century the dead, or never-living, Rosencrantz and Guildenstern were resuscitated by Tom Stoppard in a fascinating re-seeing of their existence, or its lack. In Stoppard's version, they are even more obviously two ineffectual pawns, seeking constantly to know who they are, why they are here, where they are going. Whether they "are" at all may be the ultimate question of this modern play. In *Rosencrantz and Guildenstern Are Dead*, Stoppard has given the contemporary reader or viewer a play that examines existential questions in the context of a whole world that may have no meaning at all. While it is not our intention to examine that play in great detail, suffice it to note that the essence of marginalization is here: in this view, Rosencrantz and Guildenstern are archetypal human beings caught up on a ship—spaceship Earth for the twentieth or the twenty-first century—that leads nowhere, except to death, a death for persons who are already dead. If these two characters were marginalized in *Hamlet*, they are even more so in Stoppard's handling. If Shakespeare marginalized the powerless in his own version of Rosencrantz and Guildenstern, Stoppard has marginalized us all in an era when—in the eyes of some—all of us are caught up in forces beyond our control. In other words, a cultural and historical view that was Shakespeare's is radically reworked to reflect a cultural and philosophical view of another time—our own.

And if the philosophical view of Stoppard goes too far for some, consider a much more mundane phenomenon of the later twentieth century—and times to come, we expect. We allude to the Rosencrantzes and Guildensterns, the little people, who have been caught up in the corporate downsizing and mergers in recent decades—the effects on these workers when multinational companies move factories and offices around the world like pawns on a chessboard. Not Louis XIV's "L'état: c'est moi," but "Power: it is capital."

Whether it is in Shakespeare's version or Stoppard's, Rosencrantz and Guildenstern are no more than what Rosencrantz called a "small annexment," a "petty consequence," mere nothings for the "massy wheel" of kings.

B. "To His Coy Mistress": Implied Culture versus Historical Fact

Andrew Marvell's "To His Coy Mistress" tells the reader a good deal about the speaker of the poem, much of which is already clear from earlier comments in this volume, using traditional approaches. We know that the speaker is knowledgeable about poems and conventions of classic Greek and Roman literature, about other conventions of love poetry, such as the courtly love conventions of medieval Europe, and about Biblical passages.

Indeed, if one accepts the close reading of Jules Brody (53–80), the speaker shows possible awareness of the Provençal *amor de lohn*, neo-Petrarchan "complaints," Aquinas's concept of the triple-leveled soul, Biblical echoes, a "Platonico-Christian corporeal economy" (59), and the convention of the blazon. The first stanza, says Brody, shows "its insistent, exaggerated literariness" (60). In the second stanza Brody sees not only the conventional "carpe diem" theme from Horace but also echoes from Ovid, joined by other echoes from the *Book of Common Prayer*, from the *Greek Anthology*, and from "Renaissance vernacular and neo-Latin poets" (61–64).

Brody posits the "implied reader"—as distinct from the fictive lady—who would "be able to summon up a certain number of earlier or contemporaneous examples of this kind of love poem and who [could] be counted on, in short, to supply the models which Marvell may variously have been evoking, imitating, distorting, subverting or transcending" (64). (The concept of the "implied reader," we may note, bulks large in reader-response criticism; see, for example, the work of Wolfgang Iser.)

The speaker knows all of these things well enough to parody or at least to echo them, for in making his proposition to the coy lady, he hardly expects to be taken seriously in his detailing. He knows that he is echoing the conventions only in order to satirize them and to make light of the real proposal at hand. He knows that she knows, for she comes from the same cultural milieu that he does.

In other words, the speaker—like Marvell—is a highly educated person, one who is well read, one whose natural flow of associated images moves lightly over details and allusions that reflect who he is, and he expects his hearer or reader to respond in a kind of harmonic vibration. He thinks in terms of precious stones, of exotic and distant places, of a milieu where eating, drinking, and making merry seem to be an achievable way of life.

Beyond what we know of the speaker from his own words, we are justified in speculating that his coy lady is like the implied reader, equally well educated, and therefore knowledgeable of the conventions he uses in parody. He seems to assume that she understands the parodic nature of his comments, for by taking her in on the jests he appeals to her intellect, thus trying to throw her off guard against his very physical requests. After all, if the two of them can be on the same plane in their thoughts and allusions, their smiles and jests, then perhaps they can shortly be together on a different—and literal—plane: literally bedded.

Thus might appear to be the culture and the era of the speaker, his lady—and his implied reader.

But what does he not show? As he selects these rich and multifarious allusions, what does he ignore from his culture? He clearly does not think of poverty, the demographics and socioeconomic details of which would show how fortunate his circumstances are. For example, it has been estimated that during this era at least one quarter of the European population was below the poverty line. Nor does the speaker think of disease as a daily reality that he might face. To be sure, in the second and especially in the third stanza he alludes to *future* death and dissolution. But wealth and leisure and sexual activity are his currency, his coin for present bliss. Worms and marble vaults and ashes are not present, hence not yet real.

Now consider historical reality, a dimension which the poem ignores. Consider disease—real and present disease. What has been called the "chronic morbidity" of the population. Although the speaker thrusts disease and death into the future, we know that syphilis and other sexually transmitted diseases were just as real a phenomenon in Marvell's day as in our era. What was the reality that the speaker chooses not to think about, as he pushes off death and the "vault" to some distant time?

Similarly, one might turn to a different disease that was in some ways even more ominous, more wrenching, in its grasp of the mind and body of the general population. Move ahead a few years, beyond the probable time of composition of the poem in the early 1650s: move to 1664–65. That was when the London populace was faced with an old horror, one that had ravaged Europe as early as A.D. 542. It did it again in its most thoroughgoing way in the middle of the fourteenth century (especially 1348), killing millions, perhaps 25 million in Europe alone. It was ready to strike again. It was, of course, a recurrence of the Black Death, in the Great Plague of London. From July to October, it killed some 68,000 persons, and a total of 75,000 in the course of the epidemic. Had we world enough and time, we could present the details of the plague here, its physical manifestations, its rapid spread, the quickness of death: but the gruesome horrors are available elsewhere. For example, the curious can get a sense of the lived experience by reading Daniel Defoe's *Journal of the Plague Year* (1722), an imaginative creation of what it was like.

So disease was real in the middle of the seventeenth century. There needed no ghost to come from the world of the dead to tell Marvell's speaker about the real world. Perhaps the speaker—and his lady—knew it after all. Maybe too well. Maybe that is why that real world is so thoroughly absent from the poem.

C. "The Lore of Fiends": Hawthorne and His Market

Earlier in this chapter we noted that a cultural studies approach sometimes concerns itself not only with the cultural work that is produced but also with the means of production. We noted that questions of supporting the author, of finding a publisher, and even of marketing the particular work are germane to the cultural milieu in which the work is produced.

Our present question is this: under what conditions and in what frame of mind did the younger Hawthorne handle such challenges? The answer to that question involves a review of two areas: (1) his thoughts and actions during the middle third of the nineteenth century, and (2) the world of American publication at the time.

"Young Goodman Brown" was one of Hawthorne's first published tales. It appeared in *The New England Magazine* in 1835, but it existed in draft perhaps as early as 1829. We can get some insight into his wrestling with his identity as an author if we first look at a passage that occurs early in *The Scarlet Letter*, the first and most successful of his four book-long romances. To be sure, that work was published in 1850, but the questions in his mind then pertain to the earlier work as well. In the "Custom House" section that serves as the frame for *The Scarlet Letter*, there is a lengthy meditation on how the writer's Puritan forebears would have scorned his choice to be "an idler" instead of following in the footsteps of his first "grave, bearded, sable-cloaked, and steeple-crowned progenitor[s]":

> No aim, that I have ever cherished, would they recognize as laudable; no success of mine—if my life, beyond its domestic scope, had ever been brightened by success—would they deem otherwise than worthless, if not positively disgraceful. "What was he?" murmurs one gray shadow of my forefathers to the other. "A writer of story-books! What kind of business in life,— what mode of glorifying God, or being serviceable to mankind in his day and generation,—may that be? Why, the degenerate fellow might as well have been a fiddler!"

In his anxieties about authorship, Hawthorne takes up the position of "editor" of *The Scarlet Letter* rather than author, for then he may protect both the reader's and his own "rights" and "keep the inmost Me behind its veil."

If Hawthorne seemed to suggest that he had a sense of guilt about being the equivalent of "a fiddler" in 1850, what were his feelings even earlier? The answer to this question takes us even closer to how the economic milieu of publication at this time may have influenced his selection of material. In fact, we may be getting into what a Marxist approach might call "production theory."

Hawthorne published his first story, "The Hollow of the Three Hills," a witchcraft tale, in *The Salem Gazette*, his hometown newspaper, in 1830. For the next twenty years, he wrote brief fictions and published them anonymously, except for periods in which he did not write at all, having to work as an editor, as a clerk in custom houses, and as a member of the utopian colony Brook Farm in 1841. During this period nearly a hundred of his tales appeared in print, but then his interest in these short pieces dropped completely when he produced his first full-length romance, *The Scarlet Letter* (1850). He was embarrassed by his "trifles," as he called his short stories; he felt guilty for having wasted his time on them because, as he wrote in his preface to *Mosses from an Old Manse*, they did not "evolve some deep lesson" (Hawthorne, in Pearce 1124). He was also weary of his obscurity in producing only "fitful sketches . . . but half in earnest" (1148–49). Often he would not even put his name on them, but would sign them as "by the Author of" a previous tale. His depiction of the "romantic Solitary" in several of his tales is in a way the depiction of the American writer in the changing literary market of the 1830s and 1840s.

Hawthorne wrote "Young Goodman Brown" while living as a recluse—a "romantic Solitary"—in his mother's house. Having graduated from Bowdoin College, he had as yet no income; he was a young man longing for the way up and out. But the way out was also the way into something—in the Puritan sense, evil, the self, and its curse of writing. An equation seems to be developed between writing and the devil's work: "But authors are always poor devils, and therefore Satan may take them," Hawthorne told his mother. In his early tale "The Devil in Manuscript," Oberon, a "damned author," confronts "the fiend" in his works. Burning his manuscripts, he accidentally sets fire to his village, screaming into the conflagration, "I will cry out in the loudest spirit with the wildest of the confusion." Oberon, it is important to note, was a name Hawthorne used for himself in college (it also appears in "Fragments from the Journal of a Solitary Man," published in 1837).

In addition to the burden of his self-doubt and guilt at even being an artist—a "fiddler"—it was a difficult marketplace Hawthorne entered. What would he produce? Who would buy? Because there were no international copyright laws, American publishers would pirate and sell popular British novelists of the day, which made it doubly hard for American writers to succeed. Americans felt they had to copy British forms. However, some were brave enough not to do so. For example, Herman Melville in his review "Hawthorne and His

Mosses" (1850) recognizes a fellow explorer of the murkier haunts of human psychology who is willing to experiment, a man who will "say NO in thunder" to those who wish to suppress or disguise the darkness within. Melville thus identifies one of the main reasons for Hawthorne's greatness—his willingness to return, however ambivalently, again and again to the forbidden topics that interested him, whether they would sell or not.

Another marketplace concern Hawthorne had to face was that most of his readers and competitors were women. Such authors as Harriet Beecher Stowe and Catherine Sedgwick supplied the public demand for sentimental, domestic themes. Though Hawthorne created powerful female characters and seemed to regard the artistic nature as a somewhat feminized one apart from the world of male action, he was misunderstood by some as merely sentimental. His fascination with the feminine actually took on an archetypal dimension, one that in its way allowed him to explore his own "darkness" right under the noses of readers like the contemporary Transcendentalist Margaret Fuller, who misunderstood him. Almost a century later, the English author D. H. Lawrence got closer to Hawthorne's true themes: "You *must* look through the surface of American art, and see the inner diabolism of the symbolic meaning. Otherwise it is all mere childishness. That blue-eyed darling Nathaniel knew disagreeable things in his inner soul. He was careful to send them out in disguise" (83).

Still another marketplace issue figures into Hawthorne's expressions of "inner diabolism." This particular ingredient became the key to Hawthorne's contemporary success and to his long-standing fame. For Hawthorne did find a sensational subject that was guaranteed to sell: exposure of utopian reformers and ministers, so visible in mid-nineteenth-century America, and so clearly a figure that conjoined his own sense of guilt and his attitudes toward the feminine—a connection shared to some extent by his culture. The sunlit as well as the sardonic sides of Hawthorne's authorial persona had ample opportunity for exercise when he wrote about the Puritan village of the seventeenth century, as seen in "Young Goodman Brown," and about the utopian community of the nineteenth, as seen in Brook Farm, among others.

In his comments on Brook Farm and in his treatment of reformists and millennialism, Hawthorne seems to have been taking aim at "perfectionism" as formulated by the French socialist Charles Fourier. Evidence for this view seems to be provided by the exploitation of two women, and the suicide of one, in *The Blithedale Romance,* and by the treatment of Hester Prynne in the seemingly utopian Puritan society. The dark events of "Young Goodman Brown" are in keeping with these concerns evidenced in the later romances as well as in this story. Hawthorne's linking of diabolism and reformism points to deep divisions within himself and within his nineteenth-century world.

From a cultural studies perspective, the contexts and sources of the literary work fill out the picture of literary production. In this instance, we can look at the other texts in the 1835 issue of *The New England Magazine* which contained "Young Goodman Brown," for they also appealed to the public's interest in social reform and its critics. Among the other works were fiction and poetry, the occasional travel essay, political analyses, and other popular genres. Among them appear examples of what is known as "dark reform" writing. "Dark reform" writings, also known as "immoral didacticism," might be descriptions of, for example, the horrors of prostitution or fornication, but in their tendency to dwell upon the lewdness of their subjects, they themselves become pornographic. This dichotomy has a parallel in Hawthorne. David Reynolds has identified a mixture in Hawthorne's early fiction "which manifests an almost schizophrenic split" between what Reynolds calls the Conventional and the Subversive; the works may "exemplify the post-Gothic, Subversive Hawthorne, obsessed by themes like fruitless quests, nagging guilt, crime, perversity, and so forth," and they might also employ conventional "simplified piety, patriotic history, comforting angelic visions, domestic bliss, and regenerating childhood purity" (114). Not until the great tales of the 1835–36 period, including "Young Goodman Brown," do we find Hawthorne bringing these opposing cultural forces together with mythopoeic power.

One of the most characteristic figures in dark reform writing was the secretly sinful churchgoer or the satanic preacher, the "reverend rake" (Reynolds 253–54, 262). In "Young Goodman Brown," this familiar figure is cast as a preacher, and we recall the almost lurid ways that the satanic figure speaks: he is at once chillingly diabolic and tantalizingly seductive. In that 1835 issue of *New England Magazine*, such a figure appears in an essay called "Atheism in New England." The essayist takes a dim view of literary freedoms assumed by utopian reformers, and urges the "good men" of New England to defend "the morals, the laws, and the order of society" against the devilish reform activities of the "Infidel Party." The "Free Inquirers" are associated with "licentious indulgence," misdirection of youth, and avoidance of the conventional warnings of conscience; they "strive to spread doctrines, so subversive to morality, and destructive of social order . . ." (Reynolds 54–56). There is further salivating about sexual freedom, "gratification of animal desire," and books "which are sold for filthy lucre by the priest." It is easy to forget that this essay, like "Young Goodman Brown," was not written during Puritan times but nearly two hundred years later.

In other words, sensationalism titillates, and it sells. In the midst of a publishing world that made it difficult for an American author to be rewarded on the basis of his own insights and skills; in a time when women writers and women readers were dominant; in a time when Hawthorne was wrestling, first, with being a writer at all, and, second, with his bent to inquire into the deep recesses of the individual and into the reformist societies of his day—in the midst of all this, Hawthorne was finding his own voice and themes that made him a successful author, with both a product to sell and a body of work that speaks across the generations. Within that body of work, no story speaks more eloquently or dramatically to Hawthorne's obsession with the nature of evil—the "power of blackness"—and his awareness of the marketplace than does "Young Goodman Brown."

D. Telling the Truth, "Mainly": Tricksterism in *Huckleberry Finn*

The only issue that has worried readers of *Huckleberry Finn* more than race is the ending, and the two problems are closely related. After Jim has been presented as a fully realized human being, after Huck has sworn to go to hell rather than desert his friend, after their cherished comradeship on the river, Twain again turns on the slapstick and allows Huck and Tom to torment Jim at the Phelps Farm. Furthermore, in a book that is often described as American literature's most eloquent indictment of racism, one finds racial jokes and Edward Windsor Kemble's 1885 illustrations of Jim as a shabby, servile simpleton. During his own time Twain certainly was a source of immense embarrassment to those he harpooned with his satires, and he has refused to quiet down over one hundred years since he wrote his vexing masterpiece.

The problem of the ending has been addressed by such distinguished critics as T. S. Eliot, Ernest Hemingway, Lionel Trilling, Leo Marx, James M. Cox, and Roy Harvey Pearce. Some believe the "fatal" ending is a cop-out by its author, since he quit writing the novel for two years after Huck and Jim pass Cairo in the fog in chapter 15. He must have run out of ideas and just wanted to get it finished. Or, say others, it is a brilliant indictment of Tom Sawyer's brand of romanticism; thus it is true to the book's overall satiric thrust. And it has been read as the only appropriate ending, given the antiheroic stance of the main character and his escapism, since it preserves Huck's essential freedom.

The controversies over race and the ending have gotten worse, not better. The book has been banned in a number of school districts. Of course, it was banned in many places in Twain's day, but for a different reason: it would encourage juvenile delinquency, smoking, and irreligion. It *is* a radical book, after all, attacking the conventional pieties of nineteenth-century America, not so different from those of our own day. But the questions regarding race are not easy to understand or discuss, and the disputes are sharp.

For example, in the Bedford Case Study edition of *Huckleberry Finn*, a number of critics present various sides of the question. Julius Lester calls *Huckleberry Finn* a "dangerous" book: Twain does not take Jim or black people at all seriously; Jim is childlike, only a "plaything" for Tom and Huck, and the prototypical "good nigger." The overall situation also lacks credibility: Jim's lack of knowledge and of anxiety about the trip is simply unbelievable, as is Miss Watson's deathbed release of her slave. The novel wrongfully idealizes a white male adolescent fantasy of escaping responsibility; the famous "lighting out for the territory" is a "mockery of freedom, a void," and the book as a whole reflects Twain's "contempt for humanity" (344, 347–48).

But Justin Kaplan sees it differently in "Born to Trouble: One Hundred Years of *Huckleberry Finn*": it is a "bitter irony" that the book has been called "racist"; it is in fact a "savage indictment of a society that accepted slavery as a way of life." Huck and Jim "are simply too good for us, too truthful, too loyal, too passionate, and, in a profounder sense than the one we feel easy with, too moral." Jim is "unquestionably the best person in the book," and Twain's portrait of slave times is more faithful and less stereotyped than Harriet Beecher Stowe's: "One has to be deliberately dense to miss the point Mark Twain is making here and to construe [its] passages as evidences of his 'racism'" (355–57).

Toni Morrison sees the controversy itself as what should be taught: she urges us to release the novel from "its clutch of sentimental nostrums about lighting out to the territory, river gods, and the fundamental innocence of Americanness" and instead to "incorporate its contestatory, combative critique of antebellum America." She laments the gingerly way critics have approached race in this text: "It is not what Jim seems that warrants inquiry, but what Mark Twain, Huck, and especially Tom need from him that should solicit our attention. In that sense the book may indeed be 'great' because in its structure, in the hell it puts its readers through at the end, the frontal debate it forces, it simulates and describes the parasitical nature of white freedom." In short, "freedom has no meaning to Huck or to the text without the specter of enslavement" (54–57).

One of the most surprising arguments about race in *Huckleberry Finn* is advanced by Shelley Fisher Fishkin's *Was Huck Black? Mark Twain and African-American Voices*; Fishkin argues that to a significant degree Twain modeled Huck's voice on a ten-year-old black boy named Jimmy. Two years before he published *The Adventures of Tom Sawyer* or started *Huckleberry Finn*, Twain met Jimmy, a "bright, simple, guileless little darkey boy . . . ten years old—a wide-eyed, observant little chap . . . , the most exhaustless talker I ever came across" ("Sociable Jimmy," *New York Times*, 29 November 1874). As Fishkin notes, "'Sociable Jimmy' takes the place of honor as the first piece Twain published that is dominated by the voice of a child." Clearly Twain's taking a black child named Jimmy, a white child from Hannibal named Tom Blankenship (whom Twain mentioned as a model for Huck), and a "smidgeon" of others from childhood, and transmuting them into a white child named Huck Finn "involved a measure of racial alchemy unparalleled in American literature" (Fishkin 14–15, 80).

Huck's *and* Jim's narrative voices are thus *culturally constructed* voices with sources in many places, including such African American ones as children and slaves from Twain's childhood; Jimmy, perhaps; minstrel shows; slave narratives; and diverse African American oral traditions.

These cultural sources affect interpretation. Jim's apparent superstitiousness and gullibility about being taken on a late-night ride by witches, for example, needs to be seen in the context of African American folklore instead of being merely a stereotype out of minstrelsy. The tale of being "ridden by witches" has been recorded repeatedly by folklorists. Fishkin offers this frame: in the South "night-riders" dressed as ghosts (ancestors of the Ku Klux Klan) would come to frighten the slaves. So it is no surprise that an oral tradition of "night-riders" or "witches" would have evolved among slaves. Similarly, when Jim says he has always been good to dead people, readers have picked this up as evidence of his foolishness— but in many of the cultures of the west coast of Africa there is a whole range of burial practices and spiritual beliefs involving continuing communication between the living and the dead (Fishkin 85).

Was Huck "black"? We appreciate Fishkin's answer—but we believe both the question and the answer demand an even larger cultural context. No, Huck was not black, but he was American, and that means that just as Twain absorbed the African American voices Fishkin describes, he was absorbing a lot of other things too, from American Indian folktales and other cultural practices to an array of Old World sources, including Shakespeare, the Bible, Calvinism, and Romantic poetry. Clearly the tall tale tradition influenced Twain: Davy

Crockett, Johnson Jones Hooper, and George Washington Harris. But the most comprehensive way to assess Huck's cultural role is to attend to his own voice, his narrative strategies, as presented in the novel. The feature that emerges most clearly is his comprehensive role as a Trickster.

The book is full of lies, evasions, impersonations, false leads, unexpected reversals. Huck acts as Trickster, but the figure appears in many incarnations in the story—in Tom, Jim, and the King and the Duke. Known primarily to white Americans of Twain's day and ours through the Uncle Remus stories of Joel Chandler Harris, the Trickster figure is of central importance to both African American and the American Indian folktales. As a nonwhite voice from "outside" middle-class culture in the nineteenth century, the Trickster helps construct Huck's honest, uncorrupted point of view. Paradoxically, the lying Trickster—who in folklore is ultimately redemptive—actually allows for a point of view that may just tell the truth.

The Trickster is one of the most ancient of mythical characters and, as Elizabeth Ammons notes, one of the most unruly, though his transgressions are an integral part of communal life: disruptive though the Trickster is, "the dynamic is one of interaction" (vii, ix). The basic pattern or "tale type," as folklorists call it, of the Trickster stories in American Indian literatures is this: prompted by his appetites, "Trickster the Overreacher" fixes on a particular goal, but to get it he will have to transform his identity radically or change society's norms. He attempts to accomplish his aim several times but fails; sometimes he is punished or killed, but he always survives to engage again in forbidden activities. The stories may be simple burlesques, developed scenes of dialogue, or even lengthy story cycles. They generally tell of a discrete cultural scene—hosting customs or a religious ritual—which Trickster disrupts or which are disrupted simply because of human nature (a Sunday School picnic attacked by "Spaniards and A-rabs"?). Trickster exposes institutionalized power but also addresses the limitations of being human, many tales suggesting that any attempt to impose order on human experience is presumptuous (Wiget 91, 94).

Similarly, according to John Roberts, the African American Trickster is in control of his situation; he manipulates people at will. He is indifferent to everything but making fools out of people or fellow animals; yet his is somehow a normative, heroic action. In this sense he is godlike and heroic—bigger than life. African Trickster tales emphasize the importance of creativity and inventiveness in dealing with situations peculiar to the slave-master relationship, for Trickster stories embody both the oppression of black people and their feelings of rebelliousness against white culture ("The African American Animal Trickster as Hero" 97, 100–105, 111). Roberts also notes that the focus on obtaining food was a direct result of the shortages imposed on them by the slavemasters. Tricksterism was thus a justifiable response to the dehumanizing experience they encountered as slaves (*From Trickster to Badman* 35–37). Trickster tales also assert the right of the individual to contest the irrational authority of religious ritual that benefited those at the top of the social scale while those at the bottom survived through wit (Roberts, "Animal Trickster" 105–6).

"The Signifying Monkey" is an important trope of the African Trickster. As Henry Louis Gates, Jr., points out, it "dwells at the margins of discourse, ever punning, ever troping, ever embodying the ambiguities of language" (*The Signifying Monkey* 52). "Signifying" may consist of such black vernacular practices as "testifying," playing with someone's name, rapping, playing the dozens, giving back-handed compliments, and so forth. The person signifying may goad, taunt, cajole, needle, or lie to his interlocutor. He uses what Roger D. Abrahams calls a "language of implication," a technique of "indirect argument or persuasion"; he may ask for a piece of cake by saying, "my brother wants a piece of cake," or make fun of a policeman by copying his speech or gestures behind his back (51–52). The Signifying Monkey, Gates concludes, is not only a master of technique; he *is* technique, or style (54–55). Given the strong oral element of Twain's narrative, one need only think of Huck in a dress, of his lies to the "Harelip" and others, and of the sick A-rab or Noble Prisoner to see that signifying is going on.

Tom and Huck partake of the various satiric features of these Trickster traditions, including upsetting social norms, escaping punishment, and challenging religious authority, so that at times Huck is more like the socially conscious Indian

Trickster and Tom the manipulative African Trickster; but at other times each shares in the other's "tradition." As in the African tradition in particular, the boys know the value of never *seeming* to be a Trickster, of playing dumb and retaining control of a situation that seems on the surface to have them at its mercy.

Pranks, disguises, superstitions, prayers and spells, confidence games, playacting, faked death, cross-dressing, outright rebellion, social humbuggery, social hypocrisy and delusion: from Tom Sawyer's gang of highwaymen in chapter 2 to Old Sister Hotchkiss's cabin full of forty "niggers crazy's Nebokoodneezer" in chapter 41, the folk figure of the Trickster shows himself in *Huckleberry Finn*. He is there even before the text itself begins. On the back of the title page of the book appear two bits of prefatory text: first, an "Explanatory" concerning dialects in the book: "I make this explanation for the reason that without it many readers would suppose that all these characters were trying to talk alike and not succeeding." Underneath appears a "Notice":

> Persons attempting to find a motive in this narrative will be prosecuted; persons attempting to find a moral in it will be banished; persons attempting to find a plot in it will be shot.
> BY ORDER OF THE AUTHOR
> Per G. G., CHIEF OF ORDNANCE.

Even for an avowed satirist, this is a risky way to win over readers at the beginning of a book. First, the "Explanatory" is a tongue-in-cheek warning to readers that what appears to be may not be—or *may* be, a troubling statement about the simultaneous importance of voice and its possible inauthenticity. And then the reader is threatened with extreme sanctions against "finding a moral." Do we take that as encouragement to find a moral, or should we leave it at face value and attribute to Twain a different kind of novelistic development? We do not know. The "Explanatory" doesn't explain, and the "Notice" only puts us on notice that we had better watch out.

The first paragraph of the text itself has an even more ambiguous tone:

> You don't know about me without you have read a book by the
> name of "The Adventures of Tom Sawyer," but that ain't no
> matter. That book was made by Mr. Mark Twain, and he told
> the truth, mainly. There was things which he stretched, but
> mainly he told the truth. That is nothing. I never seen anybody
> but lied, one time or another, without it was Aunt Polly, or the
> widow, or maybe Mary. Aunt Polly—Tom's Aunt Polly, she is—
> and Mary, and the Widow Douglas, is all told about in that
> book—which is mostly a true book; with some stretchers, as I
> said before.

Here is a character speaking as though he is writing the
present book (and he complains of how hard it is to do later
on), but who confesses that his existence arises from another
book by a Mark Twain, who "mainly" told the truth (but also
lied) about events which he, Huck, knows factually. We have
several layers of narrative reality here with the problem of
what "truth" might be in such an environment.

Lying forms the basis for most episodes, and obviously
these tricks point up the one huge lie of slavery. Twain's pattern of lying in *Huckleberry Finn* through his Trickster hero
poses his fiction against the big lies of society—white superiority, self-righteousness, social snobbery, confidence games,
and a thousand other falsehoods. Huck's own lying leaves a
negative space for readers to fill in the "truth" as they see it.

Like those of the American Indian and African American
Tricksters, Huck's lies are generally about personal identity,
and they are directed at survival for himself and Jim. They create alternate worlds in which he (and sometimes Jim) has a
more stable identity and a family. Sometimes he lies for the
fun of it, and occasionally he goes too far and gets caught. But
he knows when that is happening, unlike Tom, who lies purely
for fun; and, unlike the King and the Duke, he does not lie only
for profit.

But then there is a bad lie. Huck fools Jim in chapter 15 into
thinking that he only dreamed their separation in the fog, and
then lets Jim retell his dream and "'terpret" it. "Oh well, that's
all interpreted well enough," Huck says, "but what does *these*
things stand for?" Huck gestures at the leaves and rubbish on
the raft and the smashed oar: "Jim looked at the trash, and
then looked at me, and back at the trash again. . . . He

looked at me steady, without ever smiling, and says: 'What do dey stan' for? I's gwyne to tell you. . . . Dat truck dah is trash; en trash is what people is dat puts dirt on de head er dey fren's en makes 'em ashamed.'" Huck says that he has to "work himself up to go and apologize to a nigger," but that "I warn't ever sorry for it afterwards, neither. I didn't do him no more mean tricks, and I wouldn't done that one if I'd a knowed it would make him feel that way."

This moment is as morally significant to Huck as his later famous decision not to "pray a lie" and to go to hell rather than betray Jim, and it leads directly to his second episode of moral growth. Here the Trickster learns who he is and who he is not, who Jim is and who he is not. When Huck swears he will play no more "mean" tricks on Jim, he tells the truth, but the world around him will continue to lie. Trickster, as Ammons observed, lives in a "web" of the individual and the communal. When he plays tricks that appear to be "mean" later on in the story, including not telling Jim at first that the King and Duke were frauds, acquiescing in their binding Jim and dressing him up as King Lear, and cooperating with Tom's imprisonment of Jim at the Phelps Farm, we might wonder at his promise. Huck does live up to his promise (he thinks) not to do things that would make Jim feel bad. But underneath Huck's presumed rationalizing, Twain's own tricks are not so easy to explain. The "trash" scene may be a turning point in more ways than one, and Huck remains Trickster to Jim as Twain remains Trickster to us.

The general tone of the story changes after the lie to Jim; immediately afterwards, the King and Duke make their appearance. Huck's tricksterism is overshadowed by their frauds. Huck's lies become more comic in contrast; for example, there is the hilarious scene between him and the Harelip in chapter 26, in which he discusses his familiarity with William the Fourth of England, who goes to his church—which, funny though it is, illustrates how Huck's contact with the King and the Duke have led him into absurdity; he doesn't fool the Harelip for a minute. As the plot of bilking the Wilkses gets out of hand, Huck is saved from sharing the fate of the King and the Duke by his regard for Mary Jane Wilks, but of course, characteristically, he has to resort to tricks to help her. With everything sorted out, Huck says, "I judged I had done it pretty neat—I reckoned Tom Sawyer couldn't a done it no neater himself. Of course he would a throwed more style into it, but I can't do that very handy, not being brung up to it." Unconsciously, and despite all the layers of trickiness, he expresses his own basic honesty. When he tears up his letter to Miss Watson, he does so because "I was playing double. I was letting on to give up sin, but away inside of me I was holding on to the biggest one of all." But by the end of the novel, the reader perceives that the Trickster himself has been tricked: Huck fails to realize that, contrary to his own conscious perception, he is a profoundly moral human being.

E. Cultures in Conflict: A Story Looks at Cultural Change

When we turn to Alice Walker's "Everyday Use: for your grandmama," it seems easy enough to blend a multicultural view with a new historical view. We need only take note that this new historical view is contemporaneous with our present society, not a study of a piece of writing that has been with us for a long period of time, such as *Hamlet* or "To His Coy Mistress." Rather, this story represents an array of cultures and subcultures—some dominant, some lost or denied, all in some sort of conflict.

In an earlier period of American literature—the late nineteenth century, for example—Walker's depiction of the rural area with a predominantly black population might have been written as local color: the image of the house without real windows, the cow, the swept yard which is a kind of extension of the house, the conventional items found in such a house (the quilts, the benches used in place of chairs, the churn, the snuff). Alternatively, one can imagine these details as part of photographs taken for some WPA project, and now lodged in an archival collection, shown occasionally in some museum display. The timing would be about right: the mother in "Everyday Use" apparently was in the second grade in 1927, a couple of years before the crash that led to the Great Depression of the 1930s.

But this is not a local color story. Photographs are in fact being taken in the story, but they are to be part of the collection of one of the daughters, possibly just for her own use. She carefully snaps pictures that show her mother in front of the house, at one point managing to get mother, house, and cow all in the same shot. This daughter, Dee, has come back to visit her mother and her sister, but now Dee represents a culture quite different from what she left behind when she went to college. Her Polaroid and the automobile in which she has returned are distinctly different from what her mother and sister Maggie have as their conveniences and luxuries—a cool spot in the yard, some quilts, some snuff. Local color there is, but not simply as a variant of early realism. Rather, it serves to contrast a traditional culture with an emerging consciousness that African Americans are not necessarily destined to share-cropping or subsistence living.

Dee has been sent to college. She has gotten an education. Her opportunity has come from her mother and her mother's church, which had the foresight to send her away so that she could better reach her potential. The traditional culture that she has left behind is the very culture that has enabled her to be part of a different world, a fact about which she seems to be at best dimly aware. But the culture of college is not the only new culture with which she has allied herself. Somewhat to the dismay of her mother and her sister, Dee has also attached herself to a subculture within that new world of African Americans who desire not only to break with the past of economic, social, and psychological hardship (and legalized slavery before that), but also to seek to reconnect with African roots. The phenomenon of seeking one's roots is of course not unique to late-twentieth-century American life (genealogical study has been around a long time), but the particular kind of seeking that is evident in this story is a late-twentieth-century phenomenon that manifests itself especially in the use of words and names, and sometimes of hair styles and clothing, indigenous not to America but to Africa.

So we watch Dee and her friend drive up to visit the mother and Maggie. Dee's hair "stands straight up like the wool on a sheep." She says "Wa-su-zo-Tean-o!" Her friend has "hair to his navel" and says, "Asalamalakim, my mother and sister." Dee denies her earlier name: "No, Mama. Not 'Dee,' Wangero Leewanika Kemanjo!" The mother asks what happened to

"Dee," and her daughter answers, "She's dead. I couldn't bear it any longer being named after the people who oppress me." Clearly, for Dee her earlier name (in spite of her mother's effort to show its family history) represents the past, the oppressive culture of the dominant majority, from which she now seeks to separate herself so as to build on her roots as she now sees them.

Let us reflect on a couple of items in Dee's words in new historical terms.

One item is names. Particularly since the 1960s this country has seen a phenomenon that clearly Alice Walker has woven into her story—the adoption by some African Americans of names to replace their given names. The names chosen seem to reflect either an African pattern or a Muslim one, or both. The phenomenon is widespread, and various public figures have adopted such names. Among them are major athletes like Muhammad Ali, who began his career as Cassius Clay, and Kareem Abdul-Jabbar, who was Lew Alcindor when he played college basketball in the sixties. Among literary figures we have Imamu Amiri Baraka, who earlier had published dramas as LeRoi Jones.

Another item to be noted in Dee's rejoinder to her mother is the oppressiveness of the socioeconomics of their world. Dee, in urging a new name for herself upon her mother, says, "[Dee's] dead. I couldn't bear it any longer being named after the people who oppress me." "Oppression" is the operative concept here, clearly tied to the name Dee associates with her past. And with oppression we can see a connection that a Marxist or a new historical critical approach can bring to bear on the story. We need only recall the economic details of slavery, of the Jim Crow era that followed, or of the continuing disparity between income levels of white Americans and African Americans. These facts are too well known to need elaboration here. But we should emphasize that a Marxist critic would have to pay close attention to the income production or capital amassment in which slaves and later sharecroppers unwillingly participated. For that amassment of capital did not produce for African Americans the magnificent mansions associated with the capitalistic society that owned the cotton plantations of the American South. The house that Dee's mother and sister live in is obviously the antithesis of antebellum homes nearby.

Again, in a further application of a cultural approach to the story, the new historicist could easily take the story itself as a form of history, a documentary of the real world to which Alice Walker and thousands of others have borne witness. The story is a literary documentation of what photographs have preserved, of what health and demographic records have preserved—and in fact what a traveler can still observe to this day. (A side note: while the story is set in a rural area, the themes we are tracing have counterparts in virtually every city in the country.)

In review, the collocation of the name that Dee asserts and the word "oppress" clearly invites specific insights in a cultural studies approach to the story. But the story is not necessarily—or not only—a Marxist story. It is a story of cultures in conflict.

As such, it raises questions beyond oppression and economics, important though they may be. It raises a question of how one finds one's culture, one's roots. Dee has adopted a name that shows her resistance to the socioeconomic culture that she calls oppressive. Still, is a newly adopted culture with a claim on a world half a world away truly a "culture"? Rather, some would argue that a culture is something lived, part and parcel of one's everyday existence; it is almost as if one's lived culture must be below the level of consciousness if it is to be authentic. It must be natural; it must simply "be." When Dee and her friend use strange words to greet the mother and Maggie and when they announce their names (apparently recently adopted, at least by Dee), this is not the culture of the mother—nor perhaps of Africa either. But it does seem to be akin to a movement about which we hear within the story. The mother alludes to "those beef-cattle peoples down the road," who also "said 'Asalamalakim' when they met you, too." Dee's friend apparently knows of them and of some kind of movement associated with them, for he says, "I accept some of their doctrines, but farming and raising cattle is not my style." So even here we have a further complication of cultures or subcultures. Does Dee's mother see the new ideas as foreign to her? Is she more attuned to what she has known than to Dee's efforts to take on a new identity? It would seem so.

Because the story is told from the point of view of the mother, with her somewhat jaundiced view of what Dee has done and has become, we must be cautious about assuming an authorial favoritism toward any one view of which culture or subculture is "right." Rather, it seems more appropriate to say that what we have is an insight into a fact of late-twentieth-century shifts in America.

Much earlier in the century, the shift from an agrarian to an industrial-commercial base was an obvious phenomenon of American society. But for Black Americans specifically, the shift had come at a markedly slower pace, with less successful results. The mother in "Everyday Use" seems not too eager to participate in that shift, even though she and her church furthered Dee's participation. Dee, on the other hand, is clearly eager for it. The Polaroid camera is an objective symbol of that shift, just as much as keeping the quilts for Maggie suggests the mother's reticence to make the change. The situation is complex, however, because Dee is also trying to hold on to a bit of the old culture, even as she converts its objective symbols to "something artistic," thus depriving them of their original vitality as "useful" objects.

There is no person in the story who directly or indirectly represents the dominant or majority culture, but allusions to the dominant culture form an obvious and major subtext for the story. The most extended passage comes early in the story—the dream that the mother reports about seeing herself as part of a television show, something like what she associates with Johnny Carson. In that dream she would take on characteristics that daughter Dee would want her to have—"a hundred pounds lighter, my skin like an uncooked barley pancake. My hair glistens in the hot bright lights. Johnny Carson has much to do to keep up with my quick and witty tongue." But she knows that this is a dream, an entry into another culture that will not happen for her. "Who can even imagine me looking a strange white man in the eye?" There is some indication that the dominant culture was little interested in educating the blacks: "After second grade," the mother says, "the school was closed down. Don't ask me why: in 1927 colored asked fewer questions than they do now." Later, Dee directly mentions "the people who oppress me," as we have already noted. Another instance is the mother's recalling how "white folks poisoned some of the herd" of the "beef-cattle peoples down the road."

In summary, "Everyday Use" represents a variety of cultures and subcultures, in varying degrees of tension among themselves: the dominant, white majority, not directly represented in the story, but important throughout; a black culture that is somewhat typical of the agrarian South; the changing and more assertive subgroup that is entering (or creating) a different culture from that earlier tradition; and a subset of this subgroup that associates itself with a different continent—but which is not even then homogeneous, as Dee's friend indicates about not accepting all of "their doctrines." From the point of view of the new historicists, this story may not be as oriented toward action or a political agenda as some pieces of literature might be because it seems to have a certain degree of ambiguity: neither Dee nor her mother is wholly right or wholly wrong. Nevertheless, the close reader must be aware of the social, economic, and political forces at work during the latter part of the twentieth century if the full impact of the story is to be appreciated.

Quick Reference

Althusser, Louis. *For Marx*. New York: Pantheon Books, 1969.

Ammons, Elizabeth, and Annette White Parks, eds. *Tricksterism in Turn-of-the-Century American Literature: A Multicultural Perspective*. Hanover, MA: Tufts University Press, 1994.

Anzaldúa, Gloria. *Borderlands, La Frontera: The New Mestiza*. San Francisco, CA: Spinsters/Aunt Lute, 1987.

Bell, Bernard. *The Afro-African Novel and Its Tradition*. Amherst: University of Massachusetts Press, 1987.

Berlant, Lauren, and Michael Warner, eds. Introduction to *PMLA* 110 (May 1995): 343–49.

Botstein, Leon. "The De-Europeanization of American Culture," In *Opening the American Mind: Race, Ethnicity, and Gender in Higher Education*. Newark: University of Delaware Press, 1993.

Bourdieu, Pierre. *Outline of a Theory of Practice*. Trans. Richard Nice. Cambridge Studies in Social Anthropology, no. 16. Cambridge: Cambridge University Press, 1977.

Brantlinger, Patrick. *Crusoe's Footprints: Cultural Studies in Britain and America*. New York: Routledge, 1990.

Brody, Jules. "The Resurrection of the Body: A New Reading of Marvell's *To His Coy Mistress*." *ELH* 56, no. 1 (1986): 53–80.

Bruce, Susan. "The Flying Island and Female Anatomy: Gynaecology and Power in *Gulliver's Travels*." *Genders* 2 (July 1988): 60–76.

Bruster, Douglas. "Some New Light on the Old Historicism: Shakespeare and the Forms of Historicist Criticism." *Literature and History* 5, no. 1 (spring 1966): 1–18.

Christian, Barbara. *Black Feminist Criticism*. New York: Pergamon Press, 1985.

Cowan, Tom, and Jack Macquire. *Timelines of African American History: 500 Years of Black Achievement*. New York: Berkley Books, 1994.

Davidson, Cathy N., ed. *Reading in America: Literature and Social History*. Baltimore: Johns Hopkins University Press, 1989.

During, Simon, ed. *The Cultural Studies Reader*. New York: Routledge, 1993.

Eagleton, Terry. Foreword to *Social Figures: George Eliot, Social History, and Literary Representation*, by Daniel Cottom. Minneapolis: University of Minnesota Press, 1987.

Ellison, Ralph. *Shadow and Act*. New York: Random House, 1964.

Fishkin, Shelley Fisher. *Was Huck Black? Mark Twain and African-American Voices*. New York: Oxford University Press, 1993.

Gallagher, Catherine. "Marxism and the New Historicism." In *The New Historicism*. Ed. H. Aram Veeser. New York: Routledge, 1989.

Gates, Henry Louis, Jr. *"Race," Writing and Difference*. Chicago: University of Chicago Press, 1986.

———. *The Signifying Monkey*. New York: Oxford University Press, 1988.

Geertz, Clifford. *The Theory of Literature*. New York: Harcourt, 1955.

Graff, Gerald, and James Phelan, eds. *Adventures of Huckleberry Finn: A Case Study in Critical Controversy*. Boston: St. Martin's Press (Bedford), 1995.

Greenblatt, Stephen. "The Power of Forms and the Forms of Power." Introduction to *Genre* 15, nos. 1–2 (1982): 1–4.

———. "Towards a Poetics of Culture." In *The New Historicism*. Ed. H. Aram Veeser. New York: Routledge, 1989.

Groden, Michael, and Martin Krieswirth, eds. *The Johns Hopkins Guide to Literary Theory and Criticism*. Baltimore: Johns Hopkins University Press, 1994.

Grossberg, Lawrence, Cary Nelson, and Paula Treichler, eds. *Cultural Studies*. New York: Routledge, 1992.

Hemenway, Robert. "In the American Canon." In *Redefining American Literary History*. Ed. A. Lavonne Ruoff and Jerry Ward. New York: Modern Language Association, 1990.

Heyck, Denis Lynn Daly, ed. *Barrios and Borderlands: Cultures of Latinos and Latinas in the United States*. New York: Routledge, 1994.

Jameson, Frederic. *The Political Unconscious: Narrative as a Socially Symbolic Act*. Ithaca, NY: Cornell University Press, 1981.

Jenkins, Harold, ed. *The Arden Shakespeare: Hamlet*. New York and London: Routledge, 1982. Reprint, 1989–90.

Joseph, Bertram. *Conscience and the King: A Study of Hamlet*. London: Chatto and Windus, 1953.

Kaplan, Justin. "Born to Trouble: One Hundred Years of *Huckleberry Finn*." In *Adventures of Huckleberry Finn: A Case Study in Critical Controversy*. Ed. Gerald Graff and James Phelan. Boston: St. Martin's Press (Bedford), 1995.

Kingston, Maxine Hong. *The Woman Warrior: Memories of a Girlhood Among Ghosts*. New York: Random House, 1976.

Lawrence, D. H. *Studies in Classical American Fiction*. New York: Viking (Compass), 1964; first published in 1923.

Lester, Julius. "Morality and *Adventures of Huckleberry Finn*." In *Adventures of Huckleberry Finn: A Case Study in Critical Controversy*. Ed. Gerald Graff and James Phelan. Boston: St. Martin's Press (Bedford), 1995.

Lévi-Strauss, Claude. *The Raw and the Cooked*. Trans. John and Doreen Weightman. New York: Harper, 1975.

Levith, Murray J. *What's in Shakespeare's Names*. Hamden, CT: Shoe String Press (Archon), 1978.

Lim, Shirley Geok-lin, Mayumi Tsutakawa, and Margarita Donnelly, eds. *The Forbidden Stitch: An Asian American Women's Anthology*. Corvallis, OR: Calyx Books, 1989.

Ling, Amy. "Chinese American Writers: The Tradition Behind Maxine Hong Kingston." In *Redefining American Literary History*. Ed. A. LaVonne Ruoff and Jerry W. Ward. New York: Modern Language Association, 1990.

Litvak, Joseph. "Back to the Future: A Review-Article on the New Historicism, Deconstruction, and Nineteenth-Century Fiction." *Texas Studies in Literature and Language* 30 (1988): 120–49.

Madison, D. Soyini, ed. *The Woman That I Am: The Literature and Culture of Contemporary Women of Color*. New York: St. Martin's Press, 1994.

McCanles, Michael. "The Authentic Discourse of the Renaissance." *Diacritics* 10, no. 1 (spring 1980): 77–87.

Morrison, Toni. *Playing in the Dark: Whiteness and Literary Imagination*. New York: Vintage Press, 1993.

Morton, Donald. "Birth of the Cyberqueer." *PMLA* 110 (May 1995): 369–81.

Mullaney, Steven. "Brothers and Others, or the Art of Alienation." In *Cannibals, Witches, and Divorce: Estranging the Renaissance*. Ed. Marjorie Garber. Baltimore: Johns Hopkins University Press, 1987.

Paredes, Raymond A. "Autobiography and Ethnic Politics: Richard Rodriguez' *Hunger of Memory*." In *Multicultural Autobiography: American Lives*. Ed. James Robert Payne. Knoxville: University of Tennessee Press, 1992.

Pearce, Roy Harvey. *Savagism and Civilization: A Study of the Indian and the American Mind*. Berkeley: University of California Press, 1988.

Pechter, Edward. "The New Historicism and Its Discontents: Politicizing Renaissance Drama." *PMLA* 102 (May 1987): 292–303.

Porter, Carolyn. "Are We Being Historical Yet?" *South Atlantic Quarterly* 87 (fall 1988): 743–86.

Radway, Janice. *Reading the Romance: Women, Patriarchy, and Popular Literature*. Chapel Hill: University of North Carolina Press, 1984.

Rebolledo, Diana, and Eliana S. Rivera, eds. *Infinite Divisions: An Anthology of Chicana Literature*. Tucson: University of Arizona Press, 1993.

Reynolds, David S. *Beneath the American Renaissance: The Subversive Imagination in the Age of Emerson and Melville*. New York: Alfred A. Knopf, 1988.

Robinson, Forrest G. "The New Historicism and the Old West." *Western American Literature* 25, no. 2 (summer 1990): 103–23.

Roberts, John. "The African American Animal Trickster as Hero." In *Redefining American Literary History*. Ed. A. LaVonne Ruoff and Jerry W. Ward. New York: Modern Language Association, 1990.

———. *From Trickster to Badman: The Black Folk Hero in Slavery and Freedom*. Philadelphia: University of Pennsylvania Press, 1989.

Said, Edward. *Orientalism*. New York: Pantheon Books, 1978.

Sedgwick, Eve Kosofsky. *Epistemology of the Closet*. Berkeley: University of California Press, 1990.

Sill, Geoffrey M., Miriam T. Chaplin, Jean Ritzke, and David Wilson, eds. *Opening the American Mind: Race, Ethnicity, and Gender in Higher Education*. Newark: University of Delaware Press, 1993.

Sinfield, Alan. *Cultural Politics: Queer Reading*. Philadelphia: University of Pennsylvania Press, 1994.

Sumida, Stephen H. Afterword to *Growing Up Asian: An Anthology*. Ed. Maria Hong. New York: William Morrow and Co., 1993.

Tan, Amy. *Joy Luck Club*. New York: Putnam, 1989.

Tylor, Edward Burnett. *Primitive Culture*. New York: Holt, 1877.

Veeser, H. Aram, ed. *The New Historicism*. New York: Routledge, 1989.

Velie, Alan R., ed. *American Indian Literature: A Brief Introduction and Anthology*. New York: HarperCollins, 1995.

———. *American Indian Literature: An Anthology*. Norman: University of Oklahoma Press, 1979.

Vizenor, Gerald. "Introduction." *Native American Literature: A Brief Introduction and Anthology*. New York: HarperCollins, 1995.

Waxman, Barbara Frey, ed. *Multicultural Literatures Through Feminist-Postmodernist Lenses*. Knoxville: University of Tennessee Press, 1993.

Wiget, Andrew. "His Life in His Tale: The Native American Trickster and the Literature of Possibility." In *Redefining American Literary History*. New York: Modern Language Association, 1990.

Williams, Raymond. *Culture and Society: 1780–1950*. London: Chatto, 1958.

———. *Keywords*. New York: Oxford University Press, 1979.

———. *Marxism and Literature*. New York: Oxford University Press, 1977.

———. *Writing in Society*. London: Verso, 1984.

Wong, Jade Snow. *Fifth Chinese Daughter*. 1945. Reprint, Seattle: University of Washington Press, 1978.

8

Additional Approaches

In mature interpretation of a piece of literature, the reader may respond at any given moment from one particular orientation—perhaps a biographical, historical, feminist, formalistic, or psychological approach. Ideally, however, the reader's ultimate response should be multiple and eclectic. Because a work of literary art embodies a potential human experience and because human experience is multidimensional, the reader needs a variety of ways to approach and to realize (make real) that experience.

In this chapter we therefore indicate other contemporary approaches to literature, either because they are different from those already detailed or because they place different emphases upon some of the aspects of these approaches. In addition, we depart in this chapter from the established pattern in that we do not offer explications of the five works analyzed in most of the chapters. Rather, we suggest a number of approaches that may profitably be studied further.

Beside the eclectic emphasis of this chapter, we may note several other characteristics. First, after the great and salutary success of the "old" New Critics in teaching us to return to the printed text and to see it as artifact, it is not surprising—indeed, it was to be expected—that a reaction should take us somewhat away from formalism. A number of schools or approaches have suggested that in emphasizing the artifact the formalists neglected the humanness of the experience of literature, neglected the social or cultural milieux of literature, or falsified the vision of a true eclectic. Several of the approaches we survey here reflect this swing away from the allegedly objective approach of the New Critics. Second, some of the approaches in this chapter have European origins. The great movement of the New Critics was centered in America, with some ties to or even some origins in England. But other movements such as structuralism and post-structuralism that have exerted significant influence upon American criticism have predominantly Continental origins. Third, a number of the approaches in this chapter are in some respects quite traditional and are partly suggested in chapter 2. However, not all approaches could be discussed in the context of chapter 2, and some have new dimensions. Consequently, although their roots are traditional enough, their contemporary manifestations may seem quite different. We have in mind, for example, the neo-Aristotelians, the rhetorical approach, the genre approach, the history of ideas, and source and influence studies (including some aspects of "genetic" criticism).

Still another characteristic of this chapter is its special kind of utility. As already indicated, the following sections do not offer readings of *Huckleberry Finn*, *Hamlet*, "Young Goodman Brown," "Everyday Use," or "To His Coy Mistress." Rather, these sections are stepping-stones to that eclectic reading we have stressed, whatever work the reader is interested in. Each of the sections provides orientation to the approach under discussion, including something of its history, sometimes an indication of how it overlaps with other approaches, frequently the names of critics and their works associated with the approach, and occasionally some very brief examples of the approach in practice. There is usually a range within a section, so that neophytes may at the very least become aware of the existence of the approach and more advanced readers can see where they might go to learn more. It is for this last reason that the sections are consciously allusive and sometimes resemble annotated bibliographies. Not all the books and articles cited explicitly deal with the approach under consideration, but they are germane or at least suggestive and frequently contain annotations and bibliographies of their own that will lead the reader to additional materials.

In sum, this chapter describing additional approaches continues the notion that has informed this handbook throughout: because literature is the verbal artistic expression of humankind qua humankind, with all the richness, depth, and complexity that concept suggests, literary criticism is necessarily the composite of many ways of approaching that experience. It is necessarily eclectic because no one way of reading a piece of literature can capture all that is in it, just as no simplistic notion can embody all that the human being is. For that we need many approaches.

▪ I. ARISTOTELIAN CRITICISM (INCLUDING THE CHICAGO SCHOOL)

Few works of literary criticism can hope to wear so well, or so long, as Aristotle's *Poetics* (fourth century B.C.). Our theories of drama and of the epic, the recognition of genres as a way of studying a piece of literature, and our methodology of studying a work or group of works and then inducing theory from practice can all find beginnings in the *Poetics*. More specifically, from the *Poetics* we have such basic notions as catharsis, the characteristics of the tragic hero (the noble figure; tragic pride, or hubris; the tragic flaw), the formative elements of drama (action or plot, character, thought, diction, melody, and spectacle), the necessary unity of plot, and perhaps most significantly, the basic concept of mimesis, or imitation, the idea that works of literature are imitations of actions, the differences among them resulting from means, objects, and manner.

In practice, readers may be Aristotelian when they distinguish one genre from another, when they question whether Arthur Miller's Willy Loman can be tragic or affirm that Melville's Ahab is, when they stress plot rather than character or diction, or when they stress the mimetic role of literature. In formal criticism readers will do well to study Matthew Arnold's 1853 preface to his poems as a notable example of Aristotelian criticism in the nineteenth century. In the twentieth century one critic has said that the "ideal critic" would be neo-Aristotelian if he or she "scrupulously [induced] from practice" (Hyman 387).

Though Aristotelian principles are certainly a traditional

way of examining literature, their most important twentieth-century use is associated with a group of critics who were colleagues at the University of Chicago during the 1940s. While stressing their humanistic concern and their pervading hope for a broadly based literary criticism, the members of the Chicago School were in part reacting against what seemed to them to be an inadequacy in the work of the New Critics: for Ronald S. Crane, "bankruptcy" and "critical monism." Consequently, they called for an openness to critical perspectives, a "plurality" of methods, and advocated using Aristotle's principles comprehensively and systematically enough to be developed beyond what Aristotle himself had set down.

That call was made by Crane, in his introduction to *Critics and Criticism: Ancient and Modern* (18); in that book Crane and his colleagues—W. R. Keast, Richard McKeon, Norman MacLean, Elder Olson, and Bernard Weinberg—gathered papers that they had published as early as 1936. Arranged in three sections, the essays dealt with "representative critics of the present day," "figures and episodes in the history of criticism from the Greeks through the eighteenth century," and "theoretical questions relating to the criticism of criticism and of poetic forms" (1). Not all the essays were explicitly "Aristotelian," though Crane made it clear that a "major concern of the essays . . . is with the capacities for modern development and use of . . . the poetic method of Aristotle" (12).

Another work of importance produced by this movement is Crane's *The Languages of Criticism and the Structure of Poetry*. But although this book and *Critics and Criticism* are frequently alluded to by other critics, the Chicago neo-Aristotelians made less of an impact than the New Critics against whom they took up arms. Ten years after *The Languages of Criticism*, for example, Walter Sutton wrote:

> The neo-Aristotelian position developed by Crane and his colleagues is valuable for its emphasis upon theory, historical perspective, and scholarly discipline. It has, however, stimulated very little practical criticism. The active movement that the leaders hoped for never developed, although their work undoubtedly encouraged a renewal of interest in genre criticism, shared by critics like Kenneth Burke and Northrop Frye in

modified forms and by many other scholar critics within the universities. (173)

The reader will find Sutton's chapter on the neo-Aristotelians helpful because it provides not only interpretive summaries of some of their work but also comments on possible deficiencies of the neo-Aristotelians and on their relationships to other schools of criticism.

Although Sutton may have been correct in saying that the neo-Aristotelian efforts of the Chicago School stimulated very little practical criticism, renewed efforts in rhetorical criticism, and possibly in genre criticism and in some of the later stresses on fiction as a serial form, may be mutations of Aristotelian criticism. This seems to be the thought of Donald Pizer when he writes that neo-Aristotelianism can be seen in "new and influential forms." Pizer cites as examples two books, Charles C. Walcutt's *Man's Changing Mask* and Robert Scholes and Robert Kellogg's *The Nature of Narrative*. These books, according to Pizer, deal with the similarities between "all serial art" and fiction, which is seen as "a late example of . . . permanent elements" of narrative and characterization. Because of these similarities, the books by Walcutt and by Scholes and Kellogg, among others, "reflect what can be called an Aristotelian temper" (574).

Quick Reference

Crane, Ronald S., ed. *Critics and Criticism: Ancient and Modern.* Chicago: University of Chicago Press, 1952.

———. *The Languages of Criticism and the Structure of Poetry.* Toronto: University of Toronto Press, 1953.

Hyman, Stanley Edgar. *The Armed Vision.* New York: Random House (Vintage), 1955.

Pizer, Donald. "A Primer of Fictional Aesthetics." *College English* 30 (Apr. 1969): 572–80.

Scholes, Robert, and Robert Kellogg. *The Nature of Narrative.* New York: Oxford University Press, 1966.

Sutton, Walter. *Modern American Criticism.* Englewood Cliffs, NJ: Prentice Hall, 1963.

Walcutt, Charles C. *Man's Changing Mask.* Minneapolis: University of Minnesota Press, 1966.

▪ II. GENRE CRITICISM

Genre criticism, criticism of kinds or types, like several of the approaches described in this chapter (Aristotelian, rhetorical, history of ideas, and source study), is a traditional way of approaching a piece of literature, having been used in this case at least as far back as Aristotle's *Poetics* and, like some other traditional approaches, genre criticism has been given revitalized attention in modern times, modifying what was accepted as genre criticism for some two thousand years.

Since the time of the classical Greeks and especially during the neoclassical period, it was assumed that if readers knew into what genre a piece of literature fell, they knew much about the work itself. Put simply, Athenian citizens going to see a play by Sophocles knew in advance that the story would be acted out by a small group of actors, that they would be seeing and hearing a chorus as part of the production, and that a certain kind of music would accompany the chorus. When Virgil set out to write an epic for Augustan Rome, he chose to work within the genre that he knew already from Homer. According to the conventions of epic, he announced his theme in his opening line, he set his hero out on journeys and placed him in combat situations, he saw to it that the gods were involved as they had been in the *Iliad* and the *Odyssey*, and in the two halves of his *Aeneid* he even provided actions that were roughly parallel to the actions of the *Odyssey* (journey) and the *Iliad* (warfare). Because Alexander Pope and his readers were schooled in the classics, and the genres of classic literature, his parody of the epic was easily recognizable in his mock-epic, *The Rape of the Lock.* Pope took the conventions of the epic genre and deliberately reversed them: the epic theme is "mighty contests" arising from "trivial things"; the hero is a flirtatious woman with her appropriate "arms"; the journey is to Hampton Court, a place of socializing and gossip; the battle is joined over a card table, with the cards as troops; the epic weapon is a pair of scissors; the epic boast is about cutting off a lock of hair. The same use of a genre with deliberate twisting of its conventions can be found in Thomas Gray's "Ode on the Death of a Favourite Cat, Drowned in a Tub of Gold Fishes," where again high style and low matter join. Here odes, death, cats, and goldfish come together in such fashion that one genre becomes its mirror image. Instead of a serious ode (or elegy) on a serious matter, we have a humorous, even a bathetic poem.

Such are the kinds of observations that traditional genre criticism could provide. It held sway through the eighteenth century, when it was even dominant. It was less vital as a form of criticism in the nineteenth century, although the conventional types, such as drama, lyric, and romance, were still recognized and useful for terminology, as they still are. In more recent times, however, new interest has been developed in genre criticism, especially in theoretical matters.

Of major significance is Northrop Frye's *Anatomy of Criticism*. In his introduction Frye points to our debt to the Greeks for our terminology for and our distinctions among some genres, and he also notes that we have not gone much beyond what the Greeks gave us (13). This he proposes to correct in his anatomy. Although much of his book is archetypal criticism, and hence has relevance for chapter 5, much of it—especially the first essay, "Historical Criticism: Theory of Modes," and the fourth essay, "Rhetorical Criticism: Theory of Genres"—also bears upon genre criticism. Summarizing Frye is a challenge we shall gladly ignore, but two passages in particular will illustrate his technique of illuminating a critical problem and will provide insight especially into genre criticism. Calling attention to the "origin of the words drama, epic and lyric," Frye says that the "central principle of genre is simple enough. The basis of generic distinctions in literature appears to be the radical of presentation. Words may be acted in front of a spectator; they may be spoken in front of a listener; they may be sung or chanted; or they may be written for the reader" (246–47). Later he says, "The purpose of criticism by genres is not so much to classify as to clarify such traditions and affinities, thereby bringing out a large number of literary relationships that would not be noticed as long as there were no context established for them" (247–48). On the face of it these passages, though helpful, are not much different from what

Aristotle offered in the *Poetics*, but on such bases Frye ranges far and wide (much more than we can here suggest) in his study of modes and genres, classifying, describing, dividing, subdividing.

Monumental as the work is, it provoked mixed responses, and we may cite two works that differ from Frye's, sometimes explicitly, as they offer other insights into genre criticism.

E. D. Hirsch's *Validity in Interpretation* makes only small reference to Frye, and presents (among other things) a quite different approach to genre criticism (ch. 3, "The Concept of Genre"). Less concerned with the extensive anatomizing of literature and of literary criticism (Hirsch implies that Frye's classification is "illegitimate" [110–11]), Hirsch insists on the individuality of any given work. More important, he shows again and again how the reader's understanding of meaning is dependent on the reader's accurate perception of the genre that the author intended as he wrote the work. (Hirsch is not, however, thinking simplistically of short story, for example, in contrast to masque, epic, or the like.) If the reader assumes that a work is in one genre but it is really in another, only misreading can result: "An interpreter's notion of the type of meaning he confronts will powerfully influence his understanding of details. This phenomenon will recur at every level of sophistication and is the primary reason for disagreements among qualified interpreters" (75). And again: "Understanding can occur only if the interpreter proceeds under the same system of expectations" as the speaker or writer (80). Such a statement reminds us that if a person reads *The Rape of the Lock* without any previous knowledge of the epic, we must wonder whether he or she has truly read Pope's poem. For if readers do not recognize conventions, they are reading at best at a superficial level. As Hirsch says, "every shared type of meaning [every genre] can be defined as a system of conventions" (92). Elsewhere, Hirsch is helpful in showing that when we read a work with which we are not previously familiar or read a work that is creating a new genre, we operate ("triangulate") by moving back and forth from what we know to what we do not know well yet.

Still another work that qualifies Frye's treatment of genres while offering its own insights (though basically on fiction) is

Robert Scholes's *Structuralism in Literature*. Scholes's discussion (117–41) is closer to Frye's than is Hirsch's, but it brings to the treatment not only qualifications of Frye's classifications but also the influences of recent work in structuralism (see the section in this chapter), whereas Frye's emphasis is archetypal and rhetorical.

All three of these works—those of Frye, Hirsch, and Scholes—although they are challenging and stimulating, are sometimes difficult. Part of the difficulty when they are dealing with genres derives from the fact that pieces of literature do not simply and neatly fall into categories, or genres (even the folk ballad, seemingly obvious as a narrative form, partakes of the lyric, and of the drama, the latter through its dialogue). This difficulty arises from the nature of literature itself: it is original, imaginative, creative, and hence individualistic. But regardless of literature's protean quality, our interpretation of it is easier if we can recognize a genre, if we can therefore be provided with a set of "expectations" and conventions, and if we can then recognize when the expectations are fulfilled and when they are imaginatively adapted. Perhaps one of the most beneficial aspects of engaging in genre criticism is that, in our efforts to decide into what genre a challenging piece falls, we come to experience the literature more fully: "how we finally categorize the poem becomes irrelevant, for the fact of trying to categorize—even through the crudest approach—has brought us near enough to its individual qualities for genre-criticism to give way to something more subtle" (Rodway 91). More recent inquiries into genre have been carried out in the books and articles of Gérard Genette, Gary Saul Morson, and Wendy Steiner.

Quick Reference

Frye, Northrop. *Anatomy of Criticism: Four Essays*. Princeton: Princeton University Press, 1957.

Hirsch, E. D. *Validity in Interpretation*. New Haven, CT: Yale University Press, 1967.

Rodway, Allan. "Generic Criticism: The Approach Through Type, Mode, and Kind." In *Contemporary Criticism*. Stratford-Upon-Avon Studies 12. Ed. Malcolm Bradbury and David Palmer. London: Edward Arnold, 1970.

Scholes, Robert. *Structuralism in Literature: An Introduction.* New Haven, CT: Yale University Press, 1974.

▪ III. SOURCE STUDY AND RELATED APPROACHES (GENETIC CRITICISM)

The kind of approach, or the set of related approaches, discussed in this section does not have a generally accepted name. It would be pleasant but not altogether helpful if we could settle upon what Kenneth Burke called it—a "high class kind of gossip"—for Burke was describing part of what we are interested in: the "inspection of successive drafts, notebooks, the author's literary habits in general" (Gibson 171).

We might call the approach *genetic*, because that is the word sometimes used when a work is considered in terms of its origins. We would find the term appropriate in studying the growth and development of the work, its genesis, as from its sources. However, the term seems effectively to have been preempted by critics for the method of criticism that, as David Daiches says, accounts for the "characteristics of the writer's work" by looking at the sociological and psychological phenomena out of which the work grew (358–75). Similarly, the *Princeton Encyclopedia of Poetry and Poetics* uses the term *genetic* in surveying the methods of criticism that treat how the work "came into being, and what influences were at work to give it exactly the qualities that it has. Characteristically, [genetic critics] try to suggest what is in the poem by showing what lies behind it" (Preminger 167). These phrases would come near to what we are calling "source study and related approaches," except for the fact that these statements tend to have a sociological context, where the work is seen as a piece of documentary evidence for the milieu that gave rise to it. (This sort of criticism is now the province of the new historicists; see the section entitled "The New Historicism" in chapter 7.)

More precisely, then, by "source study and related approaches" we mean the growth and development of a work as seen through a study of the author's manuscripts during the stages of composition of the work, of notebooks, of sources and analogues, and of various other influences (not necessarily sociological or psychological) that lie in the background of the work. In such study, our assumption is that from the background we can derive clues to a richer, more accurate appreciation of the work. It may be that such an assumption is something of a will-o'-the-wisp, for we can never be precisely sure of how the creative process works, of the accuracy of our guesses, of the "intention" of the author (a vexed question in modern criticism). Well suited as an introduction to this kind of criticism and a pleasant indication of both the advantages and the disadvantages of this approach to literature is the collection of pieces from which we took the Kenneth Burke quotation: Walker Gibson's *Poems in the Making*. Introducing the pieces he has gathered, Gibson calls attention to the problem of the "relevance of any or all of these accounts" in our gaining a "richer appreciation of poetry," but at the same time he clearly believes that this high-class kind of gossip offers possibilities. Accordingly, he provides a variety of specific approaches—different kinds of manuscript study, essays by the original authors (for example, Edgar Allan Poe and Stephen Spender on their own works), the classic study (in part) of "Kubla Khan" by John Livingston Lowes, and T. S. Eliot's devastating attack on that kind of scholarship. Not in Gibson's compendium but of interest because of the popularity of the poem is a similar study of Robert Frost's "Stopping by Woods on a Snowy Evening." An analysis of the manuscript of the poem shows how Frost worked out his words and his rhyme scheme, crossing out words not conducive to the experience of the poem. At the same time, Frost's own (separate) comments on the writing of the poem help us to interpret what the marks in the manuscript suggest (for this study see Charles W. Cooper and John Holmes, *Preface to Poetry*). An excellent example of this kind of work is Robert Gittings's *Odes of Keats and Their Earliest Known Manuscripts*, a handsome volume that provides an essay on how five of Keats's greatest poems were written and numerous, clear facsimile pages of the manuscripts.

These examples tend to come from poems of the nineteenth and twentieth centuries, but source and analogue study has long been a staple of traditional scholarship on literature of an earlier day, such as various works on Shakespeare's plays and *Sources and Analogues of Chaucer's Canterbury Tales*, edited by

W. F. Bryan and Germaine Dempster. A work like this last, it should be noted, provides materials for the scholar or student to work with, whereas other works are applications of such materials. An example of application can be found in the study of Sir Thomas Malory's *Morte Darthur*. Study of Malory's French and English sources helps us greatly in evaluating the art of his romance and the establishment of his purposes and has contributed to the debate over whether he intended to write one book (see Lumiansky's *Malory's Originality: A Critical Study of* Le Morte Darthur) or a compendium of eight stories (see Vinaver's *The Works of Sir Thomas Malory*). Milton's notes and manuscripts over a long period of time show us how he gradually came to write *Paradise Lost* and something of his conception of what he was working toward. This and more can be seen, aided again by facsimile pages, in Allan H. Gilbert, *On the Composition of* Paradise Lost: *A Study of the Ordering and Insertion of Material*. More helpful to the beginning student is the somewhat broader view of a briefer work by Milton offered by Scott Elledge in *Milton's "Lycidas," Edited to Serve as an Introduction to Criticism*. There Elledge provides not only manuscript facsimiles of the poem, but materials on the pastoral tradition, examples of the genre, passages on the theory of monody, and information both from Milton's life and from his times.

For an example of the application of this approach to fiction, the reader might look at Matthew J. Bruccoli, *The Composition of "Tender Is the Night": A Study of the Manuscript*. Bruccoli worked from thirty-five hundred pages of holograph manuscript and typescript, plus proof sheets, which represented seventeen drafts and three versions of the novel (xv). Perhaps this is more than the beginning student cares to have in this critical approach to literature. It may be well to mention, therefore, that, like Gibson's and Elledge's works on poetry cited earlier, there are some books on pieces of fiction that are intended for the student and offer opportunities to approach a piece of fiction by means of source and influence study. Such are, for example, some of the novels (*The Scarlet Letter, Adventures of Huckleberry Finn, The Red Badge of Courage*) in the Norton Critical Editions, as in the Bedford series, where the text of the novel is accompanied by source and interpretive materials.

Similar to these is *Bear, Man, and God: Eight Approaches to William Faulkner's "The Bear"* (ed. Utley, Bloom, and Kinney). In introducing "Other Versions of 'The Bear,'" the editors point to some of the advantages of this kind of study:

> Criticism based on a close comparison of texts has recently come under attack; often such collation is seen as pedantic and fruitless. But a short time ago an examination of Mark Twain papers demonstrated that Twain had never composed "The Mysterious Stranger"; rather, an editor had combined selected fragments of his writing after his death to "make" the book. Perhaps in the same spirit of inquiry, critics have examined the various texts of "The Bear" in order to determine through textual changes something of Faulkner's evolving art: such an examination is the closest we can come to seeing Faulkner in his workshop. (121)

Perhaps that is a good place to engage in a high-class kind of gossip.

Quick Reference

Bruccoli, Matthew J. *The Composition of "Tender Is the Night": A Study of the Manuscripts.* Pittsburgh: University of Pittsburgh Press, 1963.

Bryan, W. F., and Germaine Dempster, eds. *Sources and Analogues of Chaucer's Canterbury Tales.* 1941. Reprint, New York: Humanities Press International, 1958.

Cooper, Charles W., and John Holmes. *Preface to Poetry.* New York: Harcourt, 1946.

Daiches, David. *Critical Approaches to Literature.* Englewood Cliffs, NJ: Prentice Hall, 1956.

Elledge, Scott. *Milton's "Lycidas," Edited to Serve as an Introduction to Criticism.* New York: Harper, 1966.

Gibson, Walker, ed. *Poems in the Making.* Boston: Houghton Mifflin, 1963.

Gilbert, Allan H. *On the Composition of* Paradise Lost: *A Study of the Ordering and Insertion of Material.* 1947. Reprint, New York: Octagon Press, 1966.

Gittings, Robert. *Odes of Keats and Their Earliest Known Manuscripts.* Kent, OH: Kent State University Press, 1970.

Kennedy, Beverly. "Cambridge MS. Dd. 4.24: A Misogynist Scribal Revision of the *Wife of Bath's Prologue?*" *Chaucer Review* 30 (1996): 343–58.

Lumiansky, R. M., ed. *Malory's Originality: A Critical Study of* Le Morte Darthur. Baltimore: Johns Hopkins University Press, 1964.

Preminger, Alex, ed. *Princeton Encyclopedia of Poetry and Poetics.* 3rd ed. Princeton, NJ: Princeton University Press, 1993.

Utley, Francis Lee, Lynn Z. Bloom, and Arthur F. Kinney, eds. *Bear, Man, and God: Eight Approaches to William Faulkner's "The Bear."* 2nd ed. New York: Random House, 1971.

Vinaver, Eugène, ed. *The Works of Sir Thomas Malory,* by Thomas Malory. 2nd ed. Oxford: Oxford University Press, 1967.

▪ IV. THE HISTORY OF IDEAS

Studying a piece of literature in the light of the history of ideas is somewhat similar to the historical approach presented in chapter 2. For example, the concept of revenge as found in certain Renaissance English plays can be tied directly to the study of Seneca in the universities of the sixteenth century and thus to the rise of interest in classical Greece and Rome during the Renaissance. Such a consideration must deal simultaneously with an idea, with historical developments, and with the contents of literature. Similarly, any consideration of the biography of an author may well deal with the history of his or her period and with the influence of the spirit of the times on a given work, an influence that may in turn be the result of antecedent developments. In the twentieth century the relationship between existentialism and the theater of the absurd has provided an example.

However, the history of ideas may be taken to refer more precisely to an area of philosophy than to an area of history, and to a form of study different from the traditional historical-biographical approach of chapter 2 or the more recent new historicism (see chapter 7). This subdivision of philosophy has been best described by the scholar Arthur O. Lovejoy, in his classic *The Great Chain of Being: A Study of the History of an Idea* (first published in 1936). Of the history of ideas, Stanley Edgar Hyman has said what most other readers would acknowledge: the history of ideas is a "philosophic field largely invented and pre-empted by Professor Arthur O. Lovejoy of Johns Hopkins. The history of ideas is the tracing of the unit ideas of philosophies through intellectual history, and just as it finds its chief clues in literary expression, literary criticism can draw on it for the philosophic background of literature" (187–88).

The unit ideas mentioned by Hyman are of central importance in this field of study, as we can see from Lovejoy's introductory chapter in *The Great Chain of Being*. There Lovejoy says, "By the history of ideas I mean something at once more specific and less restricted than the history of philosophy. It is differentiated primarily by the character of the units with which it concerns itself" (3). Lovejoy differentiates a unit idea from the compounds whose names usually end with -*ism*: idealism, romanticism, rationalism, transcendentalism, pragmatism, and the like. Among the principal types of ideas, that which most concerns him he describes in part as follows:

> . . . any unit-idea which the historian thus isolates he next seeks to trace through more than one—ultimately, indeed, through all—of the provinces of history in which it figures in any important degree, whether those provinces are called philosophy, science, literature, art, religion, or politics. . . . [The history of ideas] is concerned only with a certain group of factors in history, and with these only in so far as they can be seen at work in what are commonly considered separate divisions of the intellectual world; and it is especially interested in the processes by which influences pass over from one province to another. (15–16)

Lovejoy singles out the need for seeing the relationships between philosophy and modern literature:

> Most teachers of literature would perhaps readily enough admit that it is to be *studied*—I by no means say, can solely be enjoyed— chiefly for its thought-content, and that the interest of the history of literature is largely as a record of the movement of ideas. . . . [It] is by first distinguishing and analyzing the major ideas which appear again and again [in literature], and by observing each of them as a recurrent unit in many contexts, that the philosophic background of literature can best be illuminated. (16–17)

After this introduction, Lovejoy puts into practice the concept of pursuing a unit idea by studying the notion of the great chain of being in its genesis and its later diffusion in various places, eras, philosophers, and literary figures.

Lovejoy is credited also with the founding of *Journal of the History of Ideas*. In 1990, the journal entered its second half-century of publication with the lead article entitled "What Is Happening to the History of Ideas?" In that article Donald R. Kelley points to the fact that while "In its American incarnation the history of ideas has been associated above all with the work of the principal of this journal, Arthur O. Lovejoy . . . ," in fact the "field of study has had a much longer career and has been international in scope" (3). "For at least three centuries, adopting the conventions of philosophers, historians of thought have been trying to trace the trajectories of . . . enduring categories of thought and successions of speculative systems that have achieved academic recognition" (4). It is appropriate, then, that many studies can be grouped in this broad category. At the risk of extending the concept of the unit to works that Lovejoy may not have accepted as examples of the history of ideas (some may be labeled simply as comparative literature, and one even antedates *The Great Chain of Being*), our list below includes works that at least partake of Lovejoy's approach and method. The titles themselves provide glosses on how the history of ideas impinges upon literary criticism.

Quick Reference

Abrams, M. H. *Natural Supernaturalism: Tradition and Revolution in Romantic Literature.* New York: Norton, 1971.

Armstrong, Elizabeth. *Ronsard and the Age of Gold.* London: Cambridge University Press, 1968.

Barkan, Leonard. *Nature's Work of Art: The Human Body as Image of the World.* New Haven, CT: Yale University Press, 1975.

Bate, Walter Jackson. *From Classic to Romantic: Premises of Taste in Eighteenth-Century England.* 1946. New York: Harper Torchbooks, 1961.

Bercovitch, Sacvan. *The Puritan Origins of the American Self*. New Haven, CT: Yale University Press, 1975.

Boas, George. *The History of Ideas: An Introduction*. New York: Scribner's, 1969.

Conn, Peter. *The Divided Mind: Ideology and Imagination in America, 1898–1917*. Cambridge: Cambridge University Press, 1983.

Economou, George D. *The Goddess Natura in Medieval Literature*. Cambridge, MA: Harvard University Press, 1972.

Elliott, Emory. *Revolutionary Writers: Literature and Authority in the New Republic, 1752–1810*. New York: Oxford University Press, 1982.

Heminger, S. K., Jr. *Touches of Sweet Harmony: Pythagorean Cosmology and Renaissance Poetics*. San Marino, CA: Huntington Library Press, 1974.

Hyman, Stanley Edgar. *The Armed Vision*. Rev. ed. New York: Random House (Vintage), 1955.

Kelley, Donald R. "What Is Happening to the History of Ideas?" *Journal of the History of Ideas* 51, no. 1 (1990): 3–26.

Levin, Harry. *The Myth of the Golden Age in the Renaissance*. Bloomington: Indiana University Press, 1969.

Lewis, C. S. *The Allegory of Love: A Study in Medieval Tradition*. 1936. Reprint, New York: Oxford University Press (Galaxy), 1958.

Lovejoy, Arthur O. *Essays in the History of Ideas*. Baltimore: Johns Hopkins University Press, 1948.

———. *The Great Chain of Being: A Study of the History of an Idea*. 1936. Reprint, New York: Harper Torchbooks, 1960.

Marx, Leo. *The Machine in the Garden: Technology and the Pastoral Ideal in America*. New York: Oxford University Press, 1964.

Patch, H. R. *The Goddess Fortuna in Medieval Literature*. 1927. Reprint, New York: Octagon Press, 1967.

Perella, Nicolas James. *The Kiss Sacred and Profane: An Interpretive History of Kiss Symbolism and Related Religio-Erotic Themes*. Berkeley: University of California, 1969.

Poirer, Richard. *A World Elsewhere: The Place of Style in American Literature*. New York: Oxford University Press, 1966.

Quinones, Ricardo J. *The Renaissance Discovery of Time*. Cambridge, MA: Harvard University Press, 1972.

Reising, Russell J. *The Unusable Past*. New York: Metheun, 1986.

Rousseau, George S., ed. *Organic Form: The Life of an Idea.* London: Routledge, 1972.

Stewart, Stanley. *The Enclosed Garden: The Tradition and the Image of Seventeenth-Century Poetry.* Madison: University of Wisconsin Press, 1966.

Williams, Raymond. *Keywords: A Vocabulary of Culture and Society.* New York: Oxford University Press, 1979.

▪ V. RHETORIC, LINGUISTICS, AND STYLISTICS

Repeatedly in this handbook we call attention to the necessary overlapping of various approaches to any given work. Often one approach shades into another almost imperceptibly; in fact, different works on criticism will group the same approaches in different ways. Such an overlap is especially obvious when we study language and its behavior—or its effect on our own behavior—in three areas we draw together here: rhetoric, linguistics, and stylistics.

Rhetoric, or a rhetorical approach to literature, is of course a highly traditional approach to texts. The great classical critics like Aristotle and Longinus were rhetorically oriented. There were great practitioners, like Cicero. There were great teachers of rhetoric, like St. Augustine, when a knowledge of rhetoric (and necessarily of literature) was the way of training the attorneys of the day. Later, rhetoric and grammar were two-thirds of the medieval trivium (logic being the third component).

However, as traditional as they are, rhetoric, linguistics, and stylistics, like the several approaches we have just reviewed, all have their distinctly modern manifestations. And like some other "modern" approaches to criticism, the rhetorical approach has been seen as a corrective to the New Critics' tendency to set up what John C. Gerber has called a *"cordon sanitaire* between the reader and the work that distances the work almost as successfully as the historical approach" (354). Gerber ascribes the rise of this "new" rhetoric to the interest in the late 1940s in communication skills, out of which came the renewed awareness that in communication, a something must be communicated to a someone. Gradually, what was after World War II a pragmatic, elementary need in composition classes became (or became again) a method of literary criticism that preserved the New Critics' interest in the work but also directed attention to author and audience.

Looking back at that development in his very helpful introduction to a collection of rhetorical analyses, Edward P. J. Corbett has written that

> rhetorical criticism is that mode of internal criticism which considers the interactions between the work, the author, and the audience. As such, it is interested in the *product*, the *process*, and the *effect* of linguistic activity, whether of the imaginative kind or the utilitarian kind. When rhetorical criticism is applied to imaginative literature, it regards the work not so much as an object of aesthetic contemplation but as an artistically structured instrument for communication. It is more interested in a literary work for what it does than for what it *is*. (xxii)

While dealing with the work itself (hence, "internal"), rhetorical criticism considers external factors insofar as it "uses the text for its 'readings' about the author and the audience" (xviii). Particularly important is the effect of the work on its audience (what it *does*). This is not surprising, in that the original emphasis of rhetoric was on persuasion, and for that we go back to the classical Greeks.

As a matter of fact, literary criticism itself really had some of its beginnings in rhetorical analysis, for our first critics—Plato, Aristotle, Longinus, Horace—were devoted students, indeed formulators, of rhetoric. (Corbett, by the way, would stress the influence of Horace more than that of Aristotle in the later development of rhetorical criticism.) As late as the eighteenth century, rhetorical considerations played an important role in criticism, for learned men and women still knew and practiced formal rhetoric. Today much of the criticism of medieval, Renaissance, and neoclassical English and Continental literature can still profitably explore rhetorical strategies if only because we have and can work from the evidence of textbooks and manuals of rhetoric that were earnestly studied by the writers of those ages. Recently, however, the conscious and often impressive efforts to realize once again the advantages of rhetorical analyses of literature have not been limited to such earlier works. Even further, one area of rhetorical criticism—style—

has developed so much that it now deserves its own emphasis (see below). Today's new rhetoric may be expressed either in terms of classical rhetoric or through the insights gained in practical rhetoric without the use of Greek and Latin terms. Corbett, for example, points out that many a piece of practical criticism may be good rhetorical criticism even though the critic seems to be unaware of the long history of the mode within which he is operating, and may not at all use the terminology of the rhetorical critic. Similarly, creative authors may address themselves to the *audience*, while *arranging* their *argument* and working within a *style*, without realizing that these are four of the traditional concerns of rhetoricians. Readers who desire a convenient compilation of traditional terms of classical rhetoric should consult Richard A. Lanham, *A Handlist of Rhetorical Terms: A Guide for Students of English Literature*.

As already indicated, a rhetorical approach helps us to stay inside the work, although we may go outside it for terms and naming strategies, being always aware that the original author was a person who chose between available options. In this methodology, then, rhetorical analysis, on the one hand, is similar to and supportive of the formalistic approach, but, on the other, may go beyond it. Among the questions raised by the rhetorical approach are these: What can we know of the speaker or narrator? To whom is he or she allegedly speaking? What is the nature of that addressee, that audience? What setting is established or implied? How are we asked to respond to the situation created? Are we being asked to make a distinction between the *ethos* (the ethical stance) of the author and the statements of the central character (for example, a distinction between the comprehensive view of Mark Twain and the limited view of Huckleberry Finn)?

As persuasive discourse, the rhetoric of a literary work requires or invites the reader to participate in an imagined experience. If we recognize such rhetorical devices as metaphor, irony, syllogism, and induction, so much the better. But even without such terminology and accompanying sophistication, by close reading and from the experience of even a good course in freshman composition we can recognize that Marvell (or his persona) is skillfully using persuasive discourse. Consequently, "To His Coy Mistress" takes on the structure of argument. We could see just as easily that lyric poems can be structured on the basis of a definition, a process, an analysis, a causal relation; that they may provide examples; or that they may be arranged in a spatial or temporal pattern—rhetorical matters all. In every case, we can see that literature must be related to established forms of saying things; even syntax and diction, punch lines and sober conclusions, arrangement and emphasis are forms familiar to the writer before he or she begins his or her work, just as they are forms familiar to us before we read the work. The awareness of such special features and structures of words tells us a great deal about the author and the created voice. Our response to manipulated language tells us even more about the *meaning* of the work and quite a bit about ourselves as registers of meaning. Although lyric poetry seems to be the favorite genre for displays of rhetorical analysis, the method can be used effectively with fiction, as has been demonstrated by Ian Watt in "The First Paragraph of *The Ambassadors:* An Explication." There Watt examines diction and syntax in six sentences for the implications of their functions within the paragraph, the effects upon the reader, the revelations of the character of Lambert Strether, James's own attitudes toward experience, and our understanding of the meaning of the style.

Let us now look briefly at some specific aspects of linguistics and stylistics and how they fit in the overall context of rhetorical approaches. Linguistics, the study of language, has had in the twentieth century a distinctly modern approach, becoming a discipline unto itself—even, some would claim, a science. In a university it is not unusual for the department of linguistics to be separate from the department of literature (or English). As the new discipline transcended traditional philological studies, a number of new questions arose: Is literature merely a part of language? Is the object of literary criticism totally different from the object of linguistic analysis? Is the language of literature susceptible to the same kind of study that can be brought to bear on, for example, language in its spoken form? If it is so susceptible, then in what manner and in what areas can a work of art be studied by a scientific or quasi-scientific discipline? Surely this kind of study—whether it derives from structural linguistics, transformational-generative grammar, or some other modulation of modern linguistics—goes beyond the historical study of language that was important to the nineteenth- and early twentieth-century philologists, who concerned themselves with, for example, the rediscovery of the meanings of words in *Beowulf* and of Chaucer's pronunciation in such works as *The Canterbury Tales*.

Consequently, there is debate about linguistics as an approach to literature. One can find articles, for example, that say that attempts to apply modern linguistics to the study of literature are "out and out failures" (Lester 375); or that "There is no such thing as a distinctive literary language. And if this is true, it means that, though linguists may tell us a great deal about language, they tell us nothing about literature" (Schwartz 190).

But there are areas in which linguistics can further the study of literature, such as the field of sociolinguistics. At a simple and obvious level, a knowledge of historical information about language changes and about "devices which were operative at earlier stages in the development of English" is helpful (Mohr 4–6): a case in point is Shakespeare's distinction between *thou* and *you* (where distinction between social classes is a concern). Dialect study is another, for distinctions among dialects can be seen as early as in Chaucer and perhaps most famously in Mark Twain, as in *Huckleberry Finn*.

Stanley B. Greenfield has shown how linguistics is helpful in restoring a balance to the New Critics. He commented that the "new linguistics" was instrumental because it "gave rise to both linguistic and critical interest in elements of language other than diction, imagery, and symbolism, those staples of the New Criticism" (377). Especially germane to our grouping of rhetoric, linguistics, and stylistics was another observation by Greenfield to the effect that linguistics and stylistics overlap (378). Among book-length works on the application of linguistics to literary study is the one by Seymour Chatman and Samuel R. Levin, where we can read that "reconciliation" between linguists and literary critics is necessary to get us back to the view in the nineteenth and earlier twentieth century, when scholars would have seen, as a matter of course, that "linguistics and literary history were simply two peas in the philological pod" (vii).

The interest in style, always an aspect of rhetoric, has had its own modern emphasis. Defined in a most rudimentary way, stylistics is not the study of the words and grammar an author uses, but the study of the *way* the author uses words and grammar—as well as other elements—both within the sentence and within the text as a whole. To put it a different way, consider these paired statements:

1. Linguistics is a study of the materials available to users of language—materials, in other words, available to all users by virtue of the users' ability to recognize and to duplicate sentence patterns (that is, grammar can be formulated in advance of its implementation in a given sentence of a literary work).

2. Stylistics is a study of the particular choices an author makes from the available materials, choices that are largely culture-oriented and situation-bound.

The emphasis on choices is clear when Roger Fowler says, for example, "We need to make a fundamental division between the . . . linguistic materials available (grammatical facts) and the use made of them (stylistic facts)" (182). Similarly, Fowler stresses what he calls "performance," calling for a "sufficiently rich theory of linguistic performance" (187). In such an approach, stylistics concerns the full text rather than the sentence. And in that concern for the full text, some would argue that stylistics can be evaluative and judgmental of a given work, not just of language as language (e.g., Greenfield). Finally, we take note that the interest in stylistics gave rise to the founding of a journal, called *Style*, in 1967. Its expressed aim was the publication of "meritorious analyses of style, particularly those which deal with literature in the English language and which provide systematic methods of description and evaluation of style."

Quick Reference

A. Rhetoric

Bialostosky, Don H. "Dialogics as an Art of Discourse in Literary Criticism." *PMLA* 101 (Oct. 1986): 788–97.

Booth, Wayne. *The Rhetoric of Fiction*. Chicago: University of Chicago Press, 1961.

Corbett, Edward P. J. *Classical Rhetoric for the Modern Student*. 3rd edition. New York: Oxford University Press, 1990.

———. Introduction to *Rhetorical Analyses of Literary Works*. New York: Oxford University Press, 1969.

Corder, Jim. "Studying Rhetoric and Literature." In *Teaching Composition: 12 Bibliographical Essays*. Ed. Gary Tate. Fort Worth: Texas Christian University Press, 1987.

Gerber, John C. "Literature—Our Untamable Discipline." *College English* 28 (Feb. 1967): 351–58.

Halloran, S. M. "On the End of Rhetoric, Classical and Modern." *College English* 36 (Feb. 1975): 621–31.

Hirsch, E. D., Jr. "'Intrinsic' Criticism." *College English* 36 (Dec. 1974): 446–57.

Lanham, Richard A. *A Handlist of Rhetorical Terms: A Guide for Students of English Literature*. Berkeley: University of California Press, 1968.

Mailloux, Steven. "Rhetorical Hermeneutics." *Critical Inquiry* 11 (June 1985): 620–42.

Ong, Walter J., S. J. "The Writer's Audience is Always a Fiction." *PMLA* 90 (1975): 9–21.

Squires, Michael. "Teaching a Story Rhetorically: An Approach to a Short Story by D. H. Lawrence." *College Composition and Communication* 24 (May 1973): 150–56.

Watt, Ian. "The First Paragraph of *The Ambassadors*: An Explication." *Essays in Criticism* 10 (July 1960): 250–74. Reprint, in *Rhetorical Analyses of Literary Works*, ed. Edward P. J. Corbett. New York: Oxford University Press, 1969.

B. Linguistics

Blake, N. F. *Shakespeare's Language*. New York: St. Martin's Press, 1983.

Burkett, Eva. *American English Dialects in Literature*. Metuchen, N.J., London: Scarecrow, 1978.

Chatman, Seymour, and Samuel R. Levin, eds. *Essays on the Language of Literature*. Boston: Houghton Mifflin, 1967.

Esau, Helmut. "Faulkner, Literary Criticism, and Linguistics." *Language and Literature* (1982): 7–62.

Fishkin, Shelley. *Was Huck Black?* New York: Oxford University Press, 1993.

Greenfield, Stanley B. "Grammar and Meaning in Poetry." *PMLA* 82 (Oct. 1967): 377–87.

Lester, Mark. "The Relation of Linguistics to Literature." *College English* 30 (Feb. 1969): 366–75.

Milroy, James. *The Language of Gerard Manley Hopkins.* London: Deutsch, 1977.

Mohr, Eugene V. "Linguistics and the Literature Major." *CEA Forum* 3 (Apr. 1973): 4–6.

Ong, Walter J., S. J. *Orality and Literacy: The Technologizing of the Word.* London: Methuen, 1982.

Perry, Linda, Lynn Turner, and Helen Stenk, eds. *Constructing and Reconstructing Gender.* New York: SUNY Press, 1992.

Schleifer, Neil. "Melville as Lexicographer: Linguistics and Symbolism in *Moby-Dick.*" *Melville Society Extracts* 98 (1994): 1–6.

Schwartz, Elias. "Notes on Linguistics and Literature." *College English* 32 (Nov. 1970): 184–90.

Spitzer, Leo. *Linguistics and Literary History: Essays in Stylistics.* Princeton, NJ: Princeton University Press, 1948. Reprint, New York: Russell Sage Foundation, 1962.

Strauch, Eduard Hugo. *How Nature Taught Man to Know, Imagine, and Reason: How Language and Literature Recreate Nature's Lessons.* New York: Peter Lang, 1995.

Tannen, Deborah, ed. *Gender and Conversational Interaction.* New York: Oxford University Press, 1993.

Traugott, Elizabeth Closs, and Mary Louise Pratt. *Linguistics for Students of Literature.* San Diego: Harcourt Brace Jovanovich, 1980.

Whitehall, Harold. "English Verse and What it Sounds Like: From Linguistics to Criticism." *Kenyon Review* 18 (summer 1956): 411–21.

C. Stylistics

Chatman, Seymour, ed. *Literary Style: A Symposium.* New York: Oxford University Press, 1971.

Fowler, Roger. "The Structure of Criticism and the Languages of Poetry: An Approach through Language." In *Contemporary Criticism.*

Ed. Malcolm Bradbury and David Palmer. Stratford-Upon-Avon Studies 12. London: Edward Arnold, 1970.

Greenfield, Stanley. "Grammar and Meaning in Poetry." *PMLA* 82 (Oct. 1967): 377–87.

Lodge, David. *Language of Fiction.* New York: Columbia University Press, 1966.

Sebeok, Thomas A., ed. *Style in Language.* Cambridge, MA: Massachusetts Institute of Technology Press, 1960.

Steinberg, Erwin R. "Stylistics as a Humanistic Discipline." *Style* 10 (1976): 67–78.

▪ VI. THE MARXIST APPROACH

If we approach a work of literature from a sociological point of view, and even more from an economic point of view, we could well be practicing a form of historical criticism. As we saw in chapter 2, a historical view necessarily opens the possibility of seeing a work in its social and economic contexts, not just in the broad sweep of governments and wars, migrations across Europe, or the fall of Rome. We might deal with the plight of the poor in a Dickens novel, even a relatively optimistic work such as *A Christmas Carol.* Of course it is even more obvious that the deeper principles of social and economic conditions are often at the heart of cultural studies, not just those aspects that are simply the results of a given setting. It was appropriate, therefore, that some mention be made in chapter 7 of those conditions, such as the "production" and marketing of a "product"—namely, a book.

In this section we want to provide a more specific approach to economic aspects, an approach generally regarded as "Marxist." Marxist approaches to literature provide a particularly apt opportunity to note that some emphases in literary criticism ebb and flow, or evolve, with the times. We could, for example, trace some of the roots of Marxist criticism to nineteenth-century experiments in communal living. Later, the publication of the famous work of Karl Marx laid the groundwork for literary critics to look at literature from that perspective. Various authors and critics throughout the twentieth century showed interest in class conflict, the problems of the poor, and the effects of a capitalist system. But the pendulum of interest kept swinging, and what might have been popular during the Spanish Civil War was obviously less popular during the Cold War that followed World War II. Later still, after the breakup of the Soviet empire, additional views have been advanced.

But theoretical developments can come and go without necessarily being tied to specific governmental or military developments. Here we will call attention to critical developments that can stand separate from what was once seen as the alleged threat of Communist aggression.

We can find, for example, Fredric Jameson admitting that the Marxist critics of the 1930s had been "relegated to the status of an intellectual and historical curiosity"; but then Jameson stresses that "In recent years . . . a different kind of Marxist criticism has begun to make its presence felt upon the English-language horizon. This is what may be called—as opposed to the Soviet tradition—a relatively Hegelian kind of Marxism . . ." (*Marxism and Form* ix). From another perspective, this renewed interest in Marxist criticism is the result of the opinion of many that the formalistic approach, especially as practiced by the New Critics, has been inadequate. The formalistic approach, Marxists say, is elitist and deals too restrictively with the made object, with the art work's internal or aesthetic form, and not enough with the social milieu in which it was produced or the social circumstances to which it ought to speak. Consequently, among the schools of criticism that have found formalistic criticism inadequate, none have been more direct than the new Marxist criticism, challenging the formalists, in the words of Richard Wasson, "to explain how their own methodologies can come to grips with class, race, sex, with oppressions and liberation" (171).

A preeminent figure in new Marxist criticism, commanding respect regardless of one's political or philosophical leanings, is the Hungarian György Lukács (1885–1971), whose scholarly publications spanned half a century. His criticism ranges wide, and he has praise for figures as diverse as Sir Walter Scott and Alexander Solzhenitsyn. His name is associated with one particular direction of Marxist criticism: the reflection theory. Lukács and his followers stressed literature's reflection, conscious or unconscious, of the social reality surrounding it—not just a reflection of a flood of realistic detail but a reflection of the essence of a society. Detriments to social wholeness reveal themselves in the literary work as aspects of capitalism. While it is true that every work reflects to some degree the age of its composition and thus the conditions of society, the contention of the Marxist would be that fiction formed without benefit of Marxist principles can never fully show true social wholeness or meaningfulness. The Marxist critic deals with content, for in content is to be found literature's importance in the movement of history. George Levine, for example, expressed concern about the breach between the practice of criticism and any concern for society: he hoped for a "step toward healing the terrible breach between the study of literature and the life that surrounds that study" (435).

The Marxist critic wishes to go beyond mere concern with literature's inevitable disclosure of tensions and contradictions within a society. He or she may espouse the production theory of Louis Althusser. According to this theory, through the ideology that capitalism has generated—the structures of thought, feelings, and behavior that maintain its control over society—capitalism exacts of its artists undeviating reproduction of that ideology. Thus we get fictions that gloss over the contradictions in order to justify capitalism. A writer fully committed to Marxism would feel compelled to transform the modes of production so that his or her work would show the transformation of social relationships. The ideal Marxist work would present not just a powerful story but a workable solution to socioeconomic ills. Steinbeck's *Grapes of Wrath* might have the first part; the second remains to be found.

Quick Reference

Baxandall, Lee, and Stefan Morawski, eds. *Marx and Engels on Literature and Art*. Saint Louis, MO: Telos Press, 1973.

———. *Marxism and Aesthetics—An Annotated Bibliography*. New York: Humanities Press International, 1968.

Bennett, Tony. *Formalism and Marxism*. London: Metheun, 1979.

Caudwell, Christopher. *Further Studies in a Dying Culture*. London: Monthly Review, 1971.

———. *Illusion and Reality*. New York: Russell, 1955.

————. *Illusion and Reality: A Study of the Sources of Poetry*. New York: International Publishers, 1963.

————. *Romance and Realism: A Study in English Bourgeois Literature*. Ed. Samuel Hynes. Princeton, NJ: Princeton University Press, 1970.

————. *Studies in a Dying Culture*. New York: Dodd, 1938.

Demetz, Peter. *Marx, Engels and the Poets: Origins of Marxist Literary Criticism*. Chicago: University of Chicago Press, 1967.

Dowling, William. *Jameson, Althusser, Marx: An Introduction to the Political Unconscious*. Ithaca, NY: Cornell University Press, 1984.

Eagleton, Terry. *Criticism and Ideology: A Study in Marxist Literary Theory*. London: New Left, 1976.

————. *Marxism and Literary Criticism*. Berkeley: University of California Press, 1976.

Foley, Barbara. *Telling the Truth: The Theory and Practice of Documentary Fiction*. Ithaca, NY: Cornell University Press, 1986.

Frow, John. *Marxism and Literary History*. Cambridge, MA: Harvard University Press, 1986.

Hawley, Andrew. "Art for Man's Sake: Christopher Caudwell as Communist Aesthetician." *College English* 30 (Oct. 1968): 1–9.

Hicks, Granville. *Figures of Transition*. New York: Macmillan, 1939.

————. *The Great Tradition*. New York: Macmillan, 1933. Reprint, New York: Quadrangle Books, 1969.

Hyman, Stanley Edgar. *The Armed Vision*. Rev. ed. New York: Random House (Vintage), 1955.

Jameson, Fredric. *Marxism and Form: Twentieth-Century Dialectical Theories of Literature*. Princeton, NJ: Princeton University Press, 1971.

————. *The Political Unconscious: Studies in the Ideology of Form*. Ithaca, NY: Cornell University Press, 1979.

————. *The Prison-House of Language: A Critical Account of Structuralism and Russian Formalism*. Princeton, NJ: Princeton University Press, 1972.

Kennedy, James G. "The Content and Form of *Native Son*." *College English* 34 (Nov. 1972): 269–83.

Lentricchia, Frank. *Criticism and Social Change*. Chicago: University of Chicago Press, 1983.

Levine, George. "Politics and the Form of Disenchantment." *College English* 36 (Dec. 1974): 422–35.

Lukács, György. *The Historical Novel*. London: Merlin, 1962. Reprint, Boston: Beacon Press, 1962.

———. *The Meaning of Contemporary Realism*. London: Merlin, 1963. Paperback edition, *Realism in Our Time: Literature and the Class Struggle*. New York: Harper, 1964.

———. *Solzhenitsyn*. Cambridge, MA: Massachusetts Institute of Technology Press, 1971.

———. *Studies in European Realism*. New York: Grosset (Universal), 1971.

———. *The Theory of the Novel*. 1920. Reprint, Cambridge, MA: Massachusetts Institute of Technology Press, 1971.

Marcuse, Herbert. *The Aesthetic Dimension: Toward a Critique of Marxist Aesthetics*. Boston: Beacon Press, 1978.

Orwell, George. *Critical Essays*. London: Secker, 1946.

Raina, M. L. "Marxism and Literature—A Select Bibliography." *College English* 34 (Nov. 1972): 308–14.

Shor, Ira. "Questions Marxists Ask about Literature." *College English* 34 (Nov. 1972): 178–79.

Trilling, Lionel. *The Liberal Imagination: Essays on Literature and Psychology*. 1950. Reprint, Garden City, NY: Doubleday (Anchor), 1957.

Wasson, Richard. "New Marxist Criticism: Introduction." *College English* 34 (Nov. 1972): 169–72.

Williams, Raymond. *The Country and the City*. New York: Oxford University Press, 1973.

———. *Culture and Society, 1780–1950*. London: Chatto, 1958.

———. *Marxism and Literature*. New York: Oxford University Press, 1977.

Wilson, Edmund. *Axel's Castle*. 1931. Reprint, New York: Scribner's, 1961.

———. *The Triple Thinkers*. New York: Harcourt, 1948.

▪ VII. STRUCTURALISM AND POSTSTRUCTURALISM, INCLUDING DECONSTRUCTION

A. Structuralism: Context and Definition

Structuralism has been applied to linguistics, psychology, sociology, anthropology, folklore, mythology, and Biblical studies—in fact, to all social and cultural phenomena. Its attractions are considerable: structuralism is, at least seemingly, scientific and objective. It identifies *structures*, systems of relationships, which endow signs (e.g., words) or items (e.g., clothes, cars, table manners, rituals) with identities and meanings, and shows us *the ways in which we think*.

But, we note at the outset that the extent to which structuralism and its derivatives can function as an approach to interpreting a literary work is limited. It has even been said that poststructuralism cannot be applied to literary texts (Tompkins 746).

Structuralism claims intellectual linkage to the prestigious line of French rationalists stretching from Voltaire to Jean-Paul Sartre. Its representatives in Britain and the United States tend to retain French terminology and, as some say, to sound French. Structuralists emphasize that description of any phenomenon or artifact without placement in the broader systems which generate it is misleading if not impossible. Accordingly, they have developed analytical, systematic approaches to literary texts that avoid traditional categories like plot, character, setting, theme, tone, and the like. Even more significantly, however, structuralists tend to deny the text any inherent privilege, meaning, or authority; to them the text is only a system that poses the question of *how* such a construct of language can contain meaning for us.

Such a view denies any claim of privilege for any author, any school, any period, and any "correct" explication. The structuralists have encouraged us to reread, rethink, and restudy all literary works and to equate them with all other cultural and social phenomena—for example, language, landscaping, architecture, kinship, marriage customs, fashion, menus, furniture, and politics.

B. The Linguistic Model

Structuralism emerged from the structural linguistics developed by Ferdinand de Saussure, mainly in his lectures at the University of Geneva between 1906 and 1911. Not available in English until 1959, Saussure's *Course in General Linguistics* in French (1916) attracted thinkers far beyond Switzerland, linguistics, and universities: it became the model for Russian formalism, semiology or semiotics, French structuralism, and deconstruction, each of which we will treat briefly below. Saussure's model is acceptable as an analogy for the study of many systems other than language.

Saussure's theory of language systems distinguishes between *la langue* (language, the system possessed and used by all members of a particular language community—English, French, Urdu, etc.) and *la parole* (word; by extension, speech-event or any specific application of *la langue* in speech or writing). The *parole* is impossible without the support—the structural validity, generation, meaning—conferred upon it by the *langue*, the source of grammar, phonetics, morphology, syntax, and semantics. As Saussure explained, *paroles* appear as phonetic and semantic signs (*phonemes* and *semes*). A linguistic sign joins a *signifier* (a conventional sound construction) to a *signification* (semantic value, meaning). Such a sign does not join a thing and its name, but an allowable concept to a "sound image" (Pettit 6). The sign thus has meaning *only within its system*—a *langue* or some other context. An item is meaningful only within its originating system. Further, Saussure stressed the importance of considering each item in relationship to all other items within the system.

The approach to analyzing sentences is *syntagmatic*—word by word in the horizontal sequence of the parts or *syntagms* of the sentence. Saussure's "structural" linguistics furnishes a functional explanation of language according to its structural hierarchy—that is, structures within structures. He suggested that his system for studying language had profound implications for other disciplines. In the study of a literary work, Saussure's syntagmatic approach explains our usual, instinctive approach: we read the poem from its start to its finish, we see the narrative work in terms of the sequence of events or the scenes of the play, we inventory the details from the first to the last, from their start to their finish. This approach emphasizes the *surface structures* of the work, as it does for the sentence in Saussure's scheme, as opposed to the *deep structures*, those not on the surface—the understood but unexpressed signs. Saussurean linguistics applies, moreover, to *synchronic* features (i.e., language as it exists at a particular time) rather than to *dia-*

chronic features (details of language considered in their historical process of development).

C. Russian Formalism: Extending Saussure

A group of scholars in Moscow during World War I perceived the dynamic possibilities of using Saussure's work as a model for their investigations of phenomena other than language. Vladimir Propp studied Russian folktales as structural units that together contained a limited number of types of characters (*actants*) and actions (Propp called the latter "functions"). The functions recur and thus constitute in their unity the grammar or rules for such tales. To recall the Saussurean model, we can say that the entire group of functions is the *langue*; the individual tale is a *parole*. A number of these characters and functions were introduced in our chapter on mythological approaches; for example, Propp's theory identifies hero, rival or opponent, villain, helper, king, princess, and so on, and such actions as the arrival and the departure of the hero, the unmasking of the villain, sets of adventures, and the return and reward of the hero. The possibilities for applications of such a scheme to literary works are apparent.

Victor Shklovsky pointed out literature's constant tendency toward *estrangement* and *defamiliarization*, away from habitual responses to ordinary experience and/or ordinary language. In poetry, for example, we see a particular drive toward the strange and away from the familiar in its lineation of words, its rhythmic patternings, and its choice of language. Its texture is typically packed with meanings and suggestions; it might be arcane or even ritualistic, and it calls attention to itself as different. This is true of the simplest nursery rhymes. At the opposite extreme, in English Metaphysical poetry, for example, it is the defamiliarization, the estrangement, that often takes the poems well beyond the usual and into the complex intellectual and emotional experience that we associate with those poems.

Shklovsky also emphasized that narrative has two aspects: *story*, the events or functions in normal chronological sequence, and *plot*, the artful, subversive rearrangement and thus defamiliarization of the parts of that sequence. Story is the elementary narrative that seeks relatively easy recognition, as in most nursery tales, whereas plot estranges, prolongs, or complicates perception as in, say, one of Henry James's fictions.

In general, the Russian formalists adapted Saussure's syntagmatic, linear approach—examining structures in the sequence of their appearance—but showed how to use Saussure's theory in disciplines far beyond linguistics. Propp and Shklovsky demonstrated that literature can be made the equivalent of *langue* and the individual literary work the equivalent of *parole*. Finally, we may note that the work of the Russian formalists reminds us to some extent of American New Criticism in its concern for linking form to its constituent devices or conventions.

D. Structuralism, Lévi-Strauss, and Semiotics

Structuralism attracted interest in the United States after the publication of Claude Lévi-Strauss's *Structural Anthropology* in the 1950s, even though an American edition did not appear until 1963. In contrast to Saussure and the Russian formalists, Lévi-Strauss concentrated on the *paradigmatic* approach—that is, on the *deep* or *imbedded structures* of discourse that seem to evade a conscious arrangement by the artisan but are somehow embedded vertically, latently, within texts and can be represented sometimes as abstractions or as paired opposites (*binary oppositions*). Lévi-Strauss, an anthropologist who studied myths of aboriginal peoples in central Brazil, combined psychology and sociology in cross-cultural studies and found structures comparable to those discovered by Saussure in language—that is, systems reducible to structural features. He traced structural linkages of riddles, the Oedipus myth, American Indian myths, the Grail cycle, and anything else that might be found to structure codes of kinship (including codes of chastity and incest). He believed these linkages reached out to embrace the most profound mysteries of human experience and may very well remind us of the simultaneous layers of literary and mythic images in works like Eliot's *The Waste Land*, Joyce's *Ulysses* or *Finnegans Wake*, and Conrad's *Heart of Darkness*. But Lévi-Strauss warns that literary critic-scholars ought not to attempt structural studies solely from a literary fund of knowledge, for sufficient command of multidisciplinary knowledge is necessary to construct adequate models (*Structural Anthropology* 275).

The myth studies of Lévi-Strauss suggest the kind of links we infer between, say, *Oedipus Rex* and *Hamlet* (the emphases on kingship, marriage, incest, gross sexuality; the sacrificial scapegoat; the health of the society vis-à-vis the throne; the uses of reason), or between *King Lear* and *Moby-Dick* (structures of sight, the tyranny of pride, or "reason in madness"), or between the *Divine Comedy* and *Leaves of Grass* (the poet's quest, the scope of vision, and the sequence of confrontations). Lévi-Strauss recommended the semiotic approach (semiotics being the study of *signs*) because the approach links *messages* in individual works to their respective codes, the larger system which permits individual expression—connects *parole* to *langue* (*The Raw and the Cooked* 147). Like studies by the Russian formalists, Lévi-Strauss's semiotics is important for us because it prepares for mainstream structuralism; indeed, most explanations of structuralism identify Lévi-Strauss as its major founding father.

To Lévi-Strauss, the structures of myth point to the structures of the human mind common to all people—that is, to the way all human beings think (cf. our discussion in chapter 5 on the universality of myth). Myth thus becomes a language—a universal narrative mode that transcends cultural or temporal barriers and speaks to all people, in the process tapping deep reservoirs of feeling and experience. To Lévi-Strauss, even though we have no knowledge of any entire mythology, such myths as we do uncover reveal the existence within any culture of a system of abstractions by which that culture structures its life. In his study of the Oedipus myth, Lévi-Strauss found a set of *mythemes*—units of myth analogous to linguistic terms like morphemes or phonemes, and like those linguistic counterparts based in *binary oppositions*. The structural patterns of these *mythemes* invest the myth with meaning. For example, Oedipus kills his father (a sign of the undervaluation of kinship) and marries his mother, Jocasta (an overvaluation of kinship). In either case, Oedipus has choices: what he does and what he does not do are significant binary oppositions within the myth. Although Lévi-Strauss was not interested in the *literariness* of myths, some of his contemporaries saw in his work promising implications for purely literary studies, particularly studies of narrative.

E. French Structuralism: Codes and Decoding

As a response to Lévi-Strauss, the "school of Paris," as it is often called, produced a French new criticism in the 1950s and 1960s. It included the work of Roland Barthes, Jacques Derrida, Michel Foucault, and Tzvetan Todorov. Mainly these writers have been interested in relatively sophisticated narrative—the fiction of Bernanos, Proust, Balzac—and in some popular modes like mystery novels and humor, rather than in folk or naive art. Yet they too accept the Saussurean linguistic model and thus an essentially syntagmatic (horizontal) approach to texts. They have viewed narrative as a kind of analogy to the sentence: the text, like the sentence, expresses the writer's mind and is a whole composed of distinguishable parts. Instead of the Russian formalists' distinction between story and plot, the French structuralists use the term *histoire* (essentially the sequence of events from the beginning to the end) and *discours* (discourse; the narrative rearranged and reconstructed for its own purposes and aesthetic effects, as in the artful, intricate rearrangements of time and events in Faulkner's "Rose for Emily," which conceals or withholds an essential fact until the very last sentence in the work). Discursive manipulation of the raw data is another instance of the defamiliarization we associate with and expect in literary art; other kinds of estrangement are flashbacks, unequal treatment of time, alternation of dramatic and expository passages, shifts of viewpoint or speaker, or even the absence of viewpoint (as in the French *nouveau roman* of Alain Robbe-Grillet and others; see Culler, *Structuralist Poetics* 190–92).

In such an approach, the text is a *message* which can be understood only by references to the *code* (the internalized formal structure consisting of certain semantic possibilities, which explain and validate the content of a message). The reader gets the message (*parole*) only by knowing the code (*langue*) that lies behind it. Structuralist reading is essentially the quest for the code.

Todorov has assured us that structuralism cannot interpret any literary work: it can only show us how to identify a work's characteristic features and perhaps how to perceive their likenesses to or differences from structures in other works. Barthes, usually considered the preeminent structuralist (and later, a major French deconstructionist), and Todorov declared their indifference to authors, who after all cannot claim—they said—any originality, since authorship is merely the rearrangement of structures already present in the code. Any literary criticism inevitably will be totally subjective; even if a critic claims to be a Freudian or a Marxist, the artifact is irreducible to any such semiological, psychological, or political systems.

On the other hand, it is, or should be, according to Jonathan Culler, the object of a structuralist poetics "to specify the codes and conventions [i.e., the codes of art] which make . . . meanings possible" (Foreword to *The Poetics of Prose* 8). We can learn those codes and conventions, of course, only by experience. The author *encodes* a work; the reader must try to *decode* it. For example, Todorov points out, Henry James's fictions typically encode an essential secret in the narrative machinery, so subtly that it can entrap the unwary or inexperienced reader. Examples of encoded mysteries, riddles, or ambiguities could be multiplied from many works (e.g., *Hamlet*) and authors (e.g., Hawthorne).

In his often-cited analysis of a story by Balzac, Barthes classifies five literary codes in fiction:

1. The code of actions (proairetic codes) asks the reader to find meaning in the sequence of events.
2. The code of puzzles (hermeneutic code) raises the questions to be answered.
3. The cultural code refers to all the systems of "knowledge and values invoked by a text."
4. The connotative code expresses themes developed around the characters.
5. The symbolic code refers to the theme as we have generally considered it, that is, the meaning of the work.

(See Scholes 153–55 for a fuller explanation of the scheme that Barthes provided in *S/Z*.) The reader of a work need not use all codes at once, and in practice may blend codes. The awareness of the tendency of the codes to coalesce, and appear and disappear, may remind us of formalism's concentration on the theory of organic form.

In *S/Z*, Barthes also defined one other term, the *lexie*, which is the basic unit of a narrative text—"the minimal unit of reading, a stretch of text which is isolated as having a specific effect or function different from that of the neighboring stretches of text" (in Culler, *Structuralist Poetics* 202). In size the *lexie* can be anything from a single word to a nexus of several sentences which will fit into and support one of the five narrative codes.

F. British and American Interpreters

Jonathan Culler is usually credited with the greatest success in mediating European structuralism to students of critical theory in Britain and the United States, mainly through his *Structuralist Poetics*; however, Robert Scholes's *Structuralism in Literature* may have done more to simplify and clarify the issues and the practical possibilities of structuralism for nonprofessional students of literature. Although both Culler and Scholes pass along the pervasive structuralist caveat that favors theory of literature in general over analysis of particular texts, in fact they repeatedly express regret that texts are neglected in structuralist studies. (Probably the atmosphere that favors interpretation or explication established by the New Criticism also steered British and American scholar-critics and teachers of literature toward what the New Critics called practical criticism.)

However, Culler, by specifying a structuralist poetics based on the model of Saussurean linguistic theory, invites intelligent and unprejudiced readers to contribute to the expansion of that poetics, which he defines simply as the "procedures of reading" that ought to be found in any discourse *about* literature. Literature, Culler insists, can have no existence beyond a display of literary conventions which able readers identify as the sign system that they already know and that is analogous to the way we read sentences by recognizing phonetic, semantic, and grammatical structures in them. Through experience, readers acquire degrees of literary competence (just as children gradually acquire degrees of syntactical and grammatical complexity) that permit degrees of textual penetration. Culler stresses that it is the reader's business to *find* contexts that make a text intelligible and to reduce the "strangeness" or defamiliarization achieved by the text. Learning literary conventions (the equal of Saussure's *langue*) and resisting any inclination to grant the text autonomy (to privilege the text) dispose the structuralist reader to search out and identify structures within the system of the text and, if possible, expand poetics rather than to explicate the organic form of a privileged text.

G. Poststructuralism: Deconstruction

Poststructuralism and deconstruction are virtually synonymous. Deconstruction arises out of the structuralism of Roland Barthes as a reaction against the certainties of structuralism. Like structuralism, deconstruction identifies textual features but, unlike structuralism, concentrates on the *rhetorical* rather than the *grammatical*.

Deconstruction accepts the analogy of text to syntax as presented by Ferdinand de Saussure and adapted by the structuralists. But whereas structuralism finds order and meaning in the text as in the sentence, deconstruction finds disorder and a constant tendency of the language to refute its apparent sense. Hence the name of the approach: texts are found to deconstruct themselves rather than to provide a stable identifiable meaning.

Deconstruction views texts as subversively undermining an apparent or surface meaning, and it denies any final explication or statement of meaning. It questions the presence of any objective structure or content in a text. Instead of alarm or dismay at their discoveries, the practitioners of deconstruction celebrate the text's self-destruction, that inevitable seed of its own internal contradiction, as a never-ending free play of language. Instead of discovering one ultimate meaning for the text, as formalism seems to promise, deconstruction describes the text as always in a state of change, furnishing only provisional meanings. All texts are thus open-ended constructs, and sign and signification are only arbitrary relationships. Meaning can only point to an indefinite number of other meanings.

Thus, deconstruction involves taking apart any meaning to reveal contradictory structures hidden within. Neither meaning nor the text that seeks to express it has any privilege over the other, and this extends to critical statements about the text.

The break with structuralism is profound. Structuralism

claims kinship between systems of meaning in a text and structuralist theory itself: both would reveal the way human intelligence works. When deconstruction denies connections of mind, textual meaning, and methodological approach, it represents for structuralists only nihilism and anarchy. It has appeared that way to many other critics as well.

Further, deconstruction opposes logocentrism, the notion that written language contains a self-evident meaning that points to an unchanging meaning authenticated by the whole of Western tradition. It would demythologize literature and thus remove the privilege it has enjoyed in academe. In deconstruction, knowledge is viewed as embedded in texts, not authenticated within some intellectual discipline. Since meaning in language shifts and remains indeterminate, deconstructionists argue that all forms of institutional authority shift in like manner. Since there is no possibility of absolute truth, deconstructionists seek to undermine all pretensions to authority, or power systems, in language.

The most important figure in deconstruction has been the French philosopher Jacques Derrida, whose philosophical skepticism became widely adopted when his work was translated in the early 1970s. Because of the academic location of many other deconstructionists at the time, deconstruction came to be known by some as the Yale school of criticism.

Derrida claimed that the Western tradition of thought repressed meaning by repressing the limitless vitality of language and by moving some thought to the margin. Yet while Derrida argued to subvert the dominant Western mindset, he also recognized that there is no privileged position outside the instabilities of language from which to attack. Thus, deconstruction deconstructs itself; in a self-contradictory effort, it manages to leave things the way they were, the only difference being our expanded consciousness of the inherent play of language-as-thought.

The major attacks on deconstruction have responded to its seeming lack of seriousness about reading literature, and more seriously, to its refusal to privilege such reading as an act at all. Its opponents feel that it threatens the stability of the literary academy, that it promotes philosophical and professional nihilism, that it is too dogmatic, that it is wilfully obscure and clique-ridden, and that it is mostly responsible for the heavy emphasis on theory over practical criticism in recent years. Various critiques of deconstruction have pointed out that deconstructive readings all sound oddly similar, that it does not seem to matter if the author under study is Nietzsche or Wordsworth. Furthermore, deconstructive readings always seem to start out with a set conclusion, lacking any sense of suspense about the outcome of the reading.

Despite its alleged shortcomings, the value of deconstruction may be as a corrective, as some of its cautions are absorbed into other interpretive approaches.

Quick Reference

Barthes, Roland. *S/Z*. Paris: Seuil, 1970.

Culler, Jonathan. Foreword to *The Poetics of Prose*, by Tzvetan Todorov. Trans. Richard Howard. Ithaca, NY: Cornell University Press, 1977.

———. *Structuralist Poetics: Structuralism, Linguistics, and the Study of Literature*. Ithaca, NY: Cornell University Press, 1975.

Derrida, Jacques. *Of Grammatology*. Trans. Gayatri Chakravorty Spivak. Baltimore: Johns Hopkins University Press, 1976.

———. *Speech and Phenomena: And Other Essays on Husserl's Theory of Signs*. Trans. David B. Allison. Evanston, IL: Northwestern University Press, 1973.

———. *Writing and Difference*. Trans. Alan Bass. Chicago: University of Chicago Press, 1978.

Jackson, Claire. Translator's Preface to *Structural Anthropology*, by Claude Lévi-Strauss. Vol. 1. New York: Basic Books, 1963.

Lévi-Strauss, Claude. *The Raw and the Cooked*. London: Jonathan Cape, 1970.

———. *Structural Anthropology*. Vol. 2. Trans. Monique Layton. New York: Basic Books, 1976.

de Man, Paul. *Allegories of Reading: Figural Language in Rousseau, Nietzsche, Rilke, and Proust*. New Haven, CT: Yale University Press, 1979.

Neel, Jasper. "Plot, Character, or Theme? *Lear* and the Teacher." In *Writing and Reading Differently: Deconstruction and the Teaching of Composition and Literature*. Ed. G. Douglas Atkins and

Michael L. Johnson. Lawrence, KS: University Press of Kansas, 1985.

Pettit, Philip. *The Concept of Structuralism: A Critical Analysis*. Berkeley: University of California Press, 1975.

Scholes, Robert. *Structuralism in Literature: An Introduction*. New Haven, CT: Yale University Press, 1975.

Tompkins, Jane. "A Short Course in Post-Structuralism." *College English* 50 (1988): 733–47.

▪ VIII. PHENOMENOLOGICAL CRITICISM (THE CRITICISM OF CONSCIOUSNESS)

Through much of Henry James's famous novel *The Ambassadors*, the reader shares with the central intelligence, Lambert Strether, a particular set of notions and beliefs, only to find at a later time along with Strether that a considerable reorientation and reinterpretation of apparent facts is necessary. In T. S. Eliot's *Waste Land*, we are deliberately deprived of transitions and explanations, forcing us to perceive juxtapositions, to grasp allusions and echoes, and to develop patterns of relationships. In F. Scott Fitzgerald's *Great Gatsby* the reader must see the world of Gatsby through the eyes of Nick Carraway, but must simultaneously evaluate and then accept or reject Nick's judgments about Gatsby and the people around him. In William Faulkner's *The Sound and the Fury* the reader must first experience the world as perceived by Benjy, the idiot from whose point of view is told the first of four sections of Faulkner's novel; then the reader moves through the other three sections, each with its own point of view, so that we must successively reorient our consciousness to live in the world (or worlds) created. For that matter, we might take all of Faulkner, or any other writer whose works form a totality, and live not only in an individual work but in the full consciousness of the author, what has been called the living unity of their work. The mind of the artist, a consciousness, has created an art object, or a number of them, with which the mind of the reader, a different consciousness, must interact in a dynamic process of perception, so dynamic that objects may cease to exist as objects, becoming subsumed in the subjective reality of the reader's consciousness.

In other words, when we place ourselves in the hands of an author, surrendering our time and attention to the author's creation, we begin to live within the world that the author has created. Conversely, the text, which has been waiting for us, begins to come alive, for the text can live only when read. The space and time dimensions of our everyday life and the facts of that life do not cease to exist, of course, but they are augmented by the space-time relationships and the facts of the fictive world that we now inhabit. In addition, the manner in which we now live, discover, and experience in that world is akin to the manner in which we live, learn, and experience in "real" life; a subjective consciousness is involved in that world, and seemingly objective data are important to us insofar as they merge into subjective consciousness. In the first half of the twentieth century the perceptions of the phenomena of "reality" became the concern of phenomenological philosophy and psychology. In the second half of the twentieth century the phenomena of the fictive world, the perceptions within that world, the very process of reading, and the understanding of consciousness (the author's and the critic's) became the subject matter of literary criticism as well.

The development of this approach to literature is understandable because the made object (novel, play, epic), the various occurrences and realities of the fictive world, and the reader are all coexistent phenomena. David Halliburton, using a concept credited to Hans-Georg Gadamer, has suggested that art "is not a means of securing pleasure, but a revelation of being. The work is a phenomenon through which we come to know the world" (32). As he explains:

> . . . my chief concern is with the existential situation of the work—the way it stands against the horizon of interrelated phenomena that we call life. I am not speaking of some mystic spirit or *Geist*, but of everyday things: of consciousness, identity, process, body, love, fear, struggle, the material world. Phenomenology, as a philosophical discipline, has investigated these things, and, within its powers, has described and analyzed their operations and structures. "Literary phenomenology," in its own way, must, I believe, try to do the same. (34)

The philosophical discipline alluded to by Halliburton dates especially from the works of Edmund Husserl, early in the twentieth century, and includes, at least to some extent, the work of Martin Heidegger, Jean-Paul Sartre, Maurice Merleau-Ponty, and Pierre Thévenaz. Merleau-Ponty's *Phenomenology of Perception* is frequently cited. Thévenaz is not as well known as some of these others, but a useful work by him is *What Is Phenomenology? And Other Essays*. Besides "What Is Phenomenology?" the book contains other essays by Thévenaz, bibliographies, and an introduction by the editor. Near the end of the title essay, Thévenaz repeats the question, and answers: "[Phenomenology] is above all method—a method for changing our relation to the world, for becoming more acutely aware of it. But at the same time and by that very fact, it is already a certain attitude vis-à-vis the world" (90). As a method and an attitude, the philosophical discipline known as phenomenology reaches out to touch such other concerns as psychology, psychiatry, social studies, and literary criticism. In this far-reaching effect, phenomenology compares with structuralism (see section above) as a movement that has had European roots but that is now felt in America, including American literary criticism.

One of the more influential European phenomenological critics whose works are now available in English is the Belgian Georges Poulet, whose *Proustian Space* has been translated by Elliott Coleman. The emphasis on the interrelationship of space and time in Proust (time transformed into space) is consonant with the concerns with time and space in other phenomenological critics. (Other works by Poulet that Coleman has translated are *The Metamorphoses of the Circle*, *The Interior Distance*, and *Studies in Human Time*.)

This spreading from Europe to America can be further illustrated by Wolfgang Iser's *Implied Reader: Patterns of Communication in Prose Fiction from Bunyan to Beckett*, the German edition of which was subsequently published in the United States. Iser's treatment of the novel is especially important in helping us to perceive the world within which the reader can live—for the reader is involved in the world of the novel in such manner that he or she better understands that world—"and ultimately his own world—more clearly" (xi). Iser's final essay (which had appeared earlier in *New Literary History*), "The Reading Process: A Phenomenological Approach," gives a helpful overview of the process of reading as seen phenomenologically, stressing "not only the actual text but also, and in equal measure, the actions involved in responding to that text" (274). Among other things, Iser deals with time and its importance in the reading process. For example, reading a work of fiction involves us in a process that has duration, and necessarily involves a changing self as the reader reads. Similarly, subsequent rereadings of a text create an interaction between text and reader that is necessarily different, because the reader is different, because he or she now knows what is to come, and reads in a different way from the initial reading, thus experiencing the phenomena in a different way. (See section on reader-response below.)

If something of *time* can be seen in Iser's work, Cary Nelson uses *space* as his central fact and metaphor in *The Incarnate Word: Literature as Verbal Space*. Nelson sees "literature as a unique process in which the self of the reader is transformed by an external verbal structure" (4). Individual works—or even chapters of his book—set beside one another, "are a series of alternative spaces which can be entered and energized by the imagination" (5). When we read, the "word becomes flesh," for "we evacuate a space in our bodies which we . . . encircle and fill. . . . To read is to fold the world into the body's house" (6). Nelson, unlike Iser, who concentrates on fiction, offers chapters on a range of genres—a medieval poem, Shakespeare's *The Tempest*, Milton's *Paradise Regained*, and other prose and poetry from the eighteenth, nineteenth, and twentieth centuries.

Sometimes the term *criticism of consciousness* is used to describe the kind of literary criticism represented by Poulet, Iser, and Nelson, but the term often extends beyond the study of particular works. In criticism of consciousness, some critics would pursue not only the text, but the whole range of texts of an author—his or her corpus—so that the critic's consciousness tries to identify with the author's consciousness, a "union of subject with another subject," an approach not favored by W. K. Wimsatt in his "Battering the Object: The Ontological Approach" (66).

Associated with this approach is the so-called Geneva school, which includes, for example, Georges Poulet (mentioned earlier) and, in this country, J. Hillis Miller and Geoffrey H. Hartman (see, for example, Hartman's *The Unmediated Vision*). Miller and Hartman later abandoned phenomenological criticism in favor of deconstruction, but their earlier work remains influential. Poulet has written that "When reading a literary work, there is a moment when it seems to me that the subject *present* in this work disengages itself from all that surrounds it, and stands alone"; at such a time, he senses that he has "reached the common essence present in all the works of a great master," an essence that now stands out and beyond the particular manifestations in individual worlds ("Phenomenology of Reading" 68). Two of Miller's works—*The Disappearance of God: Five Nineteenth-Century Writers* and *Poets of Reality: Six Twentieth-Century Writers*—have been cited (by Halliburton [17]) as important in preparing the way for such developments in American literary thought. The following passage from Miller will help to show how criticism of consciousness derives from, or is synonymous with, the phenomenological movement:

> Literature is a form of consciousness, and literary criticism is the analysis of this form in all its varieties. Though literature is made of words, these words embody states of mind and make them available to others. The comprehension of literature is a process of what Gabriel Marcel calls "intersubjectivity." Criticism demands above all that gift of participation, that power to put oneself within the life of another person, which Keats called negative capability. If literature is a form of consciousness the task of a critic is to identify himself with the subjectivity expressed in the words, to relive that life from the inside, and to constitute it anew in his criticism. (*The Disappearance of God* ix)

Such a view compares with what Halliburton says early in his study of Poe. Calling into question the emphasis of earlier twentieth-century criticism on seeing the literary work as a "discrete object, a kind of inert and neutral 'thing,'" in the studying of which the critic need not be concerned with the author's intentions, Halliburton points out that such a view totally disconnects the text "from the consciousness that creates it and from the consciousness that interprets it." "The phenomenologist holds a different view. Without denying that the work has, in some sense, a life of its own, the phenomenologist believes that the work cannot be cut off from the intentionality that made it or from the intentionality that experiences it after it is made" (21). In stressing intention, the phenomenologist would therefore call us back to the consciousness of the author and the critic, a call that would set him or her apart from the formalistic or New Critical approach. But the phenomenologists, like the New Critics, would emphasize the text, for "The intentionality [they seek] out is not in the author but in the text" (22). In pursuing a comprehension of the work, the phenomenologist must seek out in each work "its own way of going." The interpreter must "find this way and go along with it; experiencing the process of the work *as* a process" (36).

Quick Reference

Brodtkorb, Paul, Jr. *Ishmael's White World: A Phenomenological Reading of "Moby Dick."* New Haven, CT: Yale University Press, 1965.

Halliburton, David. *Edgar Allan Poe: A Phenomenological View.* Princeton, NJ: Princeton University Press, 1973.

Hartman, Geoffrey H. *The Unmediated Vision: An Interpretation of Wordsworth, Hopkins, and Valéry.* New Haven, CT: Yale University Press, 1954.

Iser, Wolfgang. *Implied Reader: Patterns of Communication in Prose Fiction from Bunyan to Beckett.* German ed. Munich, 1972. Baltimore: Johns Hopkins University, 1974.

———. "The Reading Process: A Phenomenological Approach." *New Literary History* 3 (1972): 279–99.

Lawall, Sarah N. *Critics of Consciousness: The Existentialist Structures of Literature.* Cambridge, MA: Harvard University Press, 1968.

Magliola, Robert. *Phenomenology and Literature: An Introduction.* West Lafayette, IN: Purdue University Press, 1977.

Miller, J. Hillis. *The Disappearance of God: Five Nineteenth-Century Writers.* Cambridge, MA: Harvard University Press, 1968.

———. *Poets of Reality: Six Twentieth-Century Writers.* Cambridge, MA: Harvard University Press, 1965.

Nelson, Cary. *The Incarnate Word: Literature as Verbal Space.* Urbana: University of Illinois Press, 1973.

Poulet, Georges. "Phenomenology of Reading." *New Literary History* 1 (1969): 53–68.

———. *Proustian Space.* Trans. Elliott Coleman. Baltimore: Johns Hopkins University Press, 1977.

Thévenaz, Pierre. *What Is Phenomenology? And Other Essays.* Ed. James M. Edie. New York: Quadrangle Books, 1962.

Vernon, John. *The Garden and the Map: Schizophrenia in Twentieth-Century Literature and Culture.* Urbana: University of Illinois Press, 1973.

Wimsatt, W. K. "Battering the Object: The Ontological Approach." In *Contemporary Criticism.* Stratford-upon-Avon Studies 12. London: Edward Arnold, 1970.

IX. DIALOGICS

Dialogics is the key term used to describe the narrative theory of Mikhail Mikhailovich Bakhtin (1895–1975) and is specifically identified with his approach to questions of language in the novel. Dialogics (cf. "dialogue," "speaking across") refers to the inherent "addressivity" of all language; that is, all language is addressed to someone, never uttered without consciousness of a relationship between the speaker and the addressee. In this humanistic emphasis, Bakhtin departed from linguistically based theories of literature and from other Russian formalists. He also felt suspicious of what was to become the psychological approach to literature, for he saw such an approach as a diminishment of the human soul and an attendant sacrifice of human freedom. It is safe to say that Bakhtin would have rejected *any* "ism" as an approach to the novel if it failed to recognize the essential indeterminacy of meaning outside the dialogic—and hence open—relationship between voices. Bakhtin would call such a closed view of meaning monological (single-voiced). For him, not only the interaction of characters but also the act of reading the novel in which they exist are living events.

The writings of Bakhtin go back to the 1920s and 1930s, but he remained largely unknown outside of the Soviet Union until translations in the 1970s brought him to world attention. His thought emphasizes language as an area of social conflict, particularly in the ways the discourse of characters in a literary work may disrupt and subvert the authority of ideology as expressed in a single voice of a narrator. He contrasts the monologic novels of writers such as Leo Tolstoy with the dialogic works of Fyodor Dostoyevsky. Instead of subordinating the voices of all characters to an overriding authorial voice, a writer such as Dostoyevsky creates a polyphonic discourse in which the author's voice is only one among many, and the characters are allowed free speech. Indeed, Bakhtin seems to believe that a writer such as Dostoyevsky actually thought in *voices* rather than in *ideas* and wrote novels that were thus primarily dialogical exchanges. What is important in them is not the presentation of facts about a character, then, but the significance of facts voiced to the hero himself and to other characters. In a sense, the hero *is* a word and not a fact in himself. Bakhtin identifies such polyphony as a special property of the novel, and he traces it back to its carnivalistic sources in classical, medieval, and Renaissance cultures (for "carnivalistic," see later discussion).

Bakhtin's constant focus is thus on the many voices in a novel, especially the way that some authors in particular, such as Dostoyevsky, allow characters' voices free play by actually placing them on the same plane as the voice of the author. In recent years, as more of his works have been translated, Bakhtin has become very important to critics of many literatures and has been found to be especially appropriate to the many-voiced, open-ended American novel.

In a sense there are multiple Bakhtins. He is read differently by Marxist critics, for example, than by more traditional humanistic critics. He himself partook of both Christianity and revolutionary Marxism. Marxist critics respond more to his notions of chronotope, or how time is encoded in fiction, and to his notion of the hidden polemic in all speech, while humanistic or moral critics address themselves more to his notion of addressivity because "addressing" someone promotes human connection and community. Since his emergence inside and outside the Soviet Union, his ideas have proved attractive to critics of all sorts of ideologies, including most recently feminist critics.

Bakhtin's definition of the modern polyphonic, dialogic novel made up of a plurality of voices that avoids reduction to a single perspective indicates a concern on his part about the dangers of knowledge, whether inside or outside a text. That is, he points toward a parallel between issues of knowledge and power among the characters and those between the author and the reader. In both cases, knowledge is best thought of as dialogic rather than monologic, as open to the other rather than closed, as *addressing* rather than *defining*. Obviously Bakhtin's theory and criticism feature a powerful moral lesson about freedom.

Another of Bakhtin's key terms is carnivalization. Out of the primordial roots of the carnival tradition in folk culture, he argues, arises the many-voiced novel of the twentieth century. Dostoyevsky, for example, writes out of a rich tradition of seriocomic, dialogic, satiric literature that may be traced through Socratic dialogue and Menippian satire, Apuleius, Boethius, medieval mystery plays, Boccaccio, Rabelais, Shakespeare, Cervantes, Voltaire, Balzac, and Hugo. In the modern world this carnivalized antitradition appears most significantly in the novel. Just as the public ritual of carnival inverts values in order to question them, so may the novel call closed meanings into question. Of particular importance is the ritual crowning and decrowning of a mock king: in such actions, often through the medium of the grotesque, the people of a community express both their sense of being victims of power and their own power to subvert institutions. (One thinks of the Ugly King, El Rey Feo, of Hispanic tradition, as well as of the King of Comus in New Orleans' Mardi Gras.) As carnival concretizes the abstract in a culture, so Bakhtin claims that the novel carnivalizes through diversities of speech and voice reflected in its structure. Like carnival's presence in the public square, the novel takes place in the public sphere of the middle class. Carnival and the novel make power relative by *addressing* it. This makes the novel unique among other genres, many of which arose in the upper classes.

As Michael Holquist points out, rather than seeing the novel as a genre alongside others, such as epic, ode, or lyric, Bakhtin sees it as a supergenre that has always been present in Western culture, always breaking traditional assumptions about form. Holquist explains that "'novel' is the name Bakhtin gives to whatever force is at work within a given literary system to reveal the limits, the artificial constraints of that system. Literary systems are comprised of canons, and 'novelization' is fundamentally anticanonical." The novel, Bakhtin argues, is "the only developing genre" (Bakhtin, *The Dialogic Imagination* 261–62, 291; Holquist, Introduction to *The Dialogic Imagination* xxxi). One can easily see the importance of such a transforming or relativizing function for Bakhtin, living as he did through the oppressions of the czars, the gloomy years of Stalin's purges, and the institution of official Soviet bureaucracy. Through carnivalization in the novel, opposites may come to know and understand one another in a way not otherwise possible. The key is the unfettered but clearly addressed human voice.

In his insistence on the novel's dynamism, Bakhtin provides an instructive perspective on its history and its future. As he observes, although the novel has existed since ancient times, its full potential was not developed until after the Renaissance. A major factor was the development of a sense of linear time, past, present, and especially future, moving away from the cyclical time of ancient epochs. Whereas the epic lives in cylical time, the novel is oriented to contemporary reality. "From the very beginning, then," says Bakhtin, "the novel was structured . . . in the zone of direct contact with inconclusive present-day reality. At its core lay personal experience and free creative imagination." In its contemporaneity, the novel is "made of different clay [from] the other already completed genres," and "with it and in it is born the future of all literature." Bakhtin adds that the novel may absorb any other genre into itself and still remain a novel and that no other genre can do so. It is "ever-questing, ever examining itself and subjecting its established forms to review" (*The Dialogic Imagination* 38–40).

Bakhtin extends his ideas to dialogicity, which moves past genre to describe language. The person is always the "*subject of an address*" because one "cannot talk about him; one can only address oneself to him." One cannot understand another person as an object of neutral analysis or "master him through a merging with him, through empathy with him." The solution, dialogue, "is not the threshold to action, it is the action itself." Indeed, "to be means to communicate dialogically. When dialogue ends, everything ends." Bakhtin's principles of dialogue of the hero are by no means limited to actual dialogue in novels; they refer to a novelist's entire undertaking. Yet in a polyphonic novel, dialogues are unusually powerful (*The Dialogic Imagination* 338–39, 342).

Bakhtin's major principles of the novel include the freedom of the hero, special placement of the idea in the polyphonic design, and the principles of linkage that shape the novel into a whole—including multiple voices, ambiguity, multiple genres, stylization, parody, the use of negatives, and the function of the double address of the word both to another word and to another speaker of words. An author may build indeterminancies into his or her polyphonic design, introduce multiple voices, render ideas intersubjective, and leave novels seemingly unfinished—all to leave characters free. And no reader may "objectify an entire event according to some ordinary monologic category." The novel does not recognize any overriding monologic point of view outside the world of its dialogue, "but on the contrary, everything in the novel is structured to make dialogic opposition interminable. Not a single element of the work is structured from the point of view of a non-participating 'third person'" (*Problems of Dostoevsky's Poetics* 17).

Bakhtin describes how the novelist may voice a moral concern through narrative technique, particularly the power of knowledge to enact a design on that which is known. To think about other people "means to *talk with them; otherwise they immediately turn to us their objectivized side:* they fall silent, close up and congeal into finished, objectivized images." For this reason, the author of the polyphonic novel does not renounce his or her own consciousness but "to an extraordinary extent broaden[s], deepen[s] and rearrange[s] this consciousness . . . in order to accommodate the consciousness of others," and he or she does not turn other consciousnesses, whether character or reader, into objects of a single vision, but instead "re-creates

them in their authentic *unfinalizability*" (*Problems of Dostoevsky's Poetics* 6–7, 59, 68). In "Author and Hero in Aesthetic
Activity," an early essay, Bakhtin asks "What would I have to
gain if another were to *fuse* with me? He would see and know
only what I already see and know, he would only repeat in
himself the inescapable closed circle of my own life; let him
rather remain outside me" (quoted in Emerson 68–80).

By allowing characters their free speech, then, authors may
thus ensure that they do not perpetrate a narrowing design by
using their knowledge of the characters, a design that would
violate them by restricting their freedom. To do this the author
must create a "design for discourse" that allows the reader to
interpret the characters' actions and words without the direct
intervention of the author. Such "dialogic opposition" means
that the greatest challenge for an author, "to create out of heterogeneous and profoundly disparate materials of varying
worth a unified and integral artistic creation," cannot be realized by using a single "philosophical design" as the basis of
artistic unity, just as musical polyphony cannot be reduced to a
single accent. Contrasting this polyphony with novels in
which the hero is the "voiceless object" of the "ideologue" author's "deduction," Bakhtin describes such intrusive narrators
as those of many nineteenth-century British novelists. In the
polyphonic novel, "there are only . . . voice-viewpoints."
Through characterization, Dostoyevsky structurally dramatizes "internal contradictions and internal stages in the development of a single person," allowing his characters "to con-
verse with their own doubles, with the devil, with their alter
egos, with caricatures of themselves." Dialogicity in characterization thus leads to particular structures. A polyphonic novel
seeks to "*juxtapose* and *counterpose* [forms] dramatically," to
"*guess at their interrelationships in the cross-section of a single moment.*" Not "evolution" but "*coexistence* and *interaction*" characterize such structures. "It cannot be otherwise," Bakhtin insists, for "only a dialogic and participatory orientation takes
another person's discourse seriously, and is capable of approaching it as both a semantic position and another point of
view." It is only through such orientation that one can come
into "intimate contact with someone else's discourse" and yet
not "fuse with it, not swallow it up, not dissolve in itself the

other's power to mean" (*Problems of Dostoevsky's Poetics* 7–8, 18–20, 28–30, 63–64, 82–85).

Quick Reference

Bakhtin, Mikhail. *The Dialogic Imagination: Four Essays by M. M. Bakhtin*. Trans. Caryl Emerson and Michael Holquist. Austin: University of Texas Press, 1981.

———. *Problems of Dostoevsky's Poetics*. Ed. and trans. Caryl Emerson. Introduction by Wayne C. Booth. Minneapolis: University of Minnesota Press, 1984.

Bauer, Dale M. *Feminist Dialogics: A Theory of Failed Community*. Albany: State University of New York Press, 1988.

Clark, Katerina, and Michael Holquist. *Mikhail Bakhtin*. Cambridge, MA: Harvard University Press, 1985.

Emerson, Caryl. "The Tolstoy Connection." *PMLA* 100 (1985): 68–80.

Holquist, Michael. Introduction to *The Dialogic Imagination: Four Essays by M. M. Bakhtin*. Trans. Caryl Emerson and Michael Holquist. Austin: University of Texas Press, 1981.

———. *Dialogism: Bakhtin and His World*. New York: Routledge, 1990.

Morson, Gary Saul. "The Heresiarch of *Meta*." *PTL: A Journal for Descriptive Poetics and Theory of Literature* 3 (1978): 407–27.

———, ed. "Forum on Mikhail Bakhtin." *Critical Inquiry* 10 (Dec. 1983): 225–320.

———, ed. *Literature and History: Theoretical Problems and Russian Case Studies*. Stanford, CA: Stanford University Press, 1986.

Morson, Gary Saul, and Caryl Emerson, eds. *Rethinking Bakhtin: Extensions and Challenges*. Evanston, IL: Northwestern University Press, 1987.

Reesman, Jeanne Campbell. *American Designs: The Late Novels of James and Faulkner*. Philadelphia: University of Pennsylvania Press, 1991.

Reising, Russell J. *The Unusable Past*. New York: Methuen, 1986.

▪ X. READER-RESPONSE CRITICISM

Reader-response theory arose in large measure as a reaction against the New Criticism, or formalistic approach, which dominated literary criticism for roughly a half-century and which is treated in detail in chapter 3 of this book. At the risk of oversimplifying and thereby misrepresenting, we may say that formalism regards a piece of literature as an art object with an existence of its own, independent of or not necessarily related to its author, its readers, the historical time it depicts, or the historical period in which it was written. Formalism, then, focuses on the text, finding all meaning and value in it and regarding everything else as extraneous, including readers, whom formalistic critics regard as downright dangerous as sources of interpretation. To rely on readers as a source of meaning—precisely what reader-response criticism does—is to fall victim to subjectivism, relativism, and other types of critical madness.

Reader-response critics take a radically different approach. They feel that readers have been ignored in discussions of the reading process, when they should have been the central concern. The argument goes something like this: a text does not even exist, in a sense, until it is read by some reader. Indeed, the reader has a part in creating or actually does create the text. It is somewhat like the old question posed in philosophy classes: if a tree falls in the forest and no one hears it, does it make a sound? Reader-response critics are saying that in effect, if a text does not have a reader, it does not exist—or at least, it has no meaning. It is readers, with whatever experience they bring to the text, who give it its meaning. Whatever meaning it may have inheres in the reader, and thus it is the reader who should say what a text means.

We should, perhaps, point out here that reader-response theory is by no means a monolithic critical position. Those who give an important place to *readers* and their *responses* in interpreting a work come from a number of different critical camps, not excluding formalism, which is the target of the heaviest reader-response attacks. Reader-response critics see formalistic critics as narrow, dogmatic, elitist, and certainly wrong-headed in essentially refusing readers even a place in the reading-interpretive process. Conversely, reader-response critics see themselves, as Jane Tompkins has put it, "willing to share their critical authority with less tutored readers and at the same time to go into partnership with psychologists, linguists, philosophers, and other students of mental functioning" (223).

Although reader-response ideas were present in critical

writing as long ago as the 1920s, most notably in that of I. A. Richards, and in the 1930s in D. W. Harding's and Louise Rosenblatt's work, it was not until the mid-twentieth-century that they began to gain currency. Walker Gibson, writing in *College English* in February 1950, talked about "mock readers," who enact roles which actual readers feel compelled to play because the author clearly expects them to by the way the text is presented (265–69). By the 1960s and continuing into the present as a more or less concerted movement, reader-response criticism had gained enough advocates to mount a frontal assault on the bastions of formalism.

Because the ideas underlying reader-response criticism are complex, and because their proponents frequently present them in technical language, it will be well to enumerate the forms that have received most attention and to attempt as clear a definition of them as possible.

Let us review once again the basic premises of reader-oriented theory, realizing that individual reader-response theorists will differ on a given point but that the following tenets reflect the main perspectives in the position as a whole. First, in literary interpretation, the text is not the most important component; the reader is. In fact, there is no text unless there is a reader. And the reader is the only one who can say what the text is; in a sense, the reader creates the text as much as the author does. This being the case, to arrive at meaning, critics should reject the autonomy of the text and concentrate on the reader and the reading process, the interaction that takes place between the reader and the text.

This premise perplexes people trained in the traditional methods of literary analysis. It declares that reading-response theory is subjective and relative, whereas earlier theories sought for as much objectivity as possible in a field of study that has a high degree of subjectivity by definition. Paradoxically, the ultimate source of this subjectivity is modern science itself, which has become increasingly skeptical that any objective knowledge is possible. Einstein's theory of relativity stands as the best known expression of that doubt. Also, the philosopher Thomas S. Kuhn's demonstration (in *The Structure of Scientific Revolutions*) that scientific fact is dependent on the observer's frame of reference reinforces the claims of subjectivity.

Another special feature of reader-response theory is that it is based on rhetoric, the art of persuasion, which has a long tradition in literature dating back to the Greeks, who originally employed it in oratory. Rhetoric now refers to the myriad devices or strategies used to get the reader to respond to the literary work in certain ways. Thus, by establishing the reader firmly in the literary equation, the ancients may be said to be precursors of modern reader-response theory. Admittedly, however, when Aristotle, Longinus, Horace, Cicero, and Quintilian applied rhetorical principles in judging a work, they concentrated on the presence of the formal elements within the work rather than on the effect they would produce on the reader.

In view, then, of the emphasis on the audience in reader-response criticism, its relationship to rhetoric is quite obvious. Wayne Booth in his *Rhetoric of Fiction* was among the earliest of modern critics to restore readers to consideration in the interpretive act. The New Criticism, which strongly influenced the study of literature, and still does, had actually proscribed readers, maintaining that it was a critical fallacy, the affective fallacy, to mention any effects that a piece of literature might have on them. And while Booth did not go as far as some critics in assigning readers the major role in interpretation, he certainly did give them prominence and called rhetoric "the author's means of controlling his reader" (Preface to *Rhetoric of Fiction*). For example, in a close reading of Jane Austen's *Emma*, Booth demonstrates the rhetorical strategies that Austen uses to ensure the reader's seeing things through the heroine's eyes.

In 1925 I. A. Richards, usually associated with the New Critics, published *Principles of Literary Criticism*, in which he constructed an affective system of interpretation, that is, one based on emotional responses. Unlike the New Critics who were to follow in the next two decades, Richards conceded that the scientific conception of truth is the correct one and that poetry provides only pseudo-statements. These pseudo-statements, however, are crucial to the psychic health of humans because they have now replaced religion as fulfilling our desire—"appetency" is Richards's term—for truth, that is, for some vision of the world that will satisfy our deepest needs. Matthew Arnold had in the nineteenth century predicted that literature would fulfill this function. Richards tested his theory by asking Cambridge students to write their responses to and assessments of a number of short unidentified poems of varying quality. He then analyzed and classified the responses and published them along with his own interpretations in *Practical Criticism*. Richards's methodology is decidedly reader-response, but the use he made of his data is new critical. He arranged the responses he had received into categories according to the degrees in which they differed from the "right" or "more adequate" interpretation, which he demonstrated by referring to "the poem itself."

Louise Rosenblatt, Walker Gibson, and Gerald Prince are critics who, like Richards, affirm the importance of the reader but are not willing to relegate the text to a secondary role. Rosenblatt feels that irrelevant responses finally have to be excluded in favor of relevant ones and that a text can exist independently of readers. However, she advances a transactional theory: a poem comes into being only when it receives a proper ("aesthetic") reading, that is, when readers "compenetrate" a given text (*The Reader, the Text, the Poem*). Gibson, essentially a formalist, proposes a mock reader, a role which the real reader plays because the text asks him or her to play it "for the sake of the experience." Gibson posits a dialogue between a speaker (the author?) and the mock reader. The critic, overhearing this dialogue, paraphrases it, thereby revealing the author's strategies for getting readers to accept or reject whatever the author wishes them to. Gibson by no means abandons the text, but he injects the reader further into the interpretive operation as a way of gaining fresh critical insights. Using a different terminology, Prince adopts a perspective similar to Gibson's. Wondering why critics have paid such close attention to narrators (omniscient, first person, unreliable, etc.) and have virtually ignored readers, Prince too posits a reader, whom he calls the narratee, one of a number of hypothetical readers to whom the story is directed. These readers, actually produced by the narrative, include the real reader, with book in hand; the virtual reader, for whom the author thinks he is writing; and the ideal reader of perfect understanding and sympathy; yet none of these is necessarily the narratee. Prince demonstrates the strategies by which the narrative creates the readers (7–25).

The critics mentioned so far—except Prince—are the advance guard of the reader-response movement. While continuing to insist on the importance of the text in the interpretive act, they equally insist that the reader be taken into account; not to do so will, they maintain, either impoverish the interpretation or render it defective. As the advance guard, they have cleared the way for those who have become the principal theorists of reader-response criticism. Though there will be disagreement on who belongs in this latter group, most scholars would recognize Wolfgang Iser, Hans Robert Jauss, Norman Holland, and Stanley Fish as having major significance in the movement.

Wolfgang Iser is a German critic who applies the philosophy of phenomenology to the interpretation of literature. Phenomenology stresses the perceiver's (in this case, the reader's) role in any perception (in this case, reading experience) and asserts the difficulty, if not the impossibility, of separating anything known from the mind that knows it. According to Iser, the critic should not explain the text *as an object* but *its effect on the reader*. Iser's espousal of this position, however, has not taken him away from the text as a central part of interpretation. He also has posited an implied reader, one with "roots firmly planted in the structure of the text" (34). Still, his phenomenological beliefs keep him from the formalist notion that there is one essential meaning of a text that all interpretations must try to agree on. Readers' experiences will govern the effects the text produces on them. Moreover, Iser says, a text does not tell readers everything; there are "gaps" or "blanks," which he refers to as the indeterminacy of the text. Readers must fill these in and thereby assemble the meaning(s), thus becoming coauthors in a sense. Such meanings may go far beyond the single "best" meaning of the formalist because they are the products of such varied reader backgrounds. To be sure, Iser's implied readers are fairly sophisticated: they bring to the contemplation of the text a conversance with the conventions that enables them to decode the text. But the text can transcend any set of literary or critical conventions, and readers with widely different backgrounds may fill in those blanks and gaps with new and unconventional meanings. Iser's stance, then, is phenomenological: at the center of interpretation lies the reader's experience. Nor does this creation of text by the reader mean that the resultant text is subjective and no longer the author's. It is rather, says Iser, proof of the text's inexhaustibility.

Yet another kind of reader-oriented criticism, also rhetorically grounded, is reception theory, which documents reader responses to authors and/or their works in any given period. Such criticism depends heavily on reviews in newspapers, magazines, and journals and on personal letters for evidence of public reception. There are varieties of reception theory, one of the most important recent types promulgated by Hans Robert Jauss, another German scholar, in his *Toward an Aesthetic of Reception*. Jauss seeks to bring about a compromise between that interpretation which ignores history and that which ignores the text in favor of social theories. To describe the criteria he would employ, Jauss has proposed the term *horizons of expectations* of a reading public. These result from what the public already understands about a genre and its conventions. For example, Pope's poetry was judged highly by his contemporaries, who valued clarity, decorum, and wit. The next century had different horizons of expectations and thus actually called into question Pope's claim to being considered a poet at all. Similarly, Flaubert's *Madame Bovary* was not well received by its mid-nineteenth-century readers, who objected to the impersonal, clinical, naturalistic style. Their horizons of expectations had conditioned them to appreciate an impassioned, lyrical, sentimental, and florid narrative method. Delayed hostile reader response to firmly established classics surfaced in the latter half of the twentieth century. *Huckleberry Finn* became the target of harsh and misguided criticism on the grounds that it contained racial slurs in the form of epithets like "nigger" and demeaning portraits of Negroes. Schools were in some instances required to remove the book from curriculums or reading lists of approved books and in extreme cases from library shelves. In like manner, feminists have resented what they considered male-chauvinist philosophy and attitudes in Marvell's "To His Coy Mistress." The horizon of expectations of these readers incorporated hot partisanship on contemporary issues into their literary analyses of earlier works.

Horizons of expectations do not establish the final meaning

of a work. Thus, according to Jauss, we cannot say that a work is universal, that it will make the same appeal to or impact on readers of all eras. Is it possible, then, ever to reach a critical verdict about a piece of literature? Jauss thinks it is possible only to the extent that we regard our interpretations as stemming from a dialogue between past and present and thereby representing a fusion of horizons.

The importance of psychology in literary interpretation has long been recognized. Plato and Aristotle, for example, attributed strong psychological influence to literature. Plato saw this influence as essentially baneful: literature aroused people's emotions, especially those that ought to be stringently controlled. Conversely, Aristotle argued that literature exerted a good psychological influence; in particular, tragedy did, by effecting in audiences a catharsis or cleansing or purging of emotions. Spectators were thus calmed and satisfied, not excited or frenzied, after their emotional encounter.

As we noted in our earlier chapter on the psychological approach, one of the world's preeminent depth psychologists, Sigmund Freud, has had an incalculable influence on literary analysis with his theories about the unconscious and about the importance of sex in explaining much human behavior. Critics, then, have looked to Plato and Aristotle in examining the psychological relations between a literary work and its audience and to Freud in seeking to understand the unconscious psychological motivations of the characters in the literary work and of the author.

If, however, followers of Freud have been more concerned with the unconscious of literary characters and their creators, more recent psychological critics have focused on the unconscious of readers. Norman Holland, one such critic, argues that all people inherit from their mother an identity theme or fixed understanding of the kind of person they are. Whatever they read is processed to make it fit their identity theme, he asserts in "The Miller's Wife and the Professors: Questions about the Transactive Theory of Reading." In other words, readers interpret texts as expressions of their own personalities or psyches and thereby use their interpretations as a means of coping with life. Holland illustrates this thesis in an essay entitled *"Hamlet—My Greatest Creation."* This highly personal response to literature appears in another Holland article, "Recovering 'The Purloined Letter': Reading as a Personal Transaction." Here, Holland relates the story to his own attempt to hide an adolescent masturbatory experience.

Holland's theory, for all of its emphasis on readers and their psychology, does not deny or destroy the independence of the text. It exists as an object and as the expression of another mind, something different from readers themselves, something they can project onto. But David Bleich, in *Subjective Criticism*, denies that the text exists independent of readers. Bleich accepts the arguments of such contemporary philosophers of science as Thomas S. Kuhn who deny that objective facts exist. Such a position asserts that even what passes for scientific observation of something—of anything—is still merely individual and subjective perception occurring in a special context. Bleich claims that individuals everywhere classify things into three essential groups: objects, symbols, and people. Literature, a mental creation (as opposed to a concrete one), would thus be considered a symbol. A text may be an object in that it is paper (or other matter) and print, but its meaning depends on the symbolization in the minds of readers. Meaning is not found; it is developed. Better human relations will result from readers with widely differing views sharing and comparing their responses and thereby discovering more about motives and strategies for reading. The honesty and tolerance required in such operations is bound to help in self-knowledge, which, according to Bleich, is the most important goal for everyone.

The last of the theorists to be treated in this discussion is Stanley Fish, who calls his technique of interpretation affective stylistics. Like other reader-oriented critics, Fish rebels against the so-called rigidity and dogmatism of the New Critics and especially against the tenet that a poem is a single, static object, a whole that has to be understood in its entirety at once. Fish's pronouncements on reader-response theory have come in stages. In an early stage (*Surprised by Sin*), he argued that meaning in a literary work is not something to be extracted, as a dentist might pull a tooth; meaning must be negotiated by readers, a line at a time. Moreover, they will be surprised by rhetorical strategies as they proceed. Meaning is *what happens to readers during this negotiation*. A text, in Fish's view, could lead readers on, even set them up, to make certain interpretations, only to undercut them later and force readers into new and different readings. So, the focus is on the reader; the process of reading is dynamic and sequential. Fish does insist, however, on a high degree of sophistication in readers: they must be familiar with literary conventions and must be capable of changing when they perceive they have been tricked by the strategies of the text. His term for such readers is "informed."

Later, in *Is There a Text in This Class?*, Fish modified the method described above by attributing more initiative to the reader and less control by the text in the interpretive act. Fish's altered position holds that readers actually create a piece of literature as they read it. Fish concludes that every reading results in a new interpretation that comes about because of the strategies that readers use. The text as an independent director of interpretation has in effect disappeared. For Fish, interpretation is a communal affair. The readers just mentioned are informed; they possess linguistic competence; they form interpretive communities that have common assumptions; and, to repeat, they create texts when they pool their common reading techniques. These characteristics mean that such readers are employing the same or similar interpretive strategies and are thus members of the same interpretive community.

It seems reasonable to say that there may be more than one response to or interpretation of a work of literature and that this is true because responders and interpreters see things differently. It seems equally accurate to observe that to claim the meaning of literature rests exclusively with individual readers, whose opinions are equally valid, is to make literary analysis ultimately altogether relative. Somewhere within these two points of view most critics and interpreters will fall.

To summarize, two distinguishing features characterize reader-response criticism. One is the effect of the literary work on the reader, hence the moral-philosophical-psychological-rhetorical emphases in reader-response analysis. (How does the work *affect* the reader, and what strategies or devices have come into play in the production of those effects?) The second feature is the relegation of the text to secondary importance. (The reader is of primary importance.) Thus, reader-response criticism attacks the authority of the text. This is where subjectivism comes in. If a text cannot have any existence except in the mind of the reader, then the text loses its authority. There is a shift from objective to subjective perspective. Texts mean what individual readers say they mean or what interpretive communities of readers say they mean. If we have made the main reader-responses clear in principle to the readers of this book, we shall have accomplished our purpose. They may then apply them as they will. Thus, interpretation becomes the key to meaning—as it always is—but without the ultimate authority of the text or the author. The important element in reader-response criticism is the reader, and the effect (or affect) of the text on the reader.

When reader-response critics analyze the effect of the text on the reader, the analysis often resembles formalistic criticism or rhetorical criticism or psychological criticism. The major distinction is the emphasis on the reader's response in the analysis. Meaning inheres in the reader and not in the text. This is where reception theory fits in. The same text can be interpreted by different readers or communities of readers in very different ways. A text's interpretive history may vary considerably, as with Freudian interpretations of *Hamlet* versus earlier interpretations. Readers bring their own cultural heritage along with them in their responses to literary texts, a fact which allows for the principle that texts speak to other texts only through the intervention of particular readers. Thus, reader-response criticism can appropriate other theories—as all theories attempt to do.

Reader-response theory is likely to strike many people as both esoteric and too subjective. Unquestionably, readers had been little considered in the New Criticism; but they may have been overemphasized by the theorists who seek to give them the final word in interpreting literature. Communication as a whole is predicated on the demonstrable claim that there are common, agreed-upon meanings in language, however rich, metaphorical, or symbolic. To contend that there are, even in theory, as many meanings in a poem as there are readers strongly calls into question the possibility of intelligible discourse. That some of the theorists themselves are not altogether comfortable with the logical implications of their position is evidenced by their positing of mock readers, informed readers, real readers, and implied readers—by which they mean readers of education, sensitivity, and sophistication.

Despite the potential dangers of subjectivism, reader-response criticism has been a corrective to literary dogmatism and a reminder of the richness, complexity, and diversity of viable literary interpretations, and it seems safe to predict that readers will never again be completely ignored in arriving at verbal meaning.

Quick Reference

Bleich, David. *Subjective Criticism*. Baltimore: Johns Hopkins University Press, 1978.

Booth, Wayne. *Rhetoric of Fiction*. Chicago: University of Chicago Press, 1961.

Fish, Stanley. *Is There a Text in This Class?* Cambridge, MA: Harvard University Press, 1980.

———. *Surprised by Sin: The Reader in "Paradise Lost."* Berkeley: University of California Press, 1967.

Gibson, Walker. "Authors, Speakers, Readers, and Mock Readers." *College English* 11, no. 5 (1950): 265–69.

Holland, Norman. "*Hamlet*—My Greatest Creation." *Journal of the American Academy of Psychoanalysis* 3 (1975): 419–27.

———. "The Miller's Wife and the Professors: Questions about the Transactive Theory of Reading." *New Literary History* 17 (1986): 423–47.

———. "Recovering 'The Purloined Letter': Reading as a Personal Transaction." In *The Reader in the Text*. Ed. Susan Suleiman and Inge Crosman. Princeton, NJ: Princeton University Press, 1980.

Iser, Wolfgang. *The Act of Reading*. Baltimore: Johns Hopkins University Press, 1978.

Jauss, Hans Robert. *Toward an Aesthetic of Reception*. Trans. Timothy Bahti. Minneapolis: University of Minnesota Press, 1982.

Kuhn, Thomas S. *The Structure of Scientific Revolutions*. Chicago: University of Chicago Press, 1962.

Mailloux, Steven. *Interpretive Conventions: The Reader in the Study of American Fiction*. Ithaca, NY, and London: Cornell University Press, 1984.

————. "Reading *Huckleberry Finn*: The Rhetoric of Performed Ideology." In *New Essays on Huckleberry Finn*. Ed. Louis Budd. Cambridge: Cambridge University Press, 1985.

Prince, Gerald. "Introduction to the Study of the Narratee." In *Reader-Response Criticism*. Ed. Jane Tompkins. Baltimore: Johns Hopkins University Press, 1980.

Richards, I. A. *Practical Criticism*. New York: Harcourt, 1929.

————. *Principles of Literary Criticism*. New York: Harcourt, 1925.

Rosenblatt, Louise. *The Reader, the Text, the Poem*. Carbondale: Southern Illinois University Press, 1978.

Tompkins, Jane, ed. *Reader-Response Criticism: From Formalism to Post-Structuralism*. Baltimore: Johns Hopkins University Press, 1980.

Epilogue

"How do you learn to *read* this way? *Where* do you learn this? Do you take a course in *symbols* or something?"

With a rising, plaintive pitch to her voice, with puzzled eyes and shaking head, a college student once asked those questions after her class had participated in a lively discussion of the multiple levels in Henry James's *Turn of the Screw*. As with most students when they are first introduced to a serious study of literature, members of this group were delighted, amazed—and dismayed—as they themselves helped to unfold the rich layers of the work, to see it from perspectives of form and of psychology, to correlate it with the author's biography and its cultural and historical context.

But that particular student, who was both fascinated and dismayed by the "symbols," had not yet taken a crucial step in the learning process: she had not perceived that the practice of close reading, the bringing to bear of all kinds of knowledge, and the use of several approaches are in themselves the "course in symbols or something." What we have traced in this volume is not a course in the occult or something only for those who have access to the inner sanctum. For, after all, as Wordsworth wrote in 1800 in his preface to *Lyrical Ballads*, the poet "is a man speaking to men." A poet or a dramatist embodies an experience in a poem or a play, embodies it—usually—for us, the readers; and we respond simply by reliving that experience as fully as possible.

To be sure, not all of us may want to respond to that extent. There was, for example, the secondary school teacher who listened to a fairly long and detailed explication of "The Death of the Ball-Turret Gunner," a five-line poem by Randall Jarrell. Later she took the lecturer aside and said, with something more than asperity, "I'd *never* make my class try to see all of *that* in a poem." Perhaps not. But is the class better or worse because of that attitude?

Clearly, the authors of this book believe that we readers are the losers when we fail to see in a work of literature all that may be legitimately seen there. We have presented a number of critical approaches to literature, aware that many have been only briefly treated and that much has been generalized. But we have suggested here some of the tools and some of the approaches that enable a reader to criticize—that is, to judge and to discern so that he or she may see better the literary work, to relate it to the range of human experience, to appreciate its form and style.

Having offered these tools and approaches, we would also urge caution against undue or misdirected enthusiasm in their use, for judgment and discernment imply reason and caution. Too often even seasoned critics, forgetting the etymology of the word *critic,* become personal and subjective or preoccupied with tangential concerns. Not-so-seasoned students, their minds suddenly open to psychoanalytic criticism, run gaily through a pastoral poem and joyously find Freudian symbols in every rounded hill and stately conifer. Some read a simple poem like William Carlos Williams's "The Red Wheelbarrow" and, unwilling to see simplicity and compression as virtues enough (and as much more than mere simpleness), stray from the poem into their individual mazes. They forget that any interpretation must be supported logically and fully from the evidence within the literary work and that the ultimate test of the validity of an interpretation must be its self-consistency. Conversely, sometimes they do establish a fairly legitimate pattern of interpretation for a work, only to find something that seems to be at odds with it; then, fascinated with or startled by what they assume to be a new element, they forget that their reading is not valid unless it permits a unified picture of both the original pattern and the new insight. As the New Critics would have said, an object of literary art has its unique aesthetic experience; the reader is no more at liberty to mar it with careless extensions than the author would have been free to damage its organic unity with infelicitous inclusions.

Having noted this, we acknowledge that individual readers bring their own unique experiences to the perception of a literary work of art; since these experiences may and will be vastly different, they will color the readers' perceptions. As we have shown elsewhere in this handbook, important recent critical theories have acknowledged and furthered this potential for more subjective interpretations.

We must therefore remember to be flexible and eclectic in our choices of critical approaches to a given literary work. Our choices are determined by the same discretion that controls what we exclude, by our concern for the unique experience and nature of a piece of literature. Not all approaches are useful in all cases. Perhaps we would not be too far wrong to suggest that there are as many approaches to literary works as there are literary works. All we can do is to draw from the many approaches the combination that best fits a particular literary creation. As David Daiches said at the end of *Critical Approaches to Literature,* "Every effective literary critic sees some facet of literary art and develops an awareness with respect to it; but the total vision, or something approximating it, comes only to those who learn how to blend the insights yielded by many critical approaches" (393).

That is why we have chosen to present a variety of approaches and why some of the chapters in this book have even blended several methods. This blending is as it should be. It is not easy—and it would be unwise to try—to keep the work always separate from the life of the author and a view of his or her times; to divide the study of form from the study of basic imageries; to segregate basic imageries from archetypes or from other components of the experience of the work. And it would be unwise to ignore how, for example, a work long known and interpreted by conventional methods might yield fresh insights if examined from such newer perspectives as feminism, phenomenology, and cultural studies.

Our final word, then, is this: we admit that literary criticism can be difficult and sometimes esoteric, but it is first of all an attempt of readers to understand fully what they are reading. To understand in that manner, they do well to bring to bear whatever is in the human province that justifiably helps them to achieve that understanding. For literature is a part of the richness of human experience: it at once thrives on it, feeds it, and constitutes a significant part of it. When we realize this, we never again can be satisfied with the simple notions that a story is something only for the idler or the impractical dreamer, that a poem is merely a pretty combination of sounds and sights, that a significant drama is equivalent to an escapist motion picture or a television melodrama. Browning's Fra Lippo Lippi says:

> This world's no blot for us,
> Nor blank; it means intensely, and means good:
> To find its meaning is my meat and drink.

So, too, must be our attitude toward any worthy piece of literature in that world.

Quick Reference

Daiches, David. *Critical Approaches to Literature*. Englewood Cliffs, NJ: Prentice Hall, 1956.

Appendixes

Andrew Marvell
TO HIS COY MISTRESS

Had we but world enough, and time,
This coyness, Lady, were no crime.
We would sit down and think which way
To walk and pass our long love's day.
Thou by the Indian Ganges' side   5
Shouldst rubies find; I by the tide
Of Humber would complain. I would
Love you ten years before the Flood,
And you should, if you please, refuse
Till the conversion of the Jews.   10
My vegetable love should grow
Vaster than empires, and more slow;
An hundred years should go to praise
Thine eyes and on thy forehead gaze;
Two hundred to adore each breast,   15
But thirty thousand to the rest;
An age at least to every part,
And the last age should show your heart.
For, Lady, you deserve this state,
Nor would I love at lower rate.   20

But at my back I always hear
Time's wingèd chariot hurrying near;
And yonder all before us lie

Deserts of vast eternity.
Thy beauty shall no more be found,   25
Nor, in thy marble vault, shall sound
My echoing song; then worms shall try
That long preserved virginity,
And your quaint honor turn to dust,
And into ashes all my lust: 30
The grave's a fine and private place,
But none, I think, do there embrace.

Now therefore, while the youthful hue
Sits on thy skin like morning dew,
And while thy willing soul transpires   35
At every pore with instant fires,
Now let us sport us while we may,
And now, like amorous birds of prey,
Rather at once our time devour
Than languish in his slow-chapped power.   40
Let us roll all our strength and all
Our sweetness up into one ball,
And tear our pleasures with rough strife
Thorough* the iron gates of life:
Thus, though we cannot make our sun   45
Stand still, yet we will make him run.

*thorough: through

Nathaniel Hawthorne
YOUNG GOODMAN BROWN

Young Goodman Brown came forth at sunset into the street at Salem Village; but put his head back, after crossing the threshold, to exchange a parting kiss with his young wife. And Faith, as the wife was aptly named, thrust her own pretty head into the street, letting the wind play with the pink ribbons of her cap while she called to Goodman Brown.

"Dearest heart," whispered she, softly and rather sadly, when her lips were close to his ear, "prithee put off your journey until sunrise and sleep in your own bed to-night. A lone woman is troubled with such dreams and such thoughts that she's afeard of herself sometimes. Pray tarry with me this night, dear husband, of all nights in the year."

"My love and my Faith," replied young Goodman Brown, "of all nights in the year, this one night must I tarry away from thee. My journey, as thou callest it, forth and back again, must needs be done 'twixt now and sunrise. What, my sweet, pretty wife, dost thou doubt me already, and we but three months married?"

"Then God bless you!" said Faith, with the pink ribbons; "and may you find all well when you come back."

"Amen!" cried Goodman Brown. "Say thy prayers, dear Faith, and go to bed at dusk, and no harm will come to thee."

So they parted; and the young man pursued his way until, being about to turn the corner by the meeting-house, he looked back and saw the head of Faith still peeping after him with a melancholy air, in spite of her pink ribbons.

"Poor little Faith!" thought he, for his heart smote him. "What a wretch am I to leave her on such an errand! She talks of dreams, too. Methought as she spoke there was trouble in her face, as if a dream had warned her what work is to be done to-night. But no, no; 'twould kill her to think it. Well, she's a blessed angel on earth; and after this one night I'll cling to her skirts and follow her to heaven."

With this excellent resolve for the future, Goodman Brown felt himself justified in making more haste on his present evil purpose. He had taken a dreary road, darkened by all the gloomiest trees of the forest, which barely stood aside to let the narrow path creep through, and closed immediately behind. It was all as lonely as could be; and there is this peculiarity in such a solitude, that the traveller knows not who may be concealed by the innumerable trunks and the thick boughs overhead; so that with lonely footsteps he may yet be passing through an unseen multitude.

"There may be a devilish Indian behind every tree," said Goodman Brown to himself; and he glanced fearfully behind him as he added, "What if the devil himself should be at my very elbow!"

His head being turned back, he passed a crook of the road, and, looking forward again, beheld the figure of a man, in grave and decent attire, seated at the foot of an old tree. He arose at Goodman Brown's approach and walked onward side by side with him.

"You are late, Goodman Brown," said he. "The clock of the Old South was striking as I came through Boston, and that is full fifteen minutes agone."

"Faith kept me back a while," replied the young man, with a tremor in his voice, caused by the sudden appearance of his companion, though not wholly unexpected.

It was now deep dusk in the forest, and deepest in that part of it where these two were journeying. As nearly as could be discerned, the second traveller was about fifty years old, apparently in the same rank of life as Goodman Brown, and bearing a considerable resemblance to him, though perhaps more in expression than features. Still they might have been taken for father and son. And yet, though the elder person was as simply clad as the younger, and as simple in manner too, he had an indescribable air of one who knew the world, and who would not have felt abashed at the governor's dinner table or in King William's court, were it possible that his affairs should call him thither. But the only thing about him that could be fixed upon as remarkable was his staff, which bore the likeness of a great black snake, so curiously wrought that it might almost be seen to twist and wriggle itself like a living serpent. This, of course, must have been an ocular deception, assisted by the uncertain light.

"Come, Goodman Brown," cried his fellow-traveller, "this is

a dull pace for the beginning of a journey. Take my staff, if you are so soon weary."

"Friend," said the other, exchanging his slow pace for a full stop, "having kept covenant by meeting thee here, it is my purpose now to return whence I came. I have scruples touching the matter thou wot'st of."

"Sayest thou so?" replied he of the serpent, smiling apart. "Let us walk on, nevertheless, reasoning as we go; and if I convince thee not thou shalt turn back. We are but a little way in the forest yet."

"Too far! too far!" exclaimed the goodman, unconsciously resuming his walk. "My father never went into the woods on such an errand, nor his father before him. We have been a race of honest men and good Christians since the days of the martyrs; and shall I be the first of the name of Brown that ever took this path and kept—"

"Such company, thou wouldst say," observed the elder person, interpreting his pause. "Well said, Goodman Brown! I have been as well acquainted with your family as with ever a one among the Puritans; and that's no trifle to say. I helped your grandfather, the constable, when he lashed the Quaker woman so smartly through the streets of Salem; and it was I that brought your father a pitch-pine knot, kindled at my own hearth, to set fire to an Indian village, in King Philip's war. They were my good friends, both; and many a pleasant walk have we had along this path, and returned merrily after midnight. I would fain be friends with you for their sake."

"If it be as thou sayest," replied Goodman Brown, "I marvel they never spoke of these matters; or, verily, I marvel not, seeing that the least rumor of the sort would have driven them from New England. We are a people of prayer, and good works to boot, and abide no such wickedness."

"Wickedness or not," said the traveller with the twisted staff, "I have a very general acquaintance here in New England. The deacons of many a church have drunk the communion wine with me; the selectmen of divers towns make me their chairman; and a majority of the Great and General Court are firm supporters of my interest. The governor and I, too— But these are state secrets."

"Can this be so?" cried Goodman Brown, with a stare of amazement at his undisturbed companion. "Howbeit, I have nothing to do with the governor and council; they have their own ways, and are no rule for a simple husbandman like me. But, were I to go on with thee, how should I meet the eye of that good old man, our minister, at Salem village? Oh, his voice would make me tremble both Sabbath day and lecture day."

Thus far the elder traveller had listened with due gravity; but now burst into a fit of irrepressible mirth, shaking himself so violently that his snake-like staff actually seemed to wriggle in sympathy.

"Ha! ha! ha!" shouted he again and again; then composing himself, "Well, go on, Goodman Brown, go on; but, prithee, don't kill me with laughing."

"Well, then, to end the matter at once," said Goodman Brown, considerably nettled, "there is my wife, Faith. It would break her dear little heart; and I'd rather break my own."

"Nay, if that be the case," answered the other, "e'en go thy ways, Goodman Brown. I would not for twenty old women like the one hobbling before us that Faith should come to any harm."

As he spoke he pointed his staff at a female figure on the path, in whom Goodman Brown recognized a very pious and exemplary dame, who had taught him his catechism in youth, and was still his moral and spiritual adviser, jointly with the minister and Deacon Gookin.

"A marvel, truly, that Goody Cloyse should be so far in the wilderness at nightfall," said he. "But with your leave, friend, I shall take a cut through the woods until we have left this Christian woman behind. Being a stranger to you, she might ask whom I was consorting with and whither I was going."

"Be it so," said his fellow-traveller. "Betake you to the woods, and let me keep the path."

Accordingly the young man turned aside, but took care to watch his companion, who advanced softly along the road until he had come within a staff's length of the old dame. She, meanwhile, was making the best of her way, with singular speed for so aged a woman, and mumbling some indistinct words—a prayer, doubtless—as she went. The traveller put forth his staff and touched her withered neck with what seemed the serpent's tail.

"The devil!" screamed the pious old lady.

"Then Goody Cloyse knows her old friend?" observed the traveller, confronting her and leaning on his writhing stick.

"Ah, forsooth, and is it your worship indeed?" cried the good dame. "Yea, truly it is, and in the very image of my old gossip, Goodman Brown, the grandfather of the silly fellow that now is. But—would your worship believe it?—my broom-stick hath strangely disappeared, stolen, as I suspect, by that unhanged witch, Goody Cory, and that, too, when I was anointed with the juice of smallage, and cinquefoil, and wolf's bane—"

"Mingled with fine wheat and the fat of a new-born babe," said the shape of old Goodman Brown.

"Ah, your worship knows the recipe," cried the old lady, cackling aloud. "So, as I was saying, being all ready for the meeting, and no horse to ride on, I made up my mind to foot it; for they tell me there is a nice young man to be taken into com-munion to-night. But now your good worship will lend me your arm, and we shall be there in a twinkling."

"That can hardly be," answered her friend. "I may not spare you my arm, Goody Cloyse; but here is my staff, if you will."

So saying, he threw it down at her feet, where, perhaps, it assumed life, being one of the rods which its owner had for-merly lent to the Egyptian magi. Of this fact, however, Good-man Brown could not take cognizance. He had cast up his eyes in astonishment, and, looking down again, beheld neither Goody Cloyse nor the serpentine staff, but his fellow-traveller alone, who waited for him as calmly as if nothing happened.

"That old woman taught me my catechism," said the young man; and there was a world of meaning in this simple com-ment.

They continued to walk onward, while the elder traveller exhorted his companion to make good speed and persevere in the path, discoursing so aptly that his arguments seemed rather to spring up in the bosom of his auditor than to be sug-gested by himself. As they went, he plucked a branch of maple to serve for a walking stick, and began to strip it of the twigs and little boughs, which were wet with evening dew. The moment his fingers touched them they became strangely withered and dried up as with a week's sunshine. Thus the pair proceeded, at a good free pace, until suddenly, in a gloomy hollow of the road, Goodman Brown sat himself down on the stump of a tree and refused to go any farther.

"Friend," said he, stubbornly, "my mind is made up. Not another step will I budge on this errand. What if a wretched old woman do choose to go to the devil when I thought she was going to heaven: is that any reason why I should quit my dear Faith and go after her?"

"You will think better of this by and by," said his acquaintance, composedly. "Sit here and rest yourself a while; and when you feel like moving again, there is my staff to help you along."

Without more words, he threw his companion the maple stick, and was as speedily out of sight as if he had vanished into the deepening gloom. The young man sat a few moments by the roadside, applauding himself greatly, and thinking with how clear a conscience he should meet the minister in his morning walk, nor shrink from the eye of good old Deacon Gookin. And what calm sleep would be his that very night, which was to have been spent so wickedly, but so purely and sweetly now, in the arms of Faith! Amidst these pleasant and praiseworthy meditations, Goodman Brown heard the tramp of horses along the road, and deemed it advisable to conceal himself within the verge of the forest, conscious of the guilty purpose that had brought him thither, though now so happily turned from it.

On came the hoof tramps and the voices of the riders, two grave old voices, conversing soberly as they drew near. These mingled sounds appeared to pass along the road, within a few yards of the young man's hiding-place; but, owing doubtless to the depth of the gloom at that particular spot, neither the travellers nor their steeds were visible. Though their figures brushed the small boughs by the wayside, it could not be seen that they intercepted, even for a moment, the faint gleam from the strip of bright sky athwart which they must have passed. Goodman Brown alternately crouched and stood on tiptoe, pulling aside the branches and thrusting forth his head as far as he durst without discerning so much as a shadow. It vexed him the more, because he could have sworn, were such a thing possible, that he recognized the voices of the minister and Deacon Gookin, jogging along quietly, as they were wont to do, when bound to some ordination or ecclesiastical council. While yet within hearing, one of the riders stopped to pluck a switch.

"Of the two, reverend sir," said the voice like the deacon's, "I had rather miss an ordination dinner than to-night's meeting. They tell me that some of our community are to be here from Falmouth and beyond, and others from Connecticut and Rhode Island, besides several of the Indian powwows, who, after their fashion, know almost as much deviltry as the best of us. Moreover, there is a goodly young woman to be taken into communion."

"Mighty well, Deacon Gookin!" replied the solemn old tones of the minister. "Spur up, or we shall be late. Nothing can be done, you know, until I get on the ground."

The hoofs clattered again; and the voices, talking so strangely in the empty air, passed on through the forest, where no church had ever been gathered or solitary Christian prayed. Whither, then, could these holy men be journeying so deep into the heathen wilderness? Young Goodman Brown caught hold of a tree for support, being ready to sink down on the ground, faint and overburdened with the heavy sickness of his heart. He looked up to the sky, doubting whether there really was a heaven above him. Yet there was the blue arch, and the stars brightening in it.

"With heaven above and Faith below, I will yet stand firm against the devil!" cried Goodman Brown.

While he still gazed upward into the deep arch of the firmament and had lifted his hands to pray, a cloud, though no wind was stirring, hurried across the zenith and hid the brightening stars. The blue sky was still visible, except directly overhead, where this black mass of cloud was sweeping swiftly northward. Aloft in the air, as if from the depths of the cloud, came a confused and doubtful sound of voices. Once the listener fancied that he could distinguish the accents of townspeople of his own, men and women, both pious and ungodly, many of whom he had met at the communion table, and had seen others rioting at the tavern. The next moment, so indistinct were the sounds, he doubted whether he had heard aught but the murmur of the old forest, whispering without a wind. Then came a stronger swell of those familiar tones, heard daily in the sunshine at Salem village, but never until now from a cloud of night. There was one voice, of a young woman, uttering lamentations, yet with an uncertain sorrow, and entreating for some favor, which, perhaps, it would grieve her to obtain; and all the unseen multitude, both saints and sinners, seemed to encourage her onward.

"Faith!" shouted Goodman Brown, in a voice of agony and desperation; and the echoes of the forest mocked him, crying, "Faith! Faith!" as if bewildered wretches were seeking her all through the wilderness.

The cry of grief, rage, and terror was yet piercing the night, when the unhappy husband held his breath for a response. There was a scream, drowned immediately in a louder murmur of voices, fading into far-off laughter, as the dark cloud swept away, leaving the clear and silent sky above Goodman Brown. But something fluttered lightly down through the air and caught on the branch of a tree. The young man seized it, and beheld a pink ribbon.

"My Faith is gone!" cried he, after one stupefied moment. "There is no good on earth; and sin is but a name. Come, devil; for to thee is this world given."

And, maddened with despair, so that he laughed loud and long, did Goodman Brown grasp his staff and set forth again, at such a rate that he seemed to fly along the forest path rather than to walk or run. The road grew wilder and drearier and more faintly traced, and vanished at length, leaving him in the heart of the dark wilderness, still rushing onward with the instinct that guides mortal man to evil. The whole forest was peopled with frightful sounds—the creaking of the trees, the howling of wild beasts, and the yell of Indians; while sometimes the wind tolled like a distant church bell, and sometimes gave a broad roar around the traveller, as if all Nature were laughing him to scorn. But he was himself the chief horror of the scene, and shrank not from its other horrors.

"Ha! ha! ha!" roared Goodman Brown when the wind laughed at him. "Let us hear which will laugh loudest. Think not to frighten me with your deviltry. Come witch, come wizard, come Indian powwow, come devil himself, and here comes Goodman Brown. You may as well fear him as he fear you."

In truth, all through the haunted forest there could be nothing more frightful than the figure of Goodman Brown. On he flew among the black pines, brandishing his staff with frenzied gestures, now giving vent to an inspiration of horrid blasphemy, and now shouting forth such laughter as set all the echoes of the forest laughing like demons around him. The fiend in his own shape is less hideous than when he rages in the breast of man. Thus sped the demoniac on his course, until, quivering among the trees, he saw a red light before him, as when the felled trunks and branches of a clearing have been set on fire, and throw up their lurid blaze against the sky, at the hour of midnight. He paused, in a lull of the tempest that had driven him onward, and heard the swell of what seemed a hymn, rolling solemnly from a distance with the weight of many voices. He knew the tune; it was a familiar one in the choir of the village meeting-house. The verse died heavily away, and was lengthened by a chorus, not of human voices, but of all the sounds of the benighted wilderness pealing in awful harmony together. Goodman Brown cried out, and his cry was lost to his own ear by its unison with the cry of the desert.

In the interval of silence he stole forward until the light glared full upon his eyes. At one extremity of an open space, hemmed in by the dark wall of the forest, arose a rock, bearing some rude, natural resemblance either to an altar or a pulpit, and surrounded by four blazing pines, their tops aflame, their stems untouched, like candles at an evening meeting. The mass of foliage that had overgrown the summit of the rock was all on fire, blazing high into the night and fitfully illuminating the whole field. Each pendent twig and leafy festoon was in a blaze. As the red light arose and fell, a numerous congregation alternately shone forth, then disappeared in shadow, and again grew, as it were, out of the darkness, peopling the heart of the solitary woods at once.

"A grave and dark-clad company," quoth Goodman Brown.

In truth they were such. Among them, quivering to and fro between gloom and splendor, appeared faces that would be seen next day at the council board of the province, and others which, Sabbath after Sabbath, looked devoutly heavenward, and benignantly over the crowded pews, from the holiest pulpits in the land. Some affirm that the lady of the governor was there. At least there were high dames well known to her, and wives of honored husbands, and widows, a great multitude, and ancient maidens, all of excellent repute, and fair young girls, who trembled lest their mothers should espy them. Either the sudden gleams of light flashing over the obscure field bedazzled Goodman Brown, or he recognized a score of the church members of Salem village famous for their special sanctity. Good old Deacon Gookin had arrived, and waited at the skirts of that venerable saint, his revered pastor. But, irreverently consorting with these grave, reputable, and pious people, these elders of the church, these chaste dames and dewy virgins, there were men of dissolute lives and women of spotted fame, wretches given over to all mean and filthy vice, and suspected even of horrid crimes. It was strange to see that the good shrank not from the wicked, nor were the sinners abashed by the saints. Scattered also among their pale-faced enemies were the Indian priests, or powwows, who had often scared their native forest with more hideous incantations than any known to English witchcraft.

"But where is Faith!" thought Goodman Brown; and, as hope came into his heart, he trembled.

Another verse of the hymn arose, a slow and mournful strain, such as the pious love, but joined to the words which expressed all that our nature can conceive of sin, and darkly hinted at far more. Unfathomable to mere mortals is the lore of fiends. Verse after verse was sung; and still the chorus of the desert swelled between like the deepest tone of a mighty organ; and with the final peal of that dreadful anthem there came a sound, as if the roaring wind, the rushing streams, the howling beasts, and every other voice of the unconverted wilderness were mingling and according with the voice of guilty man in homage to the prince of all. The four blazing pines threw up a loftier flame, and obscurely discovered shapes and visages of horror on the smoke wreaths above the impious assembly. At the same moment the fire on the rock shot redly forth and formed a glowing arch above its base, where now appeared a figure. With reverence be it spoken, the apparition bore no slight similitude, both in garb and manner, to some grave divine of the New England churches.

"Bring forth the converts!" cried a voice that echoed through the field and rolled into the forest.

At the word, Goodman Brown stepped forth from the shadow of the trees and approached the congregation, with whom he felt a loathful brotherhood by the sympathy of all that was wicked in his heart. He could have well-nigh sworn that the shape of his own dead father beckoned him to advance, looking downward from a smoke wreath, while a woman, with dim features of despair, threw out her hand to warn him back. Was it his mother? But he had no power to retreat one step, nor to resist, even in thought, when the minister and good old Deacon Gookin seized his arms and led him to the blazing rock. Thither came also the slender form of a veiled female, led between Goody Cloyse, that pious teacher of the catechism, and Martha Carrier, who had received the devil's promise to be queen of hell. A rampant hag was she. And there stood the proselytes beneath the canopy of fire.

"Welcome, my children," said the dark figure, "to the communion of your race. Ye have found thus young your nature and your destiny. My children, look behind you!"

They turned; and flashing forth, as it were, in a sheet of flame, the fiend worshippers were seen; the smile of welcome gleamed darkly on every visage.

"There," resumed the sable form, "are all whom ye have reverenced from youth. Ye deemed them holier than yourselves, and shrank from your own sin, contrasting it with their lives of righteousness and prayerful aspirations heavenward. Yet here are they all in my worshipping assembly. This night it shall be granted you to know their secret deeds: how hoary-bearded elders of the church have whispered wanton words to the young maids of their households; how many a woman, eager for widows' weeds, has given her husband a drink at bedtime and let him sleep his last sleep in her bosom; how beardless youths have made haste to inherit their fathers' wealth; and how fair damsels—blush not, sweet ones—have dug little graves in the garden, and bidden me, the sole guest, to an infant's funeral. By the sympathy of your human hearts for sin ye shall scent out all the places—whether in church, bed-chamber, street, field, or forest where crime has been committed, and shall exult to behold the whole earth one stain of guilt, one mighty blood spot. Far more than this. It shall be yours to penetrate, in every bosom, the deep mystery of sin, the fountain of all wicked arts, and which inexhaustibly supplies more evil impulses than human power—than my power at its utmost—can make manifest in deeds. And now, my children, look upon each other."

They did so; and, by the blaze of the hell-kindled torches, the wretched man beheld his Faith, and the wife her husband, trembling before that unhallowed altar.

"Lo, there ye stand, my children," said the figure, in a deep and solemn tone, almost sad with its despairing awfulness, as if his once angelic nature could yet mourn for our miserable race. "Depending upon one another's hearts, ye had still hoped that virtue were not all a dream. Now are ye undeceived. Evil is the nature of mankind. Evil must be your only happiness. Welcome again, my children, to the communion of your race."

"Welcome," repeated the fiend worshippers in one cry of despair and triumph.

And there they stood, the only pair, as it seemed, who were yet hesitating on the verge of wickedness in this dark world. A basin was hollowed, naturally, in the rock. Did it contain water, reddened by the lurid light? or was it blood? or, perchance, a liquid flame? Herein did the shape of evil dip his hand and prepare to lay the mark of baptism upon their foreheads, that they might be partakers of the mystery of sin, more conscious of the secret guilt of others, both in deed and thought, than they could now be of their own. The husband cast one look at his pale wife, and Faith at him. What polluted wretches would the next glance show them to each other, shuddering alike at what they disclosed and what they saw!

"Faith! Faith!" cried the husband, "look up to heaven, and resist the wicked one."

Whether Faith obeyed he knew not. Hardly had he spoken when he found himself amid calm night and solitude, listening to a roar of the wind which died heavily away through the forest. He staggered against the rock, and felt it chill and damp; while a hanging twig, that had been all on fire, besprinkled his cheek with the coldest dew.

The next morning young Goodman Brown came slowly in

to the street of Salem village, staring around him like a bewildered man. The good old minister was taking a walk along the graveyard to get an appetite for breakfast and meditate his sermon, and bestowed a blessing, as he passed, on Goodman Brown. He shrank from the venerable saint as if to avoid an anathema. Old Deacon Gookin was at domestic worship, and the holy words of his prayer were heard through the open window. "What God doth the wizard pray to?" quoth Goodman Brown. Goody Cloyse, that excellent old Christian, stood in the early sunshine at her own lattice, catechizing a little girl who had brought her a pint of morning's milk. Goodman Brown snatched away the child as from the grasp of the fiend himself. Turning the corner by the meeting-house, he spied the head of Faith, with the pink ribbons, gazing anxiously forth, and bursting into such joy at sight of him that she skipped along the street and almost kissed her husband before the whole village. But Goodman Brown looked sternly and sadly into her face, and passed on without a greeting.

Had Goodman Brown fallen asleep in the forest and only dreamed a wild dream of a witch-meeting?

Be it so if you will; but, alas! it was a dream of evil omen for young Goodman Brown. A stern, a sad, a darkly meditative, a distrustful, if not a desperate man did he become from the night of that fearful dream. On the Sabbath day, when the congregation were singing a holy psalm, he could not listen because an anthem of sin rushed loudly upon his ear and drowned all the blessed strain. When the minister spoke from the pulpit with power and fervid eloquence, and, with his hand on the open Bible, of the sacred truths of our religion, and of saint-like lives and triumphant deaths, and of future bliss or misery unutterable, then did Goodman Brown turn pale, dreading lest the roof should thunder down upon the gray blasphemer and his hearers. Often, awaking suddenly at midnight, he shrank from the bosom of Faith; and at morning or eventide, when the family knelt down at prayer, he scowled and muttered to himself, and gazed sternly at his wife, and turned away. And when he had lived long, and was borne to his grave a hoary corpse, followed by Faith, an aged woman, and children and grandchildren, a goodly procession, besides neighbors not a few, they carved no hopeful verse upon his tombstone, for his dying hour was gloom.

Alice Walker
EVERYDAY USE

for your grandmama

I will wait for her in the yard that Maggie and I made so clean and wavy yesterday afternoon. A yard like this is more comfortable than most people know. It is not just a yard. It is like an extended living room. When the hard clay is swept clean as a floor and the fine sand around the edges lined with tiny, irregular grooves, anyone can come and sit and look up into the elm tree and wait for the breezes that never come inside the house.

Maggie will be nervous until after her sister goes: she will stand hopelessly in corners, homely and ashamed of the burn scars down her arms and legs, eying her sister with a mixture of envy and awe. She thinks her sister has held life always in the palm of one hand, that "no" is a word the world never learned to say to her.

You've no doubt seen those TV shows where the child who has "made it" is confronted, as a surprise, by her own mother and father, tottering in weakly from backstage. (A pleasant surprise, of course: What would they do if parent and child came on the show only to curse out and insult each other?) On TV mother and child embrace and smile into each other's faces. Sometimes the mother and father weep, the child wraps them in her arms and leans across the table to tell how she would not have made it without their help. I have seen these programs.

Sometimes I dream a dream in which Dee and I are suddenly brought together on a TV program of this sort. Out of a dark and soft-seated limousine I am ushered into a bright room filled with many people. There I meet a smiling, gray, sporty man like Johnny Carson who shakes my hand and tells me what a fine girl I have. Then we are on the stage and Dee is embracing me with tears in her eyes. She pins on my dress a large orchid, even though she has told me once that she thinks orchids are tacky flowers.

In real life I am a large, big-boned woman with rough, man-working hands. In the winter I wear flannel nightgowns to bed and overalls during the day. I can kill and clean a hog as mercilessly as a man. My fat keeps me hot in zero weather. I can work outside all day, breaking ice to get water for washing; I can eat pork liver cooked over the open fire minutes after it comes steaming from the hog. One winter I knocked a bull calf straight in the brain between the eyes with a sledge hammer and had the meat hung up to chill before nightfall. But of course all this does not show on television. I am the way my daughter would want me to be: a hundred pounds lighter, my skin like an uncooked barley pancake. My hair glistens in the hot bright lights. Johnny Carson has much to do to keep up with my quick and witty tongue.

But that is a mistake. I know even before I wake up. Who ever knew a Johnson with a quick tongue? Who can even imagine me looking a strange white man in the eye? It seems to me I have talked to them always with one foot raised in flight, with my head turned in whichever way is farthest from them. Dee, though. She would always look anyone in the eye. Hesitation was no part of her nature.

"How do I look, Mama?" Maggie says, showing just enough of her thin body enveloped in pink skirt and red blouse for me to know she's there, almost hidden by the door.

"Come out into the yard," I say.

Have you ever seen a lame animal, perhaps a dog run over by some careless person rich enough to own a car, sidle up to someone who is ignorant enough to be kind to him? That is the way my Maggie walks. She has been like this, chin on chest, eyes on ground, feet in shuffle, ever since the fire that burned the other house to the ground.

Dee is lighter than Maggie, with nicer hair and a fuller figure. She's a woman now, though sometimes I forget. How long ago was it that the other house burned? Ten, twelve years? Sometimes I can still hear the flames and feel Maggie's arms sticking to me, her hair smoking and her dress falling off her in little black papery flakes. Her eyes seemed stretched open, blazed open by the flames reflected in them. And Dee. I see her standing off under the sweet gum tree she used to dig gum out of; a look of concentration on her face as she watched the last dingy gray board of the house fall in toward the red-hot brick chimney. Why don't you do a dance around the ashes? I'd wanted to ask her. She had hated the house that much.

I used to think she hated Maggie, too. But that was before we raised the money, the church and me, to send her to Augusta to school. She used to read to us without pity; forcing words, lies, other folks' habits, whole lives upon us two, sitting trapped and ignorant underneath her voice. She washed us in a river of make-believe, burned us with a lot of knowledge we didn't necessarily need to know. Pressed us to her with the serious way she read, to shove us away at just the moment, like dimwits, we seemed about to understand.

Dee wanted nice things. A yellow organdy dress to wear to her graduation from high school; black pumps to match a green suit she'd made from an old suit somebody gave me. She was determined to stare down any disaster in her efforts. Her eyelids would not flicker for minutes at a time. Often I fought off the temptation to shake her. At sixteen she had a style of her own: and knew what style was.

I never had an education myself. After second grade the school was closed down. Don't ask me why: in 1927 colored asked fewer questions than they do now. Sometimes Maggie reads to me. She stumbles along good-naturedly but can't see well. She knows she is not bright. Like good looks and money, quickness passed her by. She will marry John Thomas (who has mossy teeth in an earnest face) and then I'll be free to sit here and I guess just sing church songs to myself. Although I never was a good singer. Never could carry a tune. I was always better at a man's job. I used to love to milk till I was hooked in the side in '49. Cows are soothing and slow and don't bother you, unless you try to milk them the wrong way.

I have deliberately turned my back on the house. It is three rooms, just like the one that burned, except the roof is tin; they don't make shingle roofs any more. There are no real windows, just some holes cut in the sides, like the portholes in a ship, but not round and not square, with rawhide holding the shutters up on the outside. This house is in a pasture, too, like the other one. No doubt when Dee sees it she will want to tear it down. She wrote me once that no matter where we "choose" to live, she will manage to come see us. But she will never bring her friends. Maggie and I thought about this and Maggie asked me, "Mama, when did Dee ever *have* any friends?"

She had a few. Furtive boys in pink shirts hanging about on washday after school. Nervous girls who never laughed. Impressed with her they worshiped the well-turned phrase, the cute shape, the scalding humor that erupted like bubbles in lye. She read to them.

When she was courting Jimmy T she didn't have much time to pay to us, but turned all her faultfinding power on him. He *flew* to marry a cheap city girl from a family of ignorant flashy people. She hardly had time to recompose herself.

When she comes I will meet—but there they are!

Maggie attempts to make a dash for the house, in her shuffling way, but I stay her with my hand. "Come back here," I say. And she stops and tries to dig a well in the sand with her toe.

It is hard to see them clearly through the strong sun. But even the first glimpse of leg out of the car tells me it is Dee. Her feet were always neat-looking, as if God himself had shaped them with a certain style. From the other side of the car comes a short, stocky man. Hair is all over his head a foot long and hanging from his chin like a kinky mule tail. I hear Maggie suck in her breath. "Uhnnnh," is what it sounds like. Like when you see the wriggling end of a snake just in front of your foot on the road. "Uhnnnh."

Dee next. A dress down to the ground, in this hot weather. A dress so loud it hurts my eyes. There are yellows and oranges enough to throw back the light of the sun. I feel my whole face warming from the heat waves it throws out. Earrings gold, too, and hanging down to her shoulders. Bracelets dangling and making noises when she moves her arm up to shake the folds of the dress out of her armpits. The dress is loose and flows, and as she walks closer, I like it. I hear Maggie go "Uhnnnh" again. It is her sister's hair. It stands straight up like the wool on a sheep. It is black as night and around the edges are two long pigtails that rope about like small lizards disappearing behind her ears.

"Wa-su-zo-Tean-o!" she says, coming on in that gliding way the dress makes her move. The short stocky fellow with the hair to his navel is all grinning and he follows up with "Asalamalakim, my mother and sister!" He moves to hug Maggie but she falls back, right up against the back of my chair. I feel her trembling there and when I look up I see the perspiration falling off her chin.

"Don't get up," says Dee. Since I am stout it takes something of a push. You can see me trying to move a second or two before I make it. She turns, showing white heels through her sandals, and goes back to the car. Out she peeks next with a Polaroid. She stoops down quickly and lines up picture after picture of me sitting there in front of the house with Maggie cowering behind me. She never takes a shot without making sure the house is included. When a cow comes nibbling around the edge of the yard she snaps it and me and Maggie *and* the house. Then she puts the Polaroid in the back seat of the car, and comes up and kisses me on the forehead.

Meanwhile Asalamalakim is going through motions with Maggie's hand. Maggie's hand is as limp as a fish, and probably as cold, despite the sweat, and she keeps trying to pull it back. It looks like Asalamalakim wants to shake hands but wants to do it fancy. Or maybe he don't know how people shake hands. Anyhow, he soon gives up on Maggie.

"Well," I say. "Dee."

"No, Mama," she says. "Not 'Dee,' Wangero Leewanika Kemanjo!"

"What happened to 'Dee'?" I wanted to know.

"She's dead," Wangero said. "I couldn't bear it any longer, being named after the people who oppress me."

"You know as well as me you was named after your aunt Dicie," I said. Dicie is my sister. She named Dee. We called her "Big Dee" after Dee was born.

"But who was *she* named after?" asked Wangero.

"I guess after Grandma Dee," I said.

"And who was she named after?" asked Wangero.

"Her mother," I said, and saw Wangero was getting tired.

"That's about as far back as I can trace it," I said. Though, in fact, I probably could have carried it back beyond the Civil War through the branches.

"Well," said Asalamalakim, "there you are."

"Uhnnnh," I heard Maggie say.

"There I was not," I said, "before 'Dicie' cropped up in our family, so why should I try to trace it that far back?"

He just stood there grinning, looking down on me like somebody inspecting a Model A car. Every once in a while he and Wangero sent eye signals over my head.

"How do you pronounce this name?" I asked.

"You don't have to call me by it if you don't want to," said Wangero.

"Why shouldn't I?" I asked. "If that's what you want us to call you, we'll call you."

"I know it might sound awkward at first," said Wangero.

"I'll get used to it," I said. "Ream it out again."

Well, soon we got the name out of the way. Asalamalakim had a name twice as long and three times as hard. After I tripped over it two or three times he told me to just call him Hakim-a-barber. I wanted to ask him was he a barber, but I didn't think he was, so I didn't ask.

"You must belong to those beef-cattle peoples down the road," I said. They said "Asalamalakim" when they met you, too, but they didn't shake hands. Always too busy: feeding the cattle, fixing the fences, putting up salt-lick shelters, throwing down hay. When the white folks poisoned some of the herd the men stayed up all night with rifles in their hands. I walked a mile and a half just to see the sight.

Hakim-a-barber said, "I accept some of their doctrines, but farming and raising cattle is not my style." (They didn't tell me, and I didn't ask, whether Wangero (Dee) had really gone and married him.)

We sat down to eat and right away he said he didn't eat collards and pork was unclean. Wangero, though, went on through the chitlins and corn bread, the greens and everything else. She talked a blue streak over the sweet potatoes. Everything delighted her. Even the fact that we still used the benches her daddy make for the table when we couldn't afford to buy chairs.

"Oh, Mama!" she cried. Then turned to Hakim-a-barber. "I never knew how lovely these benches are. You can feel the rump prints," she said, running her hands underneath her and along the bench. Then she gave a sigh and her hand closed over Grandma Dee's butter dish. "That's it!" she said. "I knew there was something I wanted to ask you if I could have." She jumped up from the table and went over in the corner where the churn stood, the milk in it clabber by now. She looked at the churn and looked at it.

"This churn top is what I need," she said. "Didn't Uncle Buddy whittle it out of a tree you all used to have?"

"Yes," I said.

"Uh huh," she said happily. "And I want the dasher, too."

"Uncle Buddy whittle that, too?" asked the barber.

Dee (Wangero) looked up at me.

"Aunt Dee's first husband whittled the dash," said Maggie so low you almost couldn't hear her. "His name was Henry, but they called him Stash."

"Maggie's brain is like an elephant's," Wangero said, laughing. "I can use the churn top as a centerpiece for the alcove table," she said, sliding a plate over the churn, "and I'll think of something artistic to do with the dasher."

When she finished wrapping the dasher the handle stuck out. I took it for a moment in my hands. You didn't even have to look close to see where hands pushing the dasher up and down to make butter had left a kind of sink in the wood. In fact, there were a lot of small sinks; you could see where thumbs and fingers had sunk into the wood. It was beautiful light yellow wood, from a tree that grew in the yard where Big Dee and Stash had lived.

After dinner Dee (Wangero) went to the trunk at the foot of my bed and started rifling through it. Maggie hung back in the kitchen over the dishpan. Out came Wangero with two quilts. They had been pieced by Grandma Dee and then Big Dee and me had hung them on the quilt frames on the front porch and quilted them. One was in the Lone Star pattern. The other was Walk Around the Mountain. In both of them were scraps of dresses Grandma Dee had worn fifty and more years ago. Bits and pieces of Grandpa Jarrell's Paisley shirts. And one teeny faded blue piece, about the size of a penny matchbox, that was from Great Grandpa Ezra's uniform that he wore in the Civil War.

"Mama," Wangero said sweet as a bird. "Can I have these old quilts?"

I heard something fall in the kitchen, and a minute later the kitchen door slammed.

"Why don't you take one or two of the others?" I asked. "These old things was just done by me and Big Dee from some tops your grandma pieced before she died."

"No," said Wangero. "I don't want those. They are stitched around the borders by machine."

"That'll make them last better," I said.

"That's not the point," said Wangero. "These are all pieces of dresses Grandma used to wear. She did all this stitching by hand. Imagine!" She held the quilts securely in her arms, stroking them.

"Some of the pieces, like those lavender ones, come from old clothes her mother handed down to her," I said, moving up to touch the quilts. Dee (Wangero) moved back just enough so that I couldn't reach the quilts. They already belonged to her.

"Imagine!" she breathed again, clutching them closely to her bosom.

"The truth is," I said, "I promised to give them quilts to Maggie, for when she marries John Thomas."

She gasped like a bee had stung her.

"Maggie can't appreciate these quilts!" she said. "She'd probably be backward enough to put them to everyday use."

"I reckon she would," I said. "God knows I been saving 'em for long enough with nobody using 'em. I hope she will!" I didn't want to bring up how I had offered Dee (Wangero) a quilt when she went away to college. Then she had told me they were old-fashioned, out of style.

"But they're *priceless!*" she was saying now, furiously; for she has a temper. "Maggie would put them on the bed and in five years they'd be in rags. Less than that!"

"She can always make some more," I said. "Maggie knows how to quilt."

Dee (Wangero) looked at me with hatred. "You just will not understand. The point is these quilts, *these* quilts!"

"Well," I said, stumped. "What would *you* do with them?"

"Hang them," she said. As if that was the only thing you *could* do with quilts.

Maggie by now was standing in the door. I could almost hear the sound her feet made as they scraped over each other.

"She can have them, Mama," she said, like somebody used to never winning anything, or having anything reserved for her. "I can 'member Grandma Dee without the quilts."

I looked at her hard. She had filled her bottom lip with checkerberry snuff and it gave her face a kind of dopey, hang-dog look. It was Grandma Dee and Big Dee who taught her how to quilt herself. She stood there with her scarred hands hidden in the folds of her skirt. She looked at her sister with something like fear but she wasn't mad at her. This was Maggie's portion. This was the way she knew God to work.

When I looked at her like that something hit me in the top of my head and ran down to the soles of my feet. Just like when I'm in church and the spirit of God touches me and I get happy and shout. I did something I never had done before: hugged Maggie to me, then dragged her on into the room, snatched the quilts out of Miss Wangero's hands and dumped them into Maggie's lap. Maggie just sat there on my bed with her mouth open.

"Take one or two of the others," I said to Dee.

But she turned without a word and went out to Hakim-a-barber.

"You just don't understand," she said, as Maggie and I came out to the car.

"What don't I understand?" I wanted to know.

"Your heritage." she said. And then she turned to Maggie, kissed her, and said, "You ought to try to make something of yourself, too, Maggie. It's really a new day for us. But from the way you and Mama still live you'd never know it."

She put on some sunglasses that hid everything above the tip of her nose and her chin.

Maggie smiled; maybe at the sunglasses. But a real smile, not scared. After we watched the car dust settle, I asked Maggie to bring me a dip of snuff. And then the two of us sat there just enjoying, until it was time to go in the house and go to bed.

Index

Abel, Elizabeth, 200
Abrahams, Roger D., 288
Achieved content, 75, 85
Acosta, Oscar Zeta, 262
Adler, Alfred, 128
Adorno, Theodor, 246
Aeschylus, 170–72, 255
Affective fallacy, 87, 358
Affective stylistics, 363–64
African Americans. *See* Black
    literature
Agamemnon (Aeschylus), 171
Alger, Horatio, Jr., 188
Allegory in "Young Goodman
    Brown," 57–58, 100–101
Allen, Paula Gunn, 266
Allusion
    formalistic approach and, 75
    in "To His Coy Mistress," 31,
        93–94
    in "Young Goodman Brown,"
        99–100
Althusser, Louis, 246, 329
Altick, Richard D., 24
Altschuler, Mark, 229
Ambiguity
    in "A Slumber Did My Spirit
        Seal," 72
    in "Everyday Use," 121, 297
    in *Huckleberry Finn,* 289–90

in *Moby-Dick,* 185–86
precritical response and, 8
in "Young Goodman Brown,"
    96–104
American Adam archetype,
    187–91. *See also* Hero arche-
    types
American Dream, 186–91
American Indian literature,
    263–67, 287
American multiculturalism,
    253–69
    "Everyday Use" and, 292–
        97
Ammons, Elizabeth, 287, 291
Anderson, Sherwood, 191
Angelou, Maya, 210
Anima archetype, 180–82, 183
Antagonist, 7
Anthropology. *See also* Lévi-
    Strauss, Claude
    cultural studies and, 247
    Jungian psychology and,
        184–86
    mythological criticism and,
        168–77
Anzaldúa, Gloria, 261
Archetypal approaches. *See*
    Archetypes; Mythological
    approaches

Archetypes. *See also* Hero arche-
    types; Symbols
  American Adam, 187–91
  defined, 160–61
  in "Everyday Use," 191–93
  as genres, 166–67
  in Hawthorne's fiction, 281
  in *Huckleberry Finn*, 189–91,
    287–92
  imagery and, 161–65
  Jungian psychology and,
    177–86
  motifs and patterns, 165–66
  in Oedipus myth, 170–71
  scapegoat, 166, 169, 171, 174
  in "To His Coy Mistress,"
    175–77
  of women, 163, 183, 190,
    191–93, 206
Aristocracy, Twain's condemna-
    tion of, 47–48, 49, 50–51
Aristotelian criticism, 304–7
Aristotle, 87, 126, 319, 320, 358,
    362
  Poetics, 78, 85, 304, 307, 309
Arnold, Matthew, 26, 245, 304,
    358
Asian American literature,
    267–69
Atmosphere, 10–11
Audience. *See also* Reader-
    response criticism
  rhetorical criticism and, 319–22
Augustine, St., 319
Austen, Jane, 107, 203, 358
Authenticity of text. *See* Textual
    criticism
Authorial intent, 146, 312, 359
Awkward, Michael, 210

Babcock, Weston, 40
Baird, James, 185
Baker, Houston A., Jr., 214, 233
Bakhtin, Mikhail Mikhailovich,
    246–47, 349–55
Balzac, Honoré de, 337, 338
Barthes, Roland, 246, 337–39, 340

Beardsley, Monroe, 87
Beauvoir, Simone de, 198
Bell, Bernard, 257
Berlant, Lauren, 243
Berthoff, Ann, 3
Biblical motifs, 31, 98–100
Billings, Josh, 46
Binary oppositions, 203, 243, 335,
    336
Biographical approach. *See*
    Historical-biographical
    approach
Black feminism, 208–10
Black literature, 208–10, 256–60,
    286, 287–88. *See also* "Every-
    day Use: for your grand-
    mama" (Walker)
Blair, Walter, 43
Blake, William, 175
  historical-biographical
    approach to, 23–24
  "Sick Rose," 149–50, 152
Blankenship, Benson, 46
Bleich, David, 363
Bodkin, Maud, 184
Bonaparte, Marie, 132, 148–49,
    152, 155
Bonnin, Gertrude, 265
Booth, Wayne C., 88, 214, 358
Botstein, Leon, 255
Bourdieu, Pierre, 247
Bowers, Fredson, 19
Bradley, A. C., 40
Brantlinger, Patrick, 240
Brent, Linda, 258
British cultural materialism,
    245–47
Brody, Jules, 276
Brontë, Emily, 10, 203
Brooks, Cleanth, 80, 81, 82, 84, 85
Brooks, Van Wyck, 225
Browning, Robert, 89–90, 372
Bruccoli, Matthew J., 313
Bruce, Susan, 250–52
Bruster, Douglas, 250
Bryan, W. F., 313
Burke, Kenneth, 107, 311, 312

Calvinism, 55–56, 58–59, 98, 101
Campbell, Joseph, 158
Camus, Albert, 25
Cargill, Oscar, 17
Carnival tradition, 350, 351
Carpenter, Fredric I., 187
Carson, Johnny, 153–54
Catharsis, 87, 126, 304
Central intelligence, 343. *See also* Point of view
Cervantes, Miguel de, *Don Quixote*, 44
Character, 7–8
  in *Huckleberry Finn*, 104–9
Chatman, Seymour, 323
Chaucer, Geoffrey, 26, 89
  Canterbury Tales, 19, 42–43, 49, 312–13, 323
Chesnutt, Charles W., 258
Chicago school, 304–7
Chicana/o literature, 260–63, 351
Child psychology, 133–34, 140, 204
Christian, Barbara, 231–32
Chronotope, 350
Ciardi, John, 3
Cicero, 319
Circles, symbolic meanings of, 162–63, 176
Circumlocution, 71
Cirlot, J. E., 165
Cixous, Hélène, 156, 204
Clark, Robert L., Jr., 145
Clark, Suzanne, 205
Class, socioeconomic
  culture and, 245
  in *Huckleberry Finn*, 47–48, 49–50
Classical tragedy, 42, 170–73, 307
Clemens, Olivia Langdon (Livvie), 43, 225, 226
Clemens, Orion, 47
Clemens, Samuel. *See* Twain, Mark
Close reading, 73–76

Codes
  "Hemingway code," 88
  structuralism and, 336, 337–39
Coleridge, Samuel Taylor, 78, 83, 90, 126, 184
Colors, symbolic meanings of, 161–62, 175, 185
Conflict. *See* Plot
Connolly, Thomas E., 58, 98
Connotative code, 338
Conrad, Joseph, 181, 260, 335
Consciousness
  criticism of, 343–49
  Freud's theories on, 127–31, 139
  myths and, 178–79
Content
  achieved, 75, 85
  paraphrasable, 29
Cooper, James Fenimore, 23, 187–89
Corbett, Edward P. J., 320, 321
Cornford, F. M., 168
Cowan, Tom, 253
Cox, James, M., 139–40, 284
Crane, Ronald S., 25, 82, 305
Crane, Stephen, 10
Cranfill, Thomas M., 145
Criticism of consciousness, 343–49
Cullen, Countee, 259
Culler, Jonathan, 214, 337–39
Cultural code, 338
Cultural studies approach, 239–301
  American multiculturalism, 253–69
  British cultural materialism, 245–47
  defined, 239–44
  to "Everyday Use," 292–97
  film theory and, 206
  to *Hamlet*, 270–75
  to *Huckleberry Finn*, 283–92
  limitations of, 244–45
  New Historicism and, 247–53

Cultural studies approach (*continued*)
  to "To His Coy Mistress," 276–78
  to "Young Goodman Brown," 278–83

Daiches, David, 311, 371
Dante, 182, 184, 255, 336
Dark reform writing, 282–83
Davidson, Cathy N., 242
Death imagery, 139–41, 150, 151, 161, 165
Dechend, Hertha von, 171
Deconstruction, 340–43
Deep structure, 333, 335
Defamiliarization, 334–35, 337, 339
Defoe, Daniel, 133, 278
Dempster, Germaine, 313
Dénouement, 54, 61, 75
Derrida, Jacques, 337, 341
Desert, symbolic meaning of, 165
Devil archetype, 142, 181, 224
De Voto, Bernard, 42, 46, 50, 225
Diachronic features, 333–34
Dialect in *Huckleberry Finn*, 43, 289, 323
Dialectic in *Hamlet*, 110–18
Dialogics, 349–55
Diaz, Bernal, 256
Dickens, Charles, 4, 20, 23, 44
Dickinson, Emily, 197, 211
Dictionaries, unabridged, 74
Difference, feminist criticism and, 199–200
Di Marco, Corolini, 250–51, 252
Discours (term), 337
Divine appointment, myth of, 173–74
Donne, John, 85, 90, 215
Don Quixote (Cervantes), 44, 189
Dostoyevsky, Fyodor, 260, 350, 351, 354
Drama. *See also Hamlet*
  mythological approach to, 170

Dreams, 132, 179. *See also* American Dream
Dreiser, Theodore, 188
Dryden, John, 24, 25, 42
Dunbar, Paul Laurence, 258
During, Simon, 246

Eagleton, Terry, 214, 243
Eaton, Edith, 268
Eaton, Winnifred, 268–69
Eclectic approach to criticism, 17–18, 302–4, 371
Écriture féminine, 203, 204
Ecstatics, 2–3
Edenic Possibilities myth, 186–87
Ego, 128–29, 130, 142
Ekstasis. *See* Ecstatics
Eliade, Mircea, 176, 185
Eliot, T. S., 9, 24, 189, 260, 312
  formalistic criticism and, 80, 85, 122
  on *Huckleberry Finn*, 43, 105, 284
  mythological criticism and, 168, 175
  Waste Land, The, 20, 335, 343
Elledge, Scott, 313
Ellison, Ralph, 210, 256, 257, 260
English romantics. *See* Romanticism
Epic genre, 307
Erdrich, Louise, 266
Erogenous zone, 133
Erotic poetry, 32
Estrangement, 334, 337, 339
Etymology, 74
Euripides, 184
"Everyday Use: for your grandmama" (Walker)
  cultural studies approach to, 292–97
  feminist criticism and, 230–34
  formalistic approach to, 118–21
  historical-biographical approach to, 61–65

moral-philosophical approach to, 65–68
mythological approaches to, 191–93
plot, 60–61
precritical response and, 6, 7, 8, 10, 11, 12, 13–14
psychological approach to, 153–55
text of, 388–96
traditional approaches to, 60–68
External form, 83, 118–19

Fallacy
affective, 87, 358
denying the antecedent, 29
intentional, 87
Faulkner, William, 50, 188, 223, 260, 314
"Rose for Emily, A," 337
Sound and the Fury, The, 84, 89, 343
"That Evening Sun," 10
Faust legend, 54
Female imagery. *See* Anima archetype; Motherhood; Women
Female myth figures, 207
Feminism
black, 208–10
cultural studies and, 247
defined, 196–97
French, 203–6
lesbian, 208–9, 211–12
womanism vs., 209, 234
Feminist approaches, 196–238
defined, 196–97
to "Everyday Use," 230–34
gender studies, 200–202
to *Hamlet*, 217–23
to *Huckleberry Finn*, 225–30
limitations, 212–15
Marxist, 197, 202–3
minorities and, 208–12
mythological criticism and, 206–8

psychoanalytic, 203–8
themes in, 198–200
to "To His Coy Mistress," 215–17, 361
to "Young Goodman Brown," 223–25
Fergusson, Francis, 172
Fiedler, Leslie, 2–3, 189
Fielding, Henry, *Tom Jones*, 25–26, 44
Film theory, feminist criticism and, 206
Fire, symbolic meaning of, 152
Fish, Stanley, 360, 363
Fishkin, Shelley Fisher, 225, 285–86
Fitzgerald, F. Scott, 188, 313, 343
Flaubert, Gustave, *Madame Bovary*, 361
Fogle, Richard Harter, 97
Folklore
in black literature, 256–57, 258–59, 286, 287–88
in *Huckleberry Finn*, 49
Russian, 334
Form, 74–75, 83–85. *See also* Formalistic approach; Russian formalism
dialectic as, 110
external, 83, 118–19
organic, 76–77, 78–80, 83–85, 340
repetitive, 107–9
theme and, 86, 91–96
Formalism, Russian, 334–35
Formalistic approach, 70–124. *See also* New Criticism; Russian formalism
to "Everyday Use," 118–21
example of, with poem, 70–73
feminist criticism and, 202, 213–14
to *Hamlet*, 110–18
history of, 76–82
to *Huckleberry Finn*, 104–9
key elements of, 82–91

Formalistic approach
(*continued*)
limitations of, 81–82, 86,
121–23, 202, 302–3, 328,
347–48
organic form in, 76–77, 78–80,
83–85, 340
process of, 73–76
to "To His Coy Mistress,"
91–96
to "Young Goodman Brown,"
96–104
Foucault, Michel, 211, 243, 249,
337
Fowler, Roger, 324
Franklin, Benjamin, 188
Frazer, Sir James G., 168–69
French feminist criticism, 203–6
French rationalism, 332
French structuralism, 337–39
Freud, Sigmund, 126, 159, 180,
362. *See also* Psychological
approach
feminist criticism and, 204, 205
theories of, 127–34, 179, 193
Friedan, Betty, 198–99
Fromm, Erich, 132–33
Frost, Robert, 26, 312
Frye, Northrop, 81, 166–67, 185,
207, 308–10

Gadamer, Hans-Georg, 344
Gaines, Ernest, 260
Gallagher, Catherine, 248, 249
Garden, symbolic meaning of,
165
Gates, Henry Louis, Jr., 254, 288
Gender studies, 200–202, 243
Genetic criticism, 311–15
Genette, Gérard, 310
Geneva school, 347
Genre. *See also* Drama; Novel;
Poetry; Short fiction
archetype and, 166–67
Huckleberry Finn and, 43–45
"To His Coy Mistress" and,
28–29

"Young Goodman Brown"
and, 52–53
Genre criticism, 307–11
Gerber, John C., 319
Gibson, Walker, 312, 357, 359
Gilbert, Alan H., 313
Gilbert, Sandra, 156, 203, 213
Gilder, Richard Watson, 43
Gilman, Charlotte Perkins, 198,
229
Gittings, Robert, 312
"God's plenty" (phrase), 42, 49
Goethe, Johann Wolfgang, 181
Golden Bough, The (Frazer),
168–69
Gordon, Caroline, 81
Gothic tale, 54
Graff, Gerald, 242
Grammar, 324
Grammaticus, Saxo, 171
Gramsci, Antonio, 246
Granville-Barker, Harley, 271–72
Gray, Janet, 63, 64
Gray, Thomas, 308
Great Mother. *See* Motherhood,
archetypes
Greek tragedy, 42, 170–73, 307
Greenblatt, Stephen, 248–49,
250
Greenfield, Stanley B., 323, 324
Greetham, D. C., 21
Greg, W. W., 19
Grierson, Herbert, 85
Grossberg, Lawrence, 240
Gubar, Susan, 203, 213
Guilt complex, 131, 144
Gulliver's Travels (Swift), 247,
250–53

Haggard, H. Rider, 182
Halliburton, David, 344, 347–48
Hamlet (Shakespeare), 336, 365
cultural studies approach to,
270–75
feminist criticism and, 217–23
formalistic approach to,
110–18

historical-biographical approach to, 37–41
moral-philosophical approach to, 41–42
mythological approach to, 171–75
plot, 36–37
precritical response and, 6, 7, 8, 9–10, 11, 12, 15
psychological approach to, 127, 134–37
textual criticism, 33–36, 219
traditional approaches to, 33–42
Harding, D. W., 357
Hardy, Thomas, 20, 86
Harjo, Joy, 266
Harlem Renaissance, 259
Harmon, William, 90
Harper, Frances Ellen Watkins, 258
Harrison, Jane, 168
Hartman, Geoffrey H., 347
Hathorne, John, 57
Hawthorne, Nathaniel, 188–89. *See also* "Young Goodman Brown"
female characters in, 223
"My Kinsman, Major Molineux," 134
Scarlet Letter, The, 26, 57, 143, 223, 279
Heilbrun, Carolyn, 219–20
Heilman, Robert B., 81
Helen of Troy, 182
Hemenway, Robert, 256
Hemingway, Ernest, 9, 43, 140, 188, 284
Sun Also Rises, The, 88
"Hemingway code," 88
Hermeneutic code, 338
Hero archetypes, 166. *See also* Tragic hero
American Adam, 187–91
Bakhtin and, 350, 353
Hamlet, 171–75
Hill, Hamlin, 43

Hinman, Charlton, 19
Hirsch, E. D., 309, 310
Hispanic literature, 260–63, 351
Histoire (term), 337
Historical-biographical approach, 22–25. *See also* New Historicism
to "Everyday Use," 61–65
to *Hamlet,* 37–41
to *Huckleberry Finn,* 45–50
to "To His Coy Mistress," 30–32
to "Young Goodman Brown," 54–57
Historical novel, 23
History of ideas, 315–19
Hoffman, Daniel, 49
Hoffman, Frederick, 156
Hoggart, Simon, 246
Holland, Norman N., 136, 360, 362–63
Holman, C. Hugh, 90
Holquist, Michael, 351–52
Homer, 184
Homosexuality. *See also* Lesbian feminism
cultural studies and male, 243–44
Horace, 25, 78, 320
Horizons of expectations (term), 361–62
Horkheimer, Max, 246
Housman, A. E., 21
Howells, William Dean, 43, 188, 225
Hoy, Cyrus, 35
Hubler, Edward, 37
Huckleberry Finn (Twain)
archetypal patterns in, 189–91, 287–92
cultural studies approach to, 283–92
feminist criticism and, 225–30
formalistic approach to, 104–9
historical-biographical approach to, 45–50

Huckleberry Finn (Twain)
  (*continued*)
  horizons of expectations and,
    361
  moral-philosophical approach
    to, 50–51
  mythological approaches to,
    189–91
  plot, 44–45, 107–9
  point of view in, 88, 105–6
  precritical response and, 6, 7,
    8, 9, 10–11, 12
  psychological approach to,
    137–41
  reception theory and, 361
  textual criticism, 43
  traditional approaches to,
    42–51
Hughes, Langston, 259
Humanism and cultural studies,
  242–43
Humm, Maggie, 201, 209, 214
Humor, 46, 47
Hurston, Zora Neale, 209, 232,
  256, 259
Husserl, Edmund, 345
Hyman, Stanley Edgar, 304,
  315–16

Id, 128–30, 142, 153–55
Idealism, in *Hamlet*, 113–18
Ideas, history of, 315–19
Ideological novel, 23
Imagery. *See also* Sexual imagery;
  Symbols
  archetypal, 161–65
  in "A Slumber Did My Spirit
    Seal," 72
  death, 139–41, 150, 151, 161,
    165
  female, 138–39, 147, 149, 161,
    206
  formalistic approach to, 85–86
  male, 161, 163–65, 190
  of motherhood in *Huckleberry
    Finn*, 138–40, 227–29, 230
  Romanticism and, 78, 83

of space-time, 92–96, 175–77,
    345–46
  in "To His Coy Mistress," 91–96
  of trap in *Hamlet*, 110–12
  in "Young Goodman Brown,"
    97–101, 103–4
Imagination, 78
Imitation (mimesis), 304
Immoral didacticism, 282–83
Immortality archetype, 165
Implied reader
  cultural studies and, 276, 277
  phenomenological criticism
    and, 345–46
  reader-response criticism and,
    360
Individuation
  in Jungian psychology, 180–
    81
  in "Young Goodman Brown,"
    182–84
Informed reader, 364
Initiation archetype, 166, 174–75,
  190
Innocence-betrayed theme
  American Adam and, 188
  Hamlet, 174–75
  Huckleberry Finn and, 108,
    140–41
  "Young Goodman Brown"
    and, 141
Intentional fallacy, 87
Irigaray, Luce, 204–5
Irony, 71–72, 81
  in "Everyday Use," 66, 118–21
  in *Huckleberry Finn*, 51, 109
  resolution of tension through,
    90–91
Iser, Wolfgang, 276, 345–46,
  360–61

Jackson, Shirley, 169
James, Henry, 188, 223, 260, 335,
  338
  Ambassadors, The, 322, 343
  "Art of Fiction, The," 79–80
  Turn of the Screw, The, 144–47

Jameson, Frederic, 246, 247, 249, 328
Jauss, Hans Robert, 360, 361–62
Jehlen, Myra, 201–2, 213
Jenkins, Harold, 272
Jewett, Sarah Orne, 211
Johnson, Edward, 186
Johnson, James Weldon, 258
Johnson, Samuel, 1, 25
Jones, Ernest, 134–35, 137, 148, 155
Jones, Le Roi, 260, 294
Joseph, Bertram, 274
Journey motif. *See also* Quest motif
  in *Huckleberry Finn*, 45, 104–9
Joyce, James, 155, 168, 260
  Ulysses, 84, 335
Jung, Carl Gustav, 128, 159, 161
  archetypes and, 163–64, 177–86
  feminist criticism and, 206

Kaplan, Justin, 225, 285
Keats, John, 78
Keckley, Elizabeth, 258
Kelley, Donald R., 317
Kellogg, Robert, 306
Kenton, Edna, 144
Kermode, Frank, 81
King, Stephen, 188
Kings
  divine appointment of, 173–74
  sacrifice of, 168–69, 171
Kingston, Maxine Hong, 268
Kipling, Rudyard, 247
Know-Nothingism, 48
Kolodny, Annette, 197, 213
Krieger, Murray, 81–82
Kristeva, Julia, 156, 204–6
Kuhn, Thomas S., 357, 363
Kyd, Thomas, 40

Lacan, Jacques, 126, 134, 204, 205, 246
La Llorona, 263
Langbaum, Robert, 122

Langer, Susanne, 185
Langland, William, *Piers Plowman*, 22
Language. *See also* Linguistics
  dialogics and, 349, 352–53
  feminist criticism and, 199, 204–5
Langue and *parole* (terms), 333, 334, 335, 336, 337, 340
Lanham, Richard A., 321
Lathrop, George P., 52
Latina/o literature, 260–63, 351
Lauter, Paul, 214
Law of the Father, 204
Lawrence, D. H., 188–89, 281
Lazarillo de Tormes (anonymous), 44
Leavis, F. R., 245–46
Lentricchia, Frank, 81–82
Le Sage, René, 44
Lesbian feminism, 208–9, 211–12
Lesser, Simon O., 133, 134, 152–53
Lester, Julius, 284–85
Levin, David, 52
Levin, Samuel R., 323
Levine, George, 329
Lévi-Strauss, Claude, 245, 335–36
Levith, Murray J., 271
Lewis, R. W. B., 187
Lewis, Sinclair, 23
Lexie (term), 339
Libido, 128, 129, 143, 177. *See also* Sexuality
Liminality, 261
Lin, Adet, 269
Lin, Anor, 269
Lin, Memei, 269
Ling, Amy, 268, 269
Linguistic model, 332–34. *See also* Structuralism
Linguistics and literature, 322–23, 324, 325–26
Literary criticism
  attacks on, 2–3
  importance of eclectic approach to, 17–18, 302–4, 371

"Little Red Riding Hood" (Perrault), 132–33
Litvak, Joseph, 247
Llorona, 262, 263
Local color, 292
Local texture, 84
Logical structure, 75, 84, 201
Logocentrism, 341
London, Jack, 12, 188, 191
Longfellow, Henry Wadsworth, 79
Longinus, 319
Lord, George de F., 28
Lorde, Audre, 209–10
Love-hate motif, in "Young Goodman Brown," 98–104
Lovejoy, Arthur O., 315–17
Lowes, John Livingston, 312
Lucas, F. L., 149, 156
Lukács, György, 328–29
Lumiansky, Robert M., 313
Lyotard, Jean-François, 249
Lyric poetry, 29, 79, 89–90, 97, 322

MacLean, Norman, 305
Macquire, Jack, 253
Madison, D. Soyini, 262, 263
Mailer, Norman, 9
Male imagery, 161, 163–65, 190, 204
Malinche, 262, 263
Malory, Thomas, 313
Mann, Thomas, 168
Marett, R. R., 168
Marginalization, 270–75
Martz, Louis, 28
Marvell, Andrew, 30. *See also* "To His Coy Mistress"
Marx, Karl, 202, 246, 327
Marx, Leo, 284
Marxist criticism, 327–31
    Bakhtin and, 350
    cultural studies and, 241–42, 245, 246, 249
    "Everyday Use" and, 294–95
    New Historicism and, 249–50

Marxist feminism, 202–3
Mather, Cotton, 56
McCanles, Michael, 248
McKeithan, D. M., 51
McKeon, Richard, 305
Meaning. *See also* Word meanings
    deconstruction and, 340–41
    reader-response criticism and, 356, 360–65
    symbolic, 161–65
Melancholy, 40
Melville, Herman, 188–89
    Bartleby the Scrivener, 88
    "Hawthorne and His Mosses," 280–81
    Moby-Dick, 131, 160, 185–86, 336
Men. *See* Homosexuality; Male imagery
Merleau-Ponty, Maurice, 345
Metaphor, 85
    in *Hamlet*, 110–18, 270
    in "To His Coy Mistress," 31, 92–96
Metaphysical poetry, 32, 80, 85, 334
Metonymy, 147, 192
Metrics, 72–73, 83
Mexican American literature, 260–63, 351
Michaels, Walter Benn, 248
Miller, J. Hillis, 347
Millett, Kate, 198, 199
Milton, John, 181–82, 184–85, 346
    historical-biographical approach to, 22–23
    source study and, 313
Mimesis, 304
Minority feminist criticism, 208–12
Minority literature, 256–69
Misogyny
    feminist criticism and, 198
    Gulliver's Travels and, 250–53
    in *Hamlet*, 135, 136–37, 217–18, 219–20

Mock reader, 359
Moi, Toril, 197, 214
Momaday, M. Scott, 265–66
Monologic novel, 349, 350
Montagu, Mary Wortley, 211
Montrose, Louis, 248
Morality principle, 131
Moral-philosophical approach,
    25–27
    to "Everyday Use," 65–68
    to *Hamlet*, 41–42
    to *Huckleberry Finn*, 50–51
    to "To His Coy Mistress"
        (Marvell), 32–33
    to "Young Goodman Brown,"
        57–59
Morrison, Claudia C., 137
Morrison, Toni, 226, 256, 260, 285
Morse, J. Mitchell, 3
Morson, Gary Saul, 310
Morton, Donald, 244
Motherhood
    archetypes, 161, 163, 183, 190,
        191–93, 206
    feminist criticism and, 204–5,
        207
    imagery of, in *Huckleberry
        Finn*, 138–40, 227–29, 230
Motif. *See* Archetypes; Theme
Mullaney, Steven, 274
Multiculturalism. *See* American
    multiculturalism
Mulvey, Laura, 206
Murray, Gilbert, 168, 171–72, 184
Murray, Henry A., 131
Mythemes, 336
Mythological approaches,
    158–95. *See also* Archetypes
    American Dream and, 186–91
    anthropology and, 168–77
    archetypes and, 160–67
    to "Everyday Use," 191–93
    feminist criticism and, 206–8
    to *Hamlet*, 171–75
    to *Huckleberry Finn*, 189–91
    Jungian psychology and,
        177–86

limitations of, 193, 207–8
misconceptions of, 159–60, 167
psychological approach and,
    159, 206–8
    to "To His Coy Mistress,"
        175–77
    to "Young Goodman Brown,"
        182–84
Myth studies, by Lévi-Strauss,
    335–36

Narration. *See also* Point of view
    central intelligence and, 343
    in "Everyday Use," 63, 64,
        66–67, 118–20, 121
    first-person, 88, 105
    form and, 88–89, 105–6
    in *Huckleberry Finn*, 88, 105–6
    omniscient, 88, 105
    reliability of narrator and,
        88–89, 105–6, 119, 121
Native American literature,
    263–67, 287
Nature
    Romanticism and, 78, 83
    sin synonymous with, 143–44
    unwholesomeness of, in *Ham-
        let*, 111–12, 114
    vegetation myths, 172–73
Nelson, Cary, 240, 346
Neo-Aristotelian approach,
    304–7
Neoclassicism, 25
New Criticism, 17, 80–82. *See also*
    Formalistic approach
    criticism of, 121–23, 302–3, 305,
        327–28, 335, 347–48
    old, 76–77
    reader-response criticism and,
        355–56, 358–59, 360, 363
    structuralism and, 339
New Historicism, 18, 247–53, 270
    "Everyday Use" and, 292,
        294–95
    Hamlet and, 270–75
    "To His Coy Mistriss" and,
        276–78

Norris, Frank, 23
Novel. *See also Huckleberry Finn*
   (Twain)
   Bakhtin and, 349–55
   characteristics of, 104
   as female genre, 201
   formalistic approach and, 84
   historical, 23
   ideological/propagandist, 23
   picaresque tradition and, 44
   short story compared to, 97,
      104
Numbers, symbolic meanings of,
   163

Objective correlative, 80
Objectivity. *See* Narration; Point
   of view
Occom, Samson, 265
Oedipus (Sophocles), 112, 133–34,
   170–71, 172, 336
Oedipus complex, 127, 133–34,
   336
   in *Hamlet*, 134–37, 217–23
   Poe and, 148, 149
Olsen, Tillie, 197, 226
Olson, Elder, 305
O'Neill, Eugene, 155
Organic form, 76–77, 78–80,
   83–85, 340
Ortiz, Simon, 266
Overinterpretation, 26–27

Paine, A. B., 46
Paradigmatic approach, 335
Paradox, 71–72, 84
   in "Everyday Use," 119
   in *Hamlet*, 112
   resolution of tension through,
      90–91
   in "To His Coy Mistress," 33
Paraphrasable content, 29
Paredes, Raymond A., 262
Parole. *See Langue* and *parole*
   (terms)
Pearce, Roy Harvey, 284
Pechter, Edward, 249

Penelope, Julia, 211
Persona archetype
   in Jungian psychology, 180–81,
      182
   in "Young Goodman Brown,"
      182–83
Phelan, James, 242
Phenomenological criticism,
   343–49
Phenomenology, 360–61
Philology, 323
Philosophy. *See also* Moral-philo-
   sophical approach; Phenomenological criticism
   history of ideas and, 315–17
Picaresque tradition, 44
Pierce-Baker, Charlotte, 233
Pizer, Donald, 306
Plato, 25, 77–78, 320, 362
Pleasure principle, 129
   in "Everyday Use," 153–55
Plot
   Aristotelian criticism and, 304
   of "Everyday Use," 60–61
   of *Hamlet*, 36–37
   of *Huckleberry Finn*, 44–45,
      107–9
   of *Oedipus* (Sophocles), 170
   precritical response to, 7
   Russian formalism and,
      334–35
   of *Turn of the Screw, The,* 145–46
   of "Young Goodman Brown,"
      53–54
Poe, Edgar Allan, 86, 132, 189,
   229
   death wish in fiction of,
      148–49
   "Masque of the Red Death,
      The," 12
   phenomenological approach
      to, 347–48
   "Philosophy of Composition,
      The," 79
   "Purloined Letter, The," 363
   "Tell-Tale Heart, The," 10, 148
   "Ulalume," 132, 149–50

Poetry. *See also* "To His Coy Mistress" (Marvell)
  erotic, 32
  formalistic approach to, 70–76, 83–86, 90–91
  historical-biographical approach to, 22–25
  lyric, 29, 79, 89–90, 97, 322
  metaphysical, 32, 80, 85, 334
  moral-philosophical approach to, 26
  pure vs. impure, 91
  reader-response criticism and, 358–59
  Romanticism and, 78
  Russian formalism and, 334
  social themes in, 23–24
Point of view, 87–89, 105, 119, 343, 354. *See also* Narration
Pollard, A. W., 19
Polyphony, 350, 351, 353, 354
Polysemy, 247
Pope, Alexander, 24, 361
  Essay on Man, An, 25
  Rape of the Lock, The, 29–30, 307, 309
Porter, Carolyn, 248, 250, 253
Poststructuralism, 340–43
Poulet, Georges, 345, 347
Pound, Ezra, 19, 121, 122, 240
Power structures
  Bakhtin and, 351
  cultural studies and, 241, 249–53, 270–75
  feminist criticism and, 198–99, 216, 247
Practical criticism, 339
Pratt, Annis, 206–7
Precritical response, 1–15
  to atmosphere, 10–11
  to character, 7–8
  to plot, 7
  to setting, 6–7
  to structure, 8–9
  to style, 9–10
  to theme, 11–12
Predestination, 55

Prince, Gerald, 359–60
Proairetic code, 338
Production theory, 241–42, 278, 279, 282, 329
Projection, Jungian view of, 179, 180, 183–84
Propagandist novel, 23
Propp, Vladimir, 334, 335
Protagonist, 7
Proust, Marcel, 337, 345
Psychoanalytic feminism, 199, 203–8
Psychological approach, 125–57. *See also* Freud, Sigmund; Jung, Carl Gustav; Lacan, Jacques
  to Blake's "Sick Rose," 149–50
  to "Everyday Use," 153–55
  to *Hamlet,* 134–37
  to *Huckleberry Finn,* 137–41
  limitations of, 126, 155–56
  misunderstandings of, 126–27, 132–33
  mythological approach and, 159, 206–8
  to Poe's fiction, 148–49
  principles of, 125–34
  reader-response criticism and, 362–63
  to "To His Coy Mistress," 150–53
  to *Turn of the Screw, The,* 144–47
  to "Young Goodman Brown," 141–44, 150

"Queer theory," 243–44
Quest motif, 166, 171
  in *Hamlet,* 174–75
  in *Huckleberry Finn,* 189

"Rabbet-woman" (Mary Toft), 251, 252–53
Race. *See also* American multiculturalism; "Everyday Use: for your grandmama" (Walker)

Race (*continued*)
  concept of, 254
  as issue in *Huckleberry Finn*,
    48, 51, 361
Racial memory. *See* Archetypes,
  Jungian psychology and
Radway, Janice, 241
Ransom, John Crowe, 29, 77, 80,
  84, 85
Reader-response criticism,
  355–67. *See also* Audience
  precritical response and, 13–15
Reality principle, 130
Rebellion theme, 134, 137–41
Rebirth, 139–40
Rebolledo, Diana, 262, 263
Reception theory, 361–62, 365
Reed, Ishmael, 260
Reflection theory, 328–29
Repetitive form, 107–9
Repression, 128, 136–37, 144–47,
  341
Revenge tragedy, 40–41, 42,
  114–15
Reynolds, David, 282, 283
Rhetoric, and reader-response
  criticism, 358, 361
Rhetorical criticism, 319–25
Rich, Adrienne, 196, 207
Richards, I. A., 357, 358–59
Rivera, Eliana S., 262, 263
Rivers, symbolic meanings of,
  109, 139, 161, 189–90
Robbe-Grillet, Alain, 337
Roberts, John, 287–88
Robinson, Forrest G., 248
Robinson, Lillian, 202
Robinson Crusoe (Defoe), 133
Rodriguez, Richard, 262
Rodway, Allan, 310
Romantic fiction, chivalric, 44
Romanticism, 25, 86
  organic form and, 78, 83
  psychological approach and,
    126, 149
  Twain's rejection of, 48
Rosenblatt, Louise, 357, 359

*Rosencrantz and Guildenstern Are
  Dead* (Stoppard), 112, 275
Roth, Philip, 155
Rukeyser, Muriel, 62
Russian formalism, 76, 246,
  334–35

Sacrifice, rite of, 166, 168–69,
  171
  in *Hamlet*, 171–75
Said, Edward, 267
Santillana, Giorgio de, 171
Sarton, May, 212
Sartre, Jean-Paul, 25, 332
Satan, 56, 142, 181, 224
Satires, 23, 24–25, 44
Saussure, Ferdinand de, 332–33,
  335, 339, 340
Scapegoat archetype, 166, 169,
  171, 174
Scholes, Robert, 214, 306, 310,
  338, 339
School of Paris. *See* French struc-
  turalism
Schorer, Mark, 84–85, 159–60
Scott, Sir Walter, 23, 48, 328
Sedgwick, Catherine, 281
Sedgwick, Eve Kosofsky, 243
Semiotics
  cultural studies and, 246–47
  in French feminism, 204–5
  structuralism and, 335–36
Sensationalism, in *Huckleberry
  Finn*, 45–46
Serpents, symbolic meanings of,
  142, 163
Setting, precritical response to,
  6–7
Sexual imagery
  in Blake's "Sick Rose," 149–50
  in "Everyday Use," 154
  in *Gulliver's Travels*, 251–53
  in Poe's fiction, 148–49
  psychological approach and,
    132–33
  in "To His Coy Mistress,"
    94–96, 150–53, 215–17

in *Turn of the Screw, The,*
144–47
Sexuality
cultural studies and, 243–44
Freud's theories on, 128,
132–34
Shadow archetype
in *Huckleberry Finn,* 190
in Jungian psychology, 180–81
in "Young Goodman Brown,"
183
Shakespeare, William, 84, 181,
336, 346. *See also Hamlet*
Shelley, Mary, 10, 203
Shelley, Percy Bysshe, 78–79, 83,
85–86, 126
Shklovsky, Victor, 334–35
Short fiction, 79, 97. *See also*
"Young Goodman Brown"
Showalter, Elaine, 198, 199–200,
203, 210, 213
Shumaker, Wayne, 152
Sidney, Sir Philip, 126
Signifying (term), 288
Silko, Leslie Marmon, 266
Sill, Geoffrey, 256
Sinclair, Upton, 23
Sinfield, Alan, 244
Skandera-Trombley, Laura, 226
Smith, Jeanne Rosier, 164
Snakes, symbolic meanings of,
142, 163
Social themes, 23–24, 105–9. *See
also* Marxist criticism
Solzhenitsyn, Alexander, 328
Sontag, Susan, 2, 3
Sophocles, 112, 133, 170–71,
172–73
Source study and related ap-
proaches, 311–15
Space-time imagery, 92–96,
175–77, 345–46
Speaker's voice, 89–90. *See also*
Narration; Point of view
Stallman, Robert W., 81
Stein, Gertrude, 212, 226
Steinbeck, John, 23, 329

Steiner, Wendy, 310
Stoppard, Tom, 112, 275
"Stopping by Woods on a Snowy
Evening" (Frost), 26, 312
Stowe, Harriet Beecher, 12, 23,
281, 285
Strindberg, August, "Miss Julie,"
91
Structuralism
British and American interpreters, 339–40
deconstruction and, 340–43
defined, 331–32
French structuralism, 337–39
linguistic model, 332–34
New Criticism and, 339
Russian formalism and,
334–35, 337
semiotics and, 335–36
Structure
defined, 8
formalistic approach to poetry
and, 71–72, 74
logical, 75, 84, 201
New Criticism and, 81
precritical response to, 8–9
Style (journal), 324
Style, precritical response to,
9–10
Stylistics, 323–24, 326–27
affective, 363–64
Subjective criticism. *See* Precritical response; Reader-
response criticism
Subjectivism, and reader-re-
sponse criticism, 357, 363,
364–65
Sumida, Stephen, 268
Sun, symbolic meanings of, 161,
176
Superego, 128–29, 130–31,
138–39, 142, 153, 155
Surface structure, 333
Sutton, Walter, 305–6
Swift, Jonathan, 247, 250–53
Symbolic capital, 247, 249
Symbolic code, 338

412 ▪ *Index*

Symbols. *See also* Imagery
  in "Everyday Use," 121, 192
  formalistic approach and,
    74–75, 86
  in *Huckleberry Finn*, 109,
    138–39, 140–41
  sexual. *See* Sexual imagery
  in "Young Goodman Brown,"
    97–101, 103–4, 142–43,
    224
Synchronic features of language,
    333–34
Syntagmatic approach, 333–34,
    335, 337

Taine, H. A., 22
Tan, Amy, 269
Tate, Allen, 80, 81, 85, 90, 160
Taylor, Garry, 19
Tension, 90–91, 120
Text
  authenticity of, 18–21
  reader-response criticism and,
    356, 357, 359–61, 363–65
Textual criticism, 18–21
  Hamlet (Shakespeare), 33–36,
    219
  Huckleberry Finn, 43
  "To His Coy Mistress," 27–28
  "Young Goodman Brown," 52
Texture, 72, 84, 85–86
Theme
  in "Everyday Use," 120–21
  form and, 86, 91–96
  in *Hamlet*, 40–41
  in *Huckleberry Finn*, 47–48, 49,
    139–40
  precritical response to, 11–12
  in "To His Coy Mistress,"
    92–96
  in "Young Goodman Brown,"
    51–52, 57–58, 97–104
Thévenaz, Pierre, 345
Thorpe, James, 18, 19, 20, 21
Thorpe, Thomas Bangs, 46
Time motif. *See* Space-time im-
    agery

Todorov, Tzvetan, 337–38
Toft, Mary ("rabbit-woman"),
    251, 252–53
"To His Coy Mistress" (Marvell),
    16
  cultural studies and, 276–78
  feminist criticism and, 215–17,
    361
  formalistic approach to, 91–96
  historical-biographical ap-
    proach to, 30–32
  horizons of expectations and,
    361
  moral-philosophical approach
    to, 32–33
  mythological approach to,
    175–77
  precritical response and, 6–9,
    10, 12, 14–15
  psychological approach to,
    150–53
  rhetorical criticism and,
    321–22
  text of, 373–74
  textual criticism, 27–28
  traditional approaches to,
    27–33
Tolstoy, Leo, 350
Tompkins, Jane, 332, 356
Tone, 89–90
Toomer, Nathan Eugene, 259
Topicality, 18, 22, 25, 38–39. *See
    also* Social themes
Touster, Eva, 3
Traditional approaches, 16–69.
    See also Genre; Historical-
    biographical approach;
    Moral-philosophical ap-
    proach; Textual criticism
  contemporary variants of, 303
  to "Everyday Use," 60–68
  to *Hamlet*, 33–42
  to *Huckleberry Finn*, 42–51
  limitations of, 125
  nature and scope of, 16–27
  to "To His Coy Mistress,"
    27–33

types of, 21–27
to "Young Goodman Brown,"
   51–59
Tragedy
   classical, 42, 170–73, 307
   revenge, 40–41, 42, 114–15
Tragic hero, 42, 170–71, 304. *See
   also* Hero archetypes
   in *Hamlet,* 171–75
Trap metaphor in *Hamlet,* 110–12
Tree, symbolic meaning of, 165
Treichler, Paula, 240
Trickster archetype, 164, 190, 260
   in *Huckleberry Finn,* 283–92
Trilling, Lionel, 43, 51, 156, 284
Truth
   deconstruction and, 341
   reader-response criticism and,
      358–59
Tudor myth, 173
Turn of the Screw, The (James),
   psychological approach to,
   144–47, 151
Twain, Mark, 43, 46, 188, 227,
   314. *See also Huckleberry
   Finn*
   criticism of aristocracy, 47–48,
      49, 50–51
Tylor, Edward Burnett, 245

Unconscious
   collective, 177–79
   Freud's theories on, 127–31,
      139
   language and, 204
   reader-response criticism and,
      362
Unit ideas, 316–17
Unpardonable Sin, 57
Updike, John, *Couples,* 9
Utley, Francis Lee, 314
Utopia, 204, 281–82

Veeser, H. Aram, 248, 249–50,
   270
Vegetation. *See* Nature
Velie, Alan R., 264, 265, 267

Vendler, Helen, 213–14
Verse satires, 24–25
Vinaver, Eugène, 313
Virgin of Guadalupe, 262–63
Vizenor, Gerald, 265
Voice. *See also* Narration; Point of
   view
   Bakhtin and, 349, 350, 351, 354
   of speaker, 89–90
Voice of the Mother, 204
Voltaire, 332
Vonnegut, Kurt, 9

Walcutt, Charles C., 306
Walker, Alice, 60, 61–64, 209, 259,
   260. *See also* "Everyday Use:
   for your grandmama"
   on black women's creativity,
      231
   on cycles of black women,
      231–32
   The Color Purple, 239–40
Walker, Minnie, 61–64
Walker, Nancy, 226, 230
Walker, Willie Lee, 61–63
Ward, Artemus, 46
Warner, Michael, 243
Warren, Robert Penn, 80, 81, 84,
   90–91
Wasserstein, Paulette, 226
Wasson, Richard, 328
Water, symbolic meanings of,
   139, 147, 161, 189–90
Watt, Ian, 322
Watts, Alan W., 160
Wecter, Dixon, 46
Weinberg, Bernard, 305
Welch, James, 266
Wells, Stanley, 19
West, Ray B., Jr., 81
West, Rebecca, 196, 198
Wheatley, Phillis, 256, 257–58
Wheelwright, Jane, 164
Wheelwright, Philip, 160–61,
   172–73
Whitman, Walt, 140, 244, 336
Wiget, Andrew, 287

Williams, Raymond, 240, 245, 246
Williams, Tennessee, 155
Williams, William Carlos, 370
Wilson, Edmund, 144, 146–47, 148, 156
Wilson, Harriet E., 258
Wilson, J. Dover, 35, 39, 40
Wimsatt, W. K., 81, 87, 346
Winters, Yvor, 266
Winthrop, John, 143–44
Wise old man archetype, 163–64, 190
Wister, Owen (*The Virginian*), 188
Witchcraft, 56–57
Wolfe, Susan J., 211
Wollstonecraft, Mary, 198, 211
Womanist (term), 234
Women. *See also* Feminist approaches; Misogyny; Motherhood
    archetypal, 161, 163, 183, 190, 191–93, 206
    film images of, 206
Wong, Jade Snow, 269
Woolf, Virginia, 197, 198, 212
Word meanings, 323
    formalistic approach and, 74
    in *Hamlet*, 113–14, 116–17
    in "To His Coy Mistress," 92–96
    in "Young Goodman Brown," 100–101

Wordsworth, William, 126, 369
    "A Slumber Did My Spirit Seal," 70–73, 82
Wright, Richard, 210, 259–60

Yale school of criticism. *See* Deconstruction
Yeats, William Butler, 9, 122, 175
Young, Philip, 140
"Young Goodman Brown" (Hawthorne)
    cultural studies approach to, 278–83
    feminist criticism and, 223–25
    formalistic approach to, 96–104
    historical-biographical approach to, 54–57
    moral-philosophical approach to, 57–59
    mythological approaches to, 182–84, 191
    plot, 53–54
    precritical response to, 6, 7, 8, 9, 10, 11, 12, 14
    psychological approach to, 141–44, 150
    text of, 375–87
    textual criticism, 52
    traditional approaches to, 51–59

Zimmerman, Bonnie, 211